ninth edition

ARTWORKS
FOR ELEMENTARY TEACHERS

Developing Artistic and
Perceptual Awareness

Donald Herberholz
Professor Emeritus
California State University, Sacramento

Barbara Herberholz
Art Consultant

Boston   Burr Ridge, IL   Dubuque, IA   Madison, WI   New York   San Francisco   St. Louis
Bangkok   Bogotá   Caracas   Kuala Lumpur   Lisbon   London   Madrid   Mexico City
Milan   Montréal   New Delhi   Santiago   Seoul   Singapore   Sydney   Taipei   Toronto

McGraw-Hill Higher Education ⚛

*A Division of The **McGraw-Hill** Companies*

ARTWORKS FOR ELEMENTARY TEACHERS:
DEVELOPING ARTISTIC AND PERCEPTUAL AWARENESS

Published by McGraw-Hill, an imprint of The McGraw-Hill Companies, Inc. 1221 Avenue of the Americas, New York, NY, 10020. Copyright © 2002, 1998, 1994, 1990, 1985, 1979, 1974, 1969, 1964 by The McGraw-Hill Companies, Inc. All rights reserved. No part of this publication may be reproduced or distributed in any form or by any means, or stored in a database or retrieval system, without the prior written consent of The McGraw-Hill Companies, Inc., including, but not limited to, in any network or other electronic storage or transmission, or broadcast for distance learning.
Some ancillaries, including electronic and print components, may not be available to customers outside the United States.

The book is printed on acid-free paper.
1 2 3 4 5 6 7 8 9 0 QPD/QPD 0 9 8 7 6 5 4 3 2 1

ISBN 0-07-240707-7

Editorial director: *Phillip A. Butcher*
Sponsoring editor: *Joseph Hanson*
Development editor: *Jill Gordon*
Senior marketing manager: *David Patterson*
Project manager: *Christina Thornton-Villagomez*
Production supervisor: *Rose Hepburn*
Media producer: *Shannon Rider*
Senior media producer: *Sean Crowley*
Freelance design coordinator: *Mary L. Christianson*
Freelance interior and cover designer: *Jamie O'Neal*
Cover illustrations: *Emily Scherschligt, age 10*
Photo research coordinator: *David A. Tietz*
Photo researcher: *Deborah Bull*
Supplement associate: *Kate Boyland*
Printer: *Quebecor World Dubuque Inc.*
Typeface: *10/12 Times Roman*
Compositor: *Prographics*

Library of Congress Cataloging-in-Publication Data

Herberholz, Donald W.
    Artworks for elementary teachers: developing artistic and perceptual awareness /
Donald Herberholz, Barbara Herberholz.—9th ed.
        p. cm.
    Includes bibliographical references and index.
    ISBN 0-07-240707-7 (alk. paper)
    1. Art—Study and teaching (Elementary). I. Title: Developing artistic and perceptual
awareness. II. Herberholz, Barbara J. III. Title.
N350 .H47 2002
    372.5′044–dc21   2001030545

www.mhhe.com

ARTWORKS

FOR ELEMENTARY TEACHERS

PREFACE

Artworks for Elementary Teachers is a text for a one-semester college or university course for nonart majors who plan to teach art to children. It provides future classroom teachers with introductory experiences in knowing both how to create and how to respond to art. Experiences provided in this text will enable future teachers to understand art through interaction in both response and production strategies.

The *National Visual Arts Standards* (see Appendix) clearly defines the role of art with six content standards and how they may be assessed (www.naea-reston.org/publications). The six content standards are broad in coverage and include what had become known as the four disciplines (areas of study) prescribed by Discipline-Based Art Education (DBAE): art production, aesthetics, art history, and art criticism. Comprehensive arts, a later development of DBAE, includes integration of art with other school subject areas and the development of meaning in a work of art.

In using the National Visual Arts Standards as a basis for art instruction, teachers can meet all of the six forms of art content standards. They comprise the following:

1. Understanding and applying media, techniques, and processes.

2. Using knowledge of structures and functions.

3. Choosing and evaluating a range of subject matter, symbols, and ideas.

4. Understanding the visual arts in relation to history and cultures.

5. Reflecting on and assessing the characteristics and merits of their work and the work of others.

6. Making connections between visual arts and other disciplines.

Many state curriculum guides and frameworks for art have defined the content of art in similar ways as have counties and school districts.

In the years since its introduction, DBAE has evolved from an emphasis on four areas—art criticism, art history, art production, and aesthetics—to a more integrated and inquiry-based process of searching for meaning. The defining attributes of each discipline have evolved as teachers and students embraced the philosophy and expanded it under the umbrella of Comprehensive Art Education. Education in these disciplines contributes to the creation, understanding, and appreciation of art, artists, artistic processes, and the roles, functions, and meaning of art in different cultures and society. The inquiry method involves looking, writing, thinking, discussing, looking again, reflecting, and synthesizing by relating to one's own experiences.

To address these areas of art study in a practical and concise manner, this text is now divided into seven chapters, each concluding with Interactive Extensions, thereby providing students choices in becoming engaged in productive learning. Related websites are listed in Chapter 6.

There are two separate Color Galleries in the ninth edition: the Artists' Color Gallery and the Children's Color Gallery. The Artists' Color Gallery with works by adult artists is referred to throughout the text. It contains a variety of artworks that students may study to perceive visual information regarding an element or principle of art or the different styles of art. Students will find works that show different subject matter and different styles of art by artists from diverse cultures and periods of time. The Children's Color Gallery assists students in understanding the different stages of a child's artistic growth as explained in Chapter 5, as well as how art may be integrated with other areas of the curriculum.

Chapter 1 provides students with opportunities to investigate how artists work, their early training, their childhood environment, what has inspired them, and how society has viewed them as artists. Ideas related to creativity and self-expression are discussed. Students will learn through an "Artists at Work Worksheet" and class discussion that artists are very different from each other yet often have definite similarities. Additional worksheets engage the student in becoming involved in a personal inventory of their own art background, in reviewing videos on artists, and on comparing purposes of art in diverse cultures.

Chapters 2 and 3 focus on the visual and verbal language of art—the elements and principles of design. These two chapters enable students to become fluent in the terminology and concepts related to a vocabulary that will help them both in responding to art and in producing artworks themselves. These elements and principles are used by anyone involved in drawing, painting, printmaking, photography, sculpture, crafts, architecture, the graphic arts, and the creation of clothing, jewelry, containers, furniture, utensils, automobiles, and appliances. Reproductions of artworks in these chapters have brief descriptive notations that will guide students to a deeper understanding of each element and principle of art.

The art production activities in these chapters (1) introduce students to ways of perceiving the world visually; (2) begin to help them develop skills in using materials; (3) make them actively aware of their choices in using the elements and principles of art; (4) motivate them to express visually, with some measure of confidence, their own creative ideas and feelings with paint, paper, clay, and other art media; and (5) introduce them to ways of developing meaning in their own work.

Chapter 4 is devoted to the understanding of art using response strategies in relation to art criticism and art history. Art criticism involves understanding an artwork through describing, analyzing, and interpreting it—that is, putting into words what we see and feel about it and what meaning the artwork may contain. When art criticism strategies are interwoven with art history, we also learn when, where, how, and why an artist in a specific culture created a particular artwork. Through such processes future teachers become more competent in evaluating their own artwork and, later, helping elementary children reflect upon their art. Styles of art, including the aesthetic qualities found in each, are described. This chapter discusses aesthetics as a branch of philosophy that deals with the nature of art. A section on visiting art museums, galleries, and seeing art in public places concludes the chapter.

Chapter 5 focuses on children's art production and their responses to art. The stages of their artistic growth are explained. Six strategies for integrated art lessons for lower and upper grades are included. To assist children in ways to reflect upon and assess their own artwork, questions on process and product are listed. A specific example of teacher-student response in looking at a painting is presented. A number of interactive games and activities to use with elementary students when discussing works by artists are described. Ten ways to give children greater depth and meaning to art and artists through the use of books conclude the chapter.

Chapter 6, "New Directions for the Twenty-First Century," is a new chapter devoted to technology, an integrated/interdisciplinary curriculum, current resources, and their relation to the National/State Visual Arts Standards. Included is a list of 10 productive ways to use the Internet in elementary art classes. Models of lesson plans based on color plates in the text are included. A list of websites and CD-ROMs is given for instructional purposes.

Chapter 7 is a chronological summary of the history of world art. Students should use it as a reference—to learn where, when, and in which historical context different artists lived so as to better understand their special or spe-

cific contributions. Artists' birth and death dates are provided. When we reflect on what is remembered as the highest attainments and achievements of each world culture, we refer to that culture's art. Western and non-Western achievements in art are presented in a condensed format. This chapter guides students in understanding some of the important developments and connecting links in global art. More in-depth information about art periods, diverse cultures, and specific artists can be found in libraries, media centers, and museums, and on videos and the Internet. The condensed format of Chapter 7 gives students a starting point. Extensive functional websites related to Western and non-Western art are listed.

The Resource section found at the end of this text includes a Glossary, Pronunciation Guide, Art Forms: Two- and Three-Dimensional, Resources for Art Education, a List of Children's Books, Notes and Bibliography, and the National Visual Arts Standards.

In addition to a new and colorful design, we have added chapter outlines, lesson plans, and new resources to this edition. We feel these new features will benefit both instructors and their students.

ACKNOWLEDGMENTS

We wish to express our deep appreciation to:

- The editors at McGraw-Hill whose untiring and steady hands kept us on target (and on time). Joe Hanson's positive and thoughtful ideas provided us with the energy to do our best. Jill Gordon kept it all together and unwound tangles. Mary Christianson patiently and creatively directed the design and layout of the book, the final result pleasing us immensely. Christina Thornton-Villagomez carefully managed our book from final manuscript to print-ready status. All were pleasant to work with and always promptly responded to our frequent e-mails and phone calls.

- The students at California State University, Sacramento, who, over the decades, have enhanced and reinforced our energies and beliefs in the importance of art that is sparked as they learn how to understand and respond to art and begin to produce art themselves. Their enthusiasm, excitement, and growing confidence regarding their new learnings will carry over into their elementary classrooms as they bring to their students age-old cultural themes and a grasp of the undeniable role that art plays in the human experience.

- The thousands of children, volunteer parents, and teachers whose involvement in our Art Docent Program continues to reinforce our belief that responding to and making art must be included in the elementary curriculum if students are to become critical thinkers and creative producers of art. These experiences will give them a basis for cherishing art throughout their lives.

- Our three children, now parents themselves, whose artworks, when they were kids, were photographed and played a vital part in our previous editions. Their children have carried on the family tradition of telling about their expanding world through their delightful artwork, and a few examples are included in this ninth edition. When our 10-year-old Emily showed us her drawing of "Dance Class," we were especially pleased, and when the McGraw-Hill editors selected her drawing for the cover of our book, she had a very big smile.

- The teachers and students at Sacramento Country Day School who have the privilege of regular sequential instruction in a variety of media that is integrated throughout he curriculum via the untiring and creative instruction of their art teacher, Maureen Gilli. A number of their works are included in the Color Gallery and in Chapter 5.

- The researchers and writers in the art education field whose books and articles as well as the writings in the National Art Education Association publications have spurred our thinking with their enduring and exciting new directions. These changes in the field over the years cause us all to question and debate, insisting that we agree or disagree, but that we unite in our unanimous goal of providing the very best experiences in art for all of our young students.

- The thoughtful and insightful reviewers whose comments and suggestions assisted us in the specific content that they felt should be added, deleted, or changed to make this ninth edition vital and forward-looking. These professional art educators are in the field—where it's happening, so to speak—and their reviews reflected their thoughts regarding the practical philosophy and skills that nonart majors need to attain for the teaching of art in the elementary classroom. These reviewers included:

Bonnie Bernau—University of Florida
Mary Sue Foster—Wichita State University
Marybeth Koos—Northern Illinois University
Lon R. Nuell—Middle Tennessee State University
Susan C. Power—Marshall University
Kathryn I. Pursley—University of Akron

STUDENT RESOURCE

We have also added a new student supplement—*Art Starts*. It is designed to be a companion workbook to *Artworks*—a tool that the new (or first year) elementary teacher can use to start his or her art program. *Art Starts* suggests a number of ways to respond and produce artworks, as well as tips on using a wide range of art media, games and activities, motivations, integrated lesson plans, and so on. It is divided into three parts: Looking and Learning about Art, Making Art, and Integrating Art in the Curriculum.

EDUCATIONAL CONSULTANTS

Maureen Gilli
Art Consultant, Sacramento Country Day School
KD Kurutz
California Consultancy for Arts Education, Sacramento, CA
Jill M. Pease
California Consultancy for Arts Education, Sacramento, CA
Craig Roland
Area Coordinator of Art Education, University of Florida

ABOUT THE AUTHORS

Donald W. Herberholz received his BA from Michigan State University and his MA from the University of New Mexico. After teaching elementary and secondary school art in three states for ten years, he began his college teaching at Bloomsburg State Teachers' College in Pennsylvania. He then moved to California where he taught in the Art Department of California State University for 35 years. He served as treasurer of the California Art Education Association and was named by the National Art Education Association as California's Outstanding Art Educator. He served two terms on the board of directors for the Crocker Art Museum in Sacramento. His welded metal sculptures—both freestanding and wall pieces—are in numerous private collections. He produced a film on welded sculpture as well as filmstrips on puppetry and printmaking. He and Barbara have three children and eight grandchildren.

Barbara Herberholz received her BFA and MA from the University of New Mexico and has been involved in teaching art at all levels. The National Art Education Association named her California's Outstanding Elementary Art Educator and California's Outstanding Art Educator. She is coauthor of *Early Childhood Art*, McGraw-Hill. She served as an education contributor for the elementary art texts *Art in Action* and also wrote two Art Enrichment Manuals that accompanied boxes of art reproductions. As the first editor of *The Painted Monkey*, California Art Education Association's monthly newsletter, she gave the publication its name and served for six years. She originated the Art Docent Program and trains parent volunteers to teach response and production activities in elementary schools. She is a contributing editor for *Arts and Activities* magazine.

The authors wish to thank their granddaughter, Emily Scherschligt, age 10, for contributing the drawings that appear on the cover of their book.
Photo by Nancy Pietrucha.

CONTENTS

CHAPTER 4 Art Criticism, Art History, and Aesthetics: Strategies for Understanding Artworks 83

PART THREE
CHILDREN IN THE ART CLASSROOM 101

CHAPTER 5 Children Make and Respond to Art 101

CHAPTER 6 New Directions for the Twenty-First Century Technology and Curriculum Design 131

PART FOUR
THE WORLD OF ART   153

CHAPTER 7 A Narrative Time Line of World Art: Looking at Western and Non-Western Artworks 153

RESOURCES 207

COLOR GALLERIES

1

CHAPTER

Artists and the Images They Make:
Artworks in Diverse Cultures and Times

Figure 1.1 **Stephen Kaltenbach, *A Time to Cast Away Stones*, Sacramento Convention Center.**
Owner, City of Sacramento, CA.
This piece is one in Kaltenbach's series of three monumental pieces of sculpture; he claims that they represent idols that have
been cast down and are no longer worshipped. Kaltenbach states that his artwork uses the fragmentation of sculpture throughout
the ages as metaphors for the human conditions of aging and mortality. These fragments are made from replicas of his favorite
sculptures from many cultures throughout art history. He feels that art has many levels of meaning that resonate together and with
the viewer to create poetic content.

Art objects from every culture—both past and present—are artifacts that tell us of the society and individuals that produced them. An understanding of why these artworks were created leads to a better understanding of ourselves. These objects had their foundations in the thoughts, feelings, and ideas of a society or in an individual's beliefs, perceptions, priorities, values, customs, religion, tragedies, and triumphs. Artworks take many forms and are made from a variety of processes and media. (See "Art Forms: Two- and Three-Dimensional" at the end of the book.)

ART SERVES MULTIPLE PURPOSES

Our view of art throughout the world must consider art's diverse functions—the purposes it has served and continues to serve in different cultures and in other times and places. When you view an artwork, whether it is in a museum, a book, on the internet, or a work in your community, it will have more meaning for you if you consider which of the following purposes it seems to serve:

1. ***Art serves society.***

   Art tells stories about events in history, myths, religion, and literature.

   Art may convince, inform, inspire, criticize, persuade, or move people to action in relation to religious, political, national, or social causes.

   Art objects are often used in rituals, and ceremonies that ask for protection and help in controlling or honoring natural forces.

   Art often serves as a memorial or tribute to honor a special person, place, idea, or event.

2. ***Art records images and expresses an artist's feelings and imagination.***

   Art has, over the years, shown us how people, places, and objects have looked.

   Art expresses the way artists feel about people, the land, nature, cities, the sea, and much more.

   Art expresses an individual's creativity and communi-

Figure 1.2 **Armando Alvarez, detail of *We the People*, 1994. Steel sculpture in Gallup, NM, 300-ft.-long wall with 93 life-size figures.**
This monument is unique; it does not copy other monuments. Unlike the figures on the Parthenon frieze, which are idealized expressions of the artist's melding of truth and beauty, the multiple shapes of *We the People* depict a slice of ordinary northwest New Mexico life—from flea market customers to the country club crowd. Alvarez's work celebrates ordinary people creating an extraordinary freedom.
Courtesy, Armando Alvarez, artist, 1994.

Figure 1.3 ***Korean War Memorial*, Ken Cooper and William Lecky, architects who developed the memorial design. Frank Gaylord, sculptor. Louis Nelson created a wall of etched faces. Washington, DC.**
The recently constructed Korean Memorial in Washington, DC, is a strikingly emotional monument that honors the soldiers who fought in that war. Haunting figures surge silently forward with weapons and rain gear. To honor and commemorate people who have made sacrifices and contributions has long been one of the purposes of art. Our nation's capital has a number of such sculptures—the Lincoln Memorial, the Washington Monument, the Vietnam Memorial, and soon to come, a memorial to World War II.
Photo by Herberholz.

cates an artist's innovative representation of an idea. Art can show us an artist's dreams, fantasies, and rich imagination.

Art can reveal the pure visual impact of the organization of colors, shapes, lines, and textures.

Art can delight our senses with its embellishment and decoration of objects in our environment.

Art can be used as a symbol for an idea.

3. ***Art serves our functional needs.***

Art can have functional considerations, such as architectural design, city planning, furnishings, containers, utensils, clothing, and jewelry.

Art provides us with advertising, layout, logos, and other elements of graphic design.

ARTISTS IN SOCIETY: A Brief Overview

In ancient Egypt, artists worked as a team of professional craftspeople: An outline scribe made the initial drawing, a second person chiseled the **relief**, and a third artist added paint. In a similar manner, teams of 10 to 15 artisans in India worked to create paintings and **sculptures**, with some workers painting only faces and others working on other parts. The works were usually anonymous, as dictated by tradition, and the artisans were required to work within rigid specifications as to poses and symbols. Before contact with Europe, all art in India was created for religious purposes.

Artists as a class were not high on the social scale in ancient Greece and Rome, in spite of the quality of their

work. Throughout **classical** antiquity and the Middle Ages, artists were on the same plane as laborers, since they worked with their hands. The role of artists (those who made ritual and utilitarian objects) was clearly defined in church-centered **medieval** Europe: They had the same status as weavers, bakers, and other tradespeople. Artists joined guilds during the later Middle Ages. Painters belonged to the guild of physicians and apothecaries as late as the sixteenth century, probably because their work involved obtaining and using materials that were pulverized. Michelangelo's father did not want his son to become a sculptor because he considered manual labor beneath the family's dignity.

Artists' status was elevated during the **Renaissance** when interest in artworks as aesthetic objects came to be revered. Artists viewed imagination, learning, and inspiration as necessary components to creating art. The Church was the primary patron of artists in the Middle Ages and the Renaissance. Later, the courts of kings and nobles called on artists to paint their likenesses and to otherwise embellish their courts. By the seventeenth century, court artists were given titles.

During the eighteenth century, sculpture and painting began to reflect the tastes of the upper classes. It no longer merely served utilitarian purposes but was being created to please the eye and elevate the spirit. By this time, male artists considered themselves on a higher social level and did their best to keep women from becoming artists. Nineteenth-century artists often appeared at odds with society, since the public and the critics deplored and refused to accept new ways of painting. These artists forged ahead but gained little fame or funds during their lifetimes. During the twentieth century, a great variety of art was produced, with some artists achieving fame and fortune and providing inspiration for followers who often imitated their style. In general the public has often lacked understanding and has not accepted some of the more avant garde artworks, while some artists have achieved recognition and a high status.

Studying the lives of artists and the meaning behind the images they make as well as the culture from which they sprang gives us a better understanding of the place of art in our lives. Investigating how artists work, what inspires them, and the nature of their early art education can help us as elementary teachers to provide an environment for our students' maximum growth in art.

TRIBAL ARTISTS AND FOLK ARTISTS

Within African tribes, the artists usually had status, often serving as both smith and medicine man. They were apprenticed and selected on the basis of their talent. Many tribal sculptors were farmers, but rulers assembled court artists with outstanding skills to make objects that showed the wealth and power of their kingdoms. Individual carvers are remembered by name as masters with apprentices in some areas of Africa. The African sculptor spent years of apprenticeship learning how to use tools and materials to create artworks filled with symbolism that the village people would understand. Ram horns might symbolize aggression and strength; small triangles in circular layers could show a person's rank and prestige.

Traditions Meet with Creative Changes

Folk and tribal artists master, practice, and teach the cultural arts of their communities, carrying on artistic traditions from generation to generation. They share a deep pride with the past and a desire to transmit skills and knowledge. While folk art stands on its own, an understanding of its symbols enriches our appreciation of the art objects as well as of the culture that produced them. While traditions may have ancient roots, works of folk and tribal art are often not replications of what was done before but creative interpretations of a culture's beliefs and thinking represented in more contemporary modes and often with present-day materials. Technology has had its impact. For instance, Navajo basketry is having an artistic renaissance in a remote area of northern Arizona and southern Utah where Navajo basket weavers are exploring new designs created on the computer by Damien Jim of Twin Rocks Trading Post.[1] He works with local weavers in developing new designs and variations in design using a vast array of bright colors.

Folk art and tribal art include works of high craftsmanship and beauty that were created for both personal and community use and with serious, religious, or even humorous intent. Folk art may include toys, adornments, masks, sculptures, costumes, containers, figures, and other forms. We admire the carved wooden santos in New Mexico, the handsome quilts of Hawaii, the embroidered baby shoes from China, and the paper cuts from Poland, since they show us the diversity and universality of the creative impulse. But we also delight in seeing whimsical animals and figures made from discarded materials such as bottle caps and plastic containers.

Highly regarded in America and throughout the world's diverse cultures, folk art comes in many forms. Such artists may be self-taught or they may be carrying on their culture's traditions in carving, weaving, modeling, and such. Collectors such as Michael Rockefeller, whose collection may be seen in the Metropolitan Museum of Art, and Alexander Girard, whose collection is on permanent display in the International Museum of Folk Art in Santa Fe, NM, not to mention thousands of other lovers of folk art, have relished in the freshness of approach, the imaginative and inventive use of materials, the attention to and inclusion of details, and the emphasis on repetition and pattern.

The impulse to create, whether the individual is young or old, often compels him or her to collect discarded materials and assemble them in some manner. We are reminded of the Watts Towers in Los Angeles. John Landgraf (Figure 1.4) delights in finding discarded rusty metal objects, keeping them in his studio for several years, and then seeing in them a combination that results in an animal, bird, or figure that reflects his creativity and sense of humor.

Memories of past experiences and events provide strong emotional material for some folk artists. Horace Pippin painted stories of black people in America as well as his memories of WWI, in which he was injured by a sniper, leaving his right arm badly damaged. Howard Finster's compelling religious paintings combine words and images, and Grandma Moses's works visualized her memories of years gone by.

ARTISTS, CREATIVITY, AND SELF-EXPRESSION

Artistic creativity and self-expression are rather recent concepts. Indeed, individuality was not important until the Renaissance, when most artists first began signing their work. Before then, some **mural** artists were paid by the square foot or by how many figures were included. In ancient Mesopotamia and ancient Egypt, changes in art were very slow and took place over several centuries. Amenhotep VI (ca. 1350 B.C.) being a reformer called for relaxed realistic figures instead of the idealized and rather stiff sculp-

Figure 1.4 Folk artist John Landgraf collects numerous pieces of scrap metal and welds them into whimsical and imaginary creatures. *Photo by Gene Sahs.*

Figure 1.5 **Oliver Jackson, a contemporary American artist.** "Art changes you—it is a *form* that changes you. That is why there are so many cultures that don't have a word for art. . . . Early people were not playing around with 'culture'—they weren't talking about what we are talking about—something on the wall! They were talking about those things that adjust the psyche in a way that helps you to be spiritually healthy. Those things they made were forceful and direct. One of the things that you talk about when you talk about primitive art is clarity." *Photo by McHugh.*

tures that had been created before. However, the old ways were back in style when he died.

Western art since the Renaissance has been strongly based on the creativity and self-expression of individual artists—artists who earned their place among the "greats" by having a new idea, using art materials in an inventive way, selecting unique subject matter, seeing the world in special ways, or exploring new and different materials or methods for handling color, line, and shape. Critics and the public often initially rejected these new images, but ultimately, these works inspired other artists and added another rung to the ladder of art. Artists who followed built on the inventiveness of earlier artists as they climbed this ladder and explored and created more new worlds.

Jackson Pollock achieved an important place in twentieth-century art for his action painting. Some scoff at Pollock's work and declare, "My child could do that—anyone could do it." The point, however, is that Pollock was the first to do action painting. No one else had the daring idea of dripping paint onto a canvas placed on the floor, with the artist becoming immersed in the action of the work as it progressed.

Since the Renaissance, Western artists have been far less tied to limitations imposed by tradition, and thus, individual artistic creativity has flourished. An artist's style—way of painting—is the product of both personal skills, thoughts, and feelings and important influences that occurred during the artist's career. During the Renaissance, the imagination separated art from crafts and set the precedent of the artist being in a superior position to the crafts person and being a creative intellectual. The concept of fine arts, as opposed to craft objects made for a particular function, emphasized an artwork's creative value and encouraged artistic individuality. Though individuality was admired, the people of that time generally believed that an artwork should be skillfully made, appropriate, and beautiful. However, independence and imagination in handling materials and technical problems that demonstrated inventiveness and creativity began to take on new importance.

A brief overview of this period of time in art in the Western world is marked by creative artists and groups of artists who found new ideas to express and new ways to express them. A major breakthrough in creativity occurred in the early fourteenth century when Florentine artist Giotto achieved a feeling of three-dimensional space in his **frescoes** by showing solid figures with a warm human quality placed in lifelike positions. Interestingly, however, while he used shading techniques to achieve round forms, he neglected to paint shadows that his figures cast on the ground. These new techniques were far more realistic than those of artists who had preceded Giotto—artists whose stiff, flat figures had an otherworldly quality and served as symbols. Giotto's creativity gave impetus to the Italian Renaissance as other artists emulated his ideas.

About A.D. 1350–1400, which marks the beginning of the early Renaissance, artists such as Leonardo da Vinci and Michelangelo became so interested in human anatomy

Figure 1.6 **Paul Cézanne's studio, Aix en Provence, southern France.**
A visit to Paul Cézanne's studio provides the opportunity to see some of the actual objects that he included in
his still lifes as well as easel and palette.
Photo by Barbara Herberholz.

rather than in the flat, lifeless symbolic figures that had preceded them that they dissected human corpses to improve
their knowledge of anatomy. Thus we see that a culture's
values and beliefs have a definite influence on what sort of
artworks are produced. The history of art in the Western
world is filled with other examples of artists whose creativity inspired major changes in the ways other artists perceived the world and made art.

Later, viewers demanded that noble subject matter and
elevated feelings be the proper content of art, with paintings
and sculptures telling stories in a highly realistic and traditional way. They wanted subject matter that was ennobling
or appealing, with a message that communicated courage,
patriotism, or heroism. A different type of subject matter
became prominent a bit later, with artists such as Fragonard
painting wealthy aristocrats at play on their country estates,
while artists such as the Le Nain brothers, Vermeer, Rembrandt, and Chardin began to paint peasants and ordinary
people wearing plain clothing as they engaged in everyday tasks. High-minded critics dismissed as trivial these
paintings that showed common folk engaged in ordinary
activities.

The concept that art could be a means of self-expression
first appeared during the **romantic** period in the early nineteenth century, with painters looking inward as well as outward. During the reign of Louis XIV (1661–1750), to call an
artwork "original" was to condemn it since artistic virtue at
that time upheld the long-standing tradition of copying and

emulating works by revered masters. Romantic artists challenged the idea of having only noble and heroic subject matter, believing in the exaltation of all human feelings. Their
subject matter was sometimes frightening, exotic, or myste-
rious. Romantic artists even gave **landscapes** a character
that expressed deep feelings.

In the Western world, the power of artistic tradition
declined further during the nineteenth century as experimentation and personal creative expression became the
mode—in spite of outcries from the public and critics who
scoffed at and rejected artists' new ways of perceiving and
producing paintings. Political, social, and economic factors
were instrumental in changing pictorial modes. The Catholic
Church, along with royal and aristocratic patronage in all
areas of life, declined, and the conservative attitudes and
needs of these agencies no longer restricted artists. Artists
were now free to produce art for the fast-growing middle
classes and to suit a wider range of individual tastes. Artists
began to ask themselves: In what subjects would clients
other than the church and royalty be interested? What styles
could they develop as appropriate modes? Whose needs
would they serve? Could an artist create in any way he or
she chose?

We often read or hear of the avant-garde, meaning the
"advance guard," which endeavors to establish itself as the
older, outmoded styles fade away. By the mid-nineteenth
century, a few artists had disregarded neoclassical and
romantic art and recorded life as they saw it, painting ordi-

Figure 1.7 **Kurt Edward Fishback,** *Ansel Adams,* **©1982.**
The imminent photographer is seen in his home, with several of his photographs on the wall. Ansel Adams told of breaking his nose in the 1906 San Francisco earthquake and he always planned to have it fixed when he grew up. Fishback reported that Adams laughed and said, "Since I never grew up, I didn't have it fixed." The young and often playful nature of artists often contributes to their ability to see things freshly and without preconceived notions.
Courtesy of Herberholz.

nary landscapes in an unidealized and unromantic manner. These realist painters strove to paint the real world and real life, with artists such as Millet and Courbet choosing the peasants and working classes as subject matter. A bit later, Edouard Manet shattered academic tradition with his female nudes painted as ordinary people instead of goddesses. His loose brush techniques, hard edges, and black outlines outraged the public but inspired the impressionist painters who followed him.

In the second half of the nineteenth century, the **impressionists** angered the critics and public with their dabs and daubs of unblended colors. They were endeavoring to show the sparkle of the atmosphere and the effect of light on people and landscapes; the subject of the painting (often, beautiful people in lovely landscapes) had no message. Soon, people came to realize that a painting did not need to have dramatic or heroic subject matter and that this new way of applying paint was actually quite beautiful.

The creative ferment of the **postimpressionists** firmly rejected the lighthearted world of Renoir and Monet before long, however. Postimpressionist artists such as van Gogh, Paul Gauguin, and Toulouse-Lautrec painted in highly individualistic and expressive manners. Artists such as Paul Cézanne began to see the world as made up of cubes, cylinders, and spheres. He painted it in chunky, blocky brush strokes—a creative breakthrough that caused Picasso and Braque to invent **cubism,** the real kickoff for modern twentieth-century art. Where tradition had once given artists direction, artists now took a more creative view. They trusted what they were doing and believed in their own ideas. Van Gogh, for instance, courageously painted in a different manner than anyone else, in a way that was not accepted in his time. He persevered, however, and believed that his own ideas were good and true.

A nineteenth-century invention—the camera—had a great impact on creativity's role in the development of Western art. Since the camera's debut, a number of men and women have elevated photography to an equal basis with the other fine arts. The eminent photographer Ansel Adams (Figure 1.7) once stated, "In my mind's eye, I am visualizing how a particular revelation of sight and feeling will appear on a print. If what I see in my mind excites me, there is a good chance it will make a good photograph."[2] While some artists used photographs as inspirational and visual resources, many painters concluded that **realism** was not as important as it had been previously; for realism, there was the camera. These artists began to explore new ways to paint and express their intensely personal creativity. Taken together, these individual artists created the "modern art" of the twentieth century, in which uncensored creativity and self-expression were considered rights.

Although each individual artist's creative spirit is unique and personal, the culture in which he or she lives places special values on specific activities, providing the need, the **format,** and the materials for individuals to fashion art objects. In the many and varied cultures outside of the Western world, an artist's individual creativity and inventiveness are not emphasized or desired. The needs of the particular culture or tribe supersede the artist's creativity in that art objects must carry on highly structured, inherited traditions. A particularly effective artist may come along in this setting and make a contribution that changes the tradition somewhat and causes a gradual evolution in the tribe's tradition. Tribal artists—for instance, the Native American artists along the northwest coast of North America, the Australian Aborigines, and the San Blas Indians of Panama—must work with a high degree of skill within narrow parameters established by tribe or group traditions. The ceremonial and utilitarian art that is produced is highly valued and is an integral part of that particular tribe's culture. Indeed, some cultures have no vocabulary for "art." The masks, containers, or other objects are so integrated with function and ritual as to be inseparable from life.

Figure 1.8 **Roger Vail,** *Petrochemical Tanks and Tower,* **1980.**
Photographer-professor Vail captures gradations of light reflections and detail in nocturnal images. He uses time exposures of up to several hours and lens apertures small enough to get an infinite depth-of-field sharpness. His subjects include carnival rides, moonlight, the night sky, water and piers, boats in port, oil refineries, landscapes, and structures.
Courtesy of Roger Vail.

ARTISTS ARE INSPIRED IN DIFFERENT WAYS

Artists have made many statements about what inspired their work. Art is not produced in a vacuum but by the inter-action and interrelationships of ideas, perceptions, and feelings expressed in some form. Artists are often motivated by the observation and memories of their surroundings. For example, Monet was inspired by light's changing effects on his garden and water-lily pond. Many artists can see the same object or place in many different and unique ways. This may inspire them to create a series of paintings of the same object or place because a single painting cannot express all that they see. At age 71, Henri Matisse lay in bed ill, but he had a library of images in his mind, and he continued using his memory to create bright, colorful collages. Marc Chagall based many of his fanciful paintings on memories of his childhood in a Russian village. He was also inspired by imaginative Russian folk tales. Grandma Moses did not begin painting until she was 60, but her rich storehouse of childhood memories provided plenty of material for her artworks.

Contemporary Osage Native American artist Gina Gray (see Figure 7.59) has stated that motherhood and the arts have been the priorities of her life. She said:

I have always drawn from and incorporated my Osage traditions along with my contemporary lifestyle into my paintings. I do not consider myself a traditional Native American artist, however. During my younger years, my family, along with many other Osage families at the time, was encouraged to move to a more urban settlement to experience the mainstream of society. So, technically, my cultural upbringing was very diverse. This was probably the origin of my strong usage of colors; the brilliance of the universe, the multiheritages of an urban collaboration, the personalities and the influences this multicultural lifestyle has had upon my people, however corrupt or divine.[3]

As a person trained in two cultural traditions, Brenda Louie (Figure 1.10 and Colorplate 18) seeks to demonstrate the uniqueness of each experience and to explore experiential similarities as an approach toward an artistic language. She uses elements from ancient Chinese hieroglyphs in concert with modern Western art theory. Her goal is to transcend ethnic barriers through artistic expression. She intends to extend cultural experience through interpretation. She stated:

In the works, "The River Dancing Series," I started with an idea derived from a concept of a "river." I

Figure 1.9 Maru Hoeber collects pine saplings to construct what is a recurring theme in her sculpture—a boat cast in bronze. *Photo by Barbara Herberholz.*

investigated the use of spontaneous free Chinese calligraphic brush strokes on a textured Western canvas. I am influenced by Chinese calligraphic gesture movement. The works of Mark Tobey and Brice Marden have provided a validation in the free use of Chinese writings. I am interested in an approach that once fascinated impressionists, the concept of light and color. I apply this concept through interaction with writings and brush works, to bring about the vitality and gesture of a metaphoric river.

Let's examine how their immediate surroundings influenced the following artists:

1. As a child, Louise Nevelson collected wood pieces from various sources and her family-owned lumberyards both in her native Russia and in the United States. These early childhood experiences probably influenced the art forms she produced in her adult life.

2. In his early work, David Smith collected cut pieces of metal from junkyards and welded them into sculpture. Smith was trained as a painter. To help support himself as an artist, he worked in an automotive assembly plant and welded parts together to make cars.

3. Another noted sculptor, Alexander Calder, made stabiles and mobiles out of large pieces of sheet metal. He

was trained as a mechanical engineer at a time when furnace boilers and steel bridges were riveted together. Many of his stabiles are riveted together, since the art of welding came later.

4. Japanese-American artist-teacher Yoshio Taylor draws ideas for his work from a myriad of sources—his memories, common objects, and everyday occurrences. His work consists of narrative, figurative sculpture combined with geometric shapes—shapes that relate to his impressions from architectural forms and the landscapes of Japan and America. His work is usually an extension of himself in which he tries to capture and express emotions common to all of us.

5. Artist-teacher Frank La Pena has said that his art is created to honor and show respect for those important in his life. Foremost are the elders and traditionalists—teachers who have shared with him the cultural richness and heritage of his Wintu-Nomtipom tribe and who have helped to build cultural bridges between many Northern California Valley tribes (Colorplate 28).

The works of other artists have always been a source of inspiration for artists. Contemporary artists have access to a wider range of artworks than was ever available in the past. These are in the form of books with fine color reproductions, slides, inexpensive posters and large reproductions, videos, the Internet, CD-ROMs, and exhibits in art museums, galleries, and the community at large. These sources allow access to contemporary art as well as to the art of previous centuries. Henry Moore was inspired by sculpture from many different cultures and periods, especially the sculpture of Africa and Mexico.[4] Picasso and Braque were inspired by African masks, and Mary Cassatt and van Gogh were among a number of artists who were intrigued with Japanese prints.

Darren Vigil-Gray, a Jicarilla Apache artist, was inspired by seeing his two cousins, who had returned from studying at the Institute of American Indian Arts in Santa Fe. He saw "this transformation . . . that they were exposed to something else. . . . I saw a lot of important stuff happening. So that influenced me."[5] His tribal upbringing resonates through his work, with animal figures appearing frequently. He loves birds of prey and includes half-human, half-bird figures in his paintings. His works show an ordered world of natural harmony, with humans living in accordance, but not dominating. He peers within the human psyche, his paint strokes illuminating human emotions.

When Vigil-Gray visited Europe, he found the long-established European art traditions to be equally inspiring: "Looking at European art, you understand that these people have been painting for thousands of years. They've got it down."[6] He has also adopted ideas from contemporary artists:

> What I find interesting is, for example, the **abstract expressionists** like Jackson Pollock, and even before him, Picasso, who looked toward indigenous peoples' art and found something that was so soulful, honest, and direct, and so simple that they had to use it. So why can't we do the opposite, why can't I use an element of Picasso or an element of Pollock or De Kooning."[7]

Not following the mainstream, Virgil-Gray is inspiring a new generation of artists to think beyond the regional confines of Native American art. For him, the artist's job is to "see the unseen."

Robert Bechtle, a photo-realist painter, revealed in an interview by Brian O'Doherty in *American Artists on Art from 1940 to 1980* that the inspiration to do new work came to him from a number of sources and that he became interested in figure painting because of his teacher, Richard Diebenkorn.[8] He also liked the American painters Thomas Eakins, Winslow Homer, and Edward Hopper, and he admired Vermeer and Degas very much.

Artists study the artworks of other artists, both past and present, and their work often reflects this historical knowledge. Jacob Lawrence (Colorplate 35) spoke of who his favorite artists were, and why, when he said:

> Perhaps I can explain best [what influences I have experienced] by telling who I like, Orozco, Daumier,

Figure 1.10 **Brenda Louie, *Self-Portrait*. Charcoal on paper, 81 × 24 in.**
Artist's collection, 1993.

> Goya. They're forceful. Simple. Human. In your own work, the human subject is the most important thing. Then I like Arthur Dove—I like to study the design, to see how the artist solves his problem, how he brings his subject to the public.[9]

Artists today study the works of other artists and know who their favorites are, and this visual information gives

Figure 1.12 **Robert Else, *Portraits*, 1994. Acrylic on canvas, 36 × 36 in.**
Robert Else was inspired by a family photograph of his mother when he painted this portrait. The floral bouquet is a personal symbol for the artist: His father was a gardener.
Courtesy of Robert Else.

Figure 1.11 Maria Winkler's still-life themes are directly related to her own childhood—her memories and feelings and objects that she or her parents once collected and treasured. Working in watercolors or pastels, she focuses on antique toys and games, cacti, shells, water lilies, and koi fish. Winkler first arranges her still lifes and takes a number of slides. Then she uses the images to help her perceive lines, shapes, colors, reflections, and shadows as she creates her composition.
Photo by Barbara Herberholz.

them inspiration or a basis for their work. Most painters do not start out to be abstract painters; in fact, most artists are still trained today to draw from real objects, natural or of human origin. Their training usually involves a long and intense search to find their subjects and their unique style of expression.

When children recall their own experiences, when they observe their world and its myriad sights and activities, and then use these sources for their artworks, they are working as artists. Teacher can guide students to explore these sources prior to an art activity by asking questions and making comments that activate students' thoughts, feelings, and perceptions.

Knowledge about artists and their artworks can inspire elementary students. An introduction to the many different kinds of artworks that have been created in diverse cultures

and in different times can provide elementary students not only with knowledge about art but also with the attitude that there is no one "right" or "wrong" way to make art, even though the theme or subject matter may be the same.

Artists sometimes use photographs, literary and historical references, or the Internet as resources for making art. Up through the nineteenth century, artists' links with artists in other countries and the images made by those artists were limited. Some artists traveled long distances to other places to study the paintings and sculptures being produced there. Today, the ease of travel to visit major museums as well as sophisticated technology brings cameras, videos, films, computers, and art reproductions to people everywhere. These visual influences have made artists aware of images and ideas of other artists from diverse cultures and often have an impact on artists' works.

When children compare and contrast an assortment of photographs related to a particular subject (for example, horses, flowers, buildings, figures-in-action, and so forth), they can perceive the many different varieties of a subject; analyze the shapes, colors, lines, and textures; and observe angles and proportions. Increased perceptual input results in a richer outpouring of artistic expression.

The invention of photography in the nineteenth century inspired a number of artists. For instance, Edgar Degas often cropped his compositions in the manner of snapshots. Henri Rousseau photographed his friends in a horse-drawn cart and used the picture to make a painting. Contemporary

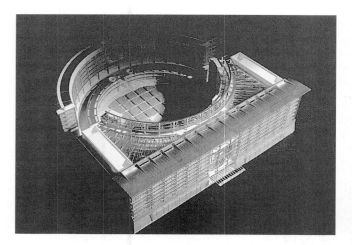

Figure 1.13 *Industrial and Commercial Bank of China,* **Beijing. Brian Lee, Architect, Skidmore, Owings & Merrill, LLP, San Francisco.**
Photograph by Fu Xing.

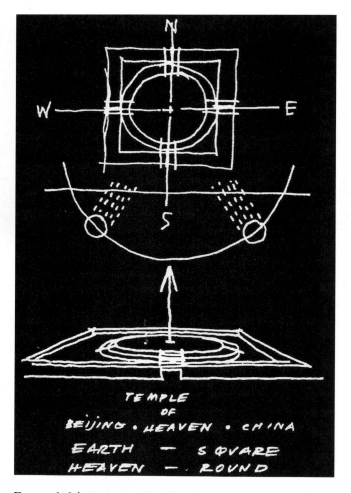

Figure 1.14 *Diagram of Building Concept, Industrial and Commercial Bank of China,* **Brian Lee, Architect, Skidmore, Owings & Merrill, LLP.**

painters Chuck Close, Maria Winkler (Figure 1.11) and (Colorplate 40), and Robert Else (Figure 1.12) are among the many artists who have created extremely diverse artworks from visual imagery in photographs.

Historical and literary references also inspire artists. Jacques Louis David used the historic account of two Roman families who swore to a fight-to-the-death battle in *Oath of the Horatii.* George Caleb Bingham told of life on the river as well as painting frontiersman *Daniel Boone* and his family as they headed westward toward Kentucky. Emmanuel Leutze's enormous painting of *Washington Crossing the Delaware* is a favorite of viewers in the National Gallery of Art in Washington, DC.

Traditional customs of a country's culture often influence the way an artist plans his or her work. Architect Brian Lee's concept for the design for the 11-story Industrial and Commercial Bank of China in Beijing (Figure 1.13 and 1.14) conforms to traditional patterns of Chinese civic architecture. Based on ancient Beijing city patterns and a symbolic circle and square geometry, the complex holds the street wall on the perimeter and carves a circular garden courtyard out of the center of the project. Following Chinese site principles, the main entry is at the south and the employee entries to the east and west.

Artists Are Collectors

Artists collect objects that excite their artistic visions. An object's uniqueness or any one of its aesthetic qualities may be attractive. For example, **pop artist** Andy Warhol collected a wide range of unusual objects. Fritz Scholder, a contemporary painter, has collected an extremely wide range of objects that attracted his fancy, even though he does not use them directly as inspiration for his paintings. Georges

Braque surrounded himself with many different collected objects, which he kept in his studio for visual inspiration: a rug, a guitar, thistles, fine art reproductions, bones, African masks, pebbles, and so on. A number of artists—for example Henry Moore, Barbara Hepworth, and Georgia O'Keeffe—have collected animal bones for inspiration. Rembrandt spent large amounts of money purchasing exotic items from around the world, later using them as costumes and props in his paintings.

Artists are usually highly selective in what they choose to view or in what might inspire them or influence their thinking. Marisol said that her art was influenced by pre-Columbian Mochica pottery jars, Mexican boxes with pictures painted inside, and early American folk art.[10] Sculptor Louise Nevelson collected "found objects" from the streets of New York because they intrigued her vision, and she later incorporated some of them in her sculptures. She also collected rugs, a Paul Klee, Mexican santos, and African sculpture.[11]

Figure 1.15 **Kurt Edward Fishback,** *Viola Frey* **©1981.**
Frey's ceramic studio is in one corner of her backyard and is filled with larger-than-life-size figures of the artist herself. Her brothers were all tall and teased her about being short, so she made the figures taller than she was because that is how she pictured herself.
Courtesy of Herberholz.

Young Pablo Picasso ignored his toys and carefully collected items that appealed to him. It is said that once, when he broke one of his seashells, he threw a temper tantrum and could not be consoled: He had discovered that each shell was unique. Children are natural collectors and need little or no encouragement to horde seashells, interesting stones, feathers, dry leaves, and other items.

Learning from Critics

Artists sometimes learn more about their works by reading or listening to an art critic's review. American artist Jasper Johns talked about how the art critic can help other people to see in a new way and can even influence the artist's future work:

There is a great deal of intention in painting; it's rather unavoidable. But when a work is let out by the artist and said to be complete, the intention loosens. Then it's subject to all kinds of use and misuse and pun. Occasionally, someone will see the work in a way that even changes its significance for the person who made it; the work is no longer "intention," but the thing being seen and someone responding to it. They will see it in a way that makes you think, that is a possible way of seeing it. Then you, as the artist, can enjoy it—that's possible—or you can lament it. If you like, you can try to express the intention more clearly in another work.[12]

The dialogue of the art critic, fellow artist, or the public stimulates the artist to change or extend an idea, and the dialogue is never-ending. Art teachers serve a similar function as art critics when they assist their students in assessing their own artwork. A teacher's comments can focus specifically on positive aspects—what the student has done that has made the painting show balance, harmony, and unity; how the student has been especially creative or imaginative; or how the student has shown a special mood or feeling. Comments and questions can also help students to focus on how they might change the painting or how they would choose to do it next time.

ARTISTS WORK IN DIFFERENT WAYS

When we study the lives of artists through the things they have said or written, or what has been written about them, we can better understand their work habits and how their thought processes evolved in creating art. When we increase our understanding of the meanings and functions of artists' work, we are better able to know how art can function in the lives of elementary students.

Artists often focus on a particular theme, **medium**, or technique for their artworks over a period of time. Photographer Kurt Fishback, who made Viola Frey's portrait (Figure 1.15), stated that her work was everywhere.[13] What was once a large living room was now her painting studio with three easels set up and paintings on each of them in various stages of completion. Upstairs rooms held a variety of styles of ceramic sculpture, one room having nothing but large plates in it.

On the other hand, artists are challenged by variety or a change in media or themes. For instance, after working intensely in oil paints over a period of time, an artist may find new inspiration and opportunities for solving aesthetic problems by switching to printmaking or, perhaps, a three-dimensional medium. Pablo Picasso, who produced an enormous number of paintings during his long and productive life, combined scrap metal and children's toys to create fanciful sculptures.

Most artists make sketches or drawings before they do their final artwork. Some make sketches or preparatory drawings on grid paper. This same grid drawing is then transferred to a canvas with a larger grid for the finished artwork. Artist Joan Miró, for example, used this grid system in planning his large paintings. A few artists, such as action painter Jackson Pollock, used a more spontaneous approach; but more often, artists mull over the idea or experience for a period of time and make sketches before they create the final artwork. Time to reflect is an important factor. Elementary students should be encouraged to make sketches and give thought to the preparation of an artwork.

Artists are totally engrossed in their work. As expressed in an old saying, inspiration comes to the prepared mind, and a lot of perspiration is involved in inspiration. To the lay person, a painting or piece of sculpture may appear to spring directly and immediately from the artist's hands and mind—a burst of genius. However, most artists develop ideas by making many sketches before beginning the final artwork. Their sketchbooks constantly freshen their vision and sharpen their skills, as well as help them select a viewpoint, frame their composition, observe nuances of light and shadow, and simplify and abstract the basic elements. They may draw the same object or pose again and again—changing, accenting, deleting, and **distorting**.

Figure 1.16 **Drawbridge in Arles in southern France.**
Artists frequently become immersed in painting their surroundings. Newly arrived in Arles, Vincent van Gogh felt a sense of nostalgia when he saw this drawbridge as it reminded him of his native Holland, and he made several paintings of it.
Photo by Barbara Herberholz.

Degas kept a wooden horse in his studio after making numerous sketches at the racetrack. Thomas Eakins made a small boat from a cigar box, placed little rag figures inside, and then tried to get the true effect by putting the box and its occupants out in the sunlight. Sculptors such as Michelangelo and Rodin always made models of clay or wax first. Modern technology has given today's artists the camera, duplicating machines, computers, and other aids to help them plan their compositions.

Some artists do not make preliminary sketches, but they have a general idea of what they wish to make, and as they progress, the work itself gives them direction. American painter Robert Motherwell, when asked what one of his pictures meant, said, "I realized there were about 10,000 brush strokes in it and that each brush stroke is a decision."[14] The work in progress becomes the inspiration as each change occurs. Or as Motherwell said, with the application of each new brush stroke, another decision is made. This is often the way younger children paint.

The medium may dictate the way the artist works. Before the invention of oil paints in tubes, artists made sketches outdoors and completed the work in their studios. Artists think in terms of the medium while they make preparatory sketches because of numerous in-depth experiences with particular media. If artists are not familiar with a new material or technique, they often approach it in a free and playful way until they can judge what they can and cannot do. Similarly, elementary students need multiple experiences with each art medium to gain knowledge of its expressive potential.

Some artists respond to their environment not only with sketches and drawings but with verbal descriptions as well. Vincent van Gogh was extremely articulate with both words and paint brush. His letters to his brother Theo testified to this, for he frequently described in vivid and lush details his perceptions and feelings about how he was drawing and painting his surroundings and about the people who inspired his artworks. One of his letters described his painting *Night Cafe*:

> I have tried to express the idea that the cafe is a place where one can ruin oneself, run mad, or commit a crime. I have tried to express the terrible passions of humanity by means of red and green. The room is blood-red and dark yellow, with a green billiard table in the middle; there are four lemon-yellow lamps with a glow of orange and green. Everywhere there is a clash and contrast of the most alien reds and greens in the figures of little sleeping hooligans in the empty dreary room, in violet and blue. The white coat of the patron, on vigil in a corner, turns lemon-yellow, or pale luminous green.[15]

ARTISTS BEGIN EARLY OR LATE IN LIFE

The starting point in the education of artists is their sensory impressions and feelings as children. These first impressions are as diverse as the individual styles manifested in their mature artworks. Some artists use their perceptions to begin drawing and painting images at a very early age; others have parents who are artists and who provide early instruction.

The age at which artists first show their exceptional abilities and intense drives to make art varies considerably. If we examine the careers of some familiar artists, we find a wide disparity in the time of life when they began to pursue a career in art. Charles Russell, the well-known artist of the American West, is said to have drawn pictures from characters that came to his mind as his mother read Bible stories. When he was four years old, he strayed from home and followed a man with a trained bear on a chain. That evening, he scraped the mud from his shoes and modeled a small figure of the bear, his first sculpture. At age 12, he received a blue ribbon for one of his drawings at the St. Louis County Fair. From his earliest years, Russell loved the West, learning of the adventures and life on the frontier from relatives who had built a fort on the Arkansas River and had been fur traders on the Upper Missouri. After receiving a pony on his tenth birthday, he decided that one day he would go West and be a cowboy. Later in military school, where he had been sent by well-meaning parents, he filled his notebooks with sketches of cowboys and Indians and then spent most of his time walking guard duty as punishment for his inattention. One term there concluded Russell's formal education.

A famous artist named Cimabue discovered young Giotto (the forerunner of the Italian Renaissance) one day when the young boy was drawing with a sharp stone on a flat rock while herding sheep. The French artist Toulouse-Lautrec, the Spanish artist Pablo Picasso, and American artists Edward Hopper, Thomas Hart Benton, John James Audubon, Winslow Homer, Georgia O'Keeffe, and Mary Cassatt are all people whose talents and ambitions bloomed early in exceptional ways. French artist Maurice Utrillo was encouraged at age 18 by his artist mother, who brought him paints and picture postcards when he was confined to a hospital for alcoholism. Southwestern artist Darren Vigil-Gray stated that he started painting as a teenager and always wanted to paint, that he never wanted to do anything else: "I didn't want to be a carpenter . . . electrician . . . plumber, I didn't want to be president."[16]

Russian artist Wassily Kandinsky began his artistic career later in life. He had obtained a law degree and was offered a professorship but left for Munich to study painting. French artist Henri Matisse was also trained to be a lawyer, but while recovering from an illness, he began to paint and soon gave up his law career. Vincent van Gogh decided to be an artist at the age of 27, after having failed at a number of other endeavors. French **naive** artist Henri Rousseau was a customs official until he retired at the age of 40 to paint. The explosive artistic energies of Paul Gauguin caused him to give up family and a prosperous stock brokerage and leave behind the confines of Parisian city life. He fled to the French countryside, and later to the South Seas, to paint.

Perhaps you know a child who loves to draw and paint, who does it regularly with skill and creativity, and whose parents are supportive; this child may already be saying that he or she wants to be an artist. Yani, a young Chinese girl, began showing her magnificent talent at the age of three. Her paintings have been widely exhibited in U.S. museums. At the other end of the age continuum, you may have a parent or grandparent who took up painting for the first time in an adult education class and found that he or she was able to achieve a lifelong goal. Americans Horace Pippin and Grandma Moses are examples of late bloomers.

The training of many artists in the past consisted of studying and copying great works of art. As youths, many artists trained as apprentices in studios of professional artists. But one thing all artists have in common, no matter what their age, is an inner drive to create art. Nothing else matters to them except the urge to produce art. It is an all-consuming passion that in most cases drastically changes their lives.

Today, in our highly technological world, most artists have formal art training. They often start their art careers at home under the guidance of an artist parent or in art classes for children. Public-supported schools provide training for the artist as well as for the doctor, lawyer, engineer, and elementary teacher. A number of outstanding contemporary artists teach at major universities.

Figure 1.17 **Malaguias Montoya, *El Profe*, 1996.**
Computer portrait of Jose Montoya from a black-and-white photograph
by Art Luna. New technology provides opportunities for the creative use
of photographs.
Courtesy of Jose Montoya.

There is no one way to train or educate an artist. Anyone who draws or paints probably has at some time or other copied from drawings, photographs, or paintings by other artists to learn and better understand color, shading, perspective, or a particular style or technique. Museums give permits to art students to make copies of pieces from their collection, albeit in a different size than the original to prevent forgery. Contemporary artist Grace Hurtigan copied the works of famous artists from history to try to understand where she really came from. She had to find her roots.

Studying to be an artist is like studying for any other profession: You study the content of the subject. Most artists have stated that they became artists because a strong inner feeling always told them that is what they wanted to be. As a nine-year-old, Louise Nevelson said when a librarian asked her what she wanted to be when she grew up, "I am going to be an artist. No. I want to be a sculptor, I don't want color to help me."[17] Nevelson did not become a world-famous artist by just wishing to be one. She received training, studied art, and enriched her understanding of herself to accomplish her goal.

In studying the lives of artists, the images they make, what inspires them, what they collect, and what they say about their artworks and their working processes, we begin to see the diversity of their individual approaches to each of these aspects of their lives. By examining their production techniques, we, as elementary teachers, can better plan studio activities for the students in our care. Through this study, we will be better able to relate this content to our students to assist them in producing and responding to their own artworks and the artworks of others.

INTERACTIVE EXTENSIONS

1. Give some thought to your own art background and fill out "My Personal Art Inventory" on page 17.

2. Using references and the form "Purposes of Art in Diverse Cultures" on page 17, select at least four purposes of art and find examples of each of these from four different global cultures.

3. Choose an artist mentioned in Chapter 7, fill out the blanks on the "Artists at Work" worksheet on page 18. Use and list at least two references (books, videos, Internet, magazine articles, CD-ROMs). During a class meeting, compare your artist with those researched by other class members.

4. Review two videos on different artists, and use the form on page 17 to make short statements that tell four things that you learned from watching each video.

5. When you draw, paint, or work in three dimensions, what sources do you use for inspiration? Are they similar to or different from those of the artists described in this chapter? If you have taken any studio art classes, were you encouraged to use similar sources of inspiration?

6. What objects do you collect? Did you collect anything as a child? What relationship do these items have to any art you might create?

7. How have recent technology and new inventions provided avenues for artists to use in creating new kinds of artworks? (See Chapter 6 for websites.)

Purposes of Art in Diverse Cultures

Refer to one or more art history books or the Internet, and select four artworks from four different global cultures that are examples of your choice of the different purposes of art listed below. Discuss your choices in class with other students.

Purposes	Culture or Country of Origin
Inspiring or instructing for religious purposes	
Ceremonial, controlling natural forces	
Recording a likeness	
Telling stories, history, myths, legends	
Propaganda, political, social comment	
Personal expression	
Utilitarian	
Decorate, embellish	
Other	

Reviewing Videos on Artists

Name _____

View two videotapes in the media center in the library. Write in the title in the space below. Then write four statements about the artist and his or her artwork that you learned from watching the video.

Name of video _____   **Librarian's stamp** _____
  1.
  2.
  3.
  4.

Name of video _____   **Librarian's stamp** _____
  1.
  2.
  3.
  4.

My Personal Art Inventory

  1. My definition of art.
  2. What do I remember about my art lessons when I was in elementary school?
  3. Courses in art that I have had in high school or college include:
  4. I would like to acquire these skills in art production during this class:
  5. I would like to acquire this knowledge as to art history and art criticism:
  6. The elements of art are:
  7. The principles of art are:
  8. Three important periods, schools, or eras in the history of art are:
  9. I have/have not visited an art museum recently. If so, what do you remember most about the experience?
 10. My favorite artist is _____ because _____ .
 11. I feel/do not feel that art is an important area of study for elementary students for the following reasons:
 12. I think that these components or disciplines should be included in the elementary art curriculum:
 13. I think that (amount of time) _____ each week should be devoted to art instruction in the elementary classroom.

Artists at Work

Choose an artist listed in Chapter 7. Use reference books, videos, and websites to supply you with the following specific information in regard to the artist you have selected. Be prepared to participate in a class discussion that will focus on how artists are different and how they are similar to each other.

1. Your name.
2. Artist's name; life span; nationality; correct pronunciation of his or her name.
3. Artist's childhood experiences; early training and influences; parents' occupations.
4. Artist's working habits, visual resources, where and how artist obtained visual information and ideas for his or her art production; items collected, if any.
5. Events of the same period of time and in the same country where artist lived that may have influenced him or her.
6. Artists that may have influenced him or her.
7. Degree of success in lifetime; degree of success later.
8. What influence did this artist have on other artists or on society?
9. Artist's main subjects and themes; style; prevalent medium used.
10. Main contribution of this artist: why is this artist notable?
11. Quotation by the artist, and your reaction to his or her quotation.
12. List a minimum of two references used for this report (excluding your textbook).

2
CHAPTER

Understanding and Using the Elements of Art:
Response and Production

Instead of using words, as authors do when they write poems or stories, artists use a visual language called the **elements of art** when they create artworks. The six elements of art are the basic ingredients, the building blocks of artist. They are **line, color, shape/form, texture, space,** and **value.** We will identify and examine each element of art, defining and describing its characteristics and properties to see how artists use it in making art. Then we will apply what we have learned to producing our own artworks.

Chapter 3 focuses on the individual **principles of art.** There, we will explore the guidelines that help us analyze an artwork and understand how it is organized and composed. We will endeavor to unravel how an artwork gives us a feeling of **informal balance,** or how different kinds of lines lead our eyes to a focal point. We will come to understand how shapes can create a pattern, or how **variety** and **unity** must be closely allied.

The elements and principles of art are universal in concept, but artists in different cultures may use them in different ways. How a particular group of people uses color or pattern, for instance, may help us identify works from that culture. A German school of design called the **Bauhaus** (bough house), which Walter Gropius founded in 1919, emphasized understanding and working with the elements and principles of art. Great masters in many fields of art and crafts taught there, all of them emphasizing the basic elements and principles of design.

The first step in understanding and responding to artworks, as well as in producing artworks, is to applaud each "performer" (each element and principle of art) individually as each one "takes a bow." Just as each actor, lighting technician, and stagehand has an important part in making a dramatic production a hit, so does each element and principle of art have an important part in making an artwork a masterpiece. Our thoughtful analysis and reflection, as well as our hands-on involvement with each art element and art principle, will start us on our way to becoming enthusiastic and interested viewers of artworks, as well as confident, eager artwork producers.

UNDERSTANDING ARTWORKS: Learning about Line

Ten to fifteen thousand years ago, when the Ice Age was ending and huge glaciers were receding, people lived in caves and used primitive weapons as they hunted the large animals on which they depended for food and clothing. This was the Stone Age, and from it came our earliest known artworks. If you had lived then, perhaps you would have looked at the ceilings and walls of your domicile one day and in the undulating bulges and rounded forms of their surfaces seen what might have suggested to you the powerful forms of bison, horses, and other animals with which you

Figure 2.1 **Henri de Toulouse-Lautrec,** *At the Circus: Trained Pony and Baboon,* **ca. 1899. Colored pencil, black pastel, and graphite, on cream wove paper: 17½ × 10½ in.**
Gift of Tiffany and Margaret Blake, 1944.581.
Lautrec's use of spontaneous, graceful contour lines suggests a lively sense of arrested motion in this drawing.
Photograph ©2002 The Art Institute of Chicago, all rights reserved.

were familiar. Do you think you might have been tempted to trace your finger around the edges of what you imagined you saw? Perhaps you would have had the desire, as well as the ingenuity, to fashion a tool of some sort from bones and plant fibers or animal fur. You would have dipped this tool into a coloring agent made by mixing animal fat with charcoal or powders from ground rocks. You might have discovered that placing your hand on a cave wall and blowing around it with dry, powdery pigment through a hollow bone or reed created the outline of your hand. That was your "signature" and, incidentally, the first stencil. You might have marveled so much at your accomplishment that you repeated and perfected your line drawings on the cave walls in an

Figure 2.2 **Alexander Calder, *Somersaulters*, 1931. Pen and ink, 22¾ × 30¾ in.**
Collection of Mr. and Mrs. Alvin S. Lane, Riverdale, NY. ©2002 Estate of Alexander Calder/Artists Rights Society (ARS) New York.
The lines in this drawing that make up these very active and limber acrobatic figures suggest wire, a medium with which the American artist Alexander Calder frequently used in his mobiles.

effort to have some control over the enormous and often frightening creatures upon which your existence depended. Your ability to make good likenesses of these creatures with your lines probably meant that you were held in high esteem by other tribe members, who thought you had special powers.

Since these early times, artists have used lines in many ways and have made many different kinds of this important element of art. Today, we certainly have many more sophistated drawing implements than the early cave artists did.

Line may be defined as the mark left by a dot or point moving continuously through space or over a surface. It starts someplace and stops someplace, and leaves a path as it is drawn across the paper or other surface.

Probably the most common use for the element of line is to show the edges—that is, the contours—of an object. The line marks the place where the object stops and the air or space around the object begins. In a **contour line drawing**, we draw both the inner and outer contours of the person or object, or else we would only be drawing a flat shape with no details. This is usually thought of as a silhouette. In a line drawing, contour lines inside the object give it a three-dimensional quality. Strong, black outlines and hard edges add clarity and interest, and sharply define the shapes in an artwork. They also make items stand out and add a decorative accent. Many painters do not use contour lines at all. They show the contour of an object by separate colors or textures. Turn to the Color Gallery, and identify two artworks in which the artist used lines to show edges; then locate two artworks in which different colors, rather than outlines, separate the edges of shape.

The drawing tool with which a line is made relates to the line's character. The thin, neat sharpness of a pen-and-ink line looks very different from the fuzzy, blurry one made with a crayon. Lines may be quickly drawn and give us a sense of movement and spontaneity as we see in Alexander Calder's lively drawing (Figure 2.2). His playful approach and his sense of fun is evidenced in the entire wire circus he once built and in the toys he made as a child. The fluid, undulating line made with a soft, sable brush is very different from a crisp, constant pencil line. Of considerable importance also is the drawing surface upon which a line is made. An absorbent, coarse paper responds to the same drawing tool in a different way than paper with a hard, smooth surface.

Line has a number of characteristics. It has direction: horizontal, vertical, and diagonal. Vertical lines suggest strength, stability, and dignity, and remind us of lofty or quiet things. They lead our eyes upward. Think of tall pine trees in a forest or a row of columns in Greek or Roman architecture, or tall skyscrapers in a city. Horizontal lines give us a restful feeling and suggest calm, peaceful things. Think of floating on your back on the smooth surface of a lake. Diagonal lines, on the other hand, tend to create tension, movement, and uneasy feelings. They suggest motion and lead our eyes in a slanting upward, downward, or forward direction. Think of waves tossing on a stormy sea, a

Figure 2.3 **Vincent van Gogh,** *Grove of Cypresses*, **1889. Reed pen and ink over pencil on paper, 62.5 × 46.4 cm.**
Gift of Robert Allerton (1927.543). Photograph ©2002 The Art Institute of Chicago. All rights reserved.
Van Gogh's characteristic swirling, curving strokes are repeated again and again to create restless trees in this landscape. The artist was skilled in achieving the utmost effect from a flexible pen.

Figure 2.4 **Kathe Kollwitz,** *Self-Portrait* **Etching, 41 × 46 cm.**
Orlando Museum of Art, Florida/Bridgeman Art Library, New York.
©2002 Artists Rights Society (ARS), New York/VG Bild-Kunst, Bonn.
Sketchy lines, some layered for dark areas, contribute to the soulful and sad self-portrait by this German expressionist artist whose life was affected by the loss of her son and grandson in world wars. The bulk of her work is in black and white prints and drawings.

skier on a steep slope, or a ride on a roller coaster. These lines draw our eyes up, across, or down. Note how Wayne Thiebaud used strong diagonal lines in *Highland River* (Colorplate 27) and how Frank La Pena relied on dominant vertical lines to lend strength to the central form and on repeated diagonal lines to direct our attention to the figure's head in *Flower Dance Spirit* (Colorplate 28).

Our eyes follow the paths made by curving, angular, or diagonal lines, or by lines that meander and intertwine. For examples of these characteristics, turn to the Color Gallery. How are Jacob Lawrence's *Vaudeville* (Colorplate 35), Maria Winkler's *Marbles Spill III* (Colorplate 40), and Franz Marc's *Yellow Cow* (Colorplate 24) different in the use of line? How are they alike?

Lines that have been repeated in a rhythmic or random manner also lead our eyes in a certain direction. Lines that capture a fleeting movement or the posture of a subject are called **gesture lines**. These lines are usually scribbled, free-flowing, and made with a quick and continuous hand movement. The popular French artist, Toulouse-Lautrec, ventured

into the late-nineteenth-century night life of Parisian cabarets, cafes, and the circus, always making quick drawings and sketches that show us his highly skillful use of line (Figure 2.1). An **implied line** also can "take our eyes for a walk" in a composition. This means that a series of unlinked lines suggests a directional path or contour that our eyes tend to connect. Because we expect a line to be continuous, our eyes follow it even beyond the format of the picture.

Line has other characteristics as well. Lines have length and width; they may be short or long, thick or thin. They may be dark or light in value, either blurred and uneven, or sharp and clear-edged. They may change from thick to thin and be called a gradated line. They may be continuous or broken. Lautrec's innovative posters with their variety of lines advertising the performers and the entertainment world were widely acclaimed in his own time.

Artists have various intentions when they utilize the element of line. They may use line realistically, or they may use it expressively to show distorted and exaggerated objects. Kathe Kollwitz has used line both realistically and expressively in her haunting self-portrait (Figure 2.4). A line is decorative when it is used to embellish surfaces. In this capacity, it is often repeated in an orderly arrangement to create a linear pattern. An abstract use of line focuses on the line quality itself, rather than the object the artist is depicting.

Artists generally use line to make drawings and etchings. Line drawings may exist as ends in themselves and be regarded as artworks, or they may be preparatory plans for paintings, pieces of sculpture, crafts, or architecture. A line

Figure 2.5 **Utagawa Hiroshige I,** *The Mie River near Yokkaichi* **(The Hurricane), Japanese, Ukiyoye School, Print, 37.9 × 25.2 cm. 1797-1858.**
©The Cleveland Museum of Art. 2002, Gift of Mrs. T. Wingate Todd (1948.307).
Movement and action are seen in the masterful use of line in this wood block print. Thick lines mark the posts on the dock. Delicate lines give a feeling of gesture in the windblown grasses and leafy tree branches. Can you find horizontal lines and diagonal lines that direct your eyes to the focal point?

drawing requires coordinating the eye, the hand, and the mind, a process that requires practice. Instruction in making contour lines can help students learn to see lines in the natural environment and to develop the necessary skills to make drawings that are personally and individually expressive.

PRODUCING ARTWORKS EMPHASIZING LINE

Drawing Contour Lines

Contour drawing is an art skill that transcends the stage of drawing the symbols associated with early childhood to achieve the more realistic drawing associated with older children and adults. This is often referred to as utilizing the resources of the right hemisphere of the brain instead of those of the left.[1] (See Colorplate 2 in the Children's Gallery, which shows a feather drawn with this process and colored with changeable markers.)

Contour drawing is an excellent way to establish contact with our visual powers of observation. It is the fastest way to establish our belief in our ability to draw. It is a way to help students start drawing and to affirm that they really can draw what they see in front of them. The success of this

technique may simply be that, due to intense visual concentration, we arrive at a state of heightened perception. When this occurs, time seems to stand still, and after a while, the drawing is accomplished with little effort. Great artists seem to take this leap naturally, with little or no outside help. Many of them do not realize that "seeing like an artist" is not something that everyone can do without instruction. The great artist Matisse was once asked if he saw a tomato the way everyone else did. He replied that if he was going to eat it, yes; if he was going to draw it, he "saw it like an artist."

Betty Edwards described an unusual technique that helps students understand this phenomenon and convinces them that they really can draw what they see in front of them.[2] A line drawing by an artist—for example, Picasso or Matisse—is placed upside down on the table in front of a student. The student is less able to see the rather complex arrangement of in-and-out lines, curving and angular lines, intersecting lines such as fingers, arms, hair, and such. The student does not name the parts of the picture and tries to eliminate words from his or her thought pattern. Then the student intently focuses on one line at a time—copying it and connecting it with another line. Gradually, the drawing is accomplished, and when turned right side up, bears a striking resemblance to the original drawing by Picasso or Matisse. Although we cannot turn landscapes, objects, and

Figure 2.6 **Pablo Picasso,** *The Bull (Le taureau),* **1973 (second state [top], fourth state [center], eleventh state [bottom]). Lithograph on Arches paper.**
National Gallery of Art, Washington, Alisa Mellon Bruce Fund, Photograph ©2002 Board of Trustees, National Gallery of Art, Washington. ©2002 Estate of Pablo Picasso/Artists Rights Society (ARS), New York.

people upside down to draw them, the intense perceptual experience of observing contours in an unaccustomed manner (upside down) can be transferred to other situations, such as when the student is drawing items as a flower, cowboy boot, or potted plant.

Our left brain is thought to label and categorize things through the use of words. Claude Monet, the great impressionist painter, said that, to see, we have to forget the name of the thing we are observing. As young children, we tend to think mostly in pictures, not in words; however, by age eight or nine, children seem to stop visualizing things freely and start putting word labels on them instead. Too often, the school's stress on verbal and digital skills rules out visualizing things to the extent that students no longer see anything with clarity and sensitivity and only recognize things by their labels.

To demonstrate how artists perceive contours, place a large sheet of clear vinyl over a large print by a great master, such as van Gogh, Gauguin, or da Vinci. Using a water-based black marking pen, slowly draw a continuous line around the outside edges of the figure or face; then draw the inside contour lines. Now place the vinyl on a white surface, and you will see a contour drawing. The pen marks may be removed with a damp paper towel and the vinyl used again.

Edwards stated that it is the left half of the brain that tells us that we cannot draw, insists on a hurried symbolic representation, and gives names to things.[3] The right side, on the other hand, is nonverbal and is fascinated with how a contour line, or edge of something, curves in here, juts out a little farther down, meets another edge at another place, and so on. Whether our right, left, or whole brain is involved, the drawing technique that follows works with adults and older children who feel that they cannot draw.

Simply stated, contour drawing is using a continuous line to draw the outer as well as inner edges of an object while intensely looking at the object. You will need some white paper, masking tape, and a soft lead pencil or fine-tipped black marking pen. (Using a pen is preferable in that the student is discouraged from stopping to erase.) Here are a few suggestions to help you make contour drawings:

1. Find several objects for practicing this technique—a leafy twig, a flower, a doll, car keys, a pair of pliers, a turkey feather, your shoe, a cross-section of an orange or apple, and so on.

2. You will be drawing on a piece of white paper. Tape it on the table in front of you so it will not move. Your concentration needs to focus on what you are observing, not on keeping your paper from moving.

3. Place the object you are going to draw in front of you. Placing it on a piece of paper of a contrasting color helps you see the edges.

4. To break the old habit of looking at your paper rather than at the object you are drawing, your first drawing

Figure 2.7 **Student work: Drawing with glue.**

will follow every little in-and-out curve, bump, wrinkle, indentation, or angle that you see. To break any old habit you may have of drawing in a rapid, sketchy manner, pretend that a very sleepy little ant is crawling along the edge of the object and that your pen is right behind it, pushing it along. Do not lift your pen while you are drawing a particular contour line. When you reach a stopping point and need to reposition your pencil to draw another contour line, stop drawing, peek under the protective shield, lift your pen, find a new starting point, and continue drawing another contour. But do not start drawing again until your eyes are on the object.

8. Draw inside contour lines also. Keep adding as many linear details as you can find. Remember that a contour is where the edge of one thing stops and something else begins. Inner contours add realism and give your artwork three-dimensional form.

9. After you have made a blind contour drawing, remove the protective shield and begin making modified contour drawings. While you do this, your eyes should focus on the object about 90 percent of the time and on the paper the remaining 10 percent of the time. Try to look at the paper only enough to keep your lines meeting in the appropriate places. A slowly drawn, sensitive line is the result of careful observation.

10. Find someplace where you can practice drawing without interruption for about 20 minutes a day. Try making a contour drawing of a landscape, a person's face (your own in a mirror or a friend's), a mounted bird, a butterfly. You can use contour drawing skills while working with photographs as well as with real objects.

Lines That Are Curving and Straight: Drawing with Glue

Students will squeeze a bottle of white glue onto black paper, leaving a trail of curving and straight lines (Figure 2.7). When the glue dries, the lines show up as black because of the dried glue's transparency. Pastels (not oil pastels) or colored chalk that is labeled for use on paper rather than chalkboards are then applied to the black paper. Use fingers to rub and blend the colors and push the dust of the pastels or chalk up close to the raised glue lines so that they will show up.

1. Make a contour drawing with a pencil on a piece of 12-by-18-inch black construction paper. Use pictures of dinosaurs or scale models of them, photos of butterflies, birds or flowers, animals, and so on as your source of visual information. Carefully observe the outer and inner edges of your subject matter. Look for curving, straight, angular, and wavy lines. Make your object large and include some background. Use lines to

will be a blind contour drawing. To prepare to do this, poke the point of a pencil through the middle of a 4-by-6-inch piece of paper. Hold the pen with your hand under the paper so that you cannot see your hand or the pen point as they move on the drawing paper. This protective shield will force you to keep your eyes on the object you are drawing and not on your paper. Plan on making your drawing at least as large as the actual object.

5. Sit comfortably and relax. Listen to soft, relaxing instrumental music (no words!) if you wish. Plan to spend about 10 minutes with each of your first contour drawings.

6. Pick a point on the object and a corresponding point on your paper. Convince yourself that your pen and eye are simultaneously following the object's outer contours. Better still, convince yourself that your pen is actually touching the object and moving along its edges, rather than touching and moving on the surface of the paper.

7. Draw slowly! The line you make will be continuous and

Figure 2.8 **Georges Rouault, *Christ Mocked by Soldiers*, 1932. Oil on canvas, 36¼ × 28½ in.**
The Museum of Modern Art, New York. Given anonymously. Photograph ©2001 The Museum of Modern Art, New York. ©2002 Artists Rights Society (ARS), New York/ADAGP, Paris.

Figure 2.9 Bold, black outlines painted with tempera in this student work enclose shapes that are filled with thick paint applied with strong, thick brush strokes. Colors appear jewel-like in their stained-glass type of enclosures.

enclose shapes and to make repeated patterns. Have some of the lines extend off the edges of the paper.

2. Go over your pencil lines by squeezing a rather thick trail of glue from the bottle. The glue tends to shrink as it dries and may be too narrow if you don't. You can make thick and thin lines, gradated lines, broken lines, and small dots. Let the glue dry several hours or overnight.

3. Use pastels (not oil pastels) to color the shapes your lines created on the black paper. Blend colors with your fingertips. Limit your color selection, and endeavor to create a contrast between the subject and background, that is, **cool colors** for the object and **warm colors** for the background. Do not leave any black paper showing or the glue lines will not show up.

Thick Black Lines: Painting with Tempera

Students will use a photo as a visual resource and use thick, black **tempera** paint to make lines to enclose shapes that will then be painted with mixtures of colors in the manner of the artist Georges Rouault. (Figures 2.8 and 2.9.)

1. Use a photograph of a butterfly, an insect, an animal, a face, an elephant, a fox, a hot air balloon, an airplane, an owl, flowers, a turtle, and so on. Look at the basic lines and shapes that you see, and simplify them as you make a large drawing of the object with a piece of chalk on a piece of white or manila drawing paper. Enclose the various shapes and parts of the object you have drawn with strong contour lines. Divide the background area with horizontal, vertical, or diagonal lines that go to the edges of the paper, creating enclosed shapes. Think of stained glass and how strips of lead enclose each separate piece of glass. This technique was used by the artist Georges Rouault.

2. Use some black tempera and a flat or round stiff-bristle brush, and paint over your chalk marks, making bold, fairly thick lines. Let the paint dry.

3. Choose two colors, or one color and white or black. Try using two primary colors together, or two colors that are next to each other on the color wheel, or a pair of complementary colors. Do not mix the paint on a palette. Brush the first color inside one of the enclosed areas, and add the second color to it. Brush until the surface of the paper inside the enclosed space is covered. Try not to brush until all the colors are smoothly mixed. Let your brush strokes show in the manner that the artist Rouault did. This manner of applying thick, opaque paint is called **impasto**, in that textural features of the paint and brushwork show on the painting's surface. Choose two more colors, and continue painting inside each of the enclosed areas until the entire surface of your paper is covered.

Figure 2.10 **Student work,** *A Street in Our Town.*
This group project by university students, using Scratch-Foam prints, shows a diversity of styles of houses, some overlapping, all placed on a ground-sky background.
Photo by Barbara Herberholz.

4. Let your painting dry. Flatten it with an iron on the reverse side before mounting or matting.

Repeated Lines: Relief Prints

Students will make a **relief print** by making indented lines in a soft sheet of Scratch-Foam (available in art supply catalogs). The final products, in this case, houses, will be used to create a group mural (Figure 2.10). Other subject matter may be used to make a class mural of birds, fish, animals, insects, and so forth.

1. Bring to class sketches you have made of the fronts of houses, or use photographs of Victorian houses. This provides you with visual information for your print.

2. Cut a sheet of Scratch-Foam into halves or quarter sizes. Use white copy paper to prepare a preliminary line drawing the same size as your Scratch-Foam. Plan areas where you will repeat long or broken lines, cross-hatched lines, or repeated lines and dots to create a pattern. Plan where you will have thick and thin lines, and where you will have white areas. Plan where you will have a center of interest. To create interest, make some of the lines extend off the sides of the composition.

Remember: Everything that is up will print black; everything that is pressed down will print white.

3. Tape your prepared sketch on top of the Scratch-Foam sheet, and go over the lines firmly with a pencil to imprint the lines on the Scratch-Foam surface. Remove the paper, and go over the lines again to be sure the imprints are deep enough. If they are not, they will fill with ink and not show on the print. Cut the house out; that is, remove the sky that is above and on the sides of the house.

4. Put about a teaspoon of black water-soluble printing ink on a small tray or metal bench hook, and roll a brayer (rubber roller) lightly over it in two directions to obtain an even coating of ink on the brayer. The brayer should roll over the surface of the tray, not slide.

5. Place the sheet of Scratch-Foam on a piece of newspaper, and roll the ink-coated brayer over the Scratch-Foam in two directions.

6. Place the inked side of the Scratch-Foam in the center of a sheet of white copy paper or a colored sheet of Astrobright or Fadeless paper. Colored construction paper has a rough, porous surface and does not make a

sharp print. Turn the paper and the Scratch-Foam over, and rub the backside of the paper. Remove the paper from the Scratch-Foam, and let the print dry. Cut out the house.

7. Re-ink the Scratch-Foam for each print you make. Try using colored and white printing inks, instead of black, for a variety of effects.

8. Arrange all the houses on a background of colored Fadeless Banner paper, adding some cut paper trees and other items to complete "Streets in Our Town."

Decorative Lines: Paper Batik

Students will use a resist technique known as **batik** to create a linear design. Batik is an ancient process of decorating fabrics. Traditionally, melted wax is applied to fabric to cause the fabric to resist the colored dyes that are applied later to the unprotected areas. In this simplified version of batik, Dippity-Dye paper (available in art supply catalogs) is used instead of fabric. Batiks can also be created by applying melted wax (candle wax or paraffin) to the surface of the paper with a brush or a special batik tool called a **tjanting** (available in art supply stores and catalogs). This tool has a wooden handle with a tiny funnel at one end. When dipped in hot wax and trailed over the surface of the paper, a tjanting creates a flowing, fluid line.

1. As a visual resource, use photographs of tropical fish, birds, flowers, and so on, or adapt a motif from Japanese family crests or from symbols used by Aztecs, Mayas, or Southwestern Native Americans, and create a linear design with a pencil on a piece of white, 12-by-18-inch butcher paper. Then place a piece of same-size Dippity-Dye paper on top of your design, and trace over your lines with a thick, black, water-soluble marking pen. You will be able to see your lines through the Dippity-Dye paper. Permanent markers will not work with this process.

2. To melt wax safely, do not use an open flame, an exposed heating element, or boiling water. Instead, melt a small amount of candle wax or pariffin in a deep-fat fryer or electric skillet. You may wish to line the skillet with foil and place in it a small, low can of wax. Dip a natural-bristle brush (synthetic bristles may melt in the hot wax) of medium size into the melted wax, and carefully brush over all your black lines. Let the wax extend on both sides of the lines. This creates a decorative white border on the sides of the lines in the finished product. Be sure to protect all the black lines with wax, or they will dissolve later when the color **washes** are applied to the paper.

3. Make a food-coloring solution by mixing about one-fourth cup of water with about one-fourth teaspoon of the highly concentrated food colorings found in cake-decorating stores. Use large brushes or the inexpensive sponge brushes found in paint and hardware stores. Brush these colors over the different parts of your design.

4. Let the Dippity-Dye paper dry. Apply more wax over the dyed areas of the paper. This will assure an even surface on the finished product after it is ironed.

5. Place the Dippity-Dye paper (and the butcher paper beneath it) between newspapers and iron it. Lift the Dippity-Dye paper off the butcher paper while they are both hot.

6. Display your paper batik with a white backing paper, or hang it in a window, since the final product is translucent.

UNDERSTANDING ARTWORKS: Learning about Color

Painters, poets, writers, actors, and scientists respond and react to the wonderful world of color. Indeed, think for a moment of living in a black, white, and gray world. Color appeals to our sense of beauty, whether we recognize and respond to it in natural objects or in works of human origin. We cannot help but be absorbed in watching the changing moods of a beautiful sunset. We delight in the incredible range of colors in flower petals, tropical fish, and butterfly wings—and in the dazzling colors of a fine impressionist painting.

Throughout history, people have used color for many purposes, one of the earliest being that of personal decoration. For centuries, individuals have decorated their bodies for special occasions or tribal ceremonies. This practice continues today in the use of cosmetics, in clown faces, and in theaters where actors and dancers have specific ways to reveal character through facial design and color. In selecting a dress or shirt, all of us probably know which colors look best on us.

Color plays an important part in our surroundings. We have color preferences in the way we furnish our homes and the color of car we purchase. And most chefs and home cooks know to plan a pleasing variety of color in the foods they arrange on a dinner plate. A dinner of halibut, mashed potatoes, cottage cheese, white bread, and vanilla ice cream would not be visually appetizing!

Besides being decorative, color has long been associated with a universal or cultural symbolism. In our country, certain colors are associated with each holiday; for example, red for Valentine's, or orange and black for Halloween. We think of light colors for spring and warm reds, oranges, and browns for fall. Red, white, and blue are patriotic colors for Americans. We tend to associate blue with truth ("true-blue"), green with hope and everlasting life, black with sorrow and death, and purple with royalty. Perhaps the latter symbolism began in Egypt many centuries ago when the sun god Ra was assigned that color because of its rarity and the difficulty people had in obtaining it. Since then, purple has symbolized kings. In American culture, white is often associated with purity and weddings, but brides in India wear red, and in Israel, yellow. Especially in artworks made hundreds of years ago, particular colors stand for certain ideas and have special meanings.

While emotions are often linked symbolically to colors (we speak of being "green with envy," and "good as gold," and of "feeling blue"), many individuals have expressed unique and personal reactions to different colors. In her book *Hailstones and Halibut Bones*, Mary O'Neill wrote poems that connected colors to feelings and also to the senses. She associated green with the smell of a country breeze and blue with the sound of the wind over water. In another poem, she said that gray is sleepiness and bad news. White is the sound of a foot walking lightly, as well as the part we cannot remember in a dream. Russian artist Wassily Kandinsky, who worked in the early part of the twentieth century, felt that each color had a corresponding musical note. He searched for a visual system in which he could express his conviction of an "inner mystical structure of the world." His splendid and often **abstract** canvases (Colorplate 30) exploded with color as he divorced himself from the necessity of using any subject matter at all. Color took on a symbolic function with Vincent van Gogh because he used colors not locally true from a realistic point of view, but colors that spoke strongly of the emotions of his intense personality. For him, yellow was the color of love, warmth, and friendship, and we see it frequently, especially in his sunflower paintings. It is dominant in the painting he made of his own bedroom in the little house in Arles in southern France.

Color often serves functional purposes, too—those of categorization and identification. When a number of related objects are "color-keyed," it simplifies sorting them out and grouping them by certain colors. Football players wear uniforms showing team colors. The colors of different pages of a catalog may denote different categories of items. Long ago, kings assigned heraldic colors to knights for their brave deeds, and thereafter, the assigned colors of armor and shields identified the knights, since visors covered their faces.

Both artists and scientists keenly observe colors in nature, each for different purposes. Natural colors inspire artists and designers to suggest blends and combinations to be matched and used to represent the things they see, or to enhance and decorate a given surface. For instance, sharp observation shows us how nature uses color to conceal, mislead, hide, attract, and warn other creatures. Flowers use their vivid colors to attract insects to help in pollination. The Gila monster warns of its venom with its colored, beady scales. The chameleon changes its color from green to brown to gray, according to its surroundings. Male birds that must seek food among flowers and leaves have more vivid colors than their duller-colored mates that remain concealed

on nests made of dried grasses. Tigers and zebras, with their highly contrasting patterns of stripes, appear almost invisible against a shadowy background. Indeed, armies have hired persons trained in art to study nature's camouflages and to help design concealing devices for machines and soldiers in wartime.

Artists may choose to use color in one of several ways. A **representational** use shows the actual or real colors of the depicted object. This is sometimes referred to as the local color. Or artists may choose to use colors decoratively to ornament or enhance a composition. Then again, they may choose to use color arbitrarily, if they wish to express a strong emotional feeling. And sometimes, they use color symbolically to express an idea.

People have always been in awe of the glowing, pure colors seen in the enormous arch of a rainbow. Hindus in India tell stories of the god Indra, who threw thunderbolts during storms and used a rainbow to shoot his lightning arrows. Polynesians believed that a rainbow was a ladder for heroes to climb to reach heaven. Some North American tribes thought that the rainbow was the beautiful bride of their rain god. Pit River Native Americans of California believed that the rainbow was a "rain-clear sign" sent by Old-Man-Above, who shaped the rainbow like the coyote's tail and colored it with the blue of the bluebird, the red of the rising sun, the yellow of the coyote's fur, and the green of the grass. The Old Testament says that the rainbow is a covenant that God made with Noah after the Flood. The rainbow's beautiful colors can, of course, be explained scientifically. Rainbows are curtains of large raindrops in front of us when the sunshine is behind us. They appear in the west in the morning and in the east late in the afternoon. When the sun strikes the rain, each drop acts like a tiny prism, separating white light into colors. The red arc is on the outside, and the purple arc is on the inside. A second rainbow is sometimes above the first. It is pale, and the colors are reversed.

Both rainbows and color wheels have orderly arrangements of colors. The color wheel is a useful tool for learning the mechanics of color and for helping us select different combinations of colors, or color schemes. The hues (another name for colors) appear on the color wheel in the same order as they do on the rainbow. Think first of an equilateral triangle placed on top of the color wheel, and then think of placing one of the three **primary colors**—red, yellow, and blue—at each corner of the triangle. (You may fill in the color wheel on page 31 with colored pencils.) These colors are called primary because they are basic and cannot be made by mixing any other colors together.

Mixing any two of the primary colors together makes another color. Doing this three times with a different pair of primary colors each time gives us the three **secondary colors**—orange, green, and purple (violet). (Red and blue make purple; yellow and blue make green; red and yellow make orange.) Each secondary color is positioned on the color wheel midway between the pair of primary colors used to make it. Mixing a secondary color with the primary color that is next to it makes one of the six **intermediate colors**: yellow-orange, red-orange, red-purple, blue-purple, yellow-green, and blue-green. This can be carried one step farther by changing the proportions of the two colors being mixed and making another complete set of colors. You then not only have yellow-orange but also orange-yellow, with the first being more yellow than orange and the second being more orange than yellow.

Analogous colors are several colors that are adjacent to each other on the color wheel. They are often called a family of colors in that they all somewhat resemble each other. They share one color in common and can mix with each other without becoming dull or gray.

Two colors that are opposite each other on the color wheel are called **complementary colors**. If these two colors are placed at their full **intensity** (strength or concentration) close together in a design, they quickly attract attention because they contrast strongly, often almost seeming to vibrate. If we mix a little of one color of paint with its complement, we find that the first paint's intensity is dulled, or grayed. The more of a color's complement that we mix with it, the duller the color becomes. Mixing two complementary colors in equal amounts results in a gray-brown color. Artists can mix a great variety of hues by using this dulling property of complementary colors. For instance, if a landscape has many different green tones—fields, trees, foliage—we can mix a great number of dull greens by adding differing amounts of red to the pure green. And, of course, we can make lighter tones or darker ones by adding either white or black to the blended color.

An interesting phenomenon occurs when our eyes become saturated by staring for a few seconds at one color. Place a small square of red paper in the center of a large piece of white paper. Stare at it for 30 seconds, and then remove the red square and look at the white paper. You will see a "ghost" square that is green, red's complement. Try this with other colors. What colors do you think you would see on a white surface after staring at the American flag?

When we plan a particular visual effect, whether we are making a painting, decorating a room, selecting clothing, or choosing a color for our car, we often think of colors as warm or cool. This is because we associate them with either warm or cool places or things in our environment. Water, lakes, ice, and snow are cool, and so we think of green, blue, and purple as cool colors. Conversely, fire and heat are associated with warm colors—red, yellow, and orange.

A color's value has to do with its lightness or darkness. We add a little bit of color to white to create a **tint**. We add a small amount of black to a color to create a **shade**. We can mix a graded scale of the tints and shades of one color. If we make a design or a composition with the tints, shades, and different intensities of one color, we call our artwork **monochromatic** (mono means "one"; chroma means "color").

Although we do not find black, white, and gray on the color wheel, we usually need them in creating artworks. They, along with tan and brown, are called **neutrals** and can be mixed with and used harmoniously with any color or set of colors on the color wheel.

Refer to the colorplates in the Color Gallery while you read the statements that follow regarding the ways the artists used color. Then choose three more artworks in the Color Gallery, and discuss how each artist used color and what emotions and feelings the colors invoke. Use the vocabulary and terminology you have just learned about color in the preceding discussion.

Colorplate 15: Seurat, *Sunday Afternoon on the Island of La Grande Jatte*
In a technique that he developed called *pointillism*, Seurat applied a myriad of tiny dots of pure color on this enormous canvas, relying on the viewer's eye to mix the colors from a distance. The numerous dots of paint create a grainy surface.

Colorplate 24: Marc, *Yellow Cow*
The artist's choice of bright, unrealistic colors creates a happy, lyrical artwork. Our eyes glide and sweep from one primary or secondary color to another.

Colorplate 29: Fonseca, *The Creation*
Fonseca used neutral earth tones to emphasize the theme of his composition.

Colorplate 30: Kandinsky, *Painting No. 198*
Primary and secondary colors fairly explode over the surface of this painting. Kandinsky was one of the first artists to express feelings through the use of color alone, not relying on subject matter for his artworks.

Colorplate 32: Renoir, *A Girl with a Watering Can*
Renoir's love of bright colors and beautiful people is seen in this impressionist artwork. A web of brilliantly colored tiny brush strokes merges at a distance to show us a realistic image of a child, roses, a garden path, and grass. The red ribbon in the child's hair attracts our attention to her face.

Colorplate 37: Chagall, *Green Violinist*
Neutral tones of gray accent and emphasize the secondary colors of green, orange, and purple in this highly imaginative painting. The orange violin accentuates the unrealistic green of the face and hand. A variety of purple shapes make up the coat and hat.

PRODUCING ARTWORKS EMPHASIZING COLOR

Daubs of Color: Impressionism

Students will create a small tempera painting in the manner of the impressionist artists, who painted their canvases with tiny daubs of color placed closely together to show how

Color Wheel

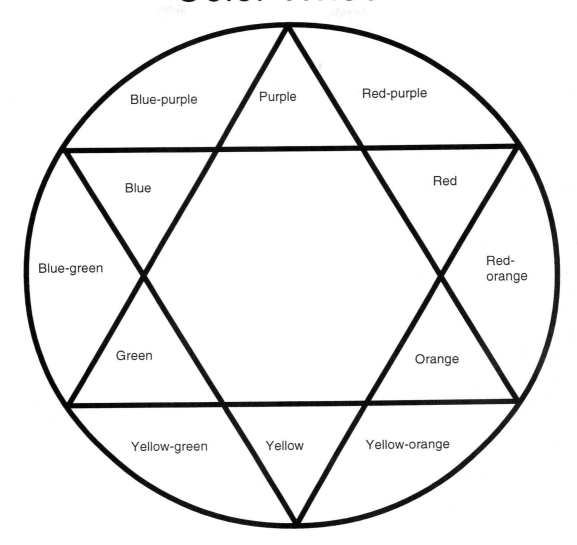

Primary colors: red, yellow, blue (with tempera paint, use magenta, yellow, and turquoise for the primary colors)

Secondary colors: orange, green, purple (made by mixing two primary colors)

Intermediate colors: red-orange; red-purple; yellow-orange; yellow-green; blue-green; blue-purple

Complementary colors: two colors opposite each other on color wheel: blue/orange; red/green; yellow/purple. When mixed together, complementary colors dull each other. Complementary colors are in contrast with each other.

Warm colors: red, orange, yellow

Cool colors: green, blue, purple

Color value: darkness or lightness of a color. When white is added to a color, it is called a **tint**. When black is added to a color, it is called a **shade**.

Monochromatic: color scheme made up of shades, tints, and intensities of one color

Intensity: brightness or dullness of a color; dull a color by adding its complement

Neutral colors: black, white, gray

Hue: another word for color

shimmering light was reflected from the surfaces of the things they saw. Impressionists did not combine and blend colors on their palettes in the traditional manner but instead depended on the viewer's eyes to mix the colors. Most impressionists did not use any black. Students will find that using turquoise, magenta, and yellow as primary colors when working with tempera paints makes richer colors.

1. Find a color photograph of a landscape. Then use L-frames (Figure 2.11) to identify a small detail of the landscape. With a pencil, lightly sketch in the major shapes and parts of the composition you have selected on a 6-by-9-inch piece of white paper.

2. Dip the tip of a small, round-bristle brush or a Q-tip in thick tempera that you have poured into a paper plate, and daub it on the paper to enlarge the detail you have framed. Do not stroke or blend the colors with your brush or Q-tip. Let several colors pile up on top of each other and be close to each other. Let each color dry before you apply another color on top of it.

3. Cover the paper in the manner described. If you seek to portray a light green, apply green and then white and perhaps some yellow or blue. If you wish to show a dull color, daub in a pair of complementary colors; if you wish to show a dark color, daub in purple or blue instead of black.

Wild Colors: Fauvism

Students will paint a person, using "wild colors" rather than realistic ones in the rather flat manner of the **fauves**, a group of artists associated with Henri Matisse around 1905 to 1907, who were dubbed "wild beasts" for their bold, startling, and unrealistic use of colors. Students will observe a posed model as the basis for the artwork.

1. Make a contour drawing (see p. 23) of a friend's face. Divide it with lines into different parts. Feel free to exaggerate and distort the shapes of the features. You may wish to draw the face with a thick, black permanent marking pen.

2. Choose bright and unrealistic colors of tempera, watercolors, or acrylic paints to paint the face in a flat manner. Be sure to paint the background, too.

Matching an Artist's Colors: A Composite Painting (Group Project)

Students will make enlarged drawings of small squares cut from a reproduction of an artwork by a well-known artist. Then students each look closely at the colors in their small squares and match the colors for painting their larger squares. When all the enlarged squares are completed and adhered to a background, the composite painting shows the famous artwork (Figure 2.12).

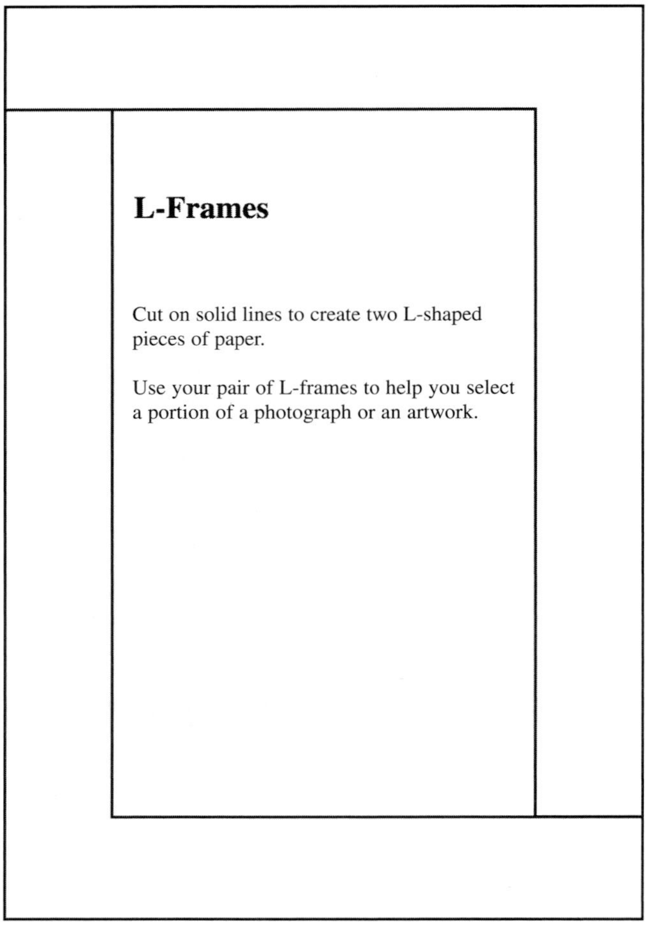

1. The instructor will photocopy a reproduction, about 8 by 10 inches or so in size, of a painting by a well-known

L-Frames

Cut on solid lines to create two L-shaped pieces of paper.

Use your pair of L-frames to help you select a portion of a photograph or an artwork.

Figure 2.11 Use a ruler and pencil and draw this diagram on a manila folder or piece of construction paper. Then cut it out and use the two large L-shapes to help you select a detail of a photograph of the part you want to use for a drawing or painting.

artist, and mark it off in approximately the same number of squares as there are students in the class. On the reverse side, number each square in sequential order. Be sure each square is marked on the reverse side as to which side is the top. Then cut the squares apart on the paper trimmer, and attach each square to a small piece of paper with clear tape.

2. Give each student a 5- or 6-inch-square piece of heavy, white drawing paper or mat board and one of the small squares from the cut-up artwork.

3. Each student should use a ruler to draw a vertical line and a horizontal line across the middle of the square of white paper, marking the paper in four equal parts. Then students should lightly draw similar lines across the small detail of the reproduction, vertically and horizontally. They have now divided the small detail of the reproduction and the larger piece of white paper into fourths. Using pencils, students then enlarge the small

Figure 2.12 Student work: Students observe color blends, tints, and shades and endeavor to match them on small squares of white paper or mat board to make a Picasso composite.

squares on the white paper, matching what they see, part by part.

4. Students should use liquid tempera (or tempera cakes, acrylics, or watercolors) and practice matching the color blends and brush strokes that they see in the great master's work. They will need to decide if a color is a greenish blue with some white added, or if it is a dulled green that can be matched by mixing some red with it. They should paint their squares carefully, trying to obtain the same color values and intensities that the great master used as well as some of the brushstrokes.

5. When everyone finishes, paste the large squares in numerical order on a large poster board or piece of paper that has been ruled off in the matching number of 5-inch squares.

6. Students can now identify the painting and evaluate how successfully they mixed and blended the colors they saw in the small squares.

Warm and Cool Colors: A Tissue Collage

Students will make a **collage** by cutting, tearing, and crumpling colored tissue paper using warm or cool colors to make a bird, fish, or flower using an opposite set of contrasting colors for the surrounding background.

1. Tissue pomps and colored tissue paper that do not bleed when wet are available. Packages of tissue pomps in 6-inch squares, all of one color, are commonly used in making parade floats.

2. Use liquid starch or a mixture of white glue and water in equal parts for adhering the tissue pieces onto a piece of 9-by-12-inch white paper.

3. Students may prepare the background first by brushing a small amount of the starch or glue/water solution on white paper. Crumple a large piece of a *very light* color of tissue, then flatten it and place it on the dampened area. Then brush a little more of the solution on top to hold it flat. Cover the entire background in this manner.

4. If you used warm colors (red, yellow, orange) for the background, then choose several cool colors (blue, green, violet) of tissue paper and cut or tear pieces to make the bird, fish, or flower. Make multiple cuts to make a lot of feathers, scales, or petals at one time. To do this, cut several thicknesses of paper at once. Adhere them to the paper with the solution, overlapping the shapes to get dark and light and blended colors.

5. Or make a warm-colored bird, fish, or flower first and then fill in the white background with small pieces of tissue paper in cool colors that you have cut or torn. This is similar to mosaics. By using these two families of colors, the bird will contrast with the background.

UNDERSTANDING ARTWORKS: Learning about Shape and Form

Do you remember as a child standing motionless between a strong light and a blank sheet of paper while someone carefully drew the shadow that your profile cast? The shape was a silhouette. It was a fairly good likeness of you after it was cut from black paper and mounted. It could even be identified as yours when all the silhouettes of your classmates were finished, even though it had no distinguishing details within its shape. We are often able to recognize an object by its shape alone. Etienne de Silhouette, who lived in the eighteenth century and served as the French controller general, introduced economic reforms that made him the object of ridicule and hostility from the nobles, who thereafter used his name to apply to a "mere outline profile drawing."

When a line moves around and comes back and meets itself, it makes a shape. You can draw the shape of an apple with a line, or you can use a paintbrush to paint an apple with no outlines at all. In an artwork, a shape is a two-dimensional area. Its length and width are defined in some way, either by an outline or boundary around it, or by being a different color or texture from the space around it.

Whether we are describing an artwork or creating one, the element of shape requires careful consideration. Shapes have size; they can be large or small. Artists can create

Figure 2.13 **Ann Dobson Palmer, *Sonoma*, 1995. Pieced silkscreen, cotton fiber.**
Sharply defined edges contrast with soft, blurry ones to create horizontal shapes in this landscape, adding to the quiet mood and feeling.
By permission of Ann Dobson Palmer.

Figure 2.14 **El Greco, *St. Martin and the Beggar*, 1597/1599. Oil on canvas, 76⅛ × 40½ in.**
Widener Collection, National Gallery of Art, Washington. Photograph ©2002 Board of Trustees, National Gallery of Art, Washington.
The elongated shapes of the horse, rider, and standing figure contribute to the intensely religious feeling of this artwork done in the mannerist tradition.

shapes that have sharp, clearly defined hard edges or soft, blurry contours that blend into surrounding shapes. If the shapes contain no interior details and are the same color or value, they are called flat shapes, such as Cham Thor's stitchery of *Mona, Hmong Daily Life* (Colorplate 42). In composing an artwork, artists know that shapes can be repeated to create a regular or irregular pattern. If they place shapes close together in an artwork, the shapes create a feeling of unity and compactness. When shapes overlap, they tend to give a feeling of depth; the one in front is seen as being close to the viewer. If an artist places similar shapes throughout a composition, our eyes tend to follow the path from shape to shape.

Artists frequently use realistic shapes in a two-dimensional artwork to represent three-dimensional objects—forms—that they see in the natural world. Sometimes, artists simplify or change the shapes they see, abstracting the important parts and planes to serve an expressive purpose, or letting the shapes stand for symbols, ideas, or concepts. Artists are sometimes more interested in the form of an object than they are in the subject matter itself. Look at Picasso's *Girl before a Mirror* (Colorplate 33) and observe how the artist simplified shapes for heads, breasts, and abdomens as he showed a young girl confronting the image of herself as she will be as an old woman. Look at the variety of open and closed shapes in Harry Fonseca's *The Creation* (Colorplate 29). Like Kandinsky, Fonseca has created shapes in his artworks that had little or no relation to things in the natural world. He was more interested in using shapes and colors to express particular feelings and emotional qualities than he was in depicting natural objects. We refer to this sort of shape as being nonobjective. Can you think how you might draw an ominous shape, a restful shape, or an exultant one?

The kinds of shapes that artists choose to use are determined by the message or visual statement they wish to con-

vey. In the Color Gallery, we see Grant Wood's *American Gothic* (Colorplate 18) and Marisol's *Women and Dog* (Colorplate 20), both artworks featuring figures. A regionalist artist who focused on life in mid-America during the Great Depression, Wood shows us a sober, stern, thoughtful couple. The repeated shape of the pitchfork and the rather elongated shapes in the figures' faces contribute to the mood of the painting. On the other hand, Marisol sought to make a different kind of visual statement, so she chose abstracted forms for the bodies of her people and showed us a group of

Figure 2.15 **Michaele LeCompte, *Parterre*, 1990.**
Flat, abstract shapes cut from thick metal were arranged to create a colorful outdoor screen.
Photo by Nikki Pahl, courtesy of Michael LeCompte.

Figure 2.16 **Jorjana Holden, *Reunion, 1986*, 1986. Bronze, 15 × 17 × 12 in.**
The artist first modeled this cast metal bronze sculpture in wax. The sculpture incorporates eye-leading movement with its diagonal forms in a composition that is pleasing when viewed from any angle or side.
Courtesy of Jorjana Holden.

individuals, along with a dog on a leash, anxiously watching for traffic as they go on yet another shopping trip.

When you wish to make a realistic drawing, the technique of blocking in the shapes can help you perceive the configuration of the object. First, look at the total, overall shape of an object or a creature—a photograph or live version of, perhaps, a hen or a squirrel. Then look for the primary smaller shapes that make up the creature's total shape. For example, the hen's body is oval—somewhat like a large egg. The tail feathers form a triangular shape. The neck is a short, tapered rectangle with a round head attached. These individual shapes could all be lightly blocked in with a pencil or charcoal and then the details of feathers, beaks, eyes, and feet added to complete the sketch. Try this technique with a squirrel, a cluster of trees, the human figure, or any object. Perceiving the small shapes that make up the big shape and then blocking them in on your paper can enhance your drawing skills. The shapes you see depend, of course, on your point of view, that is, the angle from which you see an object. Although the top of a table may be rectangular, the shape you draw will depend on where you are sitting while drawing it.

Form in art has to do with objects that have three dimensions—length, width, and depth. Generally, we speak of form in relation to sculpture, architecture, and the various craft areas, such as ceramics. Such artworks take up and enclose space. We also refer to form in two-dimensional artworks when an artist depicts solid objects on a flat surface. In the latter part of the nineteenth century, French artist Paul Cézanne rebelled against the emphasis on the surface quality of light striking objects that was the impassioned work of the impressionists; he insisted instead that everything in nature has basic forms: cylinders, cones, spheres, and cubes. His pioneering work in this field led to explorations with cubism by Picasso and Braque. Hence, Cézanne is called the "father of modern art."

When artists make sculptures, they are working with form in either the **additive** or **subtractive process**. In the first, the form is built up by adding bits and pieces of clay, soft wax, or other pliable material. Artists sometimes use an armature to support the clay or other modeling material. The final product is often cast in metal when it is finished. In subtractive works, the artist carves or takes away wood or stone from a large mass to form a figure or object.

Both shapes and forms can be classified as either geometric or free-form. Geometric shapes are two-dimensional and remind us of mathematics—circles, squares, and triangles, as well as variations and combinations of these, such as ovals, crescents, semicircles, rectangles, hexagons, and so on. Geometric forms are three-dimensional and are reminiscent of cubes, cylinders, spheres, dodecahedrons, and such. Geometric shapes and forms are often used for decoration and make up more highly organized and structured artworks. They often seem less emotional than free forms and give viewers a feeling of perfection and intellectualism. The architect is very aware of how different forms that make up his or her design must work together to make a pleasing and functional structure.

Free-form shapes and forms are irregular, uneven, and unmeasured, and they remind us of objects in nature. Many artists delight in the beauty of the natural forms of smooth, weathered driftwood, bleached bones, well-worn river rocks, and delicate seashells, and they incorporate the characteristics of these natural forms into their own artworks. British sculptor Henry Moore had a studio filled with a lifetime's collection of such forms, and his massive works show evidences of the inspiration that the forms provided him. The curving forms and carefully designed **positive shapes** and **negative spaces** of Moore's artworks bring to mind stones, rolling hills, mountain ranges, and the monumental forms at Stonehenge.

Both Moore and Georgia O'Keeffe—the former creating three-dimensional artworks, and the latter, two-dimensional—were cognizant of another important facet of working with shapes and forms, that of relating them to the negative spaces within and around the positive shapes. The positive shapes and forms in a composition are the objects themselves, while the negative spaces around the positive shapes contribute immensely to the unity, variety, and balance of an artwork.

PRODUCING ARTWORKS EMPHASIZING SHAPE AND FORM

The Shapes of Fruits and Vegetables

Students will observe the different shapes of three or four different fruits and vegetables and then cut each one out, before making multiple cuts of each one, using the first as a pattern. These are then arranged in an overlapping and pleasing composition.

1. Collect an assortment of fresh fruit and vegetables or photographs of them. Compare and contrast the different shapes. How would you describe the shapes of radishes, carrots, celery, pineapples, and green beans? How are the sizes alike or different? How is a green bean like a pea pod? How are the shapes of pears and eggplants different? Compare an apple with a slice of watermelon. Describe the shape of broccoli. Discuss how the grocer arranges the different bins in the produce section of the market. Are some vegetables and fruits stacked, overlapped, in rows, in baskets?

2. Using an assortment of colored paper, cut out the shape of one vegetable or fruit. Then make multiple cuts of the fruit or vegetable by cutting three or four pieces of paper at once.

3. Think of how produce is arranged in the market. Place your fruit or vegetable shapes on a piece of white or colored paper, overlapping and clustering the shapes in a pleasing arrangement. Do the same with several other different fruits and vegetables. Make your composition fit your paper. Paste the shapes down, and then use a

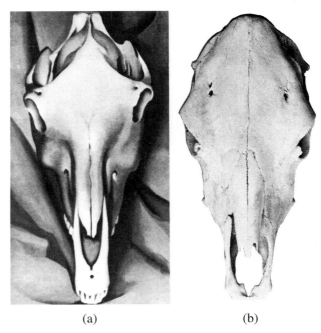

(a)   (b)

Figure 2.17 **(a) Georgia O'Keeffe, *Horse's Skull on Blue*, 1930. Oil on canvas, 30 × 16 in.**
Arizona State University Art Museum, Tempe. Gift of Oliver B. James.
©2002 The Georgia O'Keeffe Foundation/Artists Rights Society (ARS), New York.
(b) Horse skull.
Collection of the authors.
O'Keeffe collected objects that she treasured and later used as subjects for her paintings—bleached bones, smooth stones, antlers, and shells. Rather than seeing death in the clean, severe form of a horse's skull, O'Keeffe was fascinated with the positive shapes and negative spaces and painted the skull in a realistic manner.

thick, black marking pen to outline and distinguish the separate shapes.

Combining Shapes for a Tagboard Print

Students will cut geometric and free-form shapes for a composition that is pasted to a background and forms the design for a relief print (Figure 2.18). The class will choose a common theme.

1. Collect photographs of fish, space ships, trucks, birds, and so on that show varieties of the theme the class chose. Observe your selection closely to see all the different shapes that make up the whole.

2. Cut the shapes you see from tagboard. Simplify, distort, exaggerate, repeat, delete, and change the shapes to suit your purposes and intent.

3. Paste or glue them down securely. Some of the shapes may overlap. This is called your printing plate. Be sure the glue is dry before you print.

4. Place a spoonful of black, water-soluble printing ink on a printing tray. Roll a printing brayer back and forth on the tray to cover the brayer evenly with ink. Place your

Colorplate 1. Max, Still Life. This painting by an 11-year-old child shows careful and close observation of objects as well as the skillful use of tempera paint. Black lines were added with marking pen after the paint dried.

Colorplate 2. Ben Camacho, age 11.
Contour drawing develops an eye and hand partnership for making realistic drawings. When black pen lines were completed, the young artist used changeable markers to create colorful patterns.

Colorplate 3. Megan, age 5, Indian Princess. A potato-print face was the starting point for this drawing in which the child added a variety of colors, decorative patterns, and details with changeable markers.

Colorplate 4. Pam, From Above Looking Down.
An eight-year-old student imagined herself in a hot air balloon to view the shapes, colors, and patterns and to create a tempera painting of the landscape below.

Colorplate 5. Emily, age 9, used collage papers and colored markers to show her family opening Christmas gifts. Note overlapping and willingness to extend figures off the paper.

Colorplate 6.
With Jacob Lawrence's works as inspiration in her study of U.S. history, and with her knowledge of proportion and action in relation to making a 16-piece manikin, 10-year-old Carolyn made this cut and torn paper collage called "Picking Cotton."

Colorplate 7.
After hearing the story of Cobbler Clooney, Nicole, age 7, drew herself with "Sparkly shoes that roll by themselves."

Colorplate 8.
This clown on a unicycle was made by six-year-old
Colleen from geometric shapes during a lesson
that integrated art and math.

Colorplate 9. Stephen, Butterfly Wing.
Integrating art and science, this colorful painting by an nine-year-
old was the result of using a "pretend" microscope to select and
delineate a detail from a large photograph of a butterfly.

Colorplate 10. Megan, age 9, made this oil pastel drawing of a clown that shows formal balance and a sense of space and overlapping.

Colorplate 11.
This marking pen drawing shows the developing awareness of nine-year-old Emily. She shows overlapping in several places, and the previous use of baseline has evolved into a more realistic concept of ground, hills, and sky.

Colorplate 12.
Colorful painting of a cow shows six-year-old Maye's skill in handling tempera and a brush, as well as her perception of details.

Colorplate 13. Nicole, age 6, Clown.
Six-year-old Nicole used a glue line to enclose the shapes. When the glue dried as transparent lines on the black paper, she added color with chalk pastels.

Figure 2.18 Flowing repeated shapes in this tagboard print of a fish make for a unified composition. The print could be mounted singly or used in a group mural.
Photo by Barbara Herberholz.

printing plate on a piece of newspaper, and roll the brayer over it.

5. Place your inked printing plate face down on a piece of white copy, Fadeless, or Astrobright paper. These colored papers are less absorbent than colored construction paper and will produce a sharper printed image when using water-soluble printing ink.

6. Turn the printing plate and paper over, and rub the backside of the paper with your fingers to ensure an even printing. Then remove the paper from your printing plate to dry. The cut shapes will have a white shadow around them. This will accent the different shapes when you make your print. You can make several prints by re-inking the printing plate each time.

7. For a group project for a sea-life mural, use colored Fadeless banner paper and cut or tear strips to indicate different depths of water. Add cut and torn paper seaweed, and glue all the fish to this background. Simple backgrounds can be created for any theme the class has chosen.

Creating a Three-Dimensional Form: Modeling the Figure

Students will model a seated, kneeling, or reclining figure from a cylinder of clay. Six or seven students work together on a common theme, and each student models a small figure that will be displayed as part of a group. See Viola Frey's large standing ceramic figures (Figure 1.15). Fired objects may be glazed or painted with acrylics, or stained by brushing them with white tempera before scrubbing off the excess paint. Students can refer to books showing ceramic models of small figures, such as *The Spirit of Folk Art* by Henry Glassie.

Suggested themes include:

A musical group or small street band

Playing ball at the beach

A picnic in the park

Telling stories to children

A wedding party

Acrobats, clowns, and circus performers

Around the campfire

Gymnasts

The crowd around an ice-cream cart

People dancing

Football or baseball players

Playing marbles

Stranded on an island

At the market

Trick-or-treating

1. Work on a canvas mat (or piece of brown paper bag) so that you can rotate your artwork as you progress and observe it from all sides. The mat also helps keep the surface of the table clean. Form a piece of clay about the size of an orange into a 6- or 7-inch-long cylinder that is about 1½ inches in diameter.

2. With a tongue depressor, make a vertical cut at one end of the cylinder to form the legs of the figure. Form the other end of the cylinder to create a neck and head.

3. Roll a coil from another small piece of clay, and cut the coil in half at an angle to make the arms. Score the shoulders and the ends of the arms with a toothpick or toothbrush, and then apply a little bit of slip or water. Slip is a creamy, thick mixture of clay and water. Attach the arms to the body, and use the end of the tongue depressor and your fingers to smooth the joined area.

4. You have created the basic figure and are now ready to bend the knees, elbows, waist, and neck into a seated, kneeling, or reclining position. Be sure to give consideration to the negative spaces. You may add hair, clothing, a hat or helmet, shoes, and so on.

5. Smooth the surface of the form, or give it a textural quality.

6. After the figure is bisque fired, it may be glazed and fired again; or you may choose to use acrylic paints after the bisque firing. Another option is to stain or antique the figure by painting it with white tempera, letting it dry, and then holding it under the faucet and washing off most of the white tempera.

Creating Forms with Clay Slabs: Castles and Other Structures

Students will combine a variety of clay slabs to create an imaginary miniature castle or other type of building.

1. Analyze photographs of different kinds of castles to distinguish and identify the battlements, parapets, baileys, buttresses, turrets, towers, drawbridges, and so on. Then use your imagination to create a miniature castle (or a cathedral, temple, Indian pueblo, Victorian house, etc.).

2. Roll clay out on your canvas mat with a rolling pin. Make a base for your construction that is no larger than 6 inches in any direction. It may be geometric or freeform. It need not be level.

3. Using a potter's needle, a plastic knife, or a tongue depressor, cut out slabs from rolled-out pieces of clay—¼-inch thick—to make the walls, towers, and such. Score any parts to be joined, and apply slip. You may need to roll out a tiny coil of clay and apply it to the places where two pieces of clay form a right angle to ensure that no cracks appear when the piece is dry.

4. You may add roofs, but be sure to cut out windows or doors so air can escape when the finished castle is fired

in the kiln. To make a cone-shaped roof, cut out a pie-shaped section from a circle of clay, and form it into a cone.

5. Create textures by imprinting objects in the soft surface of the clay, by adding bits and pieces of clay, or by dragging a tool over the clay's surface.

6. Remember to keep looking at the form you are creating from all sides to ensure a balanced and unified design.

7. When the clay castle dries, it is called *greenware* and should be fired in a kiln. It is called *bisqueware* after it has been fired once. You can apply ceramic glaze to your castle and fire it again. Or you may choose to rinse your castle in water, apply white tempera, and then wash the tempera off under running water. This creates a stained effect, with the tempera remaining in the low areas and the color of the bisque in the higher areas. You may choose to paint your castle with acrylic paints. You can then spray it with acrylic glaze.

Creating a Three-Dimensional Form: Box Sculpture

Students will design a piece of additive sculpture by collecting small cardboard boxes, adhering them, and decorating them in the manner of the artist Marisol (Colorplate 20). Marisol imaginatively assembled a variety of materials—wood, fabric, and plaster—to create boxy sculptures that made visual comments on contemporary life.

1. Collect boxes of various sizes. You may work on a small scale with film boxes, cereal boxes, and such, or you may choose to work in several small groups on a large scale and use corrugated cardboard cartons.

2. Stack and assemble the boxes to create a figure, a group of figures, or an abstract arrangement. Attach them with masking tape.

3. Cover the boxes with newspaper or paper-toweling strips dipped in wheat paste mixture.

4. Let your box sculpture dry. Then paint it, and glue on bits of fabric, photographs, and patterned paper as finishing touches.

UNDERSTANDING ARTWORKS: Learning about Texture

Young children are very curious. They learn through their senses, and they especially have a strong urge to explore and discover through their sense of touch. Adults often move breakable or potentially harmful objects out of reach or admonish children, "Don't touch!"

But not only the very young find the impulse to touch natural objects irresistible. How many of us love to stroke the soft fur of a kitten or puppy? The silky, lustrous quality

Figure 2.19 **Vincent van Gogh, *La Maoumé*, 1888. Oil on canvas, 28⅞ × 23¾ in.**
National Gallery of Art, Washington, Chester Dale Collection, Photograph ©2002 Board of Trustees, National Gallery of Art, Washington.
The texture created by van Gogh's brush strokes contributes to the strong appeal of his works. Often intent on getting a large amount of paint on his canvas, he would squeeze colors directly from the tube, sometimes using a palette knife or even his fingers to spread the paint and achieve the rich, textural impasto.

Figure 2.20 **Navajo rug.**
Collection of authors.
The woolly texture of the fibers used to weave this decorative artwork contributes to the rug's appeal.

of satin against our skin feels better than the scratchy roughness of burlap. We learn through experience about the texture of sandpaper or cactus, and usually prefer not to touch them. Through previous association, people sometimes find the texture of a toad or snake skin repugnant.

The tactile quality of things appeals to our sense of touch, and this surface quality, whether we are describing natural objects or artworks, is referred to as *texture.* We use such words as *rough, smooth, hard, soft, slick, bumpy, fluffy,* and so on to describe texture. Our senses respond to texture in artworks as well as in nature. The smooth surface of a piece of ceramics, the rich and woolly fibers that weavers use, and the polished sheen of a pewter bowl appeal to our tactile senses. Works of sculpture in museums are often so inviting to our sense of touch that signs and even guards must be posted to ensure that museum visitors keep "hands off." Our senses are attracted to a smooth marble surface, the warm glow of polished wood, or the burnished surface of a

bronze statue. But even if we are not allowed to touch these surfaces, we know how they feel because we remember having touched similar objects.

We like variety in texture, too, and we plan our clothing as well as our interior furnishings to have different surfaces. An architect chooses several textured building materials in designing a structure—perhaps glass, stone, and wood—to achieve a pleasing effect and to create unity. Having too great a variety of textures, however, creates a chaotic effect. We enjoy variety in the textures of the foods we eat; steak and potatoes in toothpastelike tubes were abandoned when astronauts complained about the sameness of texture.

Artists are aware of tactile appeal and use texture to express a particular emotion or feeling, or to enhance their artwork in some way. They may want to use soft, fluffy textures to create a feeling of warmth, comfort, and welcome, knowing that hard, slick surfaces seem cool and less inviting. They may also choose to depict a person's character through texture, showing the rugged, wrinkled face of a sea captain or, as Renoir did, the porcelain-smooth skin of beautiful young girls and women.

In responding to and in creating artworks, we refer to two kinds of texture:

1. Actual texture is the real surface of something, one that we could feel with our eyes closed. We most often associate actual texture with three-dimensional art—sculpture, architecture, and crafts. The appeal of Navajo weaving is not only in the **symmetrical balance** of the stylized arrangement of shapes; its actual rough, woolen texture appeals to our sense of touch. A painting may also have actual texture if the artist applied paint thickly. Sometimes, artists use palette knives as well as brushes and build up several layers of paint to create a real textural quality. This is called the *impasto*

Figure 2.21 **George Catlin, *The White Cloud, Head Chief of the Iowas*, ca. 1845. Canvas, 28 × 22⅞ in.**
National Gallery of Art, Washington, Paul Mellon Collection, Photograph ©2002 Board of Trustees, National Gallery of Art, Washington.
The spiky, sharp eagle quills in the headdress and the grizzly bear claws strung around White Cloud's neck accentuate the soft texture of the white, furry wolf skin that hangs from the chief's shoulders. Catlin devoted his life to making realistic images of members of various Native American tribes

technique. Van Gogh sometimes created his thick, swirling brush strokes by squeezing the paint directly from the tube onto his canvas. Occasionally, this intense artist even painted with his fingers. Jackson Pollock created actual texture on his artworks by dripping and flinging paint on the canvas as it lay on the floor. It is, of course, easier to see this sort of actual texture when looking at an original painting rather than a reproduction. Collages, which may incorporate real pieces of burlap, string, and such, are examples of other two-dimensional artworks that can have actual texture. Artists designing sculptured works and architecture must deal with the relationships of different textures.

2. Artists sometimes create **visual texture**, or simulated texture, in two-dimensional artworks to give the illusion of real texture. A finely detailed texture in an artwork appears closer to us; blurred, indistinct textures appear farther away. Our eye is attracted to texture, so an artist may use an appealing texture or a richly textured area to focus our attention on a particular area in an artwork. Texture provides visual interest for our eyes and gives more life to a painting, drawing, or print. Such texture appeals to our tactile sense, but we do not need to touch the surfaces represented to know how they feel because we have touched the real equivalents in nature. George Catlin worked closely from direct observation to achieve the texture of the fluffy fur of a white wolf around White Cloud's shoulders, as well as the texture of the spiky, eagle-quill headdress (Figure 2.21). Artists who can create a variety of realistic textures are technically skilled.

The French term ***trompe l'oeil***, which means "to deceive the eye," describes the illusionistic skill in paintings that depicts the textures and colors of objects so realistically that we are "tricked" into thinking that the actual objects—perhaps a fly, bit of yarn, nails, pieces of wood, and such—are actually on the painting's surface. Two nineteenth-century painters often associated with **still lifes** in the trompe l'oeil manner are William Harnett and John Frederick Peto.

We often use the terms *texture* and *pattern* together in describing an artwork, since they are related but not the same thing. A pattern is usually made by repeating a line or shape many times and spacing it evenly over an area. The effect may give the illusion of texture. Repeated lines and shapes may exist as a pattern alone, however, and not refer to a surface texture at all.

PRODUCING ARTWORKS EMPHASIZING TEXTURE

Creating Actual Texture in Relief Sculpture

Students will create a variety of textures on a clay slab to make a bas-relief sculpture of a flat building, a figure, a fish, or an animal, either by imprinting the clay with a variety of objects repeatedly, by dragging an implement across the clay, or by adding bits and pieces of clay on top of the slab.

1. Decide on a theme for your textured slab project. You may wish to use visual reference materials, such as sketches you have made of Victorian houses, or you may find pictures of them in reference books. As a group, you may wish to create a frontier town, with each student making a different storefront for Main Street. Or you may wish to make a figure, vehicle, or animal. Make a paper pattern of your object's shape. Keep each clay slab 6 to 8 inches high.

2. With a rolling pin, roll out a slab of wedged clay—about ⅓-inch thick—on a piece of canvas or on a piece of brown paper bag. Place the chunk of clay between

Figure 2.22 **John Frederick Peto,** *The Old Violin,* **ca. 1890.**
Oil on canvas, 30⅜ × 22⅞ in.
The National Gallery of Art, Washington, Gift of Avalon Foundation,
Photograph ©2002 Board of Trustees, National Gallery of Art, Washington.
A passion for portraying objects exactly as the artist saw them resulted in
a form of visual realism called *trompe l'oeil.* The eye is tricked into perceiving actual objects rather than paint on a canvas. The textural qualities
of wood (both painted and varnished), metallic hinges, a key, and torn
sheet music attract and fascinate our eyes.

two thin sticks of wood to ensure that the slab will be of
an even thickness. The sticks of wood should be about
⅛-inch thick.

3. Place your paper pattern on the clay slab, and cut it out
   with a needle cutter or a plastic knife. Remove excess
   clay.

4. Imprint with different gadgets and tools to create a variety of textures on your house, storefront, figure, or animal. Try dragging a tool across the clay. Try adding tiny
   bits and pieces of clay to the surface; be sure to brush
   some slip over the surface first.

5. When you are finished, let your textured slab dry. After
   it is fired, you may glaze it and fire it again. Or you may
   paint it with acrylics or tempera. Or you may dip it
   quickly in and out of water and apply thinned tempera—white or a color; then hold it under water and
   brush off some of the excess paint to reveal a stained,

antique effect. When your slab is dry, spray it with a
clear acrylic glaze.

Using Actual and Simulated Textures

Students will use oil pastels and several differently textured
fabrics and papers to create a collage with actual and simulated textures.

1. Collect a variety of textured materials, both fabric and
   paper, such as velvet, felt, yarn, foil, corrugated paper,
   sand paper, glossy paper, corduroy, velour, ribbon,
   sponges, and so on.

2. Select a theme for your artwork, such as fishing in the
   river, walking in the rain, a robot in the lab, dancers on
   the stage, birds in a tree, and so on. Decide on several
   different textured materials, and cut from them some of
   the objects you will include in your composition. These
   will be the actual textures in your artwork. Try placing
   them on a piece of 9-by-12-inch background paper,
   white or colored, and think about how you will relate
   them to the environment and other objects in the composition. Set them aside.

3. Place your background paper on a newspaper section.
   This provides a cushioned surface and makes working
   with oil pastels easier. Use oil pastels to create several
   simulated textures. Blend several colors of oil pastels
   by rubbing them with your fingertip. Try adding black,
   white, or another color on top of a color.

4. When you have finished with the oil pastels, glue the
   objects you made in step 2 in place.

Creating a Tribal Mask with Actual Textures

Students will first research masks from different countries
and cultures around the world. They will use a variety of textured materials such as raffia, yarn, tree bark, moss, twigs,
textured papers and fabrics such as burlap and corduroy,
seashell, beads, excelsior, and so on for the hair and features. See examples of masks in Figures 7.36, 7.37, 7.54,
and 7.57.

1. Use a heavy cardboard paper plate for the background
   of your mask. You may make a short cut at the chin,
   overlapping the two sides and staple it in place to create
   a three-dimensional quality. You may choose to make a
   mask that reflects a human face or an animal face, and
   you may wish to paint it first with one or two colors.

2. Use all sorts of textured materials for the mask: hair,
   eyes, eyebrows, lips, nose, ears, and so on.

3. Try different objects and arrangements before you
   decide on your mask design. Then use white glue and
   staplers to adhere the objects to the paper plate.

Creating Actual Texture: Weaving

Students will use a variety of different-textured yarns to weave a small tapestry on a flat cardboard loom. Small chipboard looms (6½ by 13 inches) with slits already cut across the top and bottom can be purchased from art supply catalogs. Or you can make your own loom by cutting a small rectangle from chipboard, mat board, or corrugated cardboard, and then making short slits, about one-fourth inch apart, across the top and bottom. Plastic large-eyed needles and a variety of weaving yarns are also available from art supply catalogs.

1. To warp the loom, wrap the warping fiber around and around the loom through the slits at the top and bottom. Use pearl cotton, string, or other nonstretch fiber for warps. Tie the beginning of the warp to the end of the warp on the backside of the loom.

2. Select a variety of yarns with different textures (nubby, rough, smooth, shiny, fuzzy, etc.) for your wefts. Limit your selection of colors to achieve unity. Try a monochromatic color scheme. Or try using two or three neutral colors and one or two brighter colors.

3. Cut a piece of yarn about a yard long, and thread your needle. Needles should be blunt-pointed and have a large eye for the yarn to pass through. Begin weaving across the warp strings, going over and under in alternate rows. This process is called *tabby weaving*. To speed up the process, you may wish to use a pickup stick to lift the warps. To do this, use a flat stick such as a ruler and weave it across the warp fibers, going over and under each string. When you turn the stick on its side, it lifts alternate warps, enabling you to send your needle across the loom more rapidly. However, you will have to weave manually back across the loom, as the pickup stick only allows use in one direction. Pack your rows of wefts tightly and neatly together with a plastic comb, a fork, or your fingers.

4. Start or end a piece of yarn near the center of the loom, rather than at the sides. The 2–3 inches of extra yarn will then fall on the backside of the woven piece instead of projecting from the sides. These loose ends can be woven into the back of the tapestry later, or they can be glued in place.

5. You can weave the weft in curves rather than in straight rows across the loom. You can weave only partway across, leaving a slit or interlocking the wefts. You may choose to include some natural found objects—bark, lichen, twigs, and such—in your weaving.

6. When you are finished, cut the warps in the middle on the backside of the loom, and tie the first warp string to the one next to it, and so on, across the top of the loom. Tie knots in the same manner at the bottom of your woven piece.

7. Cut lengths of yarn for fringes across the bottom. Double each yarn length over, thread the loop into your needle, insert the needle through the bottom of the tapestry, and slip the yarn through the loop. Repeat across the bottom edge to add a decorative effect to your tapestry.

UNDERSTANDING ARTWORKS: Learning about Space

Raise your arms above your head. Stretch them out in front of you. Take two steps forward. You have moved in three-dimensional space—not the "outer space" frequented by spaceships, astronauts, and little green beings, but the kind that we deal with in looking at artworks and the kind that sometimes presents head-scratching problems for us in creating art, especially two-dimensional art. Natural objects—as well as those forms created by sculptors, architects, and craftspersons—exist in space. They are defined by the space around and within them. Three-dimensional space is the emptiness or areas around, above, below, and between objects, as well as the space inside hollow objects.

Architecture is concerned with enclosing actual space in a functional and unified manner. Landscape architects and people involved in city planning design spaces where people will live, work, and play. They are skilled in making practical and beautiful use of environmental spaces, and this involves how they combine forms, colors, and textures. Sculpture is also an art form that takes up actual space. It is freestanding, and viewers must move through the space and around it to view all its sides. Relief sculpture is somewhat different in that it projects outward from a flat surface and is seen from only one point of view—the front side.

One kind of actual space that we deal with in responding to artworks and in creating our own is the flat surface of the picture plane. This is the space determined by the length and width of the canvas or paper upon which the artwork is created. Artists plan carefully to achieve a feeling of balance and unity throughout a composition, leaving no spaces that do not function in harmony with the rest of the artwork. Piet Mondrian had a keen desire to order space in his stark compositions. His later works are devoid of any aspect of volume or three-dimensional form. He extracted the essence on several themes, moving from relatively naturalistic drawing, through vividly unnatural and expressive color, to a linear simplification that shows a two-dimensional space divided in perfect relationships of squares and rectangles painted with black, white, and the primary colors. Mondrian lived in Holland, where the horizon is as flat and sharp as if drawn with a ruler, and the space in his work is similarly flat, sharp, and in perfect balance.

The difference between and the close relationship of positive shapes and negative spaces in the two-dimensional space contained within the format of the picture plane are important. The figures or objects themselves are the positive

Figure 2.23 **M. C. Escher, *Belvedere*, 1958. Lithograph, 46 × 29.5 cm.**
Courtesy of Vorpal Gallery, Soho, New York. Photo by D. James Dee.
Famous for his innovative and unusual use of space, Escher created a world of wonder with his sharply delineated perspective.

Figure 2.24 **Edward Hicks, *The Cornell Farm*, 1848. Canvas, 36¾ × 49 in.**
National Gallery of Art, Washington, Gift of Edgar William and Bernice Chrysler Garbisch, Photograph ©2002 Board of Trustees, National Gallery of Art, Washington.
The Quaker preacher who painted this pastoral scene in 1848 had no formal art training, yet he knew how to create the illusion of great spatial depth with diminishing sizes, elevated placement of objects, and lighter tones and fewer details in the background.

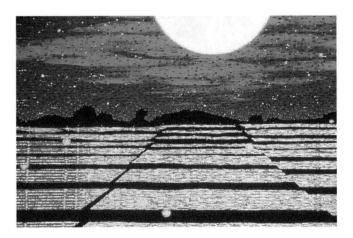

Figure 2.25 **Victoria Z. Rivers, *Bali Moon*, 1989. Mixed media on fabric, including stitching and beads.**
Courtesy of Victoria Z. Rivers, collection of Susan Matthews.
Diminishing sizes, elevated placement, and parallel lines going toward a vanishing point make for a depiction of deep space in this night landscape.

shapes, and the empty spaces between and around them are the negative spaces. In painting, we frequently refer to this as *figure-ground.* An artist creating a two-dimensional composition strives to intermingle and relate the positive shapes and negative spaces so as to achieve harmony. Placing tracing paper over a composition such as Rubens's *Lion* and drawing around all the negative spaces readily shows how, when finished, we have inadvertently drawn the positive shape of the animal.

This knowledge about the relationship of positive shapes and negative spaces can help us draw an object that otherwise might seem perplexing and complicated. Hold a

viewfinder (see Figure 2.27) very steadily in front of you. Keep one eye closed, and focus on a section of a bare-branched tree. You will see branches and the trunk creating negative spaces between each other as they extend off the four sides of the viewfinder. With a pencil, concentrate on drawing these negative spaces on a 9-by-12-inch piece of paper exactly as you see them through your viewfinder. When you finish, you will have drawn the section of the tree. The positive and negative spaces fit together like the pieces of a jigsaw puzzle. Focusing on negative spaces, rather than on the more complicated positive shapes of what you are observing, can help you solve some drawing dilemmas.

Many sculptors include negative spaces within their art-works, planning carefully to strike a pleasing balance between positive and negative areas and to create a variety of interesting open areas. In 1929, British sculptor Henry Moore pierced his first opening through a solid mass in a piece of sculpture and began exploring the many ways in which negative spaces can be integral parts of three-dimensional artwork.

Creating the illusion of actual space and giving a feeling of three-dimensional depth (**perspective**) to a two-dimensional artwork have long been challenges that have perplexed and fascinated artists, especially those in the Western world. While this photographic realism has been readily accepted in the West, Asian artists at one time might well have questioned this concept of "realism." (Do people and objects really get smaller in nature when they are farther away?) Objects in space have three dimensions—height, width, and depth—yet the flat surface of a piece of paper, a wall or ceiling, a wood panel, or a canvas has only two dimensions—height and width.

During the Renaissance, artists began studying nature much more closely to determine just how to accomplish an illusion of actual space more accurately and realistically. German artist Albrecht Dürer contrived a gridded frame through which he could look at an object directly in front of him and then copy, and even foreshorten, what he was seeing on his gridded drawing paper. Some artists puzzled over the use of converging lines and **vanishing points**. Others found that **shading** a face or arm from light to dark made the object look rounded rather than flat. These early artists attempted and succeeded in using the picture plane or surface to create a painting that made viewers feel that they were looking through a window to the real world.

Let's try this window-to-the-world idea. Look out a window, and locate which objects are nearest you. If you were making a painting of this scene, these objects would be in the *foreground*. The part that is farthest away is the *background*, and the space in between is the *middleground*. To draw or paint this window scene, you would need to create the illusion of space on your paper and would find some of the techniques that follow helpful. Sometimes, artists choose to use only a few of these techniques. Sometimes, they use all of them, depending on whether they wish to create a realistic and representational view; whether they wish to express some emotion or feeling about what they see by exaggerating, omitting, or distorting the images; and whether they are more interested in the shapes, lines, and colors of what they see than they are in the actual depiction of what is in front of them.

1. Overlapping occurs when one **opaque** object covers part of a second object. The one in front seems closer.

Figure 2.26 **Frederic Bazille,** *Negro Girl with Peonies*, **1870. Oil on canvas. 23¾ × 29¾ in.**
National Gallery of Art, Washington, Collection of Mr. and Mrs. Paul Mellon, Photograph ©2002 Board of Trustees, National Gallery of Art, Washington.
The light shining from the right on the girl's face and body gives her three-dimensional form and creates a highly realistic illusion of depth.

If only a few shapes in a composition overlap, and if that is the only way the artist uses to show depth, we say the composition has *shallow* or *flat* space.

2. Size plays a large part in depicting three-dimensional space on a flat surface. Picture two ballplayers on a field. One is several feet away from you. The other one is far away; you could raise your hand and block from your view this entire figure. In a two-dimensional art-work, large objects appear to be closer than small objects. A very small object appears to be farther away in the distance. This is often referred to as *diminishing sizes*. If our eyes are led far back in the picture plane, we say the composition has *deep* space.

3. Placement of figures and objects also plays an important part in the illusion of creating space on a flat surface. Figures and objects that are placed on the ground and lowest in the picture plane appear to be closer to the viewer than those placed higher up. Those that are farthest away are highest from the bottom of the picture, and they are found near or on the eye-level line or horizon line. Now picture what happens to this rule when we regard the sky, which is, of course, above the horizon line. The largest clouds (or balloons, helicopters, or birds) are those that are closest to us, and they are at the top of the picture. The most distant clouds (or other objects) are smaller and are seen lower and toward the horizon. Next time you drive down a highway, notice the size and placement of the clouds that you see through your windshield. Notice how the boats on the horizon line lead your eye back into the distance in

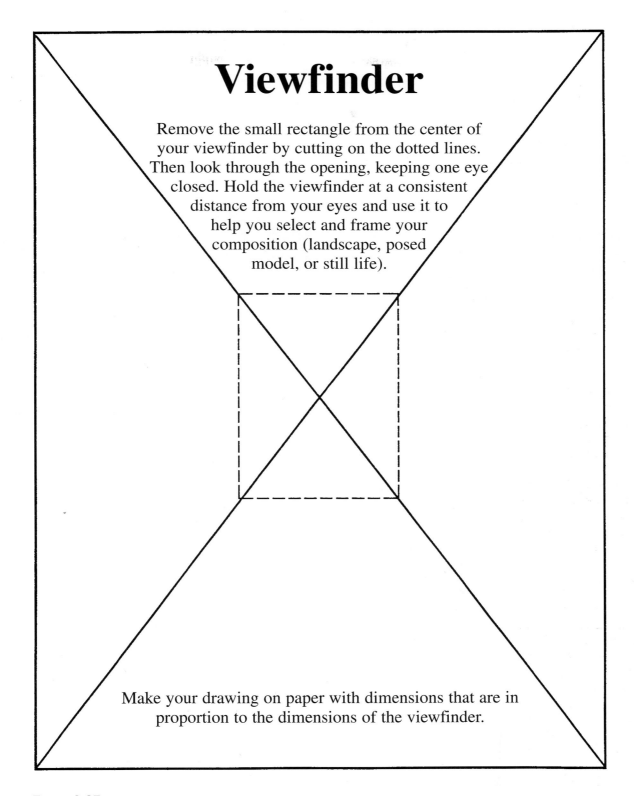

Viewfinder

Remove the small rectangle from the center of your viewfinder by cutting on the dotted lines. Then look through the opening, keeping one eye closed. Hold the viewfinder at a consistent distance from your eyes and use it to help you select and frame your composition (landscape, posed model, or still life).

Make your drawing on paper with dimensions that are in proportion to the dimensions of the viewfinder.

Figure 2.27 **Viewfinder.**
Use a manila folder or a piece of construction paper to make your viewfinder.
This 6-by-8-inch viewfinder is in correct proportion for use in making a drawing of a landscape, still life, or posed model on a piece of 9-by-12-inch paper.

Winslow Homer's *Breezing Up* (Figure 4.2). If you shield these small boats with your hand, you immediately see how the picture changes and no longer suggests deep space.

Try placing a sheet of clear vinyl over an artwork such as Georges Seurat's *Sunday Afternoon on the Island of La Grande Jatte* (Colorplate 15). Use a water-soluble black marker to trace around the largest figure and then several smaller figures that are elevated from the bottom of the composition. Remove the vinyl, and observe the size and placement of the figures. Clean the vinyl with a damp paper towel. Try tracing over photographs of figures, trees, and such to see how smaller objects are higher up to show distance.

4. Details, colors, and textures of the figures and objects closest to the viewer are clearest and brightest and have the sharpest edges and the most visible details of texture. Objects farther away lack textural detail and have hazy or blurred outlines and indistinct patterns. Lighter, less brightly colored objects seem farther away. Have you ever observed several layers of mountain ranges and noticed that the one closest to you is the darkest and that each succeeding one becomes a lighter blue? This is often called *atmospheric* or **aerial perspective**. Notice the dramatic grandeur of aerial perspective that the artist Albert Bierstadt achieved in his rendering of an American landscape in *The Rocky Mountains* (Colorplate 25).

5. Directional light gives modeled form to three-dimensional objects. When a light shines on a figure or object, the side closest to the light is shown as lighter; the side away from the light is darker. Think of a white circle on a red background. It is flat. Now think of a white sphere. What makes it appear to have three-dimensional form? A gradual change from light to dark gives the illusion of depth and form. This concept was introduced during the Italian Renaissance by such masters as Leonardo da Vinci (Colorplate 31). Note how Grant Wood's *American Gothic* (Colorplate 21) uses directional lighting to model the faces of the two figures.

6. Converging lines of **linear perspective** lead our eyes back into the deep space of the picture. The ways these lines seem to converge and where they seem to meet are somewhat rule-governed if an artist seeks to make a realistic or representational picture. But, as in all rules for creating artworks, we can distort, exaggerate, omit, or change the rules to create a desired expressive effect. At any rate, perspective with converging lines simply means that you, the artist, establish an eye-level line. This is usually an imaginary horizontal line that you project in front of you, somewhat like a horizon line. As you start to draw, notice all the vertical lines, such as the upright sides of buildings, fence posts, table legs, and so on. Draw them straight up and down, parallel to the

right and left sides of the paper. Draw the corner of the building, the table leg, or the fence post that is closest to you first. But two lines that are horizontally parallel to each other that move away from you in space will seem to converge and meet at a place on the eye-level line called the *vanishing point*. Different sets of parallel lines meet at different vanishing points. These vanishing points are often off the paper; that is, the eye-level line is extended beyond the sides of the paper.

Try placing a sheet of tracing paper over a reproduction, such as Utrillo's *Rue à Sannois* (Figure 2.28), or over a photograph or postcard of a street scene. With a ruler and pencil, trace the converging lines. Then remove the tracing paper to see how horizontal lines that are parallel to each other meet at a vanishing point on the eye-level line.

A special kind of perspective called **foreshortening** refers to the drawing or depiction of an object that appears to be projecting directly toward the viewer.

Artists in ancient Egypt were not usually concerned with aspects of visual realism as presented by perspective. Medieval art took a somewhat similar position and placed theological over physical truth. One-point perspective was common in mid-fifteenth-century artworks but was gradually replaced by two- and three-point perspectives. Systems of perspective were developed during the Renaissance in both Italy and northern Europe, and artists since then have been free to use perspective in ways of their own choosing. Some twentieth-century painters argue that perspective is a deception and deny its use on a two-dimensional canvas.

In addition to knowing these perspective rules, artists often use a sighting technique to help them draw objects in space. To do this, they hold a pencil in front of them, at arm's length, and with one eye closed, they measure objects' comparative lengths and widths. They also use sighting and the vertical and horizontal directions of the pencil to determine the angle at which lines are converging. They then draw the angles they see on paper, using the vertical and horizontal sides of the paper to guide them.

PRODUCING ARTWORKS EMPHASIZING SPACE

Three Figures in Space: Diminishing Size and Elevated Placement

Students will make an artwork that places three figures of diminishing sizes on different elevations of the picture plane to give an illusion of depth and distance.

1. Choose a subject such as one of the following: scarecrows, dancers, sailors, cowboys, robots, mermaids, mountain climbers, surfers, skiers, kings, queens, clowns, knights, farmers, and so on. Cut three figures of different sizes from colored paper. Make the largest

Figure 2.28 **Maurice Utrillo, *Rue à Sannois*, ca. 1911. Oil on canvas, 21½ × 29¼ in.**
Virginia Museum of Fine Arts, Richmond, VA. Collection of Mr. and Mrs. Paul Mellon. ©2002 Artists Rights Society (ARS), New York/ADAGP, Paris.
Utrillo frequently painted street scenes, in which he defined three-dimensional depth with sharp use of one- or two-point perspective. Here, the sides of the street converge at a vanishing point on the eye-level line. Buildings are smaller but placed higher above the bottom of the picture as they recede into space.

figure 5–6 inches tall, make the medium-sized figure several inches shorter, and make the smallest figure about 1 inch high. You can cut out the different parts for the figures separately and then paste each figure together.

2. Arrange your figures on a piece of paper. Place the largest figure low on the paper. This is the foreground. Place the medium-sized figure a little farther up. This is the middleground. Place the smallest figure farther up on the paper, in the background.

3. Cut out environmental details from other pieces of colored paper, or use oil pastels or crayons to complete your picture. If the latter, wait to paste your figures in place until you have finished using the oil pastels or crayons.

Floating Boxes: Two-Point Perspective

Students will follow step-by-step guidelines for two-point perspective to draw a series of boxes that are viewed above, on, and below the eye-level line (Figure 2.29).

Look at photographs of streets and buildings, or take a few pictures of streets and buildings with your camera and place tracing paper over several of the photographs, and draw the vertical and converging lines that you see as described above. This will help you understand how two or more horizontal lines that are parallel to each other in nature appear to converge at the same point on the eye-level line when you draw them. Vertical lines in nature are drawn vertically parallel to the sides of the paper. When you make a perspective drawing, the eye-level line is a horizontal line straight ahead of your eyes. If you are drawing objects that are below your eye level, you will see the tops of the objects. If you are drawing objects that are above your eye level, you will see the bottoms of the objects. Use a ruler or any straightedge and a pencil for this exercise. You will be drawing nine lines to complete each box. You will see three sides of the finished box. Refer to the diagram to help you draw these boxes.

1. Fold a 12-by-18-inch piece of white drawing paper horizontally a little below the middle. The fold line is the eye-level line. At both ends of the fold, mark "VP" for "vanishing point."

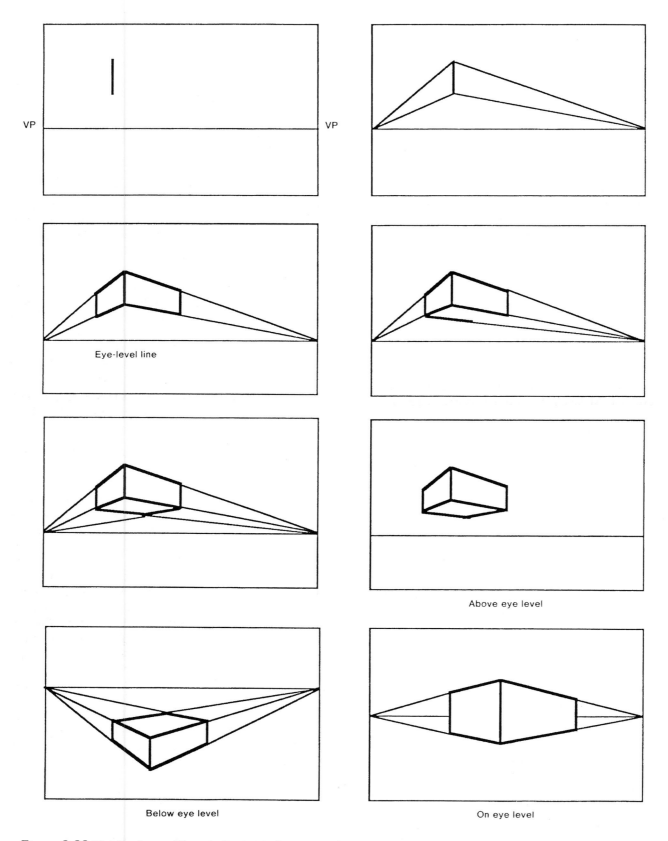

Figure 2.29 **Floating boxes: Diagram for two-point perspective.**

2. Somewhere above the eye-level line, draw a vertical 1½-inch line. This is the closest corner of a floating box that you will be drawing. It will be above the eye-level line.

3. Use your ruler and pencil to connect the bottom and top ends of this short line to the vanishing point on the left side of the paper. Draw very lightly so you can erase the lines that go beyond the box when you have finished drawing it.

4. Then connect the top and bottom ends of this short line to the vanishing point on the right side of the paper.

5. Draw two vertical lines, one on each side of the first vertical line. These two lines will be somewhere in between the long lines you drew toward the vanishing points. They will mark the two corners of your box that are the farthest away.

6. Connect the base of the vertical line that you just drew on the right with the vanishing point on the left.

7. Connect the base of the vertical line that you just drew on the left with the vanishing point on the right. This line will intersect the last line that you drew. You have completed drawing a box. Erase the lines that go beyond the box.

8. Draw more floating boxes in the space above your eye-level line. Make one box overlap another. Draw a long, narrow box piercing a large box. Try adding windows, doors, wings, and words, using the guideline of drawing the nearest vertical first and connecting its top and bottom to the vanishing points.

9. Turn your paper upside down, and your floating boxes seem to be on the ground. You can draw boxes below eye level in a similar manner as just described.

10. To draw boxes on the eye-level line, make a vertical line that intersects the eye-level line. This is the corner of the box that is nearest you. Draw lines from its top and bottom to the vanishing points. Then draw the two verticals to determine the box's dimensions. You will not see either the top or bottom of this box, just the two sides. Use your knowledge of two-point perspective to observe and draw a picture of a building.

11. Make a drawing that combines floating boxes to create a mechanical dinosaur, robot, or space city.

Drawing Negative Spaces

Make a viewfinder from tagboard as diagrammed in Figure 2.27. Hold the tagboard steadily, with one eye closed. Look through the viewfinder and concentrate on drawing the negative spaces, one by one, rather than on drawing the more complicated positive shapes of the selected subject—a bare branched tree, a potted plant, a simple still life. The positive shapes and negative spaces in a picture fit together like the pieces of a jigsaw puzzle. By drawing the more easily perceived negative spaces, you will inadvertently draw the object itself.

1. A viewfinder is like a small camera. Look through it, and adjust your view by lengthening or shortening the distance from your eyes. This will frame the parts that are touching three or four sides of the viewfinder. These four sides create negative spaces for you to draw. Your drawing paper should be proportional to the small rectangle cut in your viewfinder.

2. For your subject matter, use a bicycle, a chair, a piece of machinery, a potted plant, a portion of the trunk and branches of a tree, or some other object with clearly defined parts. Sit near it, and look through your viewfinder, keeping one eye closed. Hold the viewfinder steady and always at the same distance from your eye so that the negative areas do not shift and change.

3. As you look through the viewfinder, concentrate on seeing each negative shape. Try not to see the object itself. Then, on your paper, make a contour drawing of each negative shape, with the lines extending to the edges of your paper in the same places that they touch the edges of the viewfinder. After you have drawn all the negative spaces, you will have drawn the object.

4. Use a black marking pen or a brush and india ink to fill in the negative spaces, leaving the object itself white.

UNDERSTANDING ARTWORKS: Learning about Value

The term *value* refers to the element of lightness and darkness in an artwork. A color's value may show a range of tints and shades—that is, white may have been mixed with a pure hue to make a **gradation** of tints, and black may have been mixed with the same pure hue for a scale of shades. An artwork that uses only variations of one color has a monochromatic color scheme. Within an artwork that utilizes several colors, an artist may use a great variety of tints and shades. See the dramatic effect achieved in Salvador Dali's *The Persistence of Memory* (Colorplate 19). Note the many tints and shades of purple in the man's coat in Marc Chagall's *Green Violinist* (Colorplate 37).

But value does not always depend on a color's lightness and darkness. Many artworks that have no color at all depend on value to communicate their message. These include pen-and-ink, charcoal, and pencil drawings; etchings; block prints; and black-and-white photographs. A piece of sculpture may be all one color, or black, white, or gray; by its three-dimensional form, it catches the light in such a way as to present the viewer with an impressive range of darks and lights.

Artists use value in their artworks in several ways. In drawings, paintings, and prints, artists can create the illusion of the form of a natural object by changes in value. This technique is called *shading* or *modeling*. It was first introduced and developed during the Renaissance, when the arrangement of light and shadow was called **chiaroscuro**, an Italian word derived from *chiaro*, meaning "bright," and *oscuro*, meaning "dark." Artworks before that time tended to be flat because they lacked light and dark modeling to show three-dimensional forms. Many artworks since then have continued to use differences in value to show modeled form, but many artists show little change in value within shape, depicting forms as flat areas of color.

The angular surfaces of buildings or boxes call for the artist to make sharp changes in value from one side of the structure to the next. This helps us to see the buildings or boxes as three-dimensional. On the other hand, the curving, rounded surface of any cylindrical or spherical form must be handled differently. Think of an apple sitting on a table. The side of the apple closest to the light source is the lightest because that is where rays of light hit most directly. The other side of the apple is the darkest, with the change from light to dark very gradual. Therefore, depicting the curving, rounded surface of any cylindrical or spherical form requires a gradual change in value.

Darker values of a color are seen as being closer to us, while lighter tones are viewed as being farther away. Notice how in *The Rocky Mountains* (Colorplate 25) Albert Bierstadt used this device to create near and far. Also note the emphasis he created with light tones against dark in the middleground, where a waterfall plummets into a lake.

Four shading techniques help us create different values to show the illusion of three-dimensional form on a flat surface:

1. *Hatching* involves making a series of fine parallel lines of the same or different lengths. Hatching is best accomplished with pens or pencils since they make sharp, clean lines. The closer together the lines are, the denser and darker the value appears. When the lines are spaced farther apart, the effect is a lighter value. Several printmaking techniques, such as woodcuts and etchings, also incorporate hatching.

2. *Cross-hatching* involves making two or more intersecting sets of parallel lines. The farther apart that both hatched and crosshatched lines are, the lighter the value; the closer together they are, the darker the value. Squinting your eyes sometimes helps you to see the darks and lights and the differences and changes in value, and thus to perceive the three-dimensional illusion of the form. To effectively create the illusion of form, both hatched and crosshatched lines should follow the contours—that is, the curves of cylindrical or spherical objects. To show the flat surface of a building or box, the lines should run parallel to one edge of the surface.

3. *Stippling* is making many repeated dots with the tip of the drawing instrument. If the dots are very close

Figure 2.30 **Rembrandt van Rijn, *Self-Portrait*, 1659. Oil on canvas, 33¼ × 26 in.**
National Gallery of Art, Washington, Rosenwald Collection. Photograph ©2002 Board of Trustees, National Gallery of Art, Washington.
Deep sorrow and the troubling events in his life are reflected in this expressive portrait that the artist made of himself several years before his death. Rembrandt understood the dramatic effect of contrasting dark against light values in an artwork. He was extremely skilled in blending colors to create shading and to show form.

together, even touching each other, they present a dark value. If the dots are more widely spaced, the effect is a lighter value.

4. *Blending* consists of a gradual, smooth change from dark to light value. Lead pencils that range in their degree of softness may be used and the blending accomplished with the fingertips or a small piece of tissue. Charcoal is frequently used in black-and-white studies to create blended values. Chalks and pastels are also easily rubbed and blended. Oil paints, watercolors, acrylics, and even crayons and oil pastels also present blending possibilities.

In addition to showing the three-dimensional qualities of modeled forms, value can elicit expressive responses because of the dramatic qualities of strong darks and lights. The variety of contrasting dark and light areas often grabs our attention and provokes intense feelings. Artists can create emphasis by using the direction of light to show a strong contrast of light and dark shadows. Rembrandt's portraits,

Figure 2.31 **Utah house.**
Photo by Barbara Herberholz.
Sharp changes in value seen in the dark and light shapes define the architectural dimensions in this old house, giving it a feeling of isolation similar to paintings of houses by the American artist Edward Hopper.

Figure 2.32 **Georgio De Chirico, *The Delights of the Poet*, 1913. Oil, 27⅜ × 34 in.**
Collection of Mr. and Mrs. Leonard C. Yaseen, ©2002 Artists Rights Society (ARS), New York/SIAE, Rome.
Strange and dreamlike, this haunting composition of a broad landscape with a bright light sharply defining the shadows makes a highly dramatic use of dark, medium, and light values.

whether they were of himself or others, reveal character and grab our attention because of his heavy reliance on light sources from one direction.

PRODUCING ARTWORKS EMPHASIZING VALUE

Lights and Darks: A Monochromatic Design

Students will paint a monochromatic design that has concentric bands of one color that become either increasingly lighter or darker as they encircle the shape of an alphabet letter in the center of the paper.

1. A practice exercise: Make a value scale of one color (see Figure 2.35). Cut a 2-by-12-inch strip from a piece of white drawing paper, and mark it by inches along its length. Paint the first inch-wide strip across one end with white tempera. Then mix a tiny bit of one color with white. Brush this tint next to the white on the long strip. Then add a bit more color to the white, and paint another inch-wide strip next to the last one. Continue until you reach the middle of the strip, where you paint a strip of the pure hue. Then add a tiny bit of black to the pure color to make a shade, and paint it next to the pure hue. Continue adding a little more black to the blend until you reach the last section of the strip, which you paint pure black.

2. Now draw a letter of the alphabet with pencil or chalk in the center of a 12-by-12-inch piece of white drawing paper. Make the letter about 6 inches high and an inch or so thick. Draw five or six concentric bands encircling the letter. The bands may vary in width, and as they

reach the sides of the paper, they may form an incomplete or broken encirclement.

3. Pour a small amount of one color of tempera, as well as some black and white, on a small paper plate. Use a small- or medium-sized flat-bristle brush to mix tints and shades of the color. Be sure to wash and wipe your brush clean on a paper towel or damp sponge before you mix a new tone.

4. Either paint the letter the pure color you have chosen, or mix a tint or shade of the color. Then begin painting the bands around the letter, lightening or darkening each concentric band to make a gradated arrangement of colors around the alphabet letter. Cover the entire paper with paint.

Showing Three-Dimensional Form with Gradated Values

After completing four value scales, students will use a variety of hatched, crosshatched, stippled, and blended values to shade a small contour drawing of a leafy twig or several overlapping feathers.

1. A practice exercise: To make value scales (Figure 2.35) use a ruler and a soft lead pencil to draw four 1-by-6-inch rectangles. In the first rectangle, use hatching to show a gradation from light to dark. In the second rectangle, use cross-hatching to show such a gradation. In the third, use stippling, and in the fourth, use blending. Hold your pencil on its side rather than in the writing position when blending so you are not making lines.

Figure 2.33 Albrecht Dürer, *Melancholiah 1*, 1514.
Philadelphia Museum of Art: The Lisa Norris Elkins Fund.
In this etching, Dürer creates a variety of dark, medium, and light values by skillfully repeating fine lines. Straight line hatching shows the flat planes of geometric forms; curving lines give the illusion of rounded forms.

Figure 2.34 Suzanne Adan, detail of *Horse Sense* (Side A), 1990. Clay glaze, 4 × 8 ft. Natoma Station, Folsom, Calif.
Courtesy of Suzanne Adan.
In this tile mural, the artist dramatically contrasts dark and light shapes.

Rub the surface with your fingertip or a tissue to smoothly blend from dark to light.

2. Place a large sheet of black paper close to you on the tabletop. Then place two or three overlapping turkey feathers (these may be ordered from art supply catalogs) or a leafy twig on the black paper. Close one eye, and hold a viewfinder in front of you in such a way that part of the feathers or leaves extends off the four sides, thus creating negative spaces. Make a modified contour drawing, as explained on page 25, on a 5-by-7-inch piece of white paper. The parts of the leaves or feathers that touch the edges of your viewfinder as you look through it will be what you draw on your rectangular drawing paper. Drawing the contours of the negative spaces rather than the shape of the object itself sometimes helps you draw the object. Complete your composition by drawing inner and outer contour lines on the feathers or leaves.

3. Shade your drawing by creating gradated values. Endeavor to show the curving forms of the feathers or leaves by gradually changing from light to dark. Use all four techniques—hatching, cross-hatching, blending, and stippling—in your feather or leaf drawing. Squint your eyes at the feathers or leaves to see the darkest areas. Refer to your value scales to help you decide where to show the darkest, lightest (or white areas), and in-between values. You may need to use an eraser to keep the white areas clean. Plan on shading in the negative spaces rather than leaving them white.

Creating Value with Hatching: Scarecrows and Others

Students will form a figure such as a scarecrow by making small patches of different densities of hatches to create different gradations of dark and light values. Other subject matter may be used such as a mermaid, a magician, a witch, a sports figure, a dancer, spaceman, and so on. No outlines are used.

1. With a ballpoint pen, make a variety of practice hatches—some in which the lines are far apart and others in which the lines are close together. Make crosshatches with several layers of lines going in different directions. Squint at them. Which is the darkest? Which is the lightest? Cut them out, and arrange them in a progression from lightest to darkest value.

2. Look at real scarecrows, remember ones you have seen, or find photographs of them. Then imagine being a scarecrow, arms outstretched. Try standing in this position. Would you stand straight or be slightly tipped to one side? How would it feel to stand this way in the sun, wind, and rain day after day? Would you be lonely? Would birds be afraid of you? Or would you welcome a few friendly crows on your outstretched arms? Would

Value Scale

Use a pen or soft lead pencil for hatching, cross-hatching, and stippling. Use a soft lead pencil for blending.

Light————————————— to ——————————— Dark

Hatching

Cross-hatching

Stippling

Blending

Figure 2.35 **Value scale.**

Figure 2.36 Student work: Showing a three-dimensional form with hatching, cross-hatching, and stippling.

3. To begin, lightly draw a tall vertical axis and a crossbar for outstretched arms on a piece of 8½-by-11-inch or 9-by-12-inch white paper. Begin making hatches and crosshatches of various densities to build the form for your figure. Vary them in size, shape, and value. They may overlap. Let the hatches and crosshatches suggest details—a tattered garment, hat, scarf, hair, eyes, and so on. As hatching is added, the scarecrow (or other figure) grows. Do not use any outlines.

4. Make another hatched drawing. For example, create a rocky landscape, a cluster of flowers, a group of trees, boats on the water, and so on.

you be wearing shabby clothes? What would be on your head? What would be near you—tall cornstalks? a fence? a barn? Could you see the sun and the moon?

INTERACTIVE EXTENSIONS

1. *Making photo files*: To provide you with visual information for producing artworks, collect photographs from magazines, calendars, and such for a photo file. Look for specific categories: buildings, trees, flowers and plants, birds, fish, animals, insects, people at work, people at play, faces, machines, transportation, landscapes, seascapes, and skies. Trim the photos, and attach them to tagboard or railroad board cut to 8½-by-11 inches. Keep your collection in expandable legal folders, large envelopes, or file folders.

2. Use several different techniques or media to portray a theme or a particular subject matter. Reflect on how the technique or medium affected your interpretation of the subject matter. List the art elements you used and the effects of each on the outcome.

3. Explain how emulating an artist's style increases your understanding of the artist's technique.

4. Using the four ways of assessing a student's artwork in Chapter 5, page 120, select an artwork you have done from Chapter 2 and comment on it.

5. Select a fine art example for one of the elements of art described in this chapter. Emulate the style of the artist by creating an artwork that uses the same style but different subject matter. For instance, draw a house or bird, using van Gogh's pen-and-ink style in *Grove of Cypresses* (Figure 2.3).

6. Make a small poster about color. Include a color wheel, and clip photographs from magazines, travel folders, calendars, and such that illustrate warm colors, cool colors, primary colors, analogous colors, complementary colors, neutral colors, and so on. Also include postcard reproductions of famous artworks that demonstrate some aspect of color. Make small posters about each of the other art elements, using photographs from the natural world and the world of art. Label and use these to teach students about line, shape/form, texture, value, and space.

3

CHAPTER

Understanding and Using the Principles of Art:
Response and Production

If you have ever made a casserole or a cake, you measured, chopped, mixed, sautéed, or baked according to some directions. First, you read the list of the ingredients and then how much of each one, whether you had to slice or sift, in what order to combine the ingredients, and how long the dish or dessert had to bake before it was ready to eat.

When we make an artwork, our "ingredients" are the elements of art discussed in Chapter 2: color, line, shape/form, texture, value, and space. Some individuals organize and carefully plan their artworks; others, such as naive or **primitive** artists and young children, work more intuitively, achieving an aesthetic result almost unconsciously. Similarly, some cooks take "a pinch of this and a cup or so of that," while others read the recipe and measure each item carefully.

Whether we work intuitively or consciously, we plan, use, and control the **principles of art** when we create an artwork. We can improve our artworks by learning to recognize each principle. We can gain a richer understanding of the artworks of the great masters by analyzing how they handled the principles of art and achieved harmony in their artworks.

The principles of art are basic guidelines for producing certain effects in looking at and responding to artwork. Whether we wish to understand an artwork or improve our own art production, analyzing and using appropriate language to describe how the principles of art work are important. The seven principles of art are balance; emphasis; proportion; movement; rhythm, repetition, and pattern; variety; and unity.

UNDERSTANDING ARTWORKS: Learning about Balance

In artworks, **balance** is more a visual feeling of weight than an actual quality of being heavy or light. Our eyes seem to seek things that "feel balanced." Have you ever walked into a room in which a picture was crooked and felt a compelling urge to set it straight? Have you ever made an arrangement of flowers, then stepped back to check your work and thought, Somehow it doesn't feel balanced yet, and then added a few more zinnias to the left side? An artwork with a feeling of imbalance creates the uneasy response in viewers that something is "wrong." The imbalance might even distract us from seeing the subject matter of a painting or the artist's finely detailed textures. What causes this feeling of balance or imbalance? Balance is achieved when no one portion of an artwork seems too heavy visually or overpowers any other part of the artwork.

Artworks can have two kinds of balance. The first is called **formal** (or **symmetrical**) **balance**, and the second is called **informal** (or **asymmetrical**) **balance**. In the first, a real or an imaginary median line runs through the center of the composition. The parts, details, shapes, colors, and lines

Figure 3.1 **St. Francis Cathedral, Santa Fe, New Mexico.**
A clear example of formal balance, this type of architectural symmetry lends itself well to a feeling of dignity, stability, and enduring values. Radial symmetry is seen in the round stained-glass window in the center area.
Photo by Barbara Herberholz.

on one side are an exact duplicate or mirror image of the other side. A butterfly with its wings flattened is an example of formal balance. Our own bodies, seen from the front, show formal balance. Formal balance is the simplest kind of balance and usually produces less visual interest than does informal balance. Many pieces of traditional architecture appropriately show formal balance. Can you find examples of formal balance in buildings in your community—perhaps public buildings such as courthouses, office buildings, museums, churches, temples, and capitol buildings? Do they elicit in you a feeling that the work or worship that goes on there is dignified, stable, and enduring? Finding paintings and sculptures that show formal balance is more difficult, perhaps because artists generally strive to hold our attention by presenting less predictable parts in their compositions. The monotony of perfect balance can be offset or relieved by a variation called *approximate symmetry*. Here, the artist arranges the objects on either side of a central axis in an almost formal manner with just enough variation to hold our attention.

Another kind of formal balance, in addition to approximate symmetry, is **radial balance**. Radial balance occurs when lines, shapes, and colors radiate outward from a central point and form a circular design. Radial balance is often used for decorative purposes in architecture, textile design, jewelry, stained glass, and other crafts. Nature has many examples of radial balance—the petals of a flower, the cross section of an orange. Can you think of others? If you have ever been fascinated with the ever-changing designs in a kaleidoscope, marveled at the six-pointed symmetry of an enlarged photograph of a snowflake, or stood in awe as light streamed in through a stained-glass rose window in a cathe-

Figure 3.2 **Papercut.**
Formal balance on a vertical axis is evident in this delicately cut design
from Mexico. Paper is folded in half and then cut to create perfect symmetry before being mounted on bark paper.

Figure 3.3 **Henri Rousseau, *The Football Players*, 1908. Oil
on canvas, 39½ × 34⅝ in.**
*Solomon R. Guggenheim Museum, New York. Photo by David Heald. ©
Solomon R. Guggenheim Foundation, New York (FN 60.1583).*
Rollicking ball players seem to dance politely and gracefully between
nearly identical rows of trees in this carefully arranged composition.
Would you call its balance formal, approximately formal, or informal?

dral, you understand the basic concept of radial balance. The
city of Paris was planned as a radial design. In oriental art
and religion, the mandala is a round design that symbolizes
the universe. Some barns in Pennsylvania have large hex
signs painted on them to bring good luck to the owners.
They, too, are radial configurations.

Informal balance gives us a comfortable visual feeling
of weight, even though both sides of the artwork are dissim-
ilar. In this type of balance, the elements work to offset each
other to make a harmonious whole. When artists use informal balance, they strive to achieve a comfortable, even casual, feeling in the way they arrange the elements. Though
informal balance may seem to take less planning, it can be
complicated and difficult to achieve. Can you describe how
Picasso achieved a comfortable feeling of balance in *Girl*

before a Mirror (Colorplate 29)? Though the post of the mirror frame divides the composition in half, both halves are
different and are connected by the arm reaching toward the
reflection in the mirror. What differences in size, shape, pattern, and line can you find on either side? How does the
manner in which the artist achieved balance contribute to the
mood of the artwork?

Check your understanding of the two different kinds of
balance by tossing a handful of paper clips, erasers, car
keys, and such onto a piece of paper. First move them into a
formally balanced arrangement and then into an informally
balanced arrangement.

How are artists able to arrange the elements of art in an
informal way and still elicit a comfortable feeling of balance
in the viewer?

1. First, we know that our eyes are drawn to bright colors
   more than low-intensity colors. Therefore, an artist can
   achieve a feeling of balance by using a small area of
   bright color to balance a larger area of duller color. Also,
   warm colors appear heavier to our eyes than cool colors.

Therefore, an artist would probably choose to use a lesser amount of red and orange than blue and green.

2. A strong contrast in value between an object and its background has more visual weight than does an object that is closer in value to its background. A dark value of a color seems heavier than a light value of a color, so in making a composition, we tend to use less of a shade than a tint to achieve balance.

3. Our eyes are attracted to the more interesting textures in a composition—those that are rough or bumpy rather than those that are smooth and even. Therefore, we can balance a small, rough-textured area with a large, smooth one.

4. Shapes need to be positioned in a two-dimensional space so that large ones near the center or dominant area of a composition are balanced by smaller objects placed farther away. A large shape seems heavier than a small one, so several small shapes may be needed to balance a large one. Note in Seurat's *Sunday Afternoon on the Island of La Grande Jatte* (Colorplate 15) how the two large figures on the far right balance the groups of smaller figures on the left. Can you find other ways in which the artist has shown informal balance in this pointillistic artwork?

5. In a similar manner, shapes that are more complicated tend to catch our eye first and to appear heavier than those with simpler contours. Knowing this, we would probably choose to balance a large, simple shape with a small, complex one.

Turn to the Color Gallery, and analyze several artworks to see how artists achieved balance through one or more of the elements of art.

PRODUCING ARTWORKS EMPHASIZING BALANCE

Formal Balance: Fold-and-Blot Designs

Students will use a fold-and-blot technique (Figure 3.5) with paint and paper to create a formally balanced design based on visual observation of things in nature.

1. Fold a piece of white drawing paper in half and then unfold it. Apply watercolors or tempera paint to the paper on one side of the fold. Quickly fold the paper along the crease, and blot the painted area onto the opposite side of the paper. Think of things you have seen that show formal balance, and continue applying paint, folding, and blotting. You may wish to paint a face or mask, a butterfly, an insect or spider, a frog, reflections of trees in a lake, a full frontal figure, an alligator, and so on.

2. When the paint is dry, use a black marking pen or a small brush and black ink to add flourishes and linear details.

Figure 3.4 **Berthe Morisot, *The Artist's Sister at a Window*, 1869. Canvas, 21⅝ × 18¼ in.**
National Gallery of Art, Washington, Ailsa Mellon Bruce Collection, Photograph © 2002 Board of Trustees, National Gallery of Art, Washington. A clear example of asymmetrical balance, this painting places a dark shape on the left with a similar one on the right to give our eyes a feeling of comfortable weight. Try "erasing" any one shape in the composition to see how the informal balances change.

Informal Balance: A Cut-Paper Mural

A group of students will work together to design and complete a cut-paper mural in which the figures, animals, and objects are arranged in a harmonious, unified, asymmetrical manner. Themes for cut-paper murals can be taken from literary sources, social studies, and the sciences, as well as from other areas of the curriculum.

1. A suggested theme is "Noah's Ark" (Figure 3.6). Use books, videos, and photographs of animals, birds, and reptiles for visual information. List figures and items to include in the mural on slips of paper dropped in a box, letting each student pick one that he or she will cut from pieces of colored paper: lion, elephant, zebra, giraffe, horse, pig, cow, goat, bear, peacock, lion, camel, owl, turtle, alligator, swan, sheep, and so on. Also include Noah and his wife, a rainbow, a dove with an olive branch in its beak, a unicorn, and of course the ark itself.

2. Decide upon a scale. For an average size of class, the background should be about 3 by 4 feet with the largest

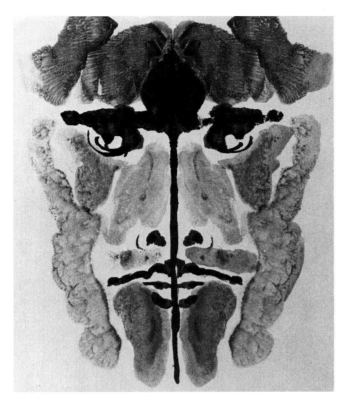

Figure 3.5 Student work: Formal balance is created by applying paint in a controlled manner before folding and blotting.

animal being about the size of one's hand and smaller animals in proportion. Of course, small animals that are actually large in life may be placed higher up in the composition to show deeper space. Colored Fadeless banner paper may be cut or torn and attached for background areas, such as a grassy area, pond, sky, hill, and so forth.

3. Students select from a variety of small, cut-up pieces of paper of various colors and surfaces. From these, they will cut and assemble the different parts for their figures and animals. A symmetrical shape can be cut from folded paper. If repeated shapes are needed, students can cut the shape from several thicknesses of paper. Fadeless banner or butcher paper may be used for the background, different colors designating areas for land, water, and sky. Place the background paper flat on a tabletop for assembling the individual items.

4. As students finish their figures and animals, they may place them temporarily on the background until all of the items for the mural are complete. Then, by shifting, moving, and overlapping the objects, the students should strive to achieve a comfortable feeling of informal balance in the arrangement—for example, a group of small creatures on one side could balance a large elephant on the other side. Give consideration to having one or more centers of interest and overlapping objects.

Remember to place objects so that the viewer's eye is led around the composition. Paste items securely in place, and hang the mural on the wall. Narrow strips of black railroad board can frame the composition, and cut-paper letters may be placed around the four sides— phrases that relate to the theme of the mural.

5. Find a photo of Edward Hicks's *Noah's Ark* and one of his *Peaceable Kingdom* paintings to further the student's interest in this American folk artist.

6. Other topics that lend themselves well to integrated group murals are the circus, jungle, the farm, the zoo, fairy tales, our town, on the playground, favorite sports, and so forth. Also students could make their own present-day version of Georges Seurat's *Sunday Afternoon on the Island of La Grande Jatte* (see Colorplate 15) or the *Peaceable Kingdom* by Edward Hicks.

UNDERSTANDING ARTWORKS: Learning about Emphasis

What catches your eye when you first look at an artwork? **Emphasis** is the principle of art that directs and centers our attention on one significant part of an artwork. This focal point or center of attention is the one object or area that is dominant over the others. Secondary areas of emphasis are subordinate to the main center of interest. Artists usually try to avoid creating too many focal points in an artwork, since this tends to be confusing. On the other hand, an artwork may not need a center of attention; for instance, fabrics, with their patterned motifs, present a repetitive, allover design with no designated focal point. A focal point or emphasis may be achieved in several ways:

1. Normally, our eyes are drawn immediately to the center of a picture, so anything placed near the center will most likely be noticed first. However, most artists do not place their focal point in the exact middle of their artwork, since the static and less interesting qualities of formal balance make for a boring composition. Most artists create emphasis by placing to the right or left of center the object or area they wish to use as a focal point. Notice that the child's face in Renoir's *A Girl with a Watering Can* (Colorplate 32) is above center. Note how Paul Cézanne (Colorplate 16) has placed the bathers in a nearly formal balance and how he positioned the branches of several trees in a triangular arrangement.

2. The subject matter of the artwork sometimes draws our attention automatically. We are naturally drawn to artworks with figures and faces in them, since as human beings, we respond to images of other human beings. Infants learn very early to focus on the faces of the people around them. The face is often the center of

Figure 3.6 *Noah's Ark*, **University art education class project.**
Look for ways in which this colored-paper mural shows informal balance. With the ark itself as a focal point, we can find the placement of creatures on either side of the ark that give us a comfortable feeling of balance. Cut-paper words form the frame.
Photo by Barbara Herberholz.

attention in an artwork, since we are already accustomed to looking at someone's face during a conversation, and we respond in the same manner when we look at a portrait. The eyes, often claimed to be "mirrors of the soul," especially rivet our attention. The farmer in the double portrait by Grant Wood and the woman in Leonardo da Vinci's work (Colorplates 21 and 31) gaze directly outward. They hold our attention in a compelling way, almost as if the personages they represent are looking at us.

3. Our attention is also drawn to faces presented in an unusual way, since we are accustomed to a more natural visage. For instance, the human face, even in a mask form, is normally symmetrical. Therefore, when we see a cubist portrait that shows both frontal and side views of the face all at once, such as Picasso's *Girl before a*

Mirror (Colorplate 33), or when we look at an Iroquois face mask with its twisted, lopsided features, or the Mexican frogman mask (Figure 7.54), we do a double take. When we look at Marisol's *Women and Dog* (Colorplate 20), we cannot help but be intrigued by the triple-faced images on two of the figures. If the subject matter of an artwork is itself surprising and presents an unusual combination of factors, or if it contains shocking material, our attention is caught. Dali grabs our attention and interest with his limp watches, one of which is covered with black ants, in *The Persistence of Memory* (Colorplate 19).

4. Another way that artists create emphasis is through lighting. Just as theatrical directors throw a spotlight on the stage to direct our attention, some artworks also use this same device. The Dutch artists Rembrandt, Leyster

Figure 3.7 **Frederic Remington, *The Apache*, 1890.**
Rockwell Gallery, Corning, New York.
What do you see first in this scene from the American West? The Apache sits astride his horse, resting his rifle on the diagonal line of rock, a slanted line that moves toward the covered wagon in the distance. The reins of the bridle are draped over his arm, creating lines that move our eyes upward to his face. He points his rifle directly at a covered wagon. Even the lines of the cactus point to the unsuspecting settlers.

Figure 3.8 **Judith Leyster, *Self-Portrait*, ca. 1630. Oil on canvas, 29⅜ × 25⅝ in.**
National Gallery of Art, Washington, Gift of Mr. and Mrs. Robert Woods Bliss, Photograph © 2002 Board of Trustees, National Gallery of Art, Washington.
Her pleasant face, off to the left, gazes at us across the centuries. Framed by her coif and bit of dark hair, we almost wait for her to speak to us. The horizontal line of her assuredly placed arm takes our eye to the diagonal of her paintbrush and upward to the secondary emphasis, the figure on the canvas that she is painting.

(Figure 3.8), and Vermeer often used light from outside the composition directed at their models.

5. Artists also direct our attention to a focal point through the use of pointers. Did you ever notice someone standing on a street and looking up at the sky? Did you then direct your gaze upward to see what had caught that person's attention? The same thing occurs if the eyes of a person in a picture are looking in a certain direction; we feel compelled to look there also. When you wish to direct someone's attention to something, do you ever point your finger? Sometimes in artworks, the subjects themselves are pointing at something or holding an object, perhaps a hockey stick or a sword, that directs our attention to the center of interest. The arrangement of these pointers may be subtle, or it may be obvious, with the lines framing the focal point. Look at Lawrence's *Vaudeville* (Colorplate 35), and decide how this artist used pointers. Then observe Homer's *Breezing Up* (Figure 4.2), and see if you can find any pointers.

6. The converging lines of perspective, as seen on a winding road or city street, often encourage our eyes to "take a walk" to a primary or secondary focal point. The converging lines of radial configurations may direct our attention to the center of a circular arrangement.

7. Our eyes also are drawn to an object that is isolated or set apart from other shapes in a composition.

8. Artists also create emphasis by using contrast—of shape, color, line, value, or texture. Think how one large rock stands out from a lot of pebbles or how one person with black hair stands out in a room of red-haired people. The ways to create such contrast in an artwork are innumerable.

9. Long used by artists as a basis for pictorial compositions, the triangle—with its base at the bottom of the canvas and its apex directing us to the focal point—emphasizes an important face or figure that becomes the center of attention.

Turn to the Color Gallery, and analyze how artists of several artworks achieved emphasis through one or more of the elements of art.

PRODUCING ARTWORKS EMPHASIZING EMPHASIS

Creating a Center of Interest: A Watercolor Landscape

Students will create a pleasing composition (Figure 3.12) either by using L-frames (Figure 2.11) and a colored photograph of a landscape, or by using a viewfinder (Figure 2.27) and an actual landscape, or by projecting a slide of a

Figure 3.9 **Hughie Lee-Smith,** *Boy with a Tire*, **1952.**
The Detroit Institute of Arts. Gift of Dr. S. B. Milton, Dr. James A. Owen, Dr.
B. F. Seabrooks, and Dr. A E. Thomas, Jr. Photograph © 1988 the Detroit
Institute of Arts © Estate of Hughie-Lee Smith/VAGA, New York, N.Y.
With his hand on a tire, the tall, isolated figure stares intently at us and
rivets our attention. The light area of concrete where he stands is framed
and defined by the fence on the left and the dark shadow on the right.
Notice how the sharp, pointed shape of the shadow of a utility pole on the
right points to the secondary focal point, the unoccupied shabby building
in the background.

landscape onto a screen and using a viewfinder to select a
portion of the landscape that clearly has a focal point. Students will make a contour drawing of the main lines in the
selected portion and then apply watercolor washes.

1. Move L-frames over the surface of a landscape photo-
    graph until you focus on a small portion of the scene. Or
    use a viewfinder to frame a portion of an actual land-
    scape or one seen on a projected colored slide. Choose
    either a vertical or horizontal format. Frame your com-
    position in such a way that a definite focal point is the
    center of attention and dominates the other parts of the
    composition.

2. Use a permanent black pen and a piece of 9-by-12-inch
    white watercolor paper or heavy white drawing paper to
    make a contour drawing of the part you selected. If you
    use a water-soluble pen, the black lines will blur when
    watercolor washes touch them.

3. Put a few drops of water on each color in the watercol-
    or tray to soften the pigments. Washes are made by mix-
    ing pigment with water in the lid of the watercolor box.
    Look for the dark and light areas in the section of the
    photograph or scene so that you can paint light and dark
    areas on your paper. Apply watercolor washes on your
    contour drawing in a loose, free manner. Paint the large
    background areas first. When the paper dries, details
    such as fence posts, windows, tree branches, and so on
    can be added with a smaller brush or your black mark-
    ing pen. Use soft sable brushes, both round and flat.

Figure 3.10 **Philip Evergood,** *Sunny Side of the Street*, **1950.**
Egg-oil varnish emulsion with marble dust, 50 × 36¼.
In the collection of the Corcoran Gallery of Art, Washington, D.C.
Museum purchase, Anna E. Clark Fund.
Converging lines of one-point perspective meet in the distance to focus
our attention on the busy activities of this city street. Within the triangular
shape they create, the white lines for children's games on the concrete, the
blind man's white cane, the white figure on the left, and the white hockey
sticks provide focal points that create a lively, active scene.

With watercolors, work for a fresh, clean, spontaneous
effect, leaving some white paper showing to create contrast and sparkle. Be sure to try the following watercol-
or techniques:

a) *Wet on wet*: The wet-on-wet technique makes the
    edges of objects look soft and blurred, which is why
    it is recommended for backgrounds, skies, and water.
    First, cover an area of your paper with clean water,
    back and front, to make it stick to the tabletop.

b) When mixing washes in the lid of your watercolor
    box, add more pigment to make a darker wash. A
    lighter color requires more water. Then smoothly
    stroke the wash onto the wet paper with your brush.
    You may flow another color in while the first color is
    still wet, but try not to scrub and overwork the

Figure 3.11 Mary Cassatt, *The Boating Party*, 1893/1894. Oil on canvas, 35⁷⁄₁₆ × 46⅛ in.
National Gallery of Art, Washington, Chester Dale Collection, Photograph © 2002 Board of Trustees, National Gallery of Art, Washington.
The artist carefully created a focal point in this painting by using the massive curving lines of the boat to sweep our eyes upward to the woman and the child she is holding. The triangular bit of sail on the left is tied to the boat by a rope that points to her sleeve. The oar in the man's hand also directs our eye to them. The dark, clearly defined shapes of the water and the man tend to contrast and frame the lighter shapes of the woman and child.

colors. To make a gradated wash from dark to light, add more water as you work down on the paper. While the paper is still wet, you can blot it with a sponge or a wad of paper towel for a special effect or sprinkle it with salt to create tiny, dark specks of color.

c) *Wet on dry*: The edges of objects done with the wet-on-dry technique will look clear and precise. Mix your washes in the lid of your watercolor box, and apply them to dry paper with a wet brush. Apply light colors first, and let them dry before adding darker layers on top. Do not scrub or brush back and forth, or the colors will become muddy and overworked. Iron your painting on the backside when it is dry for easy mounting or matting.

Showing Emphasis: A Wash-Away Painting

Students will use tempera and india ink to design a composition that places the subject matter either to the right or left of center, that uses pointers to direct the viewer's attention to the dominant object, or that uses contrast to make one object stand out from the rest. After a final application of ink is washed off, the overall effect is that of having created a focal point.

1. On watercolor paper, use a pencil to make a simple line drawing of your subject. Use a photo (or actual model

Figure 3.12 Student work: A watercolor landscape is created by applying washes over a contour pen drawing.

or object) as a visual resource. Simplify, distort, exaggerate, omit, enhance, combine. Try to make enclosed shapes.

2. Draw over your pencil lines with a black marking pen.

3. Mix tints and blends from a variety of different colors of tempera, and apply them to your composition. In mixing tints, be sure to add the color to the white paint, rather than adding white to the color. Just before you apply the paint to one of the shapes in the drawing, mix in a few drops of white glue. Try not to paint over the black pen lines. After a layer of paint dries, you can apply a second layer of color in some areas if you wish. Any areas of white paper left exposed will be black in your finished composition.

4. After the paint is thoroughly dry, brush india ink over the paper's entire surface. Let it dry thoroughly.

5. Place the paper on a cookie sheet or other flat surface, and hold it under running water. Rub gently to remove the black ink.

6. Let the paper dry. Press it with a warm iron on the backside before matting or mounting.

UNDERSTANDING ARTWORKS: Learning about Proportion

Proportion has to do with relationships—with the relationship of one part to the whole or of one part to another part. Have you ever used the phrase "out of proportion" or commented on the lines of a car as having "good proportions"? Proportion does not only have to do with size. Other elements, such as texture and color, may be used in pleasing proportions to achieve harmony, balance, variety, and unity.

Figure 3.13 **Stephanie Taylor,** *Generations*, **1994. Sacramento Regional Transit mural.**
Generations mural artist, Stephanie Taylor. Client Sacramento Regional Transit and PG & E.
Realistic and accurate proportions in these *trompe l'oeil* figures painted on an exterior wall "trick the eye" into
believing the figures are real.

In ancient Greece, when people were striving for the perfect body, the perfect mind, and perfect artworks, they began seeking an ideal for harmony and beauty that could be applied to their architecture and sculpture. They wanted a mathematical ratio of size comparisons that could be used to ensure the uniformly perfect results that they desired. In the sixth century B.C., Pythagoras found that he could apply mathematical equations to both geometric shapes and music. Then in the third century B.C., Euclid found that he could divide a line in two parts so that the smaller line is to the larger as the larger is to the sum of the two, a ratio of 1 to 1.6. When the ancient Greeks used this ratio, called the *Golden Section*, they felt they had found the perfect proportion for sculpture and architecture. Centuries later, Renaissance artists rediscovered this proportion and began consciously using it as the basis for their compositions. In the succeeding years, many artists continued to use the Golden Section, some consciously and other unconsciously, because it made things "look right." But, of course, the Golden Section's ratio is not the only arrangement of parts that presents us with harmonious relationships. Most artists do not believe in only one rule for "correct" positions.

An artwork shows realistic proportions when we see the same relationships of parts that we see in a person, a place, or a thing. One of the best ways to perceive realistic proportions is called *sighting*. This easily learned technique involves holding a pencil at arm's length with one eye closed while measuring the relative proportions of whatever it is we wish to draw. Try observing a chair from a distance of 10–12

Figure 3.14 **Elisabeth Vigée-Lebrun,** *Portrait of a Lady*, **1789. Oil on wood, 42⅛ × 32¾ in.**
National Gallery of Art, Washington, Samuel H. Kress Collection, Photograph © 2002 Board of Trustees, National Gallery of Art, Washington, DC.
This seventeenth-century artist used realistic proportions in both figure and face to show the subject to best advantage.

Figure 3.15 **Amedeo Modigliani,** *Head of a Woman,* **1910/11. Limestone, 25¾ × 7½ × 9¾ in.**
National Gallery of Art, Washington, Chester Dale Collection, Photograph © 2002 Board of Trustees, National Gallery of Art, Washington, DC.
Inspired by African masks and sculptures, this artist boldly distorted the shapes and proportions of this sculptured head.

Figure 3.16 **African face mask, nineteenth to twentieth century, Zairian. Wood and paint, ht. 17½ in.**
The Metropolitan Museum of Art, The Michael C. Rockefeller Memorial Collection of Primitive Art. Bequest of Nelson A. Rockefeller, 1979 (1979.206.83).
This example of tribal art, with its unrealistic and distorted placement of the features and decorative linear patterns, is an emphatic presence.

feet. Hold a pencil vertically as described, and use your thumb to measure the chair's overall height. Now measure the height of one of the chair legs in the same way. You can use these relative measurements when drawing the chair.

Artists do not always choose to use such realistic proportions, however (see Giacometti's sculpture in Figure 7.31). When they exaggerate, distort, or deviate from what we consider normal proportions, the effect can be powerfully expressive or quite decorative. Moods and feelings are more readily shown through elongated faces and bodies, and grace and movement through curving or spiraling forms.

Whether we choose to use realistic proportions or whether we want to achieve a special effect by exaggerating and distorting, we need to know the normal proportions of the human figure, since so much of the art in the world deals with depicting the human form and so much of what students do is related to the human figure.

The average adult is about 7½ heads high. Children,

especially infants, have larger heads in relationship to their bodies than adults. A child is 5–6 heads tall, and an infant is 3 heads long. By establishing the height of a figure's head, we have a unit of measurement for completing the rest of the figure.

Turn to the Color Gallery, and analyze how several artworks deal with proportion through one or more of the elements of art.

PRODUCING ARTWORKS EMPHASIZING PROPORTION

Proportions of the Figure: A 16-Piece Manikin

Students will cut an oval for a head and 15 rectangular pieces of paper that approximate the relationships of the different body parts. By arranging the pieces of paper, students

Figure 3.17 Student work: Crayon rubbings of a 16-piece figure. In this front view of the figure, the student adjusted the paper upon which the rubbing was being made several times to achieve a feeling of movement.

Figure 3.18 Student work: Crayon rubbing of a 16-piece figure. By cutting the torso in half vertically, the student made a profile view of the figure. Note the overlapping upper arms and upper legs.

will create a manikin for a figure in action and make a crayon rubbing.

1. From a piece of lightweight tagboard or a piece of manila folder that is approximately 6 by 8 inches in size, cut an oval about 1 inch to 1½ inches high, and place it near the top of a piece of lightweight white copy paper. This is the head. Then cut a strip that is twice as wide as the head. This is the torso. Cut the torso in two parts: The upper torso is about 1½ heads high, and the lower torso is about 1 head high. Place the two pieces beneath the oval shape of the head. Taper the sides of the upper torso from the shoulders to the waist. Taper the lower torso toward the waist also. Round the corners on all the pieces.

2. Now let your own arms drop to your side, and feel where your elbow touches your body. The upper arms are about the same length as the upper torso, that is, 1½ heads high and about ½ head wide. So cut another strip, quite a bit narrower than the strip you cut for the torso, and cut two pieces from it that are the same length as the upper torso. Place them on the shoulders. Cut two pieces for the lower arms that are the same length as the upper arms, and place them at the elbow joint. You can overlap these different pieces. Taper the rectangles from the top of the upper arm to the elbow, and from the elbow to the wrist.

3. The upper legs are also about 1½ heads high but are thicker than the upper arms—about 1 head wide—so cut another strip of paper to make the upper legs. The lower legs are thinner but are about the same length as the thighs. Taper these rectangles from the top of the thigh to the knee and from the knee to the ankle. A narrower strip will serve for the hands and feet. Try measuring your hand in relation to your head, and you will find that your hand is the same length as the face from chin to hairline. Your foot is 1 head long. Cut a small piece for the neck of your figure. Now you have a 16-piece figure that can move at the joints to perform almost any action.

4. To show a figure in a profile view, cut the two torso pieces in half vertically. Then place one upper arm and one upper leg under the torso pieces and one arm and one leg on top of the torso pieces in the position that will show the action you desire.

5. When you are satisfied with the proportions of your figure and with its action pose, use a tiny amount of glue stick to attach the 16 pieces to the white paper background. Large blobs of paste or glue will show through later on the crayon rubbing and be distracting. Then place the paper on a thick pad of newspapers, and place another piece of lightweight paper on top of it. White drawing paper is too heavy. Avoid making a crayon rubbing on the

Figure 3.19 Student work: After a crayon rubbing is completed, the student places white drawing paper over the rubbing and makes a pencil drawing of the figure, adding clothing and environment, and then completes the artwork with oil pastels, crayons, markers, or tempera paint.

hard surface of a tabletop. Use the side of a thick, black crayon, the paper having been removed by soaking the crayon in warm water, or use the edge of a black Chunk-O (available in art supply catalogs). Hold the crayon on its side, and make a number of short, firm strokes to bring out the sharply cut edges of the figure. Make the figure's silhouette stand out from the background.

6. Practice with several more pieces of paper until you are able to make a crisp rubbing with strong contrasts of dark and light. Try moving the paper over a bit and making a second and then a third rubbing on the same paper to give a feeling of motion. Combine your figure with those of several of your classmates on a larger sheet of paper. For such a group project, place a length of white butcher paper on a table, and have students bring their cut-paper figures to it to make rubbings.

7. To make a clothed and detailed figure, place a sheet of lightweight paper over your crayon rubbing, and hold them both on a window so you can see through the top paper. Draw your figure, and then add clothing, facial details, and environment. You can use crayons, felt pens, oil pastels, pencils, colored paper, and so on.

Proportions of the Face

Students will experience the realistic proportions of the face and then make a self-portrait using a variety of colors of cut paper.

As preparation, stand still in front of a mirror, and close one eye. Draw around the contour of your head on the mirror with a marking pen or crayon, starting at the top of the head. Then make a line across the center where you see your eyes in the mirror. Now step back. The eyeline is in the middle of your head. Step back to the mirror, and reposition your head in the oval shape that you drew. Mark the tip of your nose, and then make a line between your lips. This divides the bottom half of your face approximately into thirds: the tip of the nose takes up one third; from the tip of the nose to the center of the lips another third; and from the center of the lips to the tip of the chin the last third. To further experience the relationships between and the placement of the facial features, place your thumb on the bridge of your nose, and stretch your third finger up to the very top of your head. Hold your hand in this caliper-like position, and measure from the bridge of your nose to your chin. Once again, you will perceive that your eyes are halfway down from the top of your head. You might try measuring a photograph of a face in a magazine or in a realistic portrait by a great master.

Other facial proportions are also important. Use your fingers as calipers again, and measure the width of one eye, as well as the distance between your eyes. You will find both measurements to be about the same. Now place your finger directly below the center of one eye, and move the finger downward. You will find the corner of your mouth directly below the center of your eye. Now place a thumb and forefinger on the top and bottom of your nose, and then carefully move this finger measurement to one side of your head, and measure your ear. You will find that your ears are about the length of your nose and are level with it. Your neck is not as wide as your head, and it extends downward from your ears to your shoulders.

1. To make a cut-paper shape of the front view of a realistic portrait, fold a 9-by-12-inch piece of multicultural skin-colored paper in half, and draw a half-oval shape about 7 inches high on the folded side. Cut it out, unfold it, and then fold it in half horizontally. The larger end of the oval will be the top of the head and the lower, the chin. Cut a neck and shoulders separately, and place the head on the neck, either straight or tipped to one side. Place them both on a lightweight piece of white or colored paper. Now look in a mirror or at a friend's face, and cut out two pieces of paper in the shape of the eye. Be sure to observe how the lid covers a portion of the round circle of the iris. Keep looking in the mirror or at a friend's face, and cut out shapes for the eyebrows,

Figure 3.20 Student work: Self-portrait by a university student, in which she used a variety of colored papers, representing multicultural skin tones, as well as patterned papers while she concentrated on the realistic proportions for the face.
Photo by Barbara Herberholz.

nose, lips, and ears. Cut out some shapes or perhaps some fringed strips for hair. Remember that the tip of the nose and the line between the lips divide the lower half of the face into thirds. Let the cut shapes overlap, and attach them in place with a minimal amount of glue. (*Option*: Instead of using colored paper for your finished self-portrait, follow the same directions but use tagboard or manila folders instead of colored paper and make a crayon rubbing as described in making the 16-piece manikin.)

UNDERSTANDING ARTWORKS: Learning about Movement

Without **movement** there is no life. Each tiny organism is in motion. The heart pumps in a regular beat and keeps us alive. Thanks to stop-frame photography, we can see the rosebud open to a full blossom in a few seconds or the butterfly emerge from the cocoon. Our eyes are attracted to

Figure 3.22 **Rosa Bonheur,** *The Horse Fair*, **1853. Oil on canvas, 96¼ × 199½ in.**
Metropolitan Museum of Art, New York. Gift of Cornelius Vanderbilt, 1887 (87.25).
This enormous canvas is alive with the illusion of motion. The artist, who lived in the nineteenth century, was once called "the world's greatest animal painter." She was the first woman artist to receive the Cross of the Legion of Honor. Concerned with anatomical accuracy in her art, she visited slaughterhouses, attended cattle markets and horse fairs, and even dissected animal parts obtained from butcher shops.

Figure 3.21 **Marcel Duchamp,** *Nude Descending a Staircase,* **1912.**
Philadelphia Museum of Art: Louise and Walter Arensberg Collection. © 2002 Artists Rights Society (ARS), New York/ADAGP, Paris/Estate of Marcel Duchamp.
The cinema was in its infancy when Duchamp discarded completely the naturalistic appearance of a figure, keeping only the abstract shapes of some 20 different static positions in showing the successive action of descending stairs. This artwork was the hit of the Armory Show and was interpreted by thousands of Americans as the manifestation of futurism, an art movement emphasizing mechanical processes.

Figure 3.23 **Lisa Reinertson,** *MLK*, **1989. Bronze sculpture.**
Photo by Scott McCue.
Arrested movement has been caught in the forward stride and flowing garment of Martin Luther King, Jr.

moving things: The infant gazes attentively at the fluttering **mobile** suspended above her bed. We follow the antics of a playful kitten. The beauty of a vapor trail streaking across the sky in the wake of a speeding plane compels our eyes to follow its moving line. We watch with delight the ballet dancer's graceful and rhythmic movements.

Primitive cave painters made the first artworks. Their dynamic depictions show the running motion of deer, horses, and bison. Throughout the history of art, artists have endeavored to catch and simulate motion and to create the

Figure 3.24 **W. H. Brown, *Bareback Riders*, 1886. Oil on cardboard mounted on wood, 18½ × 24½ in.**
National Gallery of Art, Washington, Gift of Edgar William and Bernice Chrysler Garbisch, Photograph © 2002 Board of Trustees, National Gallery of Art, Washington.
This charming circus painting by an American naive or primitive artist portrays a rather stiff and static illusion of movement. How does it differ from Bonheur's *The Horse Fair*?

Figure 3.25 **Bridget Riley, *Current*, 1964. Synthetic polymer paint on composition board, 58⅜ × 58⅞ in.**
The Museum of Modern Art, New York. Phillip Johnson Fund. Photograph © 2001 The Museum of Modern Art, New York.
This British artist chose to explore the possibilities of optical movement inherent in curving lines. She thus created a new mode of perceiving and experiencing motion.

illusion of movement in their artworks. This has not always been easy. To draw the legs of a galloping horse realistically, you need to freeze or arrest the horse in one split second of its galloping movement because the motion is quicker than your eyes can follow. In 1878, which was some years before motion-picture cameras could show a whole sequence of multiple images and thus stop action in a single frame, California governor Leland Stanford made a $25,000 bet with a friend that a galloping horse sometimes has all four hoofs off the ground. He hired photographer Eadweard Muybridge to set up 12 still cameras, each one connected to a thread stretched across the racetrack. As the horse ran down the track, the threads clicked the camera shutters and enabled Stanford to win his bet. While the high-speed lenses of today's cameras can clearly show split-second arrested motion, photographers sometimes deliberately move the camera to make details indistinct and to enhance the feeling of great speed and energy. Perhaps you have seen other pieces of art whose streaking blurs conveyed a vibrant sense of the illusion of movement.

The **futurists** were a group of Italian artists led by Umberto Boccioni who, beginning in 1909, were obsessed with speed and the sensation of motion. Boccioni endeavored to show that living things go through constant change and growth. He liked to show everything happening at once. To do this, he created paintings and sculptures with circular forms that roll like waves, colliding and reacting with each other.

Other artists have investigated ways of making colors and shapes seem to move backward and forward. Victor Vasarely, known as the father of **op art**, was a leader in

painting optical illusions. He and other op artists took advantage of the way our eyes see things to make paintings that seem to move. After looking at one of Vasarely's paintings for a few minutes, you see colors and patterns that begin to bulge, buckle, swell, and retreat. Nothing is stable; everything moves; colors change. Bridget Riley creates movement by making her paintings undulate, push out, whirl, and push back. She achieves a sense of depth that moves up and down the painting's surface. She places dots, lines, or circles with a mathematical regularity that makes her paintings appear to dance and move. She takes advantage of the optical effect called the *afterimage*.

Some artists plan their artworks with more than the illusion of actual movement in mind. Their artworks actually move. Alexander Calder's mobiles were inventive and pioneering in their explorations of movement. The artists most concerned with actual movement in the two-dimensional area are probably involved in making films, video productions, and computer-generated images.

In addition to creating illusions of movement, artists use combinations of the different art elements to cause the viewer's eyes to move or sweep over a composition in a particular manner. Our eyes are directed to a focal point, or they sweep along an important visual channel that includes all areas of the picture plane and leaves no dead or void spots. To do this, the

Figure 3.26 **Henri Matisse, *Dance* (first version), 1909. Oil on canvas, 8 ft. 6½ in. × 12 ft. 9½ in.**
The Museum of Modern Art, New York. Gift of Nelson A. Rockefeller in honor of Alfred H. Barr, Jr. Photograph © 2001
The Museum of Modern Art, New York. © 2002 Succession H. Matisse, Paris/Artists Rights Society (ARS), New York.
Matisse simplified the human form, leaving out distracting details, to create an alternative, rhythmic motion of graceful,
curving figures and darker negative spaces for our eyes to follow.

artist exploits the direction of a line or utilizes the compelling force of a path made by repeated shapes or colors.

In van Gogh's *The Starry Night* (Colorplate 14), the triangular shape of the tall, dark cypress tree on the left echoes the tiny, centrally placed church spire, thereby stabilizing the spirally, rolling movement in the night sky. Let your eyes move along the curves, following van Gogh's definitive and characteristic brush strokes, starting on the left and moving in a dizzying roll to the horizon on the far right. Then follow the gentle diagonal movement of the hills downward to the left and back to the cypress tree and thence upward again to the starry sky.

Turn to the Color Gallery, and analyze how several artworks show movement through one or more of the elements of art.

PRODUCING ARTWORKS EMPHASIZING MOVEMENT

Varying a Cut-Paper Shape to Show Movement

Students will create a pleasing shape as the basis for an abstract cut-paper composition and vary its size, placement, and color to show movement.

1. For practice in cutting shapes, use a scissors and a 6-by-9-inch piece of paper. Place the paper deep into the V-shape of the scissor blades, and turn the paper, not the scissors, as you cut. First, make straight, angular cuts, entering the piece of paper at one side and making continuous short and long cuts until you have explored and exited the paper at its opposite side. Then take another piece of paper and make only curving cuts, entering and exiting the paper in the same manner.

2. Now practice cutting out geometric shapes of various kinds. Cut freely; do not draw the shapes first. Next, make some free-form shapes. Then make a shape that is a free-form/geometric combination. Keep your shapes fairly simple.

3. Select the shape that you like best. Using three different colors of paper, make several more of the shape you chose, varying either the shape's color or its size. Make some of the shapes small, some medium, and some large.

4. Place the shapes on a 9-by-12-inch piece of black or colored paper. Let some of the shapes overlap. Group some of them closely together to show movement. Try to place a series of small shapes so that they move your eye around the composition. When you are satisfied that your arrangement creates a feeling of movement, paste the shapes down on the background paper.

Stamped Figures Showing Movement

Students will make a figure in motion, determining action lines for different parts of the body with different lengths of strips of thick cardboard pressed on a stamp pad made with tempera.

1. Select several newspaper photographs that show figures in action: athletes, dancers, and so on. Look for the directional lines that the arms and legs make. Look at classmates in action poses; manipulate a wooden manikin into an action pose.

2. Observe the gesture and position of the legs and arms. Are the elbows and knees bent? Notice the slant or direction the body takes as it moves. Notice if the waist is bent, the head tipping to the side. Observe the angle of the feet and hands. Look at the relationships of the body's parts. Are the arms stretched up above the head? Are the hips and chest straight up and down or slanted?

3. To make the figure's head, cut out one or two small oval shapes, about an inch or two high from colored paper. Place one of them on a piece of white or colored paper, 12 by 18 inches.

4. Pour some black tempera paint down the center of several thicknesses of damp paper towels that are placed on a paper plate. If you are using black or a dark color of construction paper, you may wish to use white paint instead of black.

5. Press the edge of a strip of thick cardboard on the pad and make a print of it to begin forming the figure. You will need several different lengths of cardboard strips for different parts of the body: upper and lower torso, upper and lower legs, upper and lower arms, hands and feet. You may bend a piece of cardboard before printing it to make a bent leg or arm.

6. Keep pressing the edge of the cardboard into the paint to keep it well coated with tempera. Make many lines, repeated and close together to form each of the body parts: torso, legs, and arms. Overlap lines to make your figure have a feeling of action. Add feet and hands with very short length of cardboard.

7. Add another oval head, and print another figure in action. Part of it may extend off the paper.

UNDERSTANDING ARTWORKS: Learning about Rhythm, Repetition, and Pattern

Repetition in the world of nature and in artworks forms rhythms and patterns. From our early years, we respond to rhythm as well as create it. Small children clap their hands

Figure 3.27 **Henri Rousseau, *The Equatorial Jungle*, 1909. Oil on canvas, 55¼ × 51 in.**
National Gallery of Art, Washington, Chester Dale Collection, Photograph © 2002 Board of Trustees, National Gallery of Art, Washington.
The primitive or unschooled artist usually has an innate and intuitive sense of the decorative beauty of repeated patterns. Notice the variety of leaf motifs that overlap and intrigue the viewer in this almost dreamlike jungle scene. Note how repeated fine lines in the foreground simulate the texture of fine grasses.

to the beat of music and quickly learn the words of singsong rhymes. Who can resist the toe-tapping rhythm of a polka or the strong beat of a marching band! Our lives are governed and surrounded by tempos, beats, and rhythms of all kinds—the rising and setting sun, our heartbeats, and flashing neon lights. We see visual rhythms in the natural world as well as in artworks—on pineapples and cacti, on turtles, fish scales, and seashells. **Rhythm** is a regular or harmonious pattern that repetition of lines, shapes, and colors creates. Rhythm can create an exciting visual beat for our eyes to follow. Just as in music, rhythm and repetition in art can be smooth and flowing, or they can be sharp and staccato. It depends on the effect the artist is trying to create.

Artists use pattern that results from visual repetition of lines, colors, and shapes in many ways. In certain artworks, the repetition of a unit called a *motif* creates a decorative effect that often results in wallpaper, tile floor, fabric, and other patterns. The motif can be a line or shape, or a combination of lines and shapes. Note how the American artist Jacob Lawrence used pattern in his painting *Vaudeville* (Colorplate 35). Pattern can visually enhance both two- and three-dimensional artworks, as well as provide visual interest and focus. Sometimes, painters use a patterned area to

Figure 3.28 **Pedro Ramirez Arrazola,** *Painted Dog,* **1987.**
Collection of the authors.
This folk artist's innate love for, and understanding of, decorative pattern
is evident in this hand-carved and delicately painted wood dog from Oaxaca, Mexico.

Figure 3.29 **Grant Wood,** *Stone City, Iowa,* **1930.**
*Joselyn Art Museum, Omaha, Nebraska. © Estate of Grant Wood/VAGA,
New York, NY.*
The artist, remembering that "cornfields in spring look like black com-
forters tied in green yarn," painted the sprouting stalks in a graded or progressive pattern that leads our eyes deep into the spatial depth of this
landscape. Look for other motifs that the artist repeated. He developed
and relied on keen observational skills, researching old maps, atlases,
Currier and Ives prints, family photos, and line drawings in Sears catalogs.

simulate texture or to reveal the form of an object or figure.
Notice how the pattern of stripes on the woman's robe
shows the contours of her body in the warm and unified artwork *The Bath* by the American artist Mary Cassatt (Colorplate 36).

Pattern can also be a vital part of an object's actual
physical structure in that the material and its structure create
the pattern. Woven tapestries, baskets, and the brickwork of
a building are all examples of pattern integrating decorative
elements within a structural function.

Repetition and pattern can be simple or complex. The
simple repetition of a regular motif or element creates a regular pattern that is often used to embellish the surface of an
object. In this kind of pattern, the repeated motifs, as well as
the spaces between them, remain the same. In regular
allover patterns, the even distribution of the motif usually
follows one of several basic invisible grids or networks.
Some of these networks are based on a square, a checkerboard, bricks, or a staggered grid; others may follow a half-
drop or diamond arrangement. Sometimes, these networks
are visible and are an important element of the finished pattern (checks, stripes, lattice, and so on). Spaces between the
network lines usually interlock or connect endlessly in any
direction. This sort of allover repetition is called a *tessellation.* The Dutch artist M. C. Escher (Figure 3.34) visited the
Alhambra in Spain early in his career and became fascinated with walls and floors that were covered with repeated tile
motifs. He subsequently used the tessellation concept in
designing numerous artworks that create illusions with their
intriguing, flowing patterns.

We can achieve variety and complexity within a pattern
by changing the colors, positions, shapes, and directions or
by changing the intervals or spaces. This irregular or alter-
nating pattern is usually more interesting than a regular one,
since two or more motifs may be used instead of just one.

Artists know that the visual excitement of the unexpected
adds suspense and surprise to an artwork. Still another kind
of repeated pattern shows an orderly, step-by-step progression or gradation of the motif, perhaps in size or in color
intensity. For example, the same motif may be steadily
repeated but gradually become smaller, lighter in color, or
closer together.

However, not all visual rhythms that we see and make
in our artworks are created by a regular arrangement of the
motif and its intervals. A random pattern has no obvious
order, either of the motif or the intervening spaces. We see
random patterns in wildflowers on hillsides, cloud puffs in
the sky, and horses grazing in a pasture. Notice in the French
artist Henri Matisse's painting (Figure 3.31) the use of pattern. Scarcely any area on the surface of this large painting
does not show the repetition of shapes and colors. Matisse,
leader of Les Fauves (wild beasts), so-named because of
their use of vivid unrealistic colors, is reported to have said
that "Fauvism is not everything, but it is the beginning of
everything."

A *flowing pattern* consists of lines and shapes that are
repeated in waving or curving arrangements. Our eyes tend
to rhythmically glide along a flowing pattern as the direction
it takes makes smooth and gradual changes, or perhaps
abrupt and forceful ones. Leonardo da Vinci was fascinated
with the patterns that waves and moving water make and
sketched his observations of them carefully. If we look at the
curly ringlets that frame the face of *Ginevra dé Benci* (Colorplate 31), we see how da Vinci made a visual connection

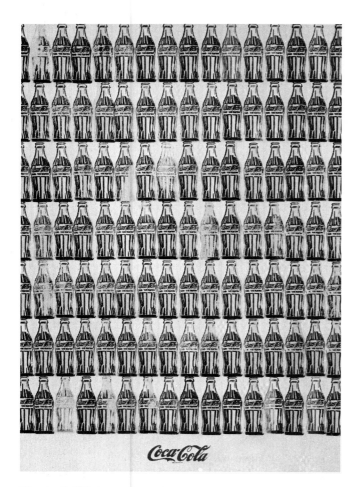

Figure 3.30 **Andy Warhol, *Green Coca-Cola Bottles*, 1962.**
Collection of Whitney Museum of American Art, New York. Purchased with funds from the Friends of the Whitney Museum of American Art (Acq. #68.25). Photograph © 2002 Whitney Museum of American Art © 2002 Andy Warhol Foundation for the Visual Arts/Artists Rights Society (ARS), New York.
Monotonous, regular repetition of a single motif purposely makes a statement about consumerism and contemporary life in this artwork classified as pop art.

between moving currents of water and the repeated pattern he used to simulate the texture of his subject's hair.

Both two- and three-dimensional artworks use the decorative principles of rhythm, repetition, and pattern. Patchwork quilts, baskets, pottery and sculpture, jewelry, masks, and many other pieces of traditional tribal and ethnic arts are often richly embellished with surface patterns. A great variety of pattern in seen in the cubist portrait by Picasso (Colorplate 33), yet the work is unified by the relationships of the cuts made with the linocutting tool. Architects plan for a variety of pattern when they design a building. How will they arrange multiple units of windows and doors? How will brick and tile patterns interact and relate with other structural surfaces? Landscape architects plan different groupings of trees, walkways, ground cover, and rocks to create har-

Figure 3.31 **Henri Matisse, *Harmony in Red*, 1908–09. Oil on canvas, 5 ft. 11 in. × 8 ft. 1 in.**
State Hermitage Museum, St. Petersburg, Russia. Giraudon/Art Resource, New York © 2002 Succession H. Matisse, Paris/Artists Rights Society (ARS), New York.
Matisse was especially intrigued with repetition and pattern, having been inspired by the designs he had seen in Persian carpets.

monious patterns of shapes, textures, and colors. City planners strive for unity, order, and balance in their arrangements of houses and streets in irregular and regular patterns.

Turn to the Color Gallery, and analyze how artworks show repetition, rhythm, and pattern through one or more of the elements of art.

PRODUCING ARTWORKS EMPHASIZING RHYTHM, REPETITION, AND PATTERN

Designing a Cityscape with Varied Patterns

Students will use direct observation of tall city buildings (Figure 3.32) and photographs of such buildings to create an imaginary cityscape. The overlapping, flat, frontal arrangement of tall buildings is drawn with a permanent black marking pen on white paper, embellished with a variety of different repeated patterns, and then painted with watercolor washes.

1. Notice the different shapes of tall and short city buildings. Observe their rooflines. Notice how closer buildings overlap those behind them. Look for repeated shapes in windows, balconies, doors, and fire escapes, as well as different patterns that bricks, tiles, and shingles make.

2. Use a black marking pen, a ruler, and assorted templates (jar lids, small blocks of wood, tongue depressors, plastic templates from art supply stores, and so on), and draw on white paper. Or you may choose to draw your cityscape freehand. Draw a large rectangle to serve as the front of the building nearest the viewer. Then draw other buildings behind and beside it, varying the rooflines. Fill most of the paper with your cityscape. Then cover the surface of each building with a different repeated pattern of windows, bricks, and so on.

3. Mix watercolor washes, and add color to your cityscape. Wet washes on wet paper are recommended for the blurry effect of skies; wet washes on dry paper create sharp edges of buildings. Let some of the white paper show to add sparkle and freshness. If you used a water-soluble black marking pen, the black lines will run when water touches them. This can add to the effect you wish to create. Permanent marking pens are unaffected by watercolor washes. (Crayons, chalk, oil pastels, or colored markers can be used to add color to your cityscape design instead of watercolors.)

Allover Patterns:
Carving a Rubber Stamp

Students will carve a design in an eraser (Figure 3.33), ink it on an office stamp pad, and print it as a repeated allover pattern. As alternatives: Safety-cut, found in art supply catalogs, is available in sheets that can be cut in small squares and used instead of erasers. Design-a-Stamp, also in art supply catalogs, may be cut with a scissors and adhered to a small block of wood in a design of the student's choice.

1. Use a small white or pink eraser that you purchase in an office, school, or art supply store. These come in square and rectangular shapes. Draw around the eraser on tracing paper, and fit a design into the shape. Try a simple geometric design, or find a design idea in books that show leaf and flower motifs, Japanese family crests, heraldic symbols, southwestern Native American pottery, Celtic art, snowflakes, the Bayeux tapestry, or Mexican or Egyptian designs. You may wish to base your design on your astrological symbol, a business logo, or your initials. Words and numbers must be carved in reverse.

2. Think in terms of raised (black) and cutout (white) areas. Go over the lines of your design with a soft lead pencil. Turn the paper over, and attach it to the eraser with tape. Go over the lines with a sharp pencil to transfer your design to the eraser. The design should be in reverse on the eraser. Hold it up to a mirror to see how the printed image will appear.

3. Now go over the fuzzy pencil lines on the eraser with a black-tipped pen. Use denatured alcohol on a tissue to

Figure 3.32 **City buildings.**
Direct observation of city buildings or collecting photographs of city skylines provides stimulus for making artwork that emphasizes repeated patterns.
Photo by Barbara Herberholz.

rub off the pencil smudges. This makes the carving much easier, since the black lines of the pen will remain. Use V- or U-shaped linocutters to carve your design.

4. Make a test print by pressing the eraser onto a well-inked office stamp pad and then pressing it onto paper. Add stamp-pad ink, if necessary. If you are not satisfied, you may wish to carve away more areas.

5. Create an allover pattern by printing your rubber stamp design on a large piece of paper many times. Avoid construction paper as its rather rough surface makes it more difficult to obtain a clear print. You may choose to make a regular pattern first and then experiment with a brick grid, checkerboard grid, and so forth, on additional paper. Use your stamped paper for bookbinding or for wrapping paper. Try other variations with your stamp, and create borders, notepaper, greeting cards, posters, labels, and so on.

Pattern by Repetition:
From Above, Looking Down

Taking a bird's eye point of view, students will design a landscape composition that shows what is seen from above, looking down, dividing the paper into areas that are then painted with repeated patterns. See American artist Wayne Thiebaud's *Highland River* (Colorplate 27).

1. Imagine yourself floating in a hot air balloon and looking down. You might see and include some of the following in your composition: fields with crops in rows; orchards; fence posts; cars on highways; cars in a parking lot; boats on a river; bridges; ships in a harbor; horses, cows, and lambs in fields; scarecrows; windmills;

Figure 3.33 Student work: The eraser print of the angel motif is repeated in a bricklike grid.
Donald Herberholz.

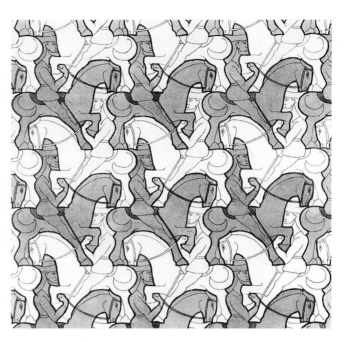

Figure 3.34 **M. C. Escher, *Symmetry Drawing E 67 (Study of Regular Division of the Plane with Horsemen)*, 1946. India ink and watercolor.**
© 2002 Cordon Art, Baarn-Holland. All rights reserved.
Interlocking dark and light horses and riders go in opposite directions, with no negative spaces remaining.

telephone poles; a family of crocodiles or turtles; the wharf and beach; and so on. Lightly sketch the main spaces and shapes with chalk.

2. Pour small amounts of tempera on a paper plate. Use another plate to mix your colors. Paint the large areas first, and let the paint dry. Then add details and patterns in the different areas, using contrasting colors and a small brush or a Q-tip. Try to include a variety of regular patterns, irregular patterns, and gradated patterns. For accents use a gold or silver marking pen.

Creating a Pattern Using Tessellations

Students will combine mathematics and art to create a template from a 3-inch square from which they will make an interlocking tessellated pattern on a larger piece of paper. A tessellation is an endlessly repeated pattern of interlocking shapes, the word being derived from the Latin word meaning tile. Tessellations have been used for more than 6,000 years by mathematicians and designers and are often seen as mosaic tiles on floors and ceilings of mosques and palaces.

1. Use a 3-inch square cut from a 3-by-5-inch index card. Using the side of the card with lines on it, draw a simple curving or jagged line that starts and stops on the top side of the square. Then draw another such line that starts and stops on the left side of the square. Then cut out the two pieces. Slide the piece you cut from the left side to the right side, matching up the blue lines on the index card and letting the cutout shape extend beyond the border of the square. Tape it in place. Do the same thing with the top piece, sliding it to the bottom, letting the cutout shape extend beyond the border of the square, and taping it in place. This is your template.

2. Use a pencil and draw around the template in the top left corner of a piece of 12-by-18-inch white paper. Move it over so it interlocks and draw it again. Keep doing this until the paper is entirely covered. Use colored pencils, markers, or paint to complete the tessellation. You may wish to add eyes, feet, tails, and so on to suggest faces, birds, turtles, animals, airplanes, or other objects.

3. An optional way to complete a tessellation is to cut out an equal number of your designs from two different pieces of colored paper. Then paste them down in an interlocking checkerboard fashion on a 12-by-18-inch piece of paper.

UNDERSTANDING ARTWORKS: Learning about Variety and Unity

Would you like to live in a room in which the walls, floor, furniture, and window coverings were all covered with red polka dots of the same size? Would you like to eat the same food for every meal, seven days a week, month after month? Would you enjoy hearing the same music played over and over again without interruption or any change to another selection? Our eyes, taste buds, and ears like variety and

Figure 3.35 **Ruth Rippon, *The Lollies*, 1978. Pavillions, Sacramento, CA.**
Photo by Barbara Herberholz. Courtesy of Ruth Rippon.
These two ceramic women pause to chat while shopping. Variety in the position of the feet and hands, the tip of the heads, and dress color and pattern is evident. Unity is achieved through similar forms, related textures, and like colors.

seek it out. For example, we may choose a solid blue carpet, a floral-patterned sofa, and tan-colored walls. We consider the different textures in the same room, striving for a harmonious blending of woods and fibers. In planning our meals, we select from a variety of vegetables and fruits, and we like to try new foods and restaurants to relieve sameness and monotony. As any good cook knows, different sauces on the same vegetables can entice and intrigue the taste buds.

Variety is the art principle that is concerned with differences. The old saying "Variety is the spice of life" also applies to art, since differences and contrasting elements enliven artworks. Sameness throughout a composition bores us, and our attention wanders elsewhere. The row of house and store fronts in American artist Romare Bearden's collage (Figure 3.36) represents the street life of Harlem. The flatness and shallow space of the composition is unified by the repetition of windows, but variety is seen in their shapes, sizes, colors, and placement. A cluster of people gather outside a funeral parlor, and our glimpses into several of the windows show a variety of figures that are harmoniously unified by the angels above the mourners.

Artists know that even if the same shape is repeated in a composition, variety can be achieved by using different

sizes of shapes or by varying the shapes' colors, surface textures, or patterns. Thick, bold lines provide striking contrast with spidery, brittle lines. Within the confines of one color, variety can consist of tints in one area, shades in another, and dulled tones in yet another. Different kinds of textures draw our attention to various areas of emphasis.

In artworks, excess variety tends to create a feel of haphazardness and even chaos, while a lack of variety invites boredom. Somewhere between these two extremes is a harmonious balance that contributes to a feeling of unity. In *Girl before a Mirror* (Colorplate 33), Picasso achieved unity and harmony through controlled and limited variety. He used a limited selection of bright colors and explored differences through changes in the sizes and placements of circular shapes. A variety of patterned areas is tightly balanced against flat, plain spaces.

Unity is the result of knowing that nothing should be changed, added, taken away, or moved to a different location when we look at a completed artwork—our own or that of a great artist. Unity is the art principle that makes all the separate elements of an artwork look as if they belong together. The elements blend harmoniously. The different parts and art elements are arranged so that they each contribute to the

Figure 3.36 Romare Bearden, *The Block*, detail, 1971. Collage; cut and pasted papers on Masonite; entire work in six panels, each 49 × 36 in.
The Metropolitan Museum of Art, New York; gift of Mr. and Mrs. Samuel Shire, 1978. © Romare Bearden Foundation/VAGA, New York.

overall effect. Nothing seems to distract our eyes or to bother us as not being quite "right." We can concentrate on the entire artwork because no one part demands our attention. The different elements help and complement each other. Nothing interrupts our conversation with the artwork. The various parts are in harmony and in accord with each other. The colors match the feeling; the shapes interact with the mood. We are led around and through the composition by any one of several devices—colors, lines, or shapes—that connect various elements. For centuries, the triangle has been an underlying structure that relates and unifies the figures or other elements in an artwork.

Several techniques contribute to a feeling of unity in an artwork:

1. We can place different shapes and objects close together, clustering and overlapping them and surrounding them with an area of negative space, while at the same time minimizing the spaces between the shapes. Contrast the appearance of a large pile of rocks with the same number of rocks scattered randomly over a large area.

2. Limiting the variety of colors, shapes, lines, or patterns within an artwork also contributes to unity. Too many different elements can lead to a feeling of chaos. Notice how Vincent van Gogh achieved unity in *The Starry Night* (Colorplate 14) through consistent and overall sameness of brush strokes. The limiting factor of using only two colors—blue and yellow—also tends to create a feeling of completeness and wholeness, and thus, unity. Now look at *The Bath* by Mary Cassatt (Colorplate 36). The artist has achieved a feeling of unity in several ways. First, the overall effect of light and limited colors matches the happy and relaxed mood. The colors have been repeated in a number of places. The pattern of stripes on the mother's robe lends unity, while variety is seen in the direction of the lines. The mother gazes downward, as does the child. Notice how the repeated circular shapes (heads, abdomen of child, washbowl) add to the consistent unity.

Turn to the Color Gallery, and analyze several artworks to see how the artists achieved variety and unity through one or more of the elements of art.

Figure 3.37 **Narcisco Abeyta (Ha-So-De) Navajo,** *Running Horses*, **1948.**
Collection of the authors.
Horses show unity through their overlapping, clustered arrangement and variety through their different positions and colors. Delicately painted plants provide fine details that harmonize with the grace and movement of the horses.

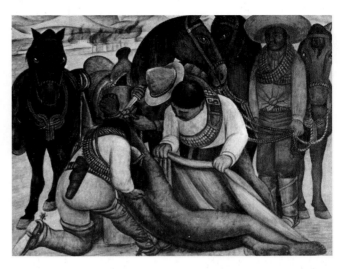

Figure 3.38 **Diego Rivera,** *The Liberation of the Peon*, **1923.**
The Philadelphia Museum of Art. Given by Mr. and Mrs. Herbert Cameron Morris. © 2002 Banco de México, Diego Rivera & Frida Kahlo Museums Trust Av., Cinco de Mayo No. 2, Col. Centro, Del. Cuahtemoc 06059, Mexico, D.F.
Closely grouped horses and figures give a feeling of unity in this artwork that was created to evoke solidarity and cooperation in the fight for agricultural and land reform in Mexico. Rounded, full forms relate to one another to add to the unified effect.

PRODUCING ARTWORKS EMPHASIZING VARIETY AND UNITY

Stitchery: Limiting Variety to Achieve Unity

Students will make a variety of stitches (Figure 3.40) with different colors and textures of yarn to create a unified artwork on burlap or other loosely woven fabric.

1. Use a 12-by-15-inch piece of plain or colored burlap, or any loosely woven fabric, through which a large-eyed plastic needle easily pulls yarn. Place masking tape around the edges of the fabric to prevent it from raveling.

2. Select a theme, such as fireworks; earth strata; a spider's web; a volcano; things that grow, above and below; jungle flowers; and so on. Sketch your idea on paper before you begin working on your fabric. Then sketch the main parts of your design on the fabric with a piece of chalk.

3. Choose appropriate colors and textures of yarns to match your theme. Limit the variety to a maximum of five. This will help give your stitchery unity.

4. Limit your stitches to an inventive use of the following: running stitch, cross-stitch, blanket stitch, couching, fly stitch, backstitch, chain stitch, satin stitch, and French knots. You can achieve variety by changing the length, size, direction, color, and placement of the stitches. Repeating them will add to the unity of your artwork. Let stitches overlap.

5. Place the stitches so that one area is emphasized, thereby creating a center of interest or focus for your composition background.

Weaving with Paper Strips

Students will weave a two-dimensional design, using a variety of widths, colors, and textures of paper strips, to create a unified artwork.

1. Collect a variety of papers—colored, foil, shiny, velour—as well as patterned wrapping paper, ribbons, brown paper bags, sandpaper, magazine pages, wallpaper, and so on.

2. Cut 9- and 12-inch strips of varying widths.

3. Spread a half-inch strip of paste along one of the 9-inch sides of a 9-by-12-inch piece of construction paper. Then attach the 12-inch strips (called the *warps*) to the pasted area, side by side, so they can be lifted up as you weave the 9-inch strips across. Select a limited but pleasing variety of widths, textures, and colors of paper strips.

4. Begin weaving over and under the warp strips with the 9-inch strips. These are called *wefts*. Push the weft strips up to the top of the warp strips. You can weave in a random or regular pattern, but try to create a composition that shows unity.

5. Fill the warps from top to bottom. Then paste the warp and weft ends to the construction paper background.

Figure 3.39 **Louise Moillon,** *Still Life with Cherries,*
Strawberries, and Gooseberries, **1630.**
The Norton Simon Foundation, Pasadena, CA.
This fresh and delectable still life shows a variety of different plump and
rounded shapes. Against a dark background, the patterned bowls and basket contain a pleasing variety of textures, color gradations and blends, and
sizes. The tiny sprig of gooseberries and droplets of water in the lower
center give contrast. Cherry stems and contours of leaves create an interesting linear note, and the horizontal edge of the table accents the rounded
shapes of the containers.

Chalk Dipped in White Tempera

Students will dip the tip of colored chalk repeatedly in thick,
white tempera and make short marks on black paper to create a design that shows both variety and unity. Photographs
of flowers, butterflies, or birds may be used for visual information.

1. Use colored chalk that is designated for use on paper,
   not chalkboards. Break pieces in half.

2. Practice first on a small piece of black construction
   paper by dipping the tip of a piece of chalk in white
   tempera and making a variety of short marks—curving,
   straight, zigzag, circular, dots, and so on. Work to make
   a mark that shows the bright color of the chalk edged
   with the white tempera.

3. Decide on your subject matter. Dip the tip of the chalk
   repeatedly in the white tempera, and make marks on a
   sheet of black construction paper until your composition is finished. Marks may overlap. The marks you
   make and the black background give your artwork a
   unified effect.

Running stitch and variations

Chain stitch and variations

Satin stitch

Cross-stitch and variations

Blanket stitch and variations

French knot

Couching variations

Fly stitch and variations

Backstitch

Figure 3.40 Basic stitches commonly used with yarn and loosely woven fabric.

INTERACTIVE EXTENSIONS

1. Select from the Color Gallery an example that clearly illustrates an aspect of each of the principles of art, and defend the reasons for your choices.

2. Save all your examples from your portfolio of "Producing Artworks" that relate to the principles of art, and show them to a student who is not in your class. See if that student can name the art principle you focused on in making each artwork.

3. Make a small poster about the principle of balance. Collect photographs from magazines, travel folders, calendars, and such that demonstrate formal and informal, approximate, and radial balance as seen in nature and in artworks. Add labels and captions, and use the poster to teach your future elementary students about the principle of balance.

4. Make individual small posters in the same manner as in number 3 about the other principles of art. Collect photographs of both natural objects and artworks that focus on aspects of each principle of art. Then use these mimi-bulletin boards to teach your future elementary students about the principles of art.

4

CHAPTER

Art Criticism, Art History, and Aesthetics:
Strategies for Understanding Artworks

Chapter Outline

Figure 4.1 Kindergarteners look at and discuss several works that depict the Old West. Here a parent volunteer docent shows the class reproductions of works by four artists that show scenes of life in those days. *Photo by Heidi Grasty*

If an artwork has ever bewildered, frustrated, or excited you, learning to perceive and think in the manner of art critics, art historians, aestheticians, and artists can help. Different questioning strategies challenge us to think about art and to clarify what we believe, what we value, and why.

An *art critic* is a professional who explains, interprets, and evaluates artworks by writing or speaking about them. An *art historian* searches for information about artworks and about artists of the past and may also write or speak about them. An *aesthetician* is a philosopher who ponders the meaning and nature of art. An *artist*, of course, creates art, whether a painting, drawing, print, sculpture, building, piece of jewelry, or film.

We can investigate and practice ways of describing, analyzing, interpreting, and judging artworks[1] that will help us evaluate their importance and artistic merit, ways that go beyond taking a quick look, and stating our personal preference ("I like it," "I don't like it"), and moving on to the next painting in a gallery or museum

When we talk about artworks, we clarify our thoughts. We make a conscious effort to receive the communication sent by the artist. We strive to be in touch with the artist's life. We come to know something of the artist's personality, the culture and time period in which the artwork was created, and for what purpose it was created. Through further explorations in art history, we learn what other artists or artworks may have influenced the artist we are studying or how

our artist may have influenced others. We take a second and then a third look at what we see in front of us and then examine what we feel inside. Seeing, investigating, and then transforming into words may be a complex and difficult process, but it is ultimately rewarding.

Just looking at artworks is often not enough. When we search for words to describe and analyze them, we progress from looking passively to seeing with greater discrimination and precision. We move from being casual, naive viewers to achieving a greater sophistication in our perceptions of and responses to artworks. We share and compare our perceptions and enthusiasms, argue our points, and formulate our judgments because when we talk about art, we better understand what we are seeing.

Strategies that help us to understand and appreciate an artwork, rather than to merely state a personal preference, intermingle two important components: art criticism and art history. When we look at an artwork and think like an art critic, we have the visual information right in front of us. We can describe what we see, analyze it, and react to it. Our personal and unique background and our experiences and attitudes may influence our interpretation. When we look at an artwork and think like an art historian, we learn about the artwork from external sources. We are on a fact-finding mission to collect available evidence, including opinions of critics and historians. To increase our knowledge in this manner, we examine books and other source materials, listen to lectures, and perhaps question a docent in a museum. Art history helps us understand what people were thinking, valuing, believing, and doing at a given period of time; it also offers insights as to why an artist painted in a particular manner and what meaning the art had or has.

Responding to artworks requires a simultaneous blend of both the art criticism and art history components. Some artworks are only understood from the fact-finding of an art history search, but all artworks can be understood, enjoyed, and cherished on a higher level when we harmonize both strategies. Therefore, art history and art criticism strategies are not sharply distinct; in fact, most conversations with an artwork are blends of both. Art criticism and art history enrich and clarify each other and help us perceive and understand what we see when we look closely at artworks.

DESCRIBING THE ARTWORK

Art Criticism

We describe what we actually see before us. We state what art form we see, whether it is two- or three-dimensional, and whether the artwork is a painting, a drawing, a sculpture, and so on. We decide if it has a vertical or horizontal format or even a round shape (called a *tondo*). We state if it is a landscape, a portrait, an abstract work, a sculpture, a mask, and so on. We state what medium was used (oil paint, watercolor, marble, metal, wood, and so on). We identify the elements of art. We observe and comment on the technical properties; that is, we may describe the manner in which paint was applied (thick, swirling brush strokes or thin washes of color) or the repeated, overlapping marks left by the chisel on a wood surface. We make an inventory of the subject matter, noting the literal details of what we see. We note the pose of the figure, the angle of the head, the facial expression, and perhaps, the viewpoint of the artist.

Art History

We describe the results of our fact-finding mission, stating the actual size of the original artwork if we are studying a reproduction of a smaller size. We relate where the artwork is located now and where it was originally meant to be housed—perhaps in a cathedral, a castle, or in the home of a wealthy seventeenth-century Dutch merchant. We tell the name of the artwork and the time and place in which it was created. We give the name of the artist and his or her birth and death dates. We check to make sure we correctly pronounce the artist's name. We consider biographical information that is pertinent to the artwork's creation. We may tell why the artwork was made—whether it is based on some historical event, was created to inspire religious thought or to record how someone looked, or is the product of the artist's imagination.

We might need to offer sociological considerations to help us reap deeper understandings and ascertain what the artwork tells us about the culture and time in which it was produced. The subject matter of Diego Rivera's frescoes in the Detroit Institute of Arts (Colorplate 26) was the automotive industry in the 1930s; the work combined Rivera's love of industrial design with his philosophical views about the industry's positive and negative contributions to society. Biographical research makes us aware of Picasso's early years in Paris, when his poverty marked his works: His haunting "blue period" from these years often depicts sad images of lonely, outcast people.

References to *iconography* (image writing) and *iconology* (image study) that we find in source materials identify specific images in artworks with symbolic content and meaning. For instance, in Christian art, a saint may be depicted by an object (attribute) that helps the viewer identify the saint. The evangelist John the Baptist is identified with a cross made from reeds, while a winged ox symbolizes Luke, the patron saint of painters. It helps to know that artists used a lighted candle to symbolize the shortness of life and ivy to symbolize eternal life, and that in Christian art, a dandelion stands for grief. To understand the complexities of a culture other than our own, we need to study the different symbols used and their meanings. Iconology helps us learn through literary and philosophical material the cultural attitudes and changes that give meaning and content to the artwork.

Consider the following questions when describing the artwork:

What is the subject matter, if any, and what is happening?

How large is the original, and where is it now?

Who was the artist, and when was the artwork created? What is the name of the artwork?

What is the medium?

What is at the top, bottom, and sides of the artwork?

If figures/portraits are seen, how much is shown, and what is the stance? Is the view three-quarter, profile, or frontal? What is the facial expression?

What is in the foreground, middleground, background?

How did the artist show the time of day or weather in the landscape?

Where is the horizon?

Do we see diagonal lines and shapes that suggest movement?

Does the artwork show deep space?

Are the contours strong and definite?

Are the edges of the object shown with an outline, or are they separated by color, texture, or value differences?

How do the lines differ? Are they the same or different widths?

How does the tool relate to the surface of the paper (or canvas or wood or plaster)? (A pencil drawing on smooth paper is different from a pencil drawing on coarse, rough paper. Bits of rough paper show through when crayons or oil pastels are rubbed over it.)

Does the color imitate natural color?

What is the light source? What is its direction?

How are the figures depicted in relation to the landscape: dwarfed by it, infused with it?

Three-dimensional artworks (sculpture/crafts/architecture): Does the artwork have a utilitarian function?

What is the effect of surface quality (highly polished wood grain, chisel marks, etc.)?

ANALYZING THE ARTWORK

Art Criticism

Art analysis involves separating the whole artwork into its parts. In analyzing a work, we note how the elements of art were used in ordering and controlling the principles of art. In a formal analysis of an artwork, we look at the elements and principles of art that have given the painting, sculpture, or piece of architecture its form as well as its content, meaning, and expression. (In this context, the term *formal* is not the opposite of *informal* or *casual*.) Formal analysis goes beyond description by seeking to show how the composition works—how it is formed.

The elements and principles of art have many possible relationships. An orderly system of looking at these relationships can help us determine how an artwork is put together. We can select any element, connect it with a principle, and then ask ourselves how this element is used. For instance, we may ask, are the colors in the painting balanced formally or informally? Has the artist used different thicknesses and kinds of lines to add variety to the artwork? How are the shapes distributed to create a feeling of movement? How does the simulation of texture create emphasis? How did the artist create a focal point or center of interest?

Art History

We compare and contrast the artwork with other works by the same artist or by other artists to determine its style and to discover what is unique and especially important about the work. Comparing and contrasting two or three artworks is an effective technique that helps us identify similarities and differences in ways that artists have used the elements and principles of art. By looking back and forth to find resemblances, differences, or things the two works have in common, we discover items we may have missed in a cursory glance at only one artwork.

Consider the following questions when analyzing the artwork:

How is unity achieved?

How did the artist vary the colors (shape, line, texture)?

Is there an illusion of movement?

Are the proportions realistic, or are they exaggerated for expressive purposes?

What is the emphasis or focal point of the composition? (The arrangements of the parts are sometimes easy to see; at other times, a closer look is warranted.)

How did the artist use dark and light contrast?

Do you know of another artist who used balance in the same way this artist did?

Do any circular, spiraling, or triangular elements lead our eyes through the composition?

Do the lines denote movement and energy?

Could your eyes "take a walk" into the distance seen in the artwork, or is the space shallow and flat?

Why do you think the artist used these colors?

Does the effect of light make strong contrasts, with some parts brightly lit while other areas are in darkness?

Is the artwork unified by gradations and a balance of light and dark?

What do repetition and pattern contribute to the artwork?

How do the positive and negative spaces relate?

INTERPRETING THE ARTWORK

Art Criticism

We respond to the artwork emotionally and try to understand the how and why we feel as we do. We interpret with more than our eyes. Our memories, emotions, and values are brought into play as we endeavor to give coherence to our perceptions. We ponder and reflect on what is in the work that evokes our feelings and sets the mood of the work—perhaps its colors, shapes, textures, or proportions. Perhaps the subject matter itself or the technical properties of the medium arouse our feelings. We look for evidence within the work of art that supports our opinions.

Just as two artists look at the same tree and render it in two entirely different manners, we can each look carefully and respond with different feelings to the content of the same artwork. We may be amused, soothed, uplifted, or repelled. We may sometimes ask ourselves questions we cannot answer. In endeavoring to interpret and understand an artwork, art critics, aestheticians, and art historians frequently find problems that they, at least for the moment, are unable to solve. Remember that we are enlarging and extending not only our knowledge about artworks but our feelings as well. We may respond by feeling that the mood of the artwork is poetic or playful, joyous or sad. It may make us feel annoyed or hostile. It may remind us of a happy or frightening experience from long ago. It may be a narrative painting that causes us to wonder and imagine beyond the actual subject matter that we see. We may feel uplifted by a religious artwork or inspired by a patriotic one. An artwork that focuses on propaganda may sway our opinions. We may enjoy an artwork for the gesture and movement of its realistic subject matter, or we may delight in its exquisite colors, lines, and shapes alone. We may find that an artwork touches the world of fantasy and dreams and makes us wonder and ask questions that are hard to answer.

Some questions dealing with aesthetics that help us interpret artworks are: Why do I feel as I do about this artwork? Why do I find the seascape (or portrait or abstraction) fascinating (or boring)? How did the artist use the medium and technique, and arrange the elements and principles of art to evoke this response in me?

Art History

We respond to the artwork by knowing how the artist's time and place and such significant events as a war or oppression were influential. We respond more fully if we know the artist's reason for creating the artwork—whether to inspire religious fervor, to record the demeanor of royalty, or to explore new ways of seeing. The artwork may reach us more eloquently if we know significant factors in the artist's life and personality. In viewing some artworks, our study of art history will greatly help our understanding of what we see and are interpreting. For instance, many artists have depicted biblical events by painting the central characters dressed in clothing and in the environment of the artist's time. In the seventeenth century, Rembrandt sought to show the human ministry of the Christian religion in this manner, and identifying the images in these artworks in their symbolic context is important. It is helpful to remember that in reading art history, we sometimes find conflicting statements about the importance or interpretation of a particular painting or school of art.

If we recognize and interpret symbols—that is, pictorial elements that stand for something—we are less likely to misinterpret what we see. Art history books can do much to enlighten us in this respect, because although the symbols had common meanings in the time and culture in which they originally appeared, those meanings may be lost to us today. Even gestures in paintings may have specific meanings, and if we know them, the artwork is richer for us. Hands open and raised to shoulder level in early Christian art represents a prayerful attitude. Playing cards may symbolize idleness. A finger placed before the mouth in Persian art means surprise. Color also often has symbolic meanings that vary

from culture to culture. Red in China stands for happiness; in ancient Egypt, it stood for evil. Renaissance depictions of Mary's robe are always blue, but in India, blue is the color of the Hindu god Krishna.

Consider the following questions when interpreting the artwork.

Is the person's personality, character, or mood revealed?

Why do you think the artist placed the horizon up high (or down low)?

If we see symmetrical or approximate balance, does this give a quiet, rigid, or monumental effect?

If we see asymmetrical balance, what makes us feel that visual balance was achieved?

If the lines and shapes are mostly vertical, what feeling does this give us?

If the lines and shapes are mostly horizontal, does this make us feel peaceful and quiet?

Is the use of deep space exaggerated and expressive?

Does the light seem natural, or theatrical and dramatic?

Does the light focus on certain symbolic areas?

Is the environment frightening, inviting, or depressing?

Does color have a symbolic meaning, realistic, or decorative effect?

Does the artwork reflect an aristocratic lifestyle or a simple, domestic one?

Are symbols used? If so, what do they symbolize?

What in the artist's personal life may have influenced the artwork? What events at the time the artwork was created may have had an impact on the artist's feelings and ideas?

JUDGING THE ARTWORK

Art Criticism

We may sometimes wonder if we are making a "correct" or "good" decision or judgment or if a critic was "on target" in an evaluation of an artwork. We may be helped by first deciding if the artist intended to create an artwork that was in one or more of the four styles of art as explained on page 89. It would be counterproductive, for instance, to judge an abstract work by its lack of realism. How can we decide if an artwork has artistic merit? Do all the parts, details, and materials harmonize with the idea behind it? Is the composition planned, and does it possess unity? Was the artwork created with skill? Do we consider expression and creativity? Is it a matter of personal taste? Does the work mean anything to you? If you like it, is it good art? If someone else hates it, does that change your opinion? Can you defend your judgment? Our responses to art are subjective and vary in intensity. You may

Figure 4.2 **Winslow Homer, *Breezing Up (A Fair Wind)*, 1876. Oil on canvas, 24⅛ × 38⅛ in.**
National Gallery of Art, Washington, Gift of the W. L. and Mary T. Mellon Foundation, Photograph © 2002 Board of Trustees, National Gallery of Art, Washington, DC.
Homer excelled in showing realistic seascapes in which people faced the forces of nature.

feel strongly positive or negative about an artwork that makes no impression one way or the other on another person.

When we say, "I don't know anything about art, but I know what I like, and I don't like that," we are most likely saying that what we are seeing is unfamiliar to us or that we do not understand what we are seeing. Hitler collected and displayed artworks that he described as "degenerate" from a number of artists of his day. Today, we look on these expressive artists as leaders in new ways to paint. What can we do to prepare ourselves to find meaning in an artwork that heretofore we have dismissed or condemned?

Art History

We thoughtfully evaluate the factors related to the artwork's importance and its place in the history of art, arriving at objective conclusions. Asking and answering questions about an artwork is a strategy that involves more than expressing our random feelings about it and stating our personal preferences—preferences that are often based on subject matter or on how realistic an artwork is. We comment on the artwork's influence on other artists, the artist's recognition or lack of recognition during his or her lifetime, or perhaps on what artworks were forerunners of the piece we are viewing. Do we consider tradition? We consider the artist's style, technical innovations, compositional originali-

ty, use of new subject matter, or variations of meanings for previously depicted subjects. We may need to research the artwork's context, history, and symbols and the artist's idea in creating the work.

Consider the following questions when judging the artwork.

Would you recognize this person in real life?

Is the landscape recognizable as a specific place?

For what purpose was the artwork made?

Is the artwork more realistic or more abstract?

Is the artwork mostly concerned with dreams and imagination?

Was the artist primarily interested in expressing a strong emotion?

Was the artist mostly concerned with formal aspects of arranging lines, shapes, and colors? Does this arrangement possess unity?

In which style of art would you categorize the artwork? What is the artwork's artistic merit within this style of art?

How did this artwork influence other artists?

How did the artist's environment and events of the time affect the work?

Figure 4.3 **John Marin,** *Phippsburg, Maine,* **1932. Watercolor, 19⅞ × 15¼ in.**
The Metropolitan Museum of Art, New York. Alfred Stieglitz Collection, 1949. (49.70.145) © 2002 Estate of John Marin/Artists Rights Society (ARS), New York.
Slashes and splashes of paint in dark and light tones make for an abstract landscape in Marin's lively watercolor.

What aspects of the artist's life and personality may have had an impact on the work?

How do the medium and technique contribute to, or distract from, the overall effect?

If this artist had lived another 100 years, how do you think his or her style might have changed? Do you think the artist will be remembered and highly regarded a century from now? Why or why not?

How do you think the painting would make you feel if the artist had used all warm colors instead of cool colors?

What does the artist's degree of skill in handling the medium contribute to the artistic merit of the work?

Does the artwork seem to have an idea, feeling, or concept within it that is indicative of the artist or culture that produced it?

FOUR STYLES OF ART AND THEIR INHERENT AESTHETIC QUALITIES

In using art criticism and art history strategies to understand paintings and sculptures, we need to determine what style of art is emphasized. Being familiar with the four styles of art and their inherent aesthetic qualities can help us evaluate a work's artistic merit. The aesthetic qualities of each of these styles provides a basis for judging a work: a representational work of art may be judged not only on its well-done realism but also on the excellent formal arrangement of its shapes, lines, and colors. It may also possess a strong feeling of loneliness, religious inspiration, and so forth.

How can we decide if an artwork is successful and has artistic merit? Personal preference alone is not an objective standard, of course, but are any standards objective? If there are objective standards, how can we use them as guidelines for evaluating an artwork? Art changes over the years and differs from culture to culture. For example, if we use beauty as a measure, we may find that others disagree on just what beauty is and that the definition of beauty changes from culture to culture and from century to century. If we judge an artwork on its success or value in conveying an important message, we need to remember that some artistic ideas have no message as such. For example, Islamic art used abstract designs to enrich and embellish functional objects. If we use the criterion of originality alone, we are valuing artists whose highly creative ideas inspired artists who followed. However, we need to consider that some

Figure 4.4 **Frank Stella, *Takhi-i-Sulayman 1*, 1967. Polymer and fluorescent polymer paint on canvas, 10 × 10 in.**
The Menil Collection, Houston, TX. Photo by Hickey-Robertson, Houston.
© 2002 Frank Stella/Artists Rights Society (ARS), New York.
Stella's interest in abstract or formal qualities is seen in this balanced nonobjective artwork, which uses a variety of brilliant colors but only one shape: a segment of a circle.

Figure 4.5 **Paul Gauguin, *Self-Portrait*, ca. 1890. Oil on canvas, 18³⁄₁₆ × 15 in.**
Photograph © 1985 The Detroit Institute of Arts. Gift of Robert H. Tannahill.
Moody, thoughtful, and piercing, Gauguin's eyes and pose give us clues to his turbulent life, during which he created many expressionist artworks both in France and the South Seas.

cultures have traditions with well-established rules that do not cherish originality. If we judge an artwork on its realism, we have a problem in that different cultures see imitation in different ways. Furthermore, an artist may have had a very different idea to convey than representing nature as he or she perceived it.

The four styles of art and their inherent aesthetic qualities are summarized as follows.

1. ***Representational or realism***: In these artworks, the emphasis is on the realistic presentation of the subject matter. The people, objects, or landscape look very real and may be considered an imitation of nature. See Colorplates 25 and 31, by Bierstadt and da Vinci, respectively. Can you identify any other artworks that fall mostly in this category?

2. ***Abstraction***: In these artworks, the emphasis is on the organization of the elements and principles of art. The artist is more interested in lines, shapes, and colors (the formal design) than in objects, people, or landscapes. See Colorplates 30 and 35, by Kandinsky and Lawrence, respectively. Can you identify any other artworks that fall mostly in this category?

3. ***Expressionism or emotionalism***: In these artworks, the emphasis is on the intense feeling, mood, or idea related to the visual image rather than on the realistic depiction of people, objects, or landscapes. See Colorplates 14 and 41, by van Gogh and Montoya, respectively. Can you identify any other artworks that fall mostly in this category?

4. ***Surrealism or fantasy***: In these artworks, the emphasis is on the imagination and the world of the subconscious. The artist often depicts objects in a realistic manner but makes unusual connections and relationships. See Colorplates 19 and 37, by Dali and Chagall, respectively. Can you find any other artworks that fall mostly in this category?

In considering an artwork in relation to the above listed styles, we may look at and reflect on the artist's principal intent. Was he or she trying to show us exactly what the person or place looked like (representationalism/realism)? Was the artist more interested in the abstract elements of lines, shapes, and colors than in showing us exactly what the scene or person looked like (abstraction)? We may decide that the artist was extremely successful and innovative in handling the elements and principles of art. Was the artist more involved in expressing an emotion or feeling (expressionism/emotionalism)? Sometimes, we are in awe of the emotional impact or mood of an artwork; the artwork's message might uplift and inspire us. Was the artist dedicated to showing us an imaginary dreamworld, a world of fantasy and of the subconscious (fantasy/surrealism)?

Many artworks do not clearly fall into only one category; they may be weighted in one direction and have overlap-

Figure 4.6 **René Magritte, *La lunette d'approche*, 1963. Oil on canvas, 69⁵⁄₁₆ × 45¼ in.**
The Menil Collection, Houston. (Hickey and Robertson, photographer).
© 2002 C. Herscovici, Brussels/Artists Rights Society/(ARS), New York.
Magritte used highly realistic images in a dreamlike manner to create sur-realistic artworks.

Figure 4.7 **Hans Hofmann, *Exuberance*, 1955. Oil on canvas, 50 × 40 in.**
Albright-Knox Art Gallery, Buffalo, NY. Gift of Seymour H. Knox, 1969.
© Estate of Hans Hofmann/VAGA, New York.
Hofmann was an abstract expressionist who combined colors, shapes, and lines in strong, bold compositions.

ping emphases. We can then look at an artwork and use the inherent qualities as a basis for judgment. For example, Grant Wood's *American Gothic* (Colorplate 21) shows us a realistic-looking man and woman standing in front of a farmhouse. Each detail is noted and painted precisely. In addition, Wood planned his composition carefully, echoing several different shapes and lines, drawing our eyes to a focal point, and creating a pleasing arrangement of the shapes and colors. His use of the formal qualities has resulted in a unified and harmonious composition. Another area to consider in Wood's famous work is the expression or emotion felt. We cannot help but gaze directly back at the farmer and read his character; then we glance at the woman's face and notice that her eyes are looking in a different direction, and we wonder what she is thinking. Thus, a strong emotion is included here. We see no fantasy or dreamworld, so we cannot judge the painting on that basis. We would give it a high evaluation in the first three qualities but would place it in realism as a work of art.

Let's use these styles or inherent qualities of art to evaluate Kandinsky's *Painting No. 198* (Colorplate 30). We are unable to evaluate this painting on its realistic qualities, since it is highly abstract, to the point of being nonobjective. However, if we contemplate the painting's expressive qualities, we

find much to respond to. And its formal qualities are reflected in the rhythm, harmony, and balance that Kandinsky achieved in his arrangement of colors, lines, and shapes. Kandinsky used two terms often associated with music to title his paintings: *improvisations* and *compositions*, the latter being more carefully planned and structured than the former.

In deciding on the artistic merit of Dali's painting (Colorplate 19), we would undoubtedly state that it looks very realistic, but we may do a double take and see things that couldn't actually be happening, placing it in the realm of surrealism. The feeling and interpretation of this artwork are many faceted. As far as formal qualities, it is well balanced; the colors and shapes are unified, and he was able to show deep space as well as details in the foreground.

You may want to compare the inherent qualities of one artwork with those of another with a similar theme or that was made in another time or culture. Your friends may not always agree with your judgments and choices. However, remember that you are evaluating the artwork on many points that go beyond stating your personal preference. Try making your judgment based on the inherent qualities in each of the four styles of art.

PUTTING IT ALL TOGETHER: Description, Analysis, Interpretation, Judgment

A Student's Sample Response: *Starry Night* by Vincent van Gogh

Below is an example of how a university student responded to Vincent van Gogh's *The Starry Night* (Colorplate 14)

This oil painting was made by Vincent van Gogh in 1889, one year before he died. The size of the original is 29 by 36¼ inches. It hangs in the Museum of Modern Art in New York. It is a nighttime landscape that is done in the thick, swirling brush strokes that are characteristic of the artist. We see the sky taking up most of the picture space, a sky that is filled with the circular, rolling, spiraling lines and shapes that represent the stars and moon. In the foreground, we see a sleeping village with the tall, dark, triangular shape of a cypress tree reaching upward on the left. Blue and yellow are the dominant colors. Since daytime scenes are far more prevalent as subjects for landscapes, we find a certain fascination in seeing a landscape at night.

Born in Holland in 1853, Vincent, as he signed his artworks and liked to be called, was a sensitive, lonely man whose behavior often alienated people. He always wanted to help people but failed at being a minister, a missionary, and at working for art dealers. Only the last 10 years of his life were devoted to art. During that time, he sold only one painting, and that was for 80 dollars. He worked at painting with a fierce intensity, all the while conveying his thoughts and feelings in correspondence with his brother Theo, who supported him financially and emotionally.

Perhaps we see Vincent's longing for a family and a home life in the peaceful village in the middleground, with its church spire pointing upward and catching our attention. We observe his feverish brush strokes in this painting and can see how he may have even squeezed the paint directly on the canvas, rather than placing it on his palette first. This created thick layers of paint that add an actual texture to the artwork. We can almost visualize Vincent working on this painting as he stood in the field at night, candles blazing on his palette and around the brim of his hat to help him see. The round, circular shapes of the stars are repeated a number of times in the dark blue sky in a random pattern with the sizes varied. Our eyes follow the movement of the rolling circles and spirals in the skies. The dark cypress in the foreground tends to stabilize the turbulence. The lightest part of the picture is the haloed crescent moon on the right. It is balanced by the deep green cypress tree on the left, a shape that reminds us of a flame writhing upward as if it were trying to reach the heavens. The gently rolling hills in the background behind the village seem restful and quiet, and tend to lead our eyes to the cypress. We see a great variety of dark and light tones of both blue and yellow used throughout the picture. These were two of Vincent's favorite colors; he believed that yellow stood for love, warmth and friendship. The limited number of colors gives unity to the painting, as do the uniform, thick, swirling brush strokes.

We feel peaceful when we look at the sleeping village with its lights glowing in the windows, even though the busy skies are alive with the restless energy of the stars. We feel uplifted, perhaps even somewhat protected, when our eyes are carried rhythmically upward by the dark form of the tree. We remember summer evenings and looking up at the clear skies and seeing stars that were especially bright. Although Vincent has painted the stars larger and more vibrant than we are accustomed to seeing them without the benefit of telescopes, he has conveyed his deep feelings. He once stated he wanted people to understand that he felt deeply and tenderly. This expressive work of art succeeds in touching our emotions and making us see night skies with perhaps a greater clarity than we would have without Vincent's special vision.

AESTHETICS

Recently, the visual arts curriculum in U.S. schools has been broadening to include more than the traditional art production base. Art educators feel that aesthetic considerations provide a firmer and more all-inclusive base for the student engaging in making art and also that the contemplative thought that relates to aesthetics leads to a fuller and more complete understanding of artworks.

Just what is **aesthetics**? The word *aesthetics* is a derivation of the Greek word *aisthetikos*, which has to do with sensory perceptions. Indeed, when we place "an" in front of it, we have the word *anesthetic*, which refers to putting the senses to sleep. Therefore, we shall begin with the premise that aesthetics must have something to do with awakening and vitalizing the senses in one way or another.

The concept of *taste* is often used in connection in aesthetic discussions, taste having to do with both a person's own perceptual skills as well as his or her life experiences.

Aesthetics is one of the four major areas in philosophy, the other being epistemology (the study of how we come to know things), ontology (the study of the nature of reality), and ethics (the study of moral good). In its broadest sense, aesthetics has to do with the philosophical study of beauty and art and all that it involves. It has to do not only with artworks such as paintings and craft objects but also with ideas and things often associated with art. When we deal with aesthetics we describe, discuss, and criticize aesthetic experiences.

More is involved in the study of aesthetics than a discussion of beauty. The rather complex concepts such as perfection, the nature of truth, and the search for meaning among our everyday experiences are involved. Our thoughts and discussions on these concepts form the base for the major part of current aesthetic theory; and these concepts have given inspiration to a great deal of art in the last 100 or so years.

We find diverse and even contradictory interpretations as to how *beautiful* can actually be defined, even among writers of the same cultural period. The classical Greek sculptor Polykleitos thought that a set of mathematical rules could be used as a guide for making ideal figures of the Greek gods with perfect proportions. His canon of proportions had to do with various relationships of the various body parts. Most classical Greek figures are about 8 and ½ heads high, called *heroic proportions*. Plato, the classical Greek, did not include artists in his definition of what an ideal state should be and had a disdain for art, stating that only through reason and logic can truth come to be known. He argued that art was a mere appearance and provided and blocked us from the truth since artists merely make copies of ideal form.

Aristotle, Plato's pupil, did not feel that art must always be beautiful, stating that imitation was the essential concept in art, caricature being useful for the purpose of moral instruction. Idealized portraits could uplift the spirit, while realism served to provide realistic historical documents.

During the Middle Ages, Christians approached art in the spirit of Plato, avoiding sensuous figures (those that might provide a case for idolatry) and instead illustrating inspirational Bible stories. During this time, many artists renounced drawing from live models as being an evil activity and copied images from old illuminated manuscripts.

By definition, then, aesthetics is a branch of philosophy that deals with the nature of art and beauty and, as such, is concerned with questions and thoughtful reflections about the meaning and purpose of artistic processes and products, concepts that help us better understand what we see and encounter. When we think, converse, and form questions on aesthetic concerns, we try to evaluate, define, and clarify different cognitive and emotional responses to artworks. Such aesthetic questions cause us to take a fresh look at some of our long-held opinions and ask us to withhold judgments until we have done some critical thinking and some careful studying to learn all we can about what we see. The deeper we delve into the issue of aesthetics, the more we find that the questions we ask, or that others ask us, cannot be answered with a simple yes or no. Often, we find that understanding aesthetics involves being able to accept answers that are neither right nor wrong and to tolerate several points of view. And we often wind up with one question leading us to yet another question.

What is art? What is an artist? How is an art object different from another object? Have you ever consulted a dictionary for a definition of art? Did the dictionary give you a clear understanding of what art is and one with which you could agree? Perhaps not. First, if we can agree that an art object is an object that human beings make and that originates in someone's mind and imagination, we have a working base, a starting point. However "beautiful" a sunset or an autumn tree may be, they are natural phenomena, not works of art. We use "art" words to describe the colors, lines, and shapes that we see in nature, and in so doing, we find parallels between art and nature. So, what is a work of art, and how is it different from other things? How does a painting of sunflowers by van Gogh differ from the actual sunflowers? The difference is that van Gogh was inspired by the visual information before him and interpreted it in his own unique way to make the painting.

Art, then, is a visible expression of perceptions, feelings, ideas, and values. It is based on human perceptions, and we recognize and understand it through our senses. A wide range of objects can be considered works of art, but all will have distinctive or valued qualities and meanings that individuals or particular cultures accept and preserve. Works of art can make us think about ideas, people, places, events, and spiritual matters, and they can make us feel and understand things in the world more deeply than we would otherwise. Some cultures have no word for art since everything the people in those cultures make, wear, and use—even the dwellings in which they live—is an artifact with significant symbolic content, skillful workmanship, and artistic style.

This, then, brings us to the word *beauty*, which usually comes up in any discussion of the word art. Can you define beauty? Perhaps we can generally agree that beauty stimulates pleasurable visual and tactile responses in the visual arts. But standards for beauty change through the centuries and from country to country, and the concept of beauty varies from individual to individual, validating the old cliché of beauty "being in the eye of the beholder." This is the position that the relativist or pluralist takes. For example, when we see Picasso's *Guernica* (Figure 7.27), with its angular, hard-edged shapes, its crisp tones of black and white, its wrenching, agonizing, twisted forms that symbolize dying people and wounded horses, we feel strongly the message that the artist wished to convey: the horror of the Nazi bombing of a small Spanish town. We probably do not describe this painting as "beautiful" in the usual sense of the word, yet it is a highly revered work of "art." The relativist point of view might note that the military personnel who instigated and implemented the bombing mission might have called the artwork "beautiful" in that their dreadful, deadly goal was accomplished.

The relativist or pluralist position, then, holds that there are multiple artistic traditions, all involving different and distinct aesthetic systems, as well as a great variety of artistic productions.[2] Therefore, it behooves teachers to be aware of the multiple artistic traditions and aesthetic values of world cultures to assist students in finding meaning and artistic merit in the many art products produced in this global diversity.

Objectivists, on the other hand, beginning with the classical Greeks and Renaissance scholars, use criteria regarding beauty, including harmony, balance, and such, and they state that actual beauty is within the artwork itself.

Ellen Dissanayake takes the ethological, or bioevolutionary, approach in relating art to human nature. This ethological view argues that art contributes something essential to the person who makes art or to the person who views it—not simply in that art brings "pleasure" but that it benefits the person's biological fitness. Dissanayake looks at art from the 4-million-year perspective of human biosocial evolution and believes that the aesthetic experience cannot be properly understood apart from the psychobiology of sense, feeling, and cognition. She feels that it is wrong to think that "being cultural exempts us from biological imperatives.... We use cultures—the elements of our cultures, like tools and language and the arts—to get what we need, biologically, as well as what we are taught to think we need." She feels that "art" has been falsely set apart from life in today's modern and postmodern societies and that this emphasis on efficiency and acquisition has forced us to devalue or ignore the aesthetic part of our nature. She feels that the arts as we know them define the universal human practice of "making special" certain objects, sounds, movements, occasions, and places. Her view is that modern society—predominantly urban, industrial, and literate—is so disengaged from nature that we have lost sight of the biosocial purposes of making art. She states that "social systems that disdain or discount beauty, form, mystery, meaning, value, and quality—whether in art or in life—are depriving their members of human requirements as fundamental as those for food, warmth, and shelter."[3]

A statement from the National Art Education Association (NAEA) in 1991 regarding the preservation of freedom of expression in the arts declared that individuals have the right to accept or reject any work of art for themselves personally, but they do not have the right to suppress works of art to which they may object or those artists with whom they do not agree.[4] The NAEA further declared that it is the duty of the art educator to provide students with a diversity of art experiences and to enable students to think critically. It endorsed the concept of allowing the students

to choose from widely conflicting images, opinions, and ideologies. While some works of art may indeed be banal and trivial, and some works may be repugnant and unacceptable to some individuals, the art educator should insist upon the right of every individual to

freely express and create in his or her own way and to experience, accept, or reject any particular work of art.

Aesthetic Points to Ponder

1. Is all art beautiful? Can art be ugly? Find an artwork in a magazine or book that you could describe as beautiful. Then find another artwork that you would describe as not beautiful. Then try to interpret each artist's message or each painting's meaning. Which artwork was more successful?

2. Must all art contain a message or have a meaningful concept behind it? Can art be an object that exists for its own sake? Can art have practical and functional uses?

3. If you like an object, is it art? If you do not like it, could it still be considered art? What part does popularity play in art?

4. How would a person who lived during the Italian Renaissance define art differently than a twentieth-century artist or a member of a tribe in Africa or Australia?

5. What is the most important art form? Art theme? Art subject? Are landscapes or still lifes as important as portraits or religious works?

6. Should art only please the artists and the culturally elite, or should it touch a wider viewing audience? Should artists be able to explain verbally the meanings of their works?

7. Is art the same thing as freedom? Is all art creative? Is anything that is creative art? Can an artist work in today's society with no restraints? Is creativity the same as doing whatever you want? Is all self-expression art?

8. What is an aesthetic experience? Does our culture value the aesthetic experience? Why or why not? What parts of our being are involved in an aesthetic experience: emotional, sensory, intellectual, social, creative, kinesthetic?

9. If a person claims to be an artist, is that person an artist? Is anything that that person creates art? How do great artists and mediocre artists differ? Can a child be an artist?

10. If an object is in an art museum, does that make the object a work of art? How do museum curators and directors decide what objects to display?

11. Should very old artworks that have deteriorated with time be restored or left as they are?

12. When you view an artwork for the first time, can you have an aesthetic experience without knowing anything about the work's history, or about the culture or artist from which the artwork sprang? Would learning more about the artwork increase your aesthetic experience?

13. Should art that is on public display be censored? If your answer is yes, what criteria should be used, and who

should make these decisions? If your answer is no, what reasons can you give for your viewpoint? Should public funds be used to buy artworks for public buildings? Why or why not? Who should make these decisions? (Many cities require that all public and corporate buildings spend a percentage of the total cost on murals, sculptures, and so on for indoors and outdoors.)

14. Do artists have any obligations to society? Does society have any obligations to artists?

15. Will an artwork that was considered beautiful several hundred years ago still be considered beautiful today?

16. Is knowing what the artist intended to create necessary for us to relate to the artwork, or can we connect with a piece of art by what we see before us?

17. People have paid millions of dollars to buy works by Monet, van Gogh, and Picasso. Who decides how much an artwork is worth? Does a higher amount of money paid for a painting make it a better artwork than one that brought in less money?

18. Is a forgery of an artwork a work of art? Suppose you visited a museum and felt that you had a legitimate aesthetic experience when you looked at a particular painting. Later, you learned that the painting was a copy of the original, placed there while the original was on loan. Was your aesthetic experience any less because you were looking at a copy?

19. Recently, a zoo in a large city gave paper, paint, and brushes to an elephant that obligingly swung its trunk, making marks on the paper. The zoo framed and sold the products that the elephant had made as art. What do you think about this?

ART MUSEUMS AND ART IN PUBLIC PLACES

Museums house many of the world's great artworks, even those that were created long before museums were built. Many artworks from the distant past were commissioned and created to serve purposes other than hanging in a museum. For instance, in the Western world, religious pieces were made for a largely illiterate populace to teach them Bible stories and to inspire them. These works were displayed in places of worship. Royalty hired court painters to record their likenesses, and these works hung in palaces. Today, museums have special exhibits that bring together groups of major artworks from many different museums and private collections. Such exhibits may feature the lifetime accomplishments of a single artist or focus on a number of artworks created during the same time period.

Frequent visits to museums can be a lifetime source of enjoyment. Most of us live reasonably close to a major museum, and many people travel in America and abroad, where wonderful museums await. Entering a museum for the first time, especially a large one, may seem bewildering, so check the maps and guides available at the front desk. These printed materials will help you know what kinds of works to expect and in which rooms they can be found. During some museum visits, you may want to gain an overview of what is there, taking a look at the major galleries and rooms and gathering impressions of the collections. You probably will not be able to take more than a quick glance at each artwork on such a visit, but when you see one that you find especially appealing, linger and enjoy the experience. You will probably finish your visit remembering several magnificent artworks and planning on returning for another look. Find what appeals to you and build on it, but keep your eyes open, and find something you are attracted to that you never liked before. Go at your own pace. Occasionally, relax for a while on a seat in a gallery, or find the gallery cafe for a snack. After several hours, you will probably leave with a satisfying feeling of exhaustion and saturation.

Another way to plan your visit to a museum is to focus on a specific gallery or collection. Most museums do not arrange their permanent collection of artworks in chronological order but instead group them geographically or by schools of art. Thus, you will find in separate sections artworks from Egypt, Greece, or perhaps the Renaissance. In addition to permanent collections, most museums have a gallery or two for changing exhibits; the museum calendar or program will tell you "what's on" at the time you are there. Popular blockbuster shows may require purchasing tickets in advance.

On a more leisurely museum visit, you can use the following approaches in responding to an artwork that particularly appeals to you:

1. Stand before a painting or sculpture, and study its use of the art elements and principles; then close your eyes and see if you can reconstruct it. If your visual memory is faulty, open your eyes and reexamine the parts more carefully. This technique helps you learn to look more carefully at the artwork, really seeing and remembering it.

2. Hold a viewfinder (page 45) before an artwork that particularly strikes your attention. Frame a significant detail, and focus on that part. Try to find a painting-within-a-painting in this manner, using your viewfinder to locate within the painting's boundaries an area that particularly appeals to you and has a center of interest and an arrangement with comfortable informal balance. Then make a small sketch of what you see through the viewfinder. You will be taking home your personalized selection of an artwork.

3. Sketch the entire artwork. You may need to obtain permission in some museums to do this. Many artists and art students have trained themselves by drawing from

artworks. A student working at an easel, copying from a masterpiece in a museum, is a frequent sight. Even if you do not feel that you are copying it skillfully, your pen or pencil acts as a magnifying glass, focusing your attention on things that you probably would not see otherwise.

4. Select three works of a similar theme but from three diverse cultures. For instance, choose three figurative works in a museum or reproduced in books, or select three such works from the Color Gallery, such as

Vaudeville by Jacob Lawrence (African-American male) (Colorplate 35)

Green Violinist by Marc Chagall (Russian Jewish male) (Colorplate 37)

Women and Dog by Marisol (Venezuelan female, living in USA/Europe) (Colorplate 20)

Flower Dance Spirit by Frank La Pena (Native-American male) (Colorplate 28)

The Bath by Mary Cassatt (American female) (Colorplate 36)

Girl before a Mirror by Pablo Picasso (Spanish male) (Colorplate 33)

Prince Riding an Elephant by Khemkaran (Indian male) (Colorplate 23)

As you study each of your three selections, reflect on the following questions:
a) How did tradition and history influence the creation of any of these artworks?
b) Which of these works show social, religious, or economic values?
c) In what way has society influenced each artwork?
d) How would each work have been different if created by another culture, in another time period, or in another style?
e) What style of art does each artwork represent?
f) What cultural or artistic standards are seen in each piece?
g) For what purpose was each piece created?

By all means, visit the museum shop, either before you enter the galleries or afterward. By stopping there first and looking at the postcards, reproductions, slides, books, and catalogs, you will discover which artworks in its collection the museum considers extraordinary enough to have reproduced. This might guide you as to what artworks you do not want to miss or those works you did not know were there. Purchasing these museum-shop reproductions allows you to take your visual memories home in a tangible way. Noted art historian Kenneth Clark has his own fine collection of original artworks in his home, but he also keeps postcard reproductions on his mantelpiece of works that currently fit his mood. If you read a museum catalog after you have seen the exhibit, your knowledge about the artworks and the artists will be enhanced.

You may visit a museum alone or with a friend or a group. Each arrangement has advantages. If you are with a friend, you will each be discovering things and sharing what you see. Being alone probably allows you to have a closer relationship with an individual artwork. Have you ever stood before a fine portrait by a seventeenth-century Dutch master and had the almost eerie feeling that the eyes of the person, long since dead, are gazing directly at you alone down through the centuries? Or perhaps you just let the pure visual impact of Kandinsky's vibrant colors drench you in a silent form of communication. Or have you sensed the eternal quality of Egyptian artifacts, or the lonely isolation of an Edward Hopper cityscape?

An audioguide can provide you with a commentary as you walk through the exhibit. Through your personal set of earphones, you are told which artwork to focus on and then are provided with interesting and revealing information. You can turn off the audioguide at any time and linger before a particular piece of art or in front of one that has caught your eye but that was not included in the audio's monologue.

Not to be overlooked as artwork is the museum itself. Many museums are spectacular pieces of architecture, and some are set in dazzling gardens and grounds that demand our attention. You will usually find outdoor sculpture to admire on the museum grounds. Notice the stately, classical columns of the Metropolitan Museum in New York; be absorbed with the buildings that were once homes and are now museums, such as the Isabella Stewart Gardner Museum in Boston and the Frick in New York. Newer museums, such as the Guggenheim in New York, the Hirshhorn in Washington, DC, and the Los Angeles County Museum, and the new Getty Museum in Los Angeles show styles of contemporary architecture and reflect the times. Contrast the new east wing of the National Gallery of Art in Washington, DC, with the older part of the gallery.

Some of the world's major museums have produced museum tour videos and interactive CD-ROMs. For instance, CD-ROMs of the New York Metropolitan Museum of Art, the Louvre in Paris, and the National Gallery of Art in Washington, DC, show some of their finest works in the museums and at the same time offer a glimpse of the museums themselves.

When Children Visit a Museum

If you plan to take a group of children on a museum field trip, make arrangements with the museum ahead of time. The museum may send you a set of slides or a video along with written information to use in preparing the children for their visit. Upon your arrival, the museum will provide you with a museum docent who is trained in talking with children. Group tours give both children and adults the opportunity to have the expertise of a trained guide. Such knowledgeable museum lectures can point out aspects of an artwork that children as well as first-time viewers might miss. They pass along pertinent historical information about

Figure 4.8 When the de Young Museum in San Francisco featured works by Claude Monet, Emily dressed as the fictional character in the children's book *Linnea in Monet's Garden* and, along with her Linnea doll, made her first museum visit.
Photo by Herberholz.

the artist and time period that gives the visit a special meaning and in-depth quality. In these situations, do not expect to see everything in one visit; rather, expect to focus on only one exhibit and especially on several works of art.

Young viewers need to understand that they may only "touch the artwork with their eyes," since the artworks are very valuable and can be damaged by physical touching. Many museums provide studio space for children to go to after seeing an exhibit to try their hand at working with a particular medium. In addition, museums often give students worksheets that enable them to go on a guided "treasure hunt," searching for specific things in specific artworks. A visit to the museum shop can give young viewers an opportunity to begin their own small-scale private art collection by purchasing postcard reproductions of the favorite artworks they have just seen.

Museum Literacy: Cracking the Code

A standard museum label by an artwork gives basic information on the artist, title, and medium/media of the work. If the artist is still living, only the birth year appears following his or her name. If the life span of this artist is unknown, other information such as the estimated years of his or her activity may be furnished instead (e.g., circa 1610–1650). If the date of the artwork is unknown, the label may read either "n.d." (no date) or the curator may provide an informed estimate of when the work was produced (circa 1840). The accession number is of primary interest to the museum itself, but it can be of interest to the general public. Most accession numbers are comprised of the date that the museum acquired the work and the order in which it was acquired. For instance, the number "1963.19" indicates that this was the nineteenth work accepted into the museum's collection in 1963. Some larger museums with encyclopedic collections may include other department or collection codes in that number. If the work is on loan from another institution or individual, this information would also appear.

Artist's name (life span)
Nationality
Title of work, date of work
Medium
Museum accession number or status

With some basic understandings of how museums work, a visitor may be able to access other information to better understand an individual work or collections of works on view. A curatorial commentary or artist's statement near the entrance to an exhibition or gallery space may provide helpful contextual information. An exhibit or grouping of artworks within a space is usually not just an arbitrary assembly of objects. Artworks are generally organized around a thesis or recognizable premise. For instance, if a museum collects Asian and European artworks, those collection areas will usually be exhibited in areas distinct from each other. Furthermore, there are different organizing elements for Western (e.g., European art) and non-Western (e.g., Asian) art. Asian works are usually subdivided into geographical (Chinese, Japanese, Indian, etc.) or religious (Buddhist, Islamic, etc.) groupings. In this way, specific cultural features become more evident to viewers as they can compare and contrast works. In Asian art, broad time periods are referenced by style or dynasties. European works are more frequently grouped by specific time periods and by country. Chronological arrangements provide opportunities to notice stylistic features of a given period and stylistic developments over time. In recent years, many curators have experimented with thematic arrangements that allow for a more dynamic installation and reveal underlying ideas across time and culture.

Figure 4.9 *Here's What We Do Inside,* **Thomas Raley Boys and Girls Club, Ray Gonzales, sculptor, Sacramento, CA, 2000.**
Ray Gonzales's public art commissions are geared toward conveying a sense of time and place reflective of the community or area. He states, "My goal is inclusion. I want my works not only to belong *in* the community in which they are installed—I want them to belong *to* that community."
Courtesy of Ray Gonzales, 2000.

Figure 4.10 **RCAF murals at Southside Park, Sacramento, CA, 1975.**
The CSU Sacramento Art Department's Barrio Art program and a nonprofit organization, the RCAF (Rebel Chicano Art Front, aka, the Royal Chicano Air Force), received a grant from the city council to finance this project. The Barrio Art program is still an important part of Sacramento's inner city, being housed at the Washington Neighborhood Center where mural classes continue to be taught. As artist/poet Jose Montoya says, "The RCAF continues to fly its adobe airplanes into the new millennium!"
Photo by Jose Montoya.

Contemporary art, which is already defined by time, but which also has less historical context, is often exhibited in more subjective groupings. Visual or aesthetic connections often guide the juxtaposition of one object to another.

All exhibits are intended to teach. Understanding how objects are arranged and considering why a given group of objects are displayed together provide the visitor with the language to access this information. Think about the following:

Where does my eye go first in this exhibition? Why? How does that object relate to other objects around it? What elements do these objects have in common? How are the objects arranged? Chronologically? Culturally? Visually? Where does my eye go next? Why? What's the connection?

Art in Public Places

Not all art is in museums. Many cities today have policies whereby a percentage of building costs for public and corporate architecture must be designated for the installation of interior or exterior artworks, including sculptures in and near the site, murals, wall hangings, fountains, memorials, and such. Local arts councils can supply visitors with lists of where to find these artworks. Arts councils often schedule "art walks" so that both students and adults can take a guided tour to view these installations.

Art in the community is many-faceted. A collaborative effort in the late 60s, 70s, and 80s resulted in a series of murals on the west facade of the band and performing shell in a park in Sacramento, CA (Figure 4.10). Built during the WPA days, the site had fallen victim to neglect and was shunned by families who saw it as a gathering place for derelicts. By the time the murals were completed, the community reclaimed the park, and festivities and celebrations have been a major part of community activity since.

Ray Gonzales, working with a grant from the Sacramento Arts Commission, met with about 40 children from the neighborhood where a new Boys and Girls Club was to be built. He photographed them playing basketball, jumping rope, running, reading a book, playing a trumpet, and painting. After selecting six photographs, he used the images of three boys and three girls as the basis for life-size silhouettes, which he then sculpted from slabs of clay. After firing and glazing them in bright colors, he installed them in large metal frames constructed by metal artist Phil Evans. The sculpture is kinetic with each pole including bearings so that the figures may shift their arrangement in the wind (Figure 4.9).

INTERACTIVE EXTENSIONS

1. Visit an art museum and complete the form on page 100. Then make a treasure hunt that elementary children could use when they go to a museum on a field trip. Think of questions that will guide the children in seeking visual information and meaning. Include games, drawings, fill-in-the-blank questions, or missing spot activities (draw a portion from a painting and ask the children to find its source).

2. Select a classmate to play the role of a friend who has just been notified of his or her inheritance. He or she must choose between two artworks from an aunt's estate (two artworks in the Color Gallery may be used). Your friend asks your advice as to which artwork to choose. How will you help him decide?

3. You own a prestigious art gallery in San Francisco and have a wealthy foreign client who wishes to purchase an American artwork. Base your interview with your client on why he or she should purchase a particular painting that you hope to sell him. Choose a classmate to play the role of the client, and brief him or her on appropriate questions and remarks.

4. Newspapers and some national newsmagazines contain reviews of current art exhibits. Select one, make a copy of it, and find statements in which the critic described, analyzed, interpreted, and judged the works. Use one color to highlight art criticism statements and another color for art history statements.

5. Each student chooses a reproduction in the Color Gallery and studies the artist and artwork. They then each write two true facts and two false statements about the artwork on separate note cards. The cards are numbered on the reverse side and put in an envelope, with the student's name written inside the envelope flap. Students trade envelopes, try to identify the false cards, and then consult with the writer to check answers.

6. Four students act as art agents presenting an artwork to a museum acquisition committee (the rest of the class). The price of each artwork is the same, and the museum budget will only allow the museum to purchase one artwork. The first student will be "selling" a realistic artwork; the second, an abstract; the third, an expressive; and the fourth, a fantasy-surrealistic artwork. Each pre-

sentation should be based on the artwork's artistic merit and historical significance. Students should describe, analyze, interpret, and make a judgment, supporting their comments with evidence seen within the artwork and with what they can find in reference books. Then the acquisition committee votes on which artwork to purchase.

7. You are the chair of the acquisitions committee at a major museum. Your committee has just used an endowment fund to purchase an artwork, and the selection that was made has caused a great deal of controversy. You are being interviewed on a local radio talk show and must justify your committee's decision. Choose a classmate to be the talk-show host who will ask you questions regarding the controversy surrounding the acquisition. Be prepared to respond to the host's questions (questions that you supply him or her with ahead of time) and those of call-in listeners (your classmates). Practice ahead of time with your talk-show host.

8. To more directly understand how a child responds to artworks, refer to recent studies about how children understand art, such as the book *Aesthetics for Young People*, edited by Ronald Moore.

9. Select a reproduction in a book or an artwork from the Color Gallery, and ask an elementary-school child to look at it with you. Ask the child questions that involve describing, analyzing, interpreting, and judging the artwork, as detailed in this chapter.

10. Select four artworks, reproductions, or ones found in books, and write a paragraph as to how a study of them may be integrated with social studies, math, language arts, or science in the elementary school.

11. Collect postcards and inexpensive reproductions of artworks. Then read Chapter 3 in *Early Childhood Art* by Barbara Herberholz and Lee Hanson and make several children's art games as described. Your game may focus on aspects of the elements and principles of art or on artists, styles of artworks, and art history.

12. Read a newspaper critic's review of an exhibit in a local gallery. Then visit the exhibit and compare your observations and reactions with those of the critic.

Visiting an Art Museum

Your name _____ Name of museum _____

List 3 resources or programs that the museum offers elementary school children.

1. _____

2. _____

3. _____

List the name of an artwork and the artist that you think

1. Tells a story _____

2. Was used in a ritual or religious ceremony _____

3. Was made to inspire religious feelings _____

4. Records how a person actually looked _____

5. Records how a place looked _____

6. Shows an artist's strong expression of his/her feelings _____

7. Was created to serve a utilitarian purpose _____

Select an artwork that is an example of the following styles of art. List the title and artist.

1. Realistic _____

2. Abstract _____

3. Expressionist _____

4. Fantasy, surrealistic _____

When you finish your tour, think about the following fantasy wish: Which artwork that you have just seen do you wish you had created? Why? Please do not base your choice on its monetary worth.

Colorplate 16. Paul Cézanne, *The Large Bathers*, 1906. Oil on canvas, 6′10″ × 8′3″ (2.08 × 2.51 m). *The Philadelphia Museum of Art, W.P. Wilstach Collection Purchase.*

Colorplate 17. Faith Ringgold, *Tar Beach*, 1988. Acrylic paint on canvas bordered with printed, painted, quilted and pieced cloth, 74⅜ × 68½″ (189.5 × 174 cm). *Solomon R. Guggenheim Museum, New York, Gift of Mr. and Mrs. Gus and Judith Lieber, 1988, (88.3620). Faith Ringgold © 1988.*

Colorplate 18. **Brenda Louie**, *River Dance #30*, date. Oil on canvas, 96 × 154″. Artist's Collection.

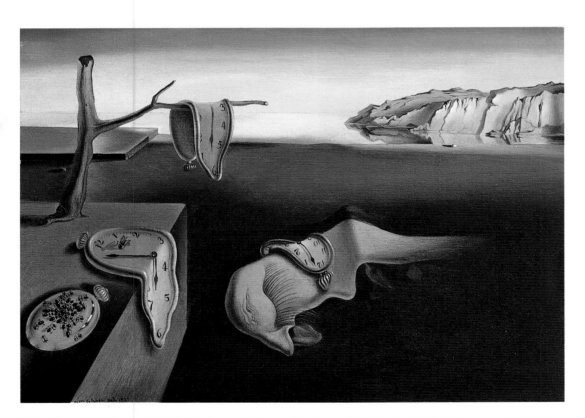

Colorplate 19. **Salvador Dali**, *The Persistence of Memory (Persistence de la Mémoire)*, 1931. Oil on canvas, 9½ × 13 in.
The Museum of Modern Art, New York, Given anonymously.
Photograph © 2001 The Museum of Modern Art, NY.
© *2002 Kingdom of Spain, Gala-Salvador Dali Foundation/Artist Rights Society (ARS), New York.*

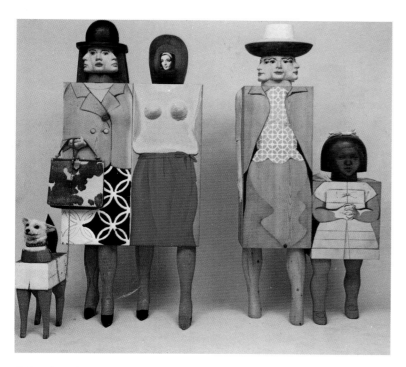

Colorplate 20. Marisol, *Women and Dog,* 1964. Wood, plaster, synthetic polymer, taxidermed dog head and miscellaneous items, 72¼ × 73 × 31 in. *Collection of Whitney Museum of American Art, New York. Purchased with funds from the Friends of the Whitney Museum of American Art (64.17 a-g). Photograph © 2002 Whitney Museum of American Art © Marisol/VAGA, NY, NY.*

Colorplate 21. Grant Wood, *American Gothic,* 1930. Oil on beaver board, 76 × 63.3 cm. © *Friends of the American Art Collection, All rights reserved by The Art Institute of Chicago and VAGA, New York, NY, 1930.934.*

Colorplate 22. **Fukaye Roshu**, *The Ivy Land (tsuta-no-hosomichi)*, Japanese, Edo Period, 1699–1755. Sixfold screen, opaque color on gold ground, 133 × 271.8 cm.
© *The Cleveland Museum of Art, 2002, John L. Severance fund, 1954.127.*

Colorplate 23. **Khemkaran**, *Prince Riding an Elephant*, period of Akbar, 1556–1605, Mughal. Leaf from an album, gouache on paper. *The Metropolitan Museum of Art, New York, Rogers Fund, 1925 (25.68.4).*
Photograph ©1988 The Metropolitan Museum of Art, NY.

Colorplate 24. **Franz Marc**, *Yellow Cow*, 1911. Oil on canvas, 55⅜ × 74¼ in. *Solomon R. Guggenheim Museum, New York. Photo by David Heald. © Solomon Guggenheim Foundation, NY (49.1210).*

Colorplate 25. **Albert Bierstadt**, *The Rocky Mountains, Lander's Peak*, 1863. Oil on canvas, 73¼ × 120¾ in. *The Metropolitan Museum of Art, New York, Rogers Fund, 1907 (07.123). Photograph © 1979 The Metropolitan Museum of Art, NY.*

Colorplate 26. Diego Rivera, detail of *Fresco in the Fountain Hall of the Detroit Institute of Arts*, 1932. *The Detroit Institute of Arts, Gift of Edsel B. Ford. Photograph © 1991 The Detroit Institute of Arts.*
© 2002 Banco de México, Diego Rivera & Frida Kahlo Museums Trust Av., Cinco de Mayo No. 2, Col. Centro, Del. Cuauhtémoc 06059, México, D.F.

Colorplate 27. Wayne Thiebaud, *Highland River*, 1996. Oil on board, 11 × 14 in. © *Wayne Thiebaud/VAGA, NY, NY.*

Colorplate 28. Frank La Pena, *Flower Dance Spirit*, 1981. *Courtesy Patty and Chris Gibson.*

Colorplate 29. **Harry Fonseca**, *The Creation*, 1991. Acrylic on canvas, 29¼ × 39¾″. *Crocker Art Museum, Sacramento, CA, Gift of Carla Hansen Hills.*

Colorplate 30. **Vasily Kandinsky**, *Panel for Edwin R. Campbell No. 1*, 1914. Oil on canvas, 64 × 36¼ in.
The Museum of Modern Art, New York, Mrs. Simon Guggenheim Fund.
Photograph © 2001 The Museum of Modern Art, NY
© 2002 Artist Rights Society (ARS), New York/ADAGP, Paris.

Colorplate 31. **Leonardo da Vinci**, *Ginevra de' Benci (obverse)*, ca. 1474. Oil on panel, 15 × 14 in.
National Gallery of Art, Washington,
Ailsa Mellon Bruce Fund.
Photograph ©2002 Board of Trustees, National Gallery of Art, Washington.

Colorplate 32. Auguste Renoir, *A Girl with a Watering Can*, 1876. Oil on canvas, 39½ × 28¾ in.
National Gallery of Art, Washington,
Chester Dale Collection.
Photograph ©2002 Board of Trustees, National Gallery of Art, Washington.

Colorplate 33. Pablo Picasso, *Girl Before a Mirror*, 1932. Oil on canvas, 64 × 51¼ in. *The Museum of Modern Art, New York, Gift of Mrs. Simon Guggenheim.*
Photograph © 2001 The Museum of Modern Art, NY

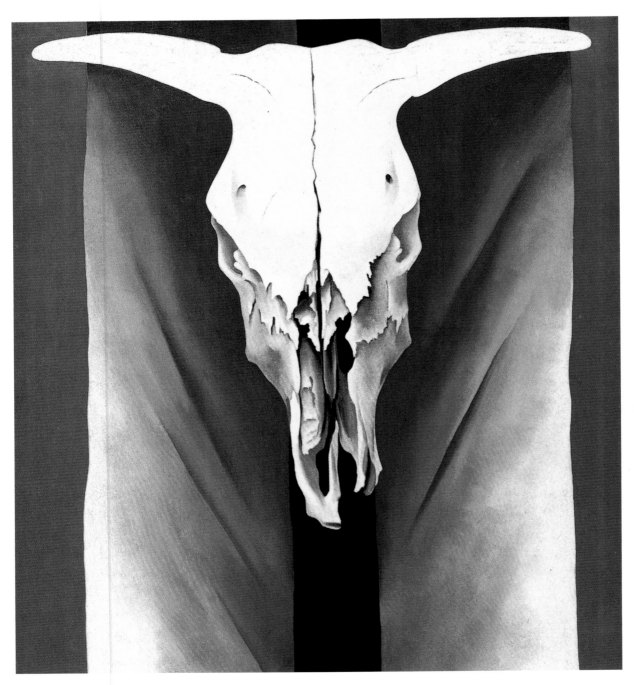

Colorplate 34. **Georgia O'Keeffe**, *Cow's Skull: Red, White and Blue*, 1931. Oil on canvas, 39⅞ × 35⅞ in. *The Metropolitan Museum of Art, New York, The Alfred Stieglitz Collection, 1949. (52.203). Photograph © 1994 The Metropolitan Museum of Art, NY.* © 2002 The Georgia O'Keeffe Foundation/Artist Rights Society (ARS), New York.

Colorplate 35. Jacob Lawrence. *Vaudeville*, 1951. Egg tempera on hardboard, 29⅞ × 19¹⁵⁄₁₆ ". *Collection of the Hirshhorn Museum Sculpture Garden, Smithsonian Institution. Gift of Joseph H. Hirshhorn, 1966. (c) Gwendolyn Knight Lawrence, courtesy of Jacob and Gwendolyn Lawrence Foundation.*

Colorplate 36. Mary Cassatt, *The Bath*, ca. 1891–92. Oil on canvas, 39½ × 26 in. *The Art Institute of Chicago. Robert A. Waller Fund (1910.2). Photograph © 2002 The Art Institute of Chicago, All rights reserved.*

Colorplate 37. **Marc Chagall**, *Green Violinist*, 1923–24. Oil on canvas, 78 × 42¾ in. *Solomon R. Guggenheim Museum, New York, Gift of Solomon R. Guggenheim, 1937. Photo by David Heald © Solomon R. Guggenheim Foundation, NY (37.446).* © *2002 Artist Rights Society (ARS), New York/ADAGP, Paris.*

Colorplate 38. Raymond Saunders, *Joseph Fitzpatrick Was Our Teacher*, 1991. Mixed media on canvas, 114 × 82½″. *Crocker Art Museum, Sacramento, CA, Gift of the Crocker Art Museum Association.*

Colorplate 39. Frida Kahlo, *Fulang-Chang and I*, 1937. Two part ensemble assembled after 1939. Part one: 1937, Oil on composition board, 15¾ × 11 in.; painted mirror frame (added after 1939), 22¼ × 17⅞ × 1¾ in. Part two: (after 1939) mirror with painted mirror frame, 25¼ × 19⅛ × 1¾ in., including frame. 1A. Composition board: 15¾ × 11 in. 1B. Mirror frame: 22¼ × 17⅞ × 1¾ in. 2. Mirror with mirror frame: 25¼ × 19⅛ × 1¾ in.
The Museum of Modern Art, New York, Mary Sklar Bequest. Photograph © 2001 The Museum of Modern Art, NY.
© 2002 Banco de México, Diego Rivera & Frida Kahlo Museums Trust Av., Cinco de Mayo No. 2, Col. Centro, Del. Cuahtémoc 06059, México, D.F.

Colorplate 40. **Maria Winkler**, *Marbles Spill III*, 1996. Chalk pastel, 22 × 33 in. *From the collection of the artist.*

Colorplate 41. Jose Montoya, *Court Appearance*, 1976. Oil, 28 × 36 in. *From the Ricardo Favela Collection.*

Colorplate 42. Cham Thor, detail of *Mona, Hmong Daily Life*, 1994. Stitchery, 30 × 30 in. *From the collection at University of California, Davis, Medical Center.*

Colorplate 43. **Pablo Picasso**, *Portrait of a Young Girl after Cranach the Younger, II*, 1958. Linoleum cut, printed in color, composition, 25¼ × 21¼ in. *The Museum of Modern Art, New York, Gift of Mr. and Mrs. Daniel Saidenberg.*
Photograph © 2001 The Museum of Modern Art, NY.

5

C H A P T E R

Children Make and Respond to Art

CHANGES IN ART EDUCATION OVER THE YEARS

The place of art in the schools has not remained static over the years. In the nineteenth century, drawing skills were emphasized in public schools, in large part because of the Industrial Revolution, to help students to acquire skills for factory work, to sketch portraits, to encourage good penmanship, and to improve hand-eye coordination. This early art curriculum was originally called *freehand drawing* and was popular for decades.

By the turn of the century other areas of art appeared in schools, including a study of pictures, reproductions of paintings, and sculpture, which were usually historic or sentimental. It was believed that they taught moral values and socially productive behavior in coordination with language texts. Another area in the art curriculum at this time was manual arts, which taught students to make practical and useful gifts or items for the home.

In the late nineteenth century, the emerging science of psychology and human behavior led to the child study movement with its interest in children's drawings and what they could reveal about mental and emotional growth. This was the beginning of art as a source of personal and creative expression. Franz Cizek and others held the view that art could be used for play and creativity in children's lives. In the progressive era in the 1920s and 1930s, John Dewey influenced many to place an increasing emphasis on the child-centered curriculum and on creativity and play. At the same time Arthur Wesley Dow at Columbia University believed not only that the elements and principles of art were important for the industrial crafts and manual arts but that they could help students appreciate artworks.

The last third of the twentieth century was influenced by psychologist and art educator Viktor Lowenfeld, who emphasized creative self-expression and how art could integrate and contribute to the growth of the child—emotionally, intellectually, physically, perceptually, socially, aesthetically, and creatively. He also explored the visual and haptic types of child artists as well as asserting the importance of creativity through art in the child's development: sensitivity, fluency, flexibility, originality, rearrangement, analysis, and synthesis.

However, most schools provided minimal time for art, especially in the upper elementary grades. Even then the "art" was often devoted to holiday-based projects and decorating the room with just-alike adult-directed projects. Not only were these activities detrimental to the child's growth in art in that they did not foster any learning about art, but they took away from the child's confidence in his or her own expression.

In 1972, the California Department of Education first published its Visual Arts Framework. This was before the emergence of the DBAE movement, which first appeared in 1984. This document outlined a comprehensive approach organized around four components: artistic perception, creative expression, historical and cultural context, and aesthetic valuing. The National Art Education Association published a booklet that explained the four areas of art study called *Quality Art Education, Goals for Schools: An Interpretation*. These four areas were aesthetics, art production, art criticism, and art history.[1] Most states were revising their art frameworks by the 1990s in order to recommend content for schools to use in adopting a policy for their curricula.

In the 1980s and 1990s, the Getty Center for Education in the Arts began supporting a comprehensive approach to art called *discipline-based art education*. The effort to uphold the DBAE approach was supported and followed by the creation of the National Standards for Visual Arts Education. This comprehensive or multifaceted approach is one in which students learn about art through multiple ways as well as integrating art throughout the school curriculum. (The National Standards for Visual Arts Education are printed at the end of this book.)

CHILD ART: Production and Response

Children come into this world with the desire to draw, or we might say that they have the impulse for art in their genetic fuel. Children are intrinsically motivated in kindergarten through the third grade, and their continual searching, experimenting, and questioning are striking evidence of this fact. We have all seen the results of art that young children make without instruction. They begin by making marks and proceed to drawing graphic symbols (geometric schemas). Some continue on to artistic representation (realism). For most children, this natural progression in graphic expression is sequential. The questions, then, are: How do we as teachers and parents instruct children in art to enhance and deepen their artistic growth? What is the content of art that children can learn through instruction? In the past, giving children materials and telling them to create was thought to be sufficient. Art educators today believe that instruction in both art production and art appreciation is important. This position was expressed by Tom Anderson, who stated

> That expression in art and understanding of artworks should be taught in close relation to each other is fundamentally sound; more insights will be gained in both areas when one is interrelated to the other. In addition, seizing opportunities to have one activity lead organically into another creates a sense of connectedness in the minds of students between making and perceiving art.[2]

Figure 5.1 A shield protected the African warrior in battle and the hunter from attack by dangerous animals. Here, a young student models the personal shield that he designed and painted on cardboard. *Photo by Maureen Gilli.*

Figure 5.2 **Dorothy,** *Playing in the snow.*
Six-year-old Dorothy combines cut-paper shapes and tempera paint in this work.

Anderson further stated that he is referring to two different types of art talk. One is "largely for instruction to further students' artistic development," and the other is discussion of the formal qualities and thematic content of the larger realm of understanding. As students learn through study and instruction in art, they grasp the expressive and formal content of artworks as well as grow in their own art expression. The development of students' creativity in general by encouraging creativity in art denigrates the importance of art, since each art discipline—art production, aesthetic judgment, art criticism, and art history—possesses a unique content and body of knowledge. Yet one art discipline should not take precedence over another. They should be intermingled in the instructional period so that students learn to produce and understand art simultaneously.

Howard Gardner, director of Harvard's Project Zero, took a similar position on the value and importance of art production when he said that "making art is central to artistic learning and . . . perception and reflection activities must be linked directly to student production of art." Gardner sees school as a place that should develop different components of the mind, and he believes that "artistic thinking—thinking in artistic symbols—is a distinctive way of using the mind." He said that all the arts represent separate sets of cognitive skills and that "if we omit those areas from the curriculum, we are, in effect, shortchanging the mind." He strongly believes that art production should remain central in the teaching of art to young children: "That is, we think artistic learning should grow from kids doing things: not just imitating, but actually drawing, dancing, performing, singing on their own." Production is "central to our approach—and it's very different from just learning traditions from the past or just talking about art." He emphasizes that "production should be linked intrinsically to perception

and reflection. Perception means learning to see better, to hear better, to make finer discriminations, to see connections between things. Reflection means to be able to step back from both your production and your perceptions." He urges using questioning strategies that require the student to ask "what, why, and how well am I doing this?"[3]

Art production should be central to the art program because it provides, as Gardner said, a "distinctive way of using the mind." Perception and reflection in both art production and art appreciation must be intermingled in art lessons to offer the greatest opportunity for the child's artistic growth.

Jean Piaget's theories of cognitive development have had a lasting impact on understanding child development.[4] His studies dealt with perception (how we take in information) and conception (how we form ideas, use symbols, and understand abstract relationships), and they revealed that a child's cognitive development occurs in stages. Art educators, most notably Viktor Lowenfeld, have identified and described a child's art production in stages of creative and mental growth that manifest themselves beginning at about two years of age.[5]

HOW CHILDREN GROW IN MAKING ART

To effectively teach elementary art, a teacher needs to know how children develop in their art production. Let's take a close-up view of each of the sequential stages of a child's artistic growth in creating visual images in order to understand and assist in the child's development.

Stages of a Child's Artistic Development

Stage 1. Making Marks: Two to Four Years:
> Manipulation, scribbling
a) Uncontrolled, kinesthetic.
b) Controlled, repeated, longitudinal, circular.
c) Naming of marks.
d) Color important but not related to object.
e) Process is more important than product.

2. Repetition of lines radiating from an enclosed shape are typical for two-and-a-half-year-old children.

1. Controlled circular marks by Mallory, a two-and-a-half-year-old, show vigor and confidence.

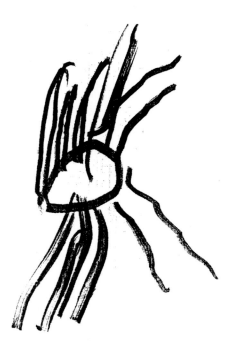

3. Heads with two legs, two eyes, and a mouth are typical beginning drawings of figures by three- and four-year-olds.

Stage 2. Making Symbols: Four to Eight Years: Figure:
a) Head/feet; closed shapes with lines; radial configurations.
b) Body usually made up of geometric shapes.
c) Works largely from memory rather than direct observation.
d) Shows emotionally and physically significant concepts, exaggeration or omission of body parts, concentration of details on important parts.
> Space:
e) Little or no overlapping.
f) Random placement of items in picture space.
g) Simple baseline appears.
> Deviations: bent, multiple, mixture of plane and elevation, x-ray, foldover.

4. A three-and-a-half-year-old elaborates on the head-with-two-legs figure by enclosing it at the bottom and adding hair, arms, and hands with multiple fingers. A zigzag decoration has been added to the body.

5. This drawing by a six-year-old shows attention to the position of arms and legs. The dress is colored in, and bows are added to the hair.

6. Elaborate schema by a six-year-old who included a hat, details on the shirt and arms, and five fingers on each hand.

7. Spatial schemas of six-year-olds often show a mixed plane and elevation view; also note beginning development of a baseline.

8. Six-year-old Megan solves a spatial problem by using mixed plane and elevation to show the tabletop and table legs. Note food arranged on the table.

9. Five-year-old Daniel drew this train after constructing one with wood scraps and glue.

10. This five-year-old began to make her own house by cutting and drawing with a pen; she then continued making houses and called it "My Neighborhood."

Stage 3. Realism: Eight to Twelve Years

a) More attention to body proportion, action of figure, details of clothing.

b) Closer observation of environment; gradual disappearance of baseline and emergence of horizon; shadows, shading may appear.

c) Shows depth through diminishing sizes and overlapping.

d) Uses realistic colors.

e) More critical of own work.

13. Schemas in profile are in action positions. Some overlapping is seen in this eight-year-old's drawing of Halloween trick-or-treaters.

15. The nine-year-old who made this detailed contour drawing observed a posed model very carefully.

11. A trip to the circus stimulated this nine-year-old to draw a balanced bareback rider on the back of a horse. Her spatial concept allowed her to add the audience and a clown to finish the composition.

14. The three overlapping figures by this nine-year-old show the child's sense of size and proportion as well as different body poses.

12. Note the more realistic way this nine-year-old drew the table and chair legs, showing her developing sense of perspective.

The Teacher's Role Questions to activate thinking, feeling, perceiving. Dialogues, a verbal interchange of a remembered event; on location; photographic materials; actual objects; acting it out; pretending to be someone/something else; specific enrichment of schema (one bodily part at a time); word images (poems, songs, stories); fantasy and humor; large drawings on sidewalk; theme-related to reproductions of artworks; integrated with other areas of the curriculum.

Materials Markers, crayons, chalk on paper and sidewalk, tempera with stiff brushes, pencils, simple printmaking (gadget, potato, tag, foam), collage with papers and collected items, clay, baker's dough, salt ceramic, edible art projects, simple weaving (soda straw, cardboard looms, paper), wood constructions, paper mâché, simple stitchery.

Figure 5.3 Intense concentration and prolonged focus are seen in this five-year-old's drawing, resulting in a richly detailed schema. Baseline provides a place for flowers.
Photo by Barbara Herberholz.

Making Marks: Two to Four Years of Age

Very young children embark on their first adventures with art by making lines. The toddler's earliest mark-making is often referred to as *scribbling*. Dictionaries tend to define scribbling as meaningless marks and lines; hence, the term has negative connotations that belittle the importance of this activity in the child's development: "Lori is just scribbling." At about two years of age, a child begins to enjoy the kinesthetic pleasure of moving his or her hand and arm around while holding a crayon or marking pen; thus begins the first stage in the child's artistic development. The child also enjoys arranging, cutting, and manipulating art materials. At this point in their development children are not attempting to make realistic images. Soon, young children realize that they can control the lines they are making, and they proceed to make a variety of repeated movements that are generally referred to as circular and longitudinal marks. They discover that they can make repeated lines, some short, some long,

and some round; putting these circles and lines together stirs their imagination into seeing something they recognize and call "mommy," "daddy," or "me."

Soon they are making all sorts of linear symbols and calling them "houses," "my dog," "a tree," "the sun," and telling stories about their marks. This naming of marks is an important step in their thinking because it means that they have established a connection between the lines they are making and the surrounding world. They are now set to explore the world through the use of line, making marks that will show their degree of perception and their emotional involvement with an experience. Parents and teachers should remember that children develop at different rates in both their physical and mental development. Some have had many opportunities to manipulate art materials and have been encouraged in their art activities at home; such children will demonstrate this in more sophisticated art production and in talking about their artworks. Children of this stage often select a particular color as their favorite and do not relate the color they are using to the actual color of the object.

In summary, the child's artistic growth in the earliest years has four recognizable stages:

1. No control and no deliberate repetition; emphasis on kinesthetic movement.

2. Line is controlled and can be repeated; longitudinal and circular.

3. Closed shapes are made and can be repeated.

4. The child names the mark or shape, sometimes before it is made and sometimes afterward.

Making Symbols: Four to Eight Years of Age

During these years, referred to as the *symbolic* or *schematic stage*, children develop their line- and shape-making skills as well as their muscular coordination in handling drawing tools, scissors, glue sticks, and modeling clay. If encouraged and motivated appropriately, they maintain a confident, flexible, fluent, and original approach to the creation of images of things that are important to them.

Children usually begin by drawing simple, recognizable images called *symbols*, often nothing more complicated than a head-feet figure. Producing a recognizable symbol with a meaning is now a deliberate and controlled act, and the symbols tell us what people, events, or objects impressed the child at a particular moment. While children develop a variety of symbols for objects in their environments, such as people, dogs, houses, flowers, and such, they most frequently draw people. The first figures usually are of themselves, their parents, siblings, and friends. They rely heavily on geometric shapes rather than on realistic or free-form shapes. They often make a round shape and add an oval or triangle for a body and perhaps two long rectangles for legs and two more for arms. A hand is often a circle, with lines or loops symbolizing fingers. Houses are squares and rectangles topped with a triangular roof and a square chimney, balanced precariously, perpendicular to the roof line. At this time, a tree is often drawn as a long rectangle topped with a circle—a "lollipop tree."

At first children are content to fill the paper with variations of head-feet people, letting them randomly float on the picture plane with little or no relationship in space or to one another. Sometime during the fourth or fifth year, children begin to connect objects in space in their drawings and they begin to tell and show us what they know about spatial relationships in artworks with such topics as taking the dog for a walk and how a clown sits on a swing: they begin to organize objects and to show more relationships and connections between objects in the picture space.

A child whose thinking is flexible and fluent will be able to deviate from his or her fixed symbol and will enrich and change the schema, perhaps to exaggerate an important body part or omit an unimportant part. "I am picking flowers" will call for an extra long arm. "I stubbed my toe" will be evidenced by a large toe with a negligence of arms and hands. A concentration of details on a figure of him- or herself may be seen by a child with newly painted fingernails and earrings.

Some children tend to repeat their symbols in a stereotyped manner if they are not motivated to remember specific experiences and physical motions and encouraged to make more detailed sensory observations. The adult may talk to them about playing ball, roller skating, skipping rope, losing their first tooth, getting a new pair of shoes, telling whispered secrets, wearing new dark glasses, swinging on the playground—any familiar experience that involves different body parts. This encourages the child to include ears, teeth, and whatever parts he or she may have previously omitted.

When children first begin drawing symbolic representations of people, trees, houses, and such, they usually do not relate the color they are using to the actual color of the object. A figure may have a green face and purple hair. Adults can point out particular colors in the environment in the course of normal conversations with these children rather than correcting the choices that the children have made in their drawings: "I like your red sweater, Maria." "Jim has made a fine painting of a brown dog." "Thank you for the pretty bouquet of pink and yellow roses." Children can take "color discovery walks," identifying colors and making lists when they return of everything that was a particular color.

Another avenue to pursue in increasing children's perceptual and cognitive awareness of color is to ask them to describe the colors they see in an artwork, whether it is their own or one by a great artist. For instance, we could ask children to point out and identify all the places where Wayne Thiebaud used different colors in his painting of *Dark Green River* (Colorplate 27). They could decide which color they see first when they look at the painting and which color is used most. They could find a dark blue and a light blue. When they also notice the areas of green, yellow, red, and violet colors, they could then be told that the artist mostly used the primary and secondary colors for his composition. If children have multiple occasions to observe artworks and to describe the colors they see, they will soon begin to consciously use more realistic or expressive colors in their symbolic representations of things that are important to them in their artwork.

At this time children may explore texture in a number of ways—cutting and pasting a variety of papers, fabrics, yarn, and so on to make an abstract collage design. Bits of textured materials may be idea starters for young children, since the concept appeals to their sense of touch. In this activity, children choose a scrap of textured material and wonder about what it suggests to them or of what it reminds them. For instance, a scrap of sandpaper may make them think of a beach or a sandbox, and after they paste it onto a piece of paper, they can use crayons or marking pens to make the rest of their picture. A bit of foil might be the beginning of a drawing about a spaceship. Another avenue for children to pursue with texture is that of making a variety of crayon rubbings of different textures found around home and school. Students can then cut and paste the found textures into pictures and designs.

These first images often do not relate to other images in the same drawing. Children are intent on drawing one symbol at a time, and before long they relate symbols within the same drawing by using a baseline or ground line upon which objects and figures are placed. This is a significant spatial discovery. This represents the child's ability to relate objects to one another in space as this line symbolizes the ground. Six-year-olds may see the sky as a line or band across the top of the picture, with the space between the baseline and the sky thought of as "air." At this time in their development, children are drawing what they logically know about space rather than what they are visually aware of perceiving.

Since the baseline concept of six- and seven-year-olds is based more on nonvisual and expressive uses of space than on realistic representations, their thinking in regard to space must be kept flexible and fluent. If children are limited in their depictions of space to a rigid, straight line drawn across the bottom of the paper to represent the ground and another across the top for the sky, they will be restricted in solving a number of spatial problems in their picture-making. To encourage and stimulate their thinking and expression in regard to the pictorial space, the following themes or topics are suggested as teaching strategies:

1. "We are climbing a mountain, going skiing, or riding our bikes on a hill." This calls for the baseline to be bent

in a curve or placed on a diagonal. ("Did you ever climb a mountain? Was the trail flat or steep? Did you get tired and out of breath as you climbed higher and higher? How tall were the trees? Did you see any rocks, rabbits, or squirrels? Was there a waterfall? How were you dressed?")

2. "Picking fruit in an orchard." This topic needs several baselines in order to place the rows of trees on separate lines. ("Did you ever pick apples or cherries in an orchard? Do you remember how the trees grew in straight rows? You could walk up and down between the rows of trees. Did you climb a ladder to pick the fruit, or could you reach it standing on the ground?")

3. "Under the sea, inside a mine, ants under the ground." An elevated baseline is required to show the subject matter that is below the surface, it being more important than what is actually on the surface. ("If you could be a deep-sea diver and explore underneath the ocean, what do you think you would see? Probably a lot of different kinds of fish, shell creatures, and plants. You could leave your boat on the surface of the water and descend downward and see all kinds of sea life. What shapes would they be? How would you be dressed?")

4. "We are having a picnic at the beach or we are playing a board game on the table." The child frequently mixes plane and elevation; that is, the top of the picnic table (or table and checkerboard) is drawn as if we are looking down at it, while other objects are drawn on eye level. ("Taking a picnic to the beach is a lot of fun. We can spread a cloth on the sand or put it on a table and then put our food on it and sit around it to eat. What kind of food would you take on your picnic? Would you take a friend or two? Would you set up near the water and maybe take along an umbrella to protect you from the hot sun?")

5. In another conceptualization of space, the child mixes plane and elevation in such a manner that, if the sides of the paper were folded upright, the picture would be quite realistic three-dimensionally. For instance, the child may solve the spatial dilemma when drawing a topic such as "floating down the river on a raft" or a "parade on Main Street" by mixing the plane and elevation and showing the river or street lying flat in the middle of the composition with the objects on each side drawn perpendicular to it. If the sides of the paper are folded up, the buildings and trees on the sides of the river or street appear as they do in the natural world. ("Did you ever go with your family on a raft and float down the river on a hot summer day? You wore a life jacket and bathing suit and you probably used a paddle to make the raft move. As you floated down the river what did you see when you looked to the left of the raft? Houses, docks, trees? What was on the right side?")

Realism: Eight to Twelve Years of Age

A newfound realistic approach to making pictures begins at about eight or nine years of age. Students may still retain the remnants of the uncritical blissfulness of childhood fantasy, but their thinking about what they see and how they make their art changes dramatically. The geometric symbols that they have used to represent people, animals, and other objects and that satisfied them in their earlier artworks no longer suffice. Children begin to show in their drawings that they perceive that the sky meets the horizon and that objects can overlap and create new spatial effects. When students become dissatisfied with the simple linear symbols they have been using, they are ready for instruction in how to draw more realistically. Here, teachers should provide experiences that develop the children's perceptual skills and numerous opportunities for the student to draw from direct observation. They should introduce and demonstrate media techniques that enable children to create artworks that are acceptable to their maturing, critical eyes.

At this stage students want to draw more realistic figures with a greater sense of visual proportion and less exaggeration of body parts. They give attention to the hair and clothing of the figures they draw and also show figures in action, overlapping, in profile view, and extending off the page. Making the 16-piece manikin as described in Chapter 3 helps the child's cognitive awareness of the proportions of the body and how the body looks in profile and in action. More perceptive children attempt to shade objects, to draw shadows, and to make distant objects smaller with less detail. They are ready to learn about visual space and perspective.

During this period, as in other levels, a single artwork may exhibit a mixture of stages. Most children of this age benefit from close observation of the objects they wish to draw. They can gain the visual information that they need from actual objects, landscapes, posed costumed models, and photographs. A study of artworks can help students understand how artists have perceived and depicted similar subjects, moods, and themes, as well as how artists have used media and solved aesthetic problems dealing with space, shading, and color changes. If children of this age are to continue in their artwork they need to learn realistic drawing skills, or in frustration, they may stop drawing altogether.

Frequent exercises in contour drawing as described in Chapter 2 are extremely helpful in teaching the child how to draw realistically. Using a small viewfinder (Figure 2.27) can help the student isolate and to frame a composition in the same way that a camera does. Frequent opportunities to draw a posed model are invaluable. Mounted birds and animals are also excellent subject matter for careful observation while drawing. Still-life setups can help students perceive relative proportions and sizes, relationships, directional angles, and three-dimensional forms. Guided exercises in linear perspective are helpful for giving students the information they need to depict space more realistically.

At the realism stage, children are rather insistent about using representational colors. The teacher can discuss the variety of colors seen in landscapes, posed models, and still lifes. The children can profit from a familiarity with the color wheel and from learning the nuances of mixing light and dark hues, dull colors, and blends of analogous colors to match the colors the children see in trees, houses, streets, animals, and such. The children may decide, however, to make an expressive rather than a realistic use of color and choose colors that communicate a particular emotion or a dramatic or fantasy event. Once again a study of several artworks in which artists use expressive coloring can help the children grasp the concept that different modes of expression call for personalized color choices. In describing Chagall's *Green Violinist* (Colorplate 37), for example, we might ask the children to find where the artist used unrealistic colors. We then might ask the children to imagine how the feeling of the picture would be changed had Chagall used realistic colors.

During the realism stage, as in other levels, a single artwork may exhibit a mixture of stages. Most children of this age benefit from close observation of the objects they wish to draw, gaining visual information that they need not only from actual objects, models, and landscapes but also from photographs.

A study of artworks can help students understand how artists have perceived and depicted similar subjects, moods, and themes, as well as how artists have used media and solved aesthetic problems dealing with space, shading, and color changes. If children of this age are to continue in their artwork, they need to learn realistic drawing skills, or in frustration, they may stop drawing altogether.

MOTIVATING ARTISTIC PRODUCTION

Strategies in which students are actively and enthusiastically engaged and motivated are the basic means teachers have of evoking artistic responses in them. Such strategies provide a focus—an open-ended structure within which students are free to express their own ideas about the subject or theme as well as how to grow in their understanding of the elements and principles of art and gain skills in using art materials.

Teachers have at their disposal a number of different ways of evoking and stimulating artistic responses in elementary students. A strategy is composed of a dialogue prior to the art activity, a time that is usually enriched with visual images for analysis—for example, actual objects, posed models (perhaps in a costume), and photographs, for instance, of horses that show close-up views, horses

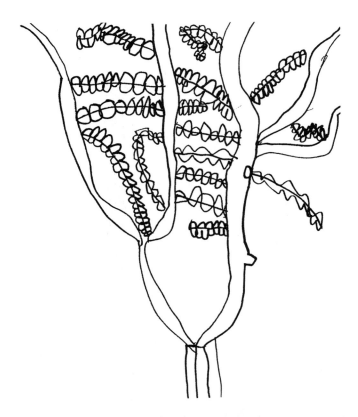

Figure 5.4 **Jacob,** *Tree.*
Seven-year-old Jacob used a viewfinder to define the detailed portion of a tree that he observed on the playground.

engaged in a number of activities, and so on. Other strategies may include a visually stimulating story, song, or poem that motivates the child to imagine and fantasize while listening to the selection and then to draw or paint an expressive response to it. Some strategies may involve remembering and discussing the details of an experience the students have had and recalling where it took place, how they were dressed, who was there, what action may have been involved, and so on.

Regularly and sequentially presented motivational strategies allow children to repeat and sharpen their skills with each art material through repeated use. They provide an environment that nurtures each child's artistic potential. Regular and sequential art lessons allow students to create images based on their perceptions, the life experiences of their culture, and the events and objects of importance in their world.

To produce and respond to artworks, students need guidance in how to see and select with finer discrimination. The sequential growth of manipulative skills requires time and instruction. If media are changed too often, students will never master the world of tools and materials. Understanding the nature and degree of assistance that each student needs requires teacher observation of individual children.

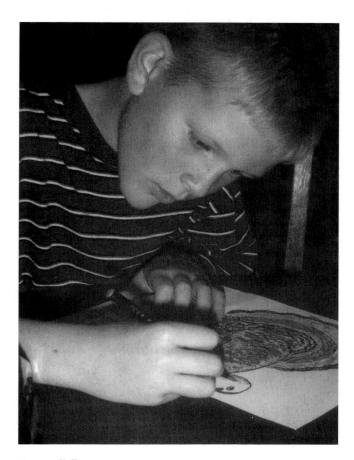

Figure 5.5 Jesse, age 11, uses his observation skills and concentrates on feather patterns as he draws his turkey at Murwood Elementary School. *Photo by Harry Marsh.*

Keeping a portfolio of each student's work to assess progress over the school year is helpful. In this way, the teacher can note if developmental stages—for example, with regard to depictions of figures, houses, and space—are in general alignment with those expected at that age level. For instance, a child who draws rather realistic figures running and throwing a football, but who persists in drawing the sky as a strip across the top of the paper, may be helped by the teacher to see clouds moving along behind the treetops.

Teacher-student conversations need to be ongoing while children are drawing. A teacher may notice that a child continues to draw very small objects even though the paper is quite large. This usually signals a lack of confidence or knowledge about, and perceptual experience with, the subject. The teacher can help such students to realize how much more they actually know or feel about the subject in a technique called *accretion*, which means extending, expanding, or adding onto the original tiny figure, house, or animal that the child has drawn.[6] Questioning strategies can direct the child's attention, memory, or perception: "What a fine rabbit! Do you remember what Alice did when she saw the rab-

bit? How tall was Alice? How big was the rabbit? Where was the hole she fell through? What happened next?" and so on. Or "You made the lion look like he's roaring. Good for you! When we went to the zoo, do you remember what the lion's cage looked like? How big was it? Was there a tree in the cage? Was there another lion? How large was he? What animals were to the left and to the right of the cage? Where did you walk next? What else did you see?" and so on.

In summary, children have the inborn capacity to transform their primary means of knowing—that is, their experiences of feeling, thinking, and perceiving—into unique art forms. Strategies may have one or more emphases, which culminate in the child's art product. The activity may focus on and underscore the following:

1. Direct observation of objects (still lifes, posed figures, landscapes).

2. Recalling past experiences (when we visited the zoo).

3. Having empathy (if I were a grasshopper; if I were a parachute jumper).

4. Becoming involved with the formal aspects of the elements and principles of art (collage using only geometric shapes).

5. Delving into diverse cultures as well as one's own art heritage (cut paper such as papel picado from Mexico).

6. Exploring feelings, fantasy, and the imagination (a trip to Mars).

7. Being inventive and experimental with art materials (wood scraps and glue).

8. Integrating the art activity with other areas of the curriculum (social studies, language arts, science, math).

9. Creating art in the manner of a particular artist or school of art (painting a flower as Georgia O'Keeffe did or painting a cubist-type portrait).

10. Visually and imaginatively interpreting a song, poem, or story.

While a strong self-motivation can transform perceptions, feelings, and thoughts into an art form, the teacher usually needs to provide the arena for the students and to help them order their impressions and concepts. In responding to a strategy, students are challenged to reflect, to observe, to imagine, and to form ideas. They are encouraged to be inventive, imaginative, and original. They are guided in exercising judgment and self-discipline as they choose and arrange their visual images.

A strategy that calls on students to remember, imagine, and observe what they see—as well as to give visual form to their observations and feelings about objects, figures, and places—may include the following:

1. A theme or subject that is clear to the students at the outset.

2. An open-ended discussion with students that activates thoughts and feelings that they already have about the subject and also provides them with new information. This interaction encourages children's imaginative responses, helping them reflect on thoughts and feelings before they create their artwork.

3. A discussion on perception can direct students to observe what they see more closely—perceiving differences and similarities of shapes, colors, lines, proportions, angles, and so on. Teachers will find it helpful to use real objects, posed models, or a variety of photographs that relate to the motivation. Visual information is essential when children make art; therefore, students need to perceive the many different colors, shapes, sizes, and patterns seen in nature. Students may surf the Internet to seek out visual information for the subject or theme they are analyzing. Photographic images can provide a vast wealth of information to assist children with their visual thinking about:
    a) The many varieties of a single subject (houses, animals, trees, birds, flowers, etc.) for comparing shapes, sizes, colors, and patterns.
    b) Details, via close-ups, that could be perceived no other way.
    c) The subject engaged in a variety of activities—birds, for instance, feeding the young in a nest, flying, and so on.

4. Thought-provoking questions, comments, and observations can help students formulate plans for what they will select from what they see and feel, and how they will arrange their compositions. Each student individualizes information gathered from visual research—whether the research involved a posed model, an object, or a photographic file—as he or she chooses, changes, combines, and deletes shapes, sizes, colors, lines, and textures in creating a personal and unique solution to the motivational challenge.

5. Reproductions of artworks that relate to the subject, theme, medium, or technique can involve students in description, analysis, and interpretation. They also introduce students to the concept that artists from diverse cultures have many ways to make art that focus on similar themes.

The following six guided tours are model lesson plans designed to elicit a variety of open-ended approaches for lower- and upper-grades art activities. Students will have the opportunity to increase their art skills while integrating the lesson with another area of the curriculum. The strategies are structured in the following format:

Focus—mapping the directions, concepts, and skills that will be covered.

Curriculum Integration—relating the art activity to literature, science, math, and so on.

The Journey—explaining, commenting, informing, and providing directions to assure that students understand the focus of the lesson and how to handle the art materials.

Side Trips—spin-off lessons, reproductions, and books that are related to the focus.

The Destination—in which the student is challenged to make a personal assessment of his or her artwork, based on (1) the degree of technical skill (Did I handle the brush and paint well?); (2) organizing the artwork (Did I show a variety of shapes and colors and achieve unity?); (3) emotional qualities (What feeling does one have when looking at my artwork?); and (4) creative imagination (In what way did I show inventiveness and originality?).

STUDENTS' GUIDED TOURS: Lower Grades

Lesson 1

Cobbler Clooney and the Art of Storytelling

See Colorplate 7 in Children's Gallery.

Focus: Mapping the Directions

Students will collect shoes as well as find pictures of shoes in magazines and books to discover how styles have changed or stayed the same throughout history. They will learn that before there were books, people listened to storytellers. They will listen to "The Story of Cobbler Clooney" while they visualize the images presented and then make a drawing of themselves wearing an imaginative pair of shoes.

They will use broad and fine-line markers on a piece of white drawing paper, about 6-by-18-inches, which is large enough for a standing figure plus space to emphasize the shoes.

Curriculum Integration

Literature: Storytellers in cultures throughout the world have been important members of society. Through their stories they have passed on legends and tales that tell of past events. In recent years storytelling has been revived, and in almost every community can be found individuals who are skilled in telling stories at special events. Some stories have been written down, and library books may be searched for such tales.

The Journey

Shoes tell us of where and how people lived, if they were rich or poor, and sometimes what kind of work they did. There are several museums dedicated entirely to shoes. A Roman empress might wear a pair of sandals with soles of gold. A Chinese woman in the nineteenth century embroidered her own silk slippers. Today, people who work on buildings and bridges protect their feet with leather boots that have steel toes. There are different shoes for different sports. Sometimes shoes are made and worn just for fun and would be very difficult for walking. Long ago, a shoemaker, sometimes called a *cobbler*, would use his special tools to make shoes, sandals, or boots. Early American settlers' shoes were made the same for both feet, that is, not a right and a left.

Look at the different shoes or pictures of shoes and make comparisons. Find shoes made from cloth, plastic, rubber, leather, or wood. Find shoes with high heels, low heels, or no heels. Do you see shoes with laces, buttons, straps, or buckles? Find shoes that would be suitable for running, dancing, or hiking.

Mr. Clooney, the cobbler of Crockerville, made all kinds of shoes for all kinds of people. He was a tall, thin man with a moustache that twitched when he talked, and he wore glasses that sat on the middle of his nose. His leather apron had pockets of all sizes and shapes that were filled with tools he used for making shoes. He made shoes with strings and straps, laces and cuffs, buckles and flaps. He made shoes with eyes and tongues, and heels and soles; shoes that were high and shoes that were low; and even shoes that were open-toed.

Listen to the following story and then make a drawing of yourself wearing special shoes.

> Cobbler Clooney made shoes for everyone in Crockerville—boots for hiking, slippers for dancing, and shoes for running. But Cobbler Clooney was tired of making the same kind of shoes. He wanted some new ideas. One day as he walked past the schoolyard, the children stopped playing to call hello to their friend. That's when Cobbler Clooney was struck with an idea! He told the children of his dilemma—that he needed new ideas for making shoes. All the children started to speak at once. "I want shoes with bright blue feathers." "I want shoes of pink and green leather." "I want shoes with zebra stripes." "I want shoes that will help me dance all night." "I want shoes that will make me jump." "I want shoes like an elephant's." "I want shoes that sparkle and glitter." "I want shoes that are long and slithery." "I want shoes that will match my hat." "I want boots for a rainy day." "I want purple polka-dot shoes just for play." "I want shoes with pockets and secret places, shoes with wings to take me places." "I want slippers with precious jewels." "I want shoes of rainbow hues." "I want shoes to store a snack." "I want shoes with matching socks." "I want slippers that are warm and fuzzy." "I want shoes that tell the time." "I want shoes that help me climb." Cobbler Clooney laughed and said, "I can't remember all these wonderful ideas." So he told the children to draw themselves wearing the pair of shoes that they dreamed of owning.

Choose a fine-line marker and draw a picture of yourself wearing a very special pair of shoes. Draw your head near the top of your paper, add your body, arms, and legs, saving enough space near the bottom for your shoes. Draw clothing that matches your shoes. Use broad markers, holding them on their sides, making strokes that are close together, to fill in large areas such as clothing and a big hat—and fine-line markers for details on your face or designs on your shoes. When your drawing is finished tell your classmates the story of your shoes.

Side Trips

Students may make up their own imaginative stories, perhaps about a special kind of train, a caterpillar, or snake that would fit a long horizontal format. Students should look at photos of the subject they have chosen (trains, caterpillars, or snakes) in order to become familiar with the main shapes, colors, and parts. They then illustrate one part of the story, using crayons or oil pastels and finishing with a watercolor wash. Use reproductions or look in books to find such imaginative works as *Feathers in Bloom*, Marc Chagall; *Tar Beach*, Faith Ringgold; *Head of a Man*, Paul Klee; or similar fantasy artworks. Look how these artists used their imagination and pretended. The children in Ringgold's quilt-painting are on a rooftop on a hot summer night. See how the little girl imagines herself flying above the bridge. Chagall combined things in *Feathers in Bloom* that don't really exist: blossoms for a rooster's tail and human feet on a blue donkey. Paul Klee's *Head of a Man* looks more like a balloon because of its shapes and warm bright colors.

Destination: Personal Assessment

1. Where did I use broad markers for big areas and fine markers to show details? Did I fill in any large areas with broad strokes all going in one direction rather than scribbling?

2. What warm or cool colors did I use, and how did I repeat them?

3. What is the feeling expressed by my self-portrait—silly, fright, happiness, and so on?

4. How are my shoes different from others? What did I do to make them special?

Lesson 2
A Teapot Still Life

Focus: Mapping the Directions

Students will make a still-life drawing of a teapot, using close direct observation. They will use watercolors to paint their teapot. They will learn how several famous artists painted still-life subjects realistically or abstractly, and they will learn of the tea ceremony that is part of Japanese culture.

Curriculum Integration

Social Studies: The elaborate four-hour tea ceremony ritual is performed in a small wooden teahouse in a Japanese garden. It is believed to have its roots in the sixteenth century. Guests are served special foods and then invited to stroll in the garden, admire Japanese painted scrolls or traditional flower arrangements called *ikibana*. Then they sit quietly in

Figure 5.6 Kathryn, age 6, sat closely to the teapot, rendering what she observed with a black marker and then painting with watercolors.

the teahouse as a tea master uses special utensils to carefully prepare two servings of tea called *thick tea* and *thin tea*. As the guests sip their tea and engage in conversation with one another, they feel relaxed and calm as they reflect on the beauty of the art, the garden, and the preparation of tea.

The Journey

Students will need a school-grade piece of watercolor paper, 8-by-10-inches, or a piece of white drawing paper, 9-by-12-inches; practice paper; pencil; set of school watercolors; container for water; paper towels; watercolor brushes (small and medium); and a fine black permanent marker. A selection of teapots, one for each four to six students.

Students will be introduced to still lifes and learn that they are made up of objects that don't move, usually arranged on a table top. Citizens in seventeenth-century Holland delighted in decorating their homes with still-life paintings that reflected their own possessions. Later some artists used still lifes to "trick the eye" and make the viewer believe that the objects were actually there and not a painting. In recent years, artists have used still lifes for abstract paintings.

Students will observe, draw, and paint a teapot and learn about the Japanese tea ceremony. Sit close to a teapot and observe its basic shape, including the sizes of the handle, the spout, and the lid. Look for the curving edges of the shapes, and use a pencil very lightly to carefully draw the teapot and any inside designs you see. Your teapot should almost touch

all four sides of your paper. Use a fine black marker and draw over the pencil lines that you want to keep. Then use watercolors to complete your artwork.

The teacher will demonstrate the following techniques for using watercolors:

- Moisten the watercolor cakes with a few drops of water.
- Choose three or four colors. Mixing two colors together will make a third color.
- To make a wash: Load the brush with water and place it in the lid of the watercolor box. Then dip the brush in a color and add it to the water. Apply one or more washes to the drawing.
- For darker colors, use more paint; for lighter colors, use more water.
- To use a smaller brush, dip the tip in a little clean water and then dip it into a color. Paint lines and details on top of the dry wash unless you wish the colors to run together.
- Let painting dry and iron on the backside to flatten before mounting or matting.

Side Trips

Students may have their own tea ceremony patterned after the Japanese and invite their parents to visit the class. *Artistic Trickery: The Tradition of Trompe L'Oeil Art* by Michael Capek shows examples by William Harnett, John F. Peto, and others of this amazing way of painting in which the still-life objects depicted appear to be real rather than painted on a flat surface. Look at reproductions of books containing still-life paintings by Jan van Huysum, who painted very realistically in the early eighteenth century; Paul Cezanne, who tirelessly painted fruit and jugs on table tops to show their solidity; Pablo Picasso and Georges Braque, who turned their still-lifes into cubist abstractions; and pop artists such as Andy Warhol and Wayne Thiebaud, who depicted familiar foods and objects from everyday life.

Destination: Personal Assessment

1. Where did I use washes of color? How was I skillful in using a fine brush?
2. What kinds of lines did I make to create variety and interest?
3. What is the feeling of my teapot—elegant and formal, or whimsical and funny? Does it look like an animal or bird?
4. What colors did I mix to make a new color?

Lesson 3

Circus Clowns, Geometry, and Fractional Parts

See Colorplate 8 in Children's Gallery.

Focus: Mapping the Directions

Students will select from an assortment of precut geometric shapes: circles, squares, rectangles, and triangles, of varying sizes and colors; 12-by-18-inch background paper; scissors; paper edgers; paper punches; and glue sticks. They will be encouraged to learn fractional parts by cutting some of the shapes, as needed, into halves and quarters.

Curriculum Integration

Mathematics: Students will learn to identify and use basic geometric shapes (circles, squares, rectangles, triangles). They will also learn about fractional parts by cutting one of these shapes in two equal parts to create halves and cutting one of these shapes in four equal parts to create quarters.

Students will look at photographs of clowns in action poses and compare the different parts of the clowns' bodies and costumes to basic geometric shapes—perhaps a medium-size circle or oval for the head, a large rectangle for the torso, a triangle for a hat, or a rectangle cut in half for arms and legs. They will become aware that clown costumes are made of bright colors that attract our attention. Students will brainstorm clown acts: juggling balls, riding a unicycle, jumping rope, flying on a trapeze, twirling an umbrella, turning a cartwheel, or performing tricks with a small dog. After they have selected a variety of geometric shapes of different sizes and colors they will be encouraged to show action and movement by using diagonals and by making right angles for elbows and knees. They may use humorous

exaggeration by enlarging the hands, feet, and facial features. Paper-edger scissors and hole punches may be used for the costume and props. After they have arranged the geometric shapes and fractional parts that make up their clown on a paper of contrasting color, they will use a glue stick to adhere the pieces. Letting the figure extend off the paper at a slight angle helps emphasize the action.

Side Trips

Look in books for paintings by Pablo Picasso and Georges Braque who worked together more than 100 years ago to create a style of painting called cubism. They would take their subjects apart—such as a still life or a person—and reassemble them, using cubes and basic geometric shapes. These two artists also practiced the art of *collage* (a French word meaning "to paste").

Write a haiku about clowns (a Japanese poem with three lines: the first line has five syllables; the second, seven syllables; and the third, five syllables).

Destination: Personal Assessment

1. Where did I effectively and skillfully cut and divide a geometric shape to make two or four fractional parts?
2. How did I create details on my clown's costume?
3. Where are diagonal shapes that create a feeling of action and excitement?
4. What parts of my clown did I distort or exaggerate to make him humorous?

STUDENTS' GUIDED TOURS: Upper Grades

Lesson 4

Butterflies and Microscopes

See Colorplate 5 in Children's Gallery.

Focus: Mapping the Directions

Students will use the negative space of a circle, pretending it is a microscope or magnifying glass, selecting a detail of a photograph of a butterfly wing or a model of a butterfly. They will enlarge the shapes and patterns first on a 9-inch circle of cardboard and then use tempera paint for the colors.

Curriculum Integration

Science: Scientists observe the world very closely and in detail. They sometimes use a microscope or magnifying glass to help them see things that are small. Many scientists make drawings of the things they see. There are many different kinds of butterflies, all with different patterns and colors on their wings. Look in a reference book to find what they are named.

The Journey

Each student needs a large photograph of a butterfly or some artificial butterflies, a piece of black paper with a 2- or 3-inch circle cut from it. This may be accomplished by drawing around a plastic cup and cutting out the circle. Each student needs a 9- or 10-inch circle of white cardboard (cake-decorating stores) or heavy paper, tempera, and brushes. Children will pretend that they are entomologists (scientists who study insects) and move their small circles around on the photograph of the butterfly or on the artificial one until they find a part of it that they like. They then draw that detail on the 9- or 10-inch circle, perceiving its patterns and including the repeated shapes. Note the colors and paint it with tempera.

Side Trips

Martin Heade was an artist who observed nature very closely and made very realistic paintings. One of his paintings showed orchids and hummingbirds. John James Audubon carefully painted hundreds of birds, placing them in their natural environment and in lifelike positions. Paul Klee has painted abstract fish, basing their shapes and patterns on his observations. Find pictures in reference books that these artists have made. Oceanographers study fish. Wouldn't it be fun to snorkel and see a world of different shapes and kinds of fish? Look in books to see the many varieties of sea life. Then cut out a fish from tagboard or manila folders. Make it about 6 or 8 inches long. Paste on details, such as fins, scales, and eyes. Then use a brayer and water-soluble printing ink and make a print. Cut it out and paste it along with those of your classmates on a "water" (paper) background.

Destination: Personal Assessment

1. Did I handle the brush and paint well?
2. Did I show a variety of shapes and colors and achieve unity?
3. What feeling does one have when looking at my artwork?
4. What did I do that is unique and shows ingenuity?

Lesson 5

The Figure in Action and Jacob Lawrence

See Colorplate 6 in Children's Gallery.

Focus: Mapping the Directions

Students will make a cut-and-torn-paper collage based on a 16-piece manikin of a person in an action pose. Students will learn the basics of realistic body proportion as well as how exaggeration and diagonal lines and shapes can suggest movement and emotion. They will explore how Jacob Lawrence exaggerated or distorted the torso and emphasized the hands and feet. Torn-paper clothing will add to the design interest as well as emphasizing the sense of despair and poverty in the life of a black slave. Fine white lines will be used for contrast and details.

Curriculum Integration

Social Studies: Students will study the life and work of African-American artist Jacob Lawrence (Colorplate 35) and his depictions of black history in the United States. They will make a collage of a figure in action. Jacob Lawrence painted a series about his heroes such as Toussaint L'Ouverture, who freed Haiti from slavery; Frederick Douglass, a slave who learned to read and write and spent his life working against slavery; Harriet Tubman, who escaped and risked her life to free 300 slaves via the Underground Railroad, which had safe places to hide and rest; and John Brown, who believed he had been chosen by God to overthrow slavery in America. Many of Lawrence's paintings show entertainers, dancers, basketball players, and people at work using a variety of tools.

The Journey

Students will need a 6-by-9-inch piece of tagboard or manila folder to make a manikin showing a frontal or profile view; they will also need bond or copy paper, glue stick, scissors, a newspaper pad, and an unwrapped black crayon. For the clothed figure they will need dark multicultural skin-tone paper, bright-colored paper for clothing and background, and white gel markers.

Their collage pictures will be in the manner of Jacob Lawrence (1917–2000), a black American artist who has shown us an important segment of U.S. history by championing his people and their stories of enslavement and freedom, their migration north, and the Harlem Renaissance. He used bright, flat areas of color and added fine white lines to bring attention to the facial expressions and to add details on the hands and feet.

Place the tagboard manikin as described in Chapter 3 in a working pose on a piece of 8½-by-11-inch copy paper. The figure may be chopping wood, picking cotton, wielding a pick, balancing a bale of cotton, washing clothes in a tub, hoeing, hammering and sawing wood, reaching, or lifting. Remember to use diagonal lines and shapes to show action. Students posing for each other is helpful. Emphasize the hands and feet by making them large. Use a glue stick to adhere the figure to copy paper. To make a crayon rubbing, place another piece of copy paper on top of the figure. Then place both papers on a pad of newspaper and use the side of a black crayon, rubbing carefully in short strokes in one direction to reveal the figure. Staple the rubbing to a piece of skin-tone paper and cut it out, rounding the elbows and knees.

Now dress the figure with pants, a shirt, dress, or blouse and skirt. To do this, place the figure on a piece of colored paper and with a very light pencil line draw the outline of the clothing. Clothes should fit loosely, leaving a little space between the body and the clothes. Use a pinch-and-tear technique, keeping your fingers close together for control, and slowly tear out the shapes for clothes. Glue your cut-and-torn-paper figure on a contrasting background color. Add hair, perhaps a hat, patches on clothing, and so forth. Cut out a farmer's or carpenter's tool, a bale of cotton or other items to complete the composition. Remember that the figure is the dominant shape and focal point of your composition. Use fine white lines to draw facial features that might express an emotion or define fingers and details on clothing.

Side Trips

Check your library for these books and others about Jacob Lawrence:

American Scenes, American Struggles by Nancy Shroyer Howard

Story Painter: The Life of Jacob Lawrence by John Duggleby

Harriet and the Promised Land by Jacob Lawrence

Create an international parade of Olympic athletes. Pose your manikin in running, jumping, or leaping position and make a rubbing. Add clothing, and staple two or three thin pieces of colored copy paper and cut out all figures at once to make silhouettes. Glue all figures in a parade on a long piece of background paper. Add cut-paper flags from around the world and a cut-paper caption.

Destination: Personal Assessment

1. Did I achieve a realistic use of proportion in making my figure? Is the head in proportion to the torso? Did I exaggerate any part of the body? Why?

2. Where did I use diagonal shapes to express movement, action, or an emotion?

3. What in my composition captures a feeling—despair, hardship, fright, and so on?

4. How did I show unity and balance with my use of colored paper?

Lesson 6
King-Size Puppets Based on Australian Aboriginal Art and Myths

Focus: Mapping the Direction

After reading the Australian Aboriginal myth "The Drought-maker," students will make large painted paper puppets (Figure 5.7) to represent the main characters. They will learn how to use tempera paint and stiff bristle brushes to make line designs and patterns. They will base their puppets on the indigenous animals of Australia and how Aboriginal artists make bark paintings. They will also be introduced to the history of puppetry.

Curriculum Integration

Social Studies: For hundreds of years, the Aboriginal artists of Australia have made vibrant and intricately patterned paintings of animals and designs on tree bark that is prepared and used like an artist's canvas. Paints are made from colored clays, burnt wood, and plants; paintbrushes are made from fiber, hair, pounded sticks, and feathers. Sometimes these paintings are used for special ceremonies and

then destroyed. Today, they are in museum collections. Both sides of the puppet should be painted.

History of Puppetry: Tracing back to the Egyptians, puppets are enjoyed by children and adults in many cultures and countries using a variety of materials and techniques. Story legends and myths from Africa, North America, Asia, and Europe bring characters to life with puppets made from clay, fabric, wood, or paper.

The Journey

Students will study photographs of the animals in the story as well as seeing the Aboriginal style of design illustrated in "The Droughtmaker" and other books on Aboriginal art. They will then draw their puppet-animal with chalk on a large piece of brown wrapping paper, 24 inches wide, that is stapled to another piece of paper of the same size. Students will study the shapes that make up the body of the animal they have chosen for their puppet and lightly draw it on the

Figure 5.7 A king-size puppet based on a folktale is being finished by this young student as she applies decorative dots and lines in the manner of the Australian Aborigine's paintings.
Photo by Maureen Gilli.

Figure 5.8 These clay Mudheads by fifth graders were the result of an art lesson that was integrated with a study of Southwestern Indians. Students combined pinch pots with slab-constructed cylinders.
Photo by Barbara Herberholz.

One of the dancers is called a Mudhead and is the designated clown of the dance. Students can make a Mudhead using clay (Figure 5.8) rather than the traditional carved wood. They will roll out about half of the clay to make a cylinder about 1½ inches in diameter and about 6 inches long. Use the edge of a stick to divide half of the cylinder lengthwise to form the legs. Use the remainder of clay to make a ball shape for the head, and roll shapes for arms, hands, and feet. Bond clay parts together with slip before pressing together and smoothing the joints. Make a clay skirt and headpiece, and use a toothpick to poke holes in the top of the head for adding feathers after it is fired. Position your Mudhead in a clown-like pose, making sure it is stable enough to stand up. Mudheads may be painted or glazed or simply left bisque.

Destination: Personal Assessment

1. Where was I skillful in capturing a likeness of the animal? The shape of the head? The position of the legs? The type of tail—long, short, or bushy?

2. How are the painted patterns most like that of the original Aboriginal art?

3. What parts of my animal will look the most alive as a puppet? The expression on the face? The bending legs or long swishy tail?

4. Where did I use a different pattern or color scheme that is unusual, and how is it effective? Did I accent the eyes? How did I unify the puppet with a pattern?

double thickness of brown paper, making sure that it almost touches all four sides of the paper. After cutting their animal out through both thicknesses of paper, they will use two or three colors of tempera paint plus black and white. To avoid diluting the paint with water, students should wipe their brush with a sponge or paper towel after rinsing it in water. Students may use a separate piece of paper to practice painting outlines, curving lines, and combinations of thick and thin lines and dots in the Aboriginal style. To assemble, staple the puppet together, leaving an opening large enough to stuff with tissue paper. Insert an 18-inch stick into the puppet for support and to create a handle, then staple and glue it in place. Students may wear black or neutral colors when they perform with their puppets to make the puppets the center of interest.

Side Trips

Students are introduced to pictures of or actual Kachina dolls carved by the Hopi artists of the American southwest.

ASSESSING THE ARTWORKS OF ELEMENTARY STUDENTS

In responding to and evaluating students' artistic growth, elementary teachers should plan on brief discussion periods with small groups or with individual students. Artistic growth is best measured by each student's individual progress rather than a comparison with other students' work. It would be counterproductive to single out one or two students' works as the best or the worst; rather, focus on the following four areas:

1. *The degree of technical skill seen in the artwork.* This is the extent to which the student has demonstrated increasing mastery in handling and controlling a given material. For example, do artworks have puddles of excessive paint? Do cut-paper collages show evidence of messy glue handling? Artworks should be evaluated on the basis of increasing skills over time. Very young children are not expected to be highly developed in controlling materials, but an improvement in this area, along with a desire to develop more control, are suitable areas to evaluate.

2. *The manner in which the student has organized the artwork.* This has to do with artistic considerations related to the elements and principles of design. When variety and unity are seen in an artwork, the colors, lines, shapes, and so on give us a feeling of completeness. The different parts are organized so that the work offers a feeling of wholeness, balance, and harmony.

3. *The extent to which the student has shown feelings and emotional qualities in the artwork.* This has to do with the expressive qualities of showing happiness, sadness, anger, and so on in an artwork. It is governed not only by color choices and the expressive use of lines and shapes but by the subject matter as well.

4. *The degree of creative imagination and ingenuity that the student has shown.* This is seen when a student makes unusual connections, relating two ordinarily unrelated ideas, or when a student depicts an original theme, worked in a humorous or insightful way, or finds a fresh new way to express an idea, solve a visual problem, or use a material.

Comparing the artworks of several children in a negative manner is inappropriate, but teachers can use questioning strategies when students complete a project to help each student understand not only what is pleasing and good about his or her product but also what important things happened during the process of making the artwork. Teachers will find that some of the following questions are helpful after an art activity. Select questions from this list that apply to the focus of the art lesson. First, guide students to reflect on the process they have undergone in making their art. Then ask them to talk about the successful aspects of their art products and to evaluate those aspects that could be improved.

Helping Students to Perceive and Reflect on Their Artwork

Process

Before you began drawing, what contours (edges), darks and lights, shapes, and colors did you observe when you took a careful look at the object (horse, tree, figure, flower) that you were going to draw?

Where did you think about placing it on the paper before you started? Did you play around with your idea, maybe making a sketch before you started?

What new ways to work with this art material did you discover?

In what ways did you improve your skill in handling this medium?

How long did you work at your artwork? Longer than you usually do? Would you like to repeat this activity? Why or why not?

When you stopped to take a critical look while you were working, what did you discover?

How would you draw this subject another time?

What artist do you know who painted this same theme or used this medium?

Product

Did you keep the format of your paper in mind? How would you change your composition to fill spaces and allow some lines to extend off the paper?

How did you make your negative spaces interesting?

What shape of paper would fit this picture better—tall paper, larger paper, smaller paper?

Did you make the figures or important shapes large enough for your idea?

How could you make the ground, sky, or background more interesting?

What other details could you include to tell what you had in mind?

What is your center of interest? How did you make it a focal point?

What colors give your picture the feeling you wanted? Would you use the same colors next time?

How did you show variety—in sizes, shapes, colors, line thicknesses, patterns, and so on?

What makes your composition feel balanced? Or does it feel balanced?

How did you show contrast—texture, color, value, shape?

Would some exaggeration or distortion have helped to create a stronger emotion?

How did you show deep space? Are distant objects higher up and smaller?

What parts of your picture did you make in a new or different way?

If you could make this picture again, what would you change?

SETTING UP FOR DIRECT OBSERVATION

1. Sit comfortably close to the subject matter to perceive its details and relationships of its parts. Try moving your chair until you have an interesting point of view.

2. Use a viewfinder (Figure 2.27) to help you frame your composition. This will help you select your subject and place it within the format of your paper. The positive shapes bump the sides of the viewfinder, creating negative spaces that you can draw on your paper. Viewfinders eliminate distracting, irrelevant, and confusing elements in the environment.

3. Have the supplies you will need conveniently at hand.

4. Take time for a visual analysis of the subject matter:
   Look at the proportions and the relationships of sizes of various parts: larger than, smaller than, twice as tall as, wider than, the same as, and so on.
   Look at the relationship of the locations of parts: halfway up, to the left of, below, in the upper right, in front of, behind, overlapping, and so on.
   Look for inner and outer contour lines and angles.
   Look for significant basic shapes of the principal objects and then of smaller parts of those objects: cones, circles, squares, rectangles, cylinders, and so on.
   Look for different colors and different values of each color: Where is the red darker?
   Where is the lightest area?
   Look for different patterns: repeated shapes and lines, regular or irregular repeats.
   Look for cast shadows.

5. Decide if you will make a highly realistic artwork, interpreting what you see in a personal way. For instance, if you apply paint with little overlapping daubs to create a feeling of sparkling sunlight, you will be painting as the impressionists did. If you apply your paint with tiny dots, placing several colors so close together that your eyes blend the colors, you will be painting as the pointillists did. You may create a fantasy, painting in a realistic manner but creating an unlikely relationship or environment, as surrealists do. You may choose to work like an expressionist, emphasizing the mood and emotion of your subject matter. Or you may focus on creating a more abstract artwork, emphasizing the formal aspects of color, line, shape, texture, and so on. If you break up what you see into planes and cubes, creating a new structure from several viewpoints, you will be working as the cubists do.

6. You may exaggerate and distort. You may change and delete and repeat what you see. You, the artist, will make decisions as you compose your artwork—selecting, refining, combining, eliminating, and repeating the elements you need to give meaning to your artwork and to create balance, pattern, direction, emphasis, and movement.

7. Make several different drawings or paintings of the subject matter, changing your viewpoint and trying to see it in a different way each time.

Still Lifes

Still lifes are drawings or paintings of objects that do not move—books, candles, pitchers, musical instruments, baskets, containers, toys, fruit, vegetables, flowers, and such—usually arranged on a table top. Still lifes have been a popular subject for artists for many years. An old legend tells of a Greek painter in the fifth century B.C. who painted a bunch of grapes that looked so real that birds tried to peck them.

The expression "still life" appeared about 1650 in Holland, where artists loved to use vivid accuracy. Citizens in seventeenth-century Holland delighted in decorating their homes with beautiful still-life paintings that reflected their possessions. These still-life objects were often selected for their symbolic value, reminding the viewer not only to remember death and the passage of time, but also to celebrate life. A number of still lifes of this time made symbolic references to the five senses. A later group of artists used still lifes to "trick the eye" and make the viewer believe that the objects in the composition were actually there and not painted.

In the nineteenth century, Paul Cézanne used still lifes in his search for ways to show solidity. He spent a great deal of time arranging the fruit and objects he was going to paint, stacking some of them on coins so they would be high enough for the effect he wished to create in his composition. Then the cubists took still lifes apart, viewed them from several directions, and reconstructed them in geometric shapes. Recently, pop artists have used common, ordinary, but popular objects for their subjects.

Artists who paint still lifes are interested in the shapes and colors they see before them. They look carefully at the objects and determine relationships, proportions, and angles so that their pictures have unity, balance, and harmony, whether painted in a realistic manner or not. See Maria Winkler's painting of marbles in Colorplate 40.

1. A still life may be just one object, or it may be made up of several items. Collect a variety of items that appeal to you for a resource bank for still-life setups. The following are suggested because of the variety of their shapes, colors, and textures and because they appeal to most people:

    Fruits and vegetables (real or artificial): Gourds, pumpkins, squash, apples, citrus fruits, grapes, mushrooms, cross sections of oranges or cabbages, eggplants, broccoli, cauliflower, potatoes.

    Flowers and plants: Cacti, fresh flowers, twigs, dried plants, silk plants.

    Containers: Bottles, jars, jugs, teapots, pitchers, bowls, ceramic items, baskets.

    Tools, implements: Spoons, typewriters, hammers, pliers, C-clamps, wrenches, can openers.

    Other items: Musical instruments, dolls, toys, gloves, hats, shoes, assorted antiques, feathers, butterflies, bones, shells, driftwood, mounted birds and animals, pieces of candy, ribbons, books.

    Backdrops: Butcher paper, felt, fabric (plain, patterned, striped, textured), blankets, shawls, beach towels, sheets.

    Lighting: Floor lamp or tripod with strong bulb placed on one side to create shadows.

2. Hang the backdrop on the wall behind the table, and let it drape over the surface in a smooth or slightly rumpled manner. Backdrops eliminate distracting elements and can provide an interesting pattern for your still-life background. They also help unify the composition.

3. Select several items of differing height and width for your still-life setup. Balance something tall with several items close together. Balance something large with several smaller items. Try several combinations, moving and rearranging until you have a pleasing and unified composition. Strive for a satisfying relationship of proportions. Let some objects stand in front of others. You may want to group and isolate some items. Select objects with a variety of textures and colors.

4. For making value studies and drawings in which the emphasis is on showing modeling and basic forms, spray with white paint items such as the following: plastic maple syrup jugs, bottles, rolling pins, croquet balls, square and rectangular blocks of wood or styrofoam, pinecones, seashells, old cowboy boots, and so on. This eliminates color and helps students to concentrate on drawing, shading, and showing modeling through tonal values.

5. When the class is drawing a single object, such as a turkey feather, pliers, wrench, or car keys, rather than an arrangement of still-life objects, each student should have an object in order to be very close to it. A magnifying glass provides a close-up look at details and makes for a larger-than-life composition of such small items as insects, seed pods, and so on. A curved reflecting mirror can provide a pleasingly distorted image that is interesting to draw.

6. After choosing and arranging your materials, find the best viewpoint. Then use your viewfinder to focus on your composition, and orient the viewfinder to the format of your drawing paper. Make several quick thumbnail sketches of the outlines that the shapes as a mass make, shading in the solid parts. This will help you see the positive and negative shapes, their relation to the background, and their position on the paper. Next, consider the individual shapes of the objects, drawing the contours of each as they overlap one another.

7. Blocking in the main vertical, horizontal, and diagonal lines often helps you get started. Then you can draw in the entire shape of the object or objects and more carefully delineate the roundness and contours. Observe the shapes that cast shadows make. Add details that characterize each object: the delicate gills on a mushroom, the woven texture of a basket. Add any decorative patterns you see in the backdrop. Use hatching, cross-hatching, stippling, and blending to create a modeled form. You might try filling in the background solidly to accent the individual shapes in the still life.

Costumed Models

The figure has long been an important subject matter for artists to draw, paint, and sculpt. In both Western and non-Western cultures, artists have depicted portraits and the full figure. The mother and child have been a favorite subject. Paintings of royalty recorded the power and dignity of the ruler, with artists often being employed as official court painters. National heroes, as well as gods and goddesses, were frequent subject matter. Families often had their portraits painted to record likenesses. In Japan, artists frequently depicted the figure in interior views of homes.

In the Western world, certain artists are well known for their paintings of people. Rembrandt, for instance, wanted to show more than a likeness when he painted a portrait; he wanted to show the person's character. Modigliani stretched and elongated faces and figures to achieve his distinctive style. Expressionist artists showed strong emotions and feelings in their portraits, while the fauves chose wildly unrealistic colors when they painted people. Cubists distorted the figure and showed it from several viewpoints all at once.

Students need to make careful observations when they are drawing—noting proportions, relationships, angles, and contour lines.

1. Have the model wear several costume items, dressing as a character from literature, history, or another country. Costume items may include a hat or bonnet, scarf, cape, skirt, belt, sash, blanket, shawl, beads, crown, helmet, armor, bridal gown, and so on.

2. Add interesting and appropriate props: a cloth-covered table beside the seated model's chair, saddle, musical instrument, bicycle, large basket, ladder, cane, tennis racquet, fan, lasso, broom, sword, banjo, shovel, flowers, and so on. Consider a fabric backdrop to soften or eliminate distracting elements.

3. Two models may pose together, seated and playing cards at a table, sweeping the floor, playing musical instruments, and so on.

4. Think about the emotional aspects, or the character and personality of the figure. Does he or she look tired, ferocious, humorous, wise, proud, arrogant, humble?

5. Look carefully at the gesture and posture of the pose. Use your viewfinder. Try several different points of view. Find angles and curves. Notice the relationship of the figure to the background. Decide if you will draw the entire figure or from the waist or shoulders up.

Landscapes, Seascapes, and Cityscapes

Although bits of landscapes appear as backgrounds for portraits as early as the late Middle Ages, European landscape painting as such appeared as late as the seventeenth century in Holland. Critics ridiculed landscapes, calling them meaningless, and landscape painting was not accepted until the nineteenth century. The artist usually made sketches on location and created the final artwork in the studio. By mid-century, a few artists began to feel that they could capture the atmosphere and the effects of light by painting outdoors in front of their subject. The invention of tubes for holding paint made this possible.

Meanwhile, the Chinese had long practiced landscape painting and considered it their highest expression. To them, human beings were small within the natural order, with nature being a living cosmic spirit. Tradition in China called on people to contemplate nature directly or through paintings as a way of achieving harmony with that cosmic spirit. To understand this difference in attitude, we need to know that Christians during the Middle Ages were seeking to look beyond this world to the next; later, during the Renaissance, the natural world was considered the setting for human actions, with artists examining it closely to paint it more realistically.

Beginning in the fifteenth century, oil paints were used in the Western world. Slow-to-dry oil paints provided artists with a broad range of color and allowed them to blend strokes and achieve three-dimensional illusions. On the other hand, Chinese landscapes were made with ink and showed washes and skillful, distinct brush strokes that evoked natural forms and attempted to convey the essence or inner nature of the scene. The viewer usually has an aerial view, with objects not diminishing in a photographic way. One is drawn into the scene and invited to walk through it. If a figure is seen in a Western landscape, it often dominates; figures in Chinese landscapes are small and a part of the world around them.

Students may use pens and pencils, colored pencils, charcoal, and watercolors for on-the-spot sketching of landscapes. They will find that frequent use of a sketchbook improves their perceptual and drawing skills.

1. You will need a drawing board on which to tape your drawing paper. A viewfinder will help you select your subject and frame your composition in the same manner that a camera does. It will stop your eye from taking in too much from a panoramic view and will help you find a focal point. Start by selecting a subject with fairly shallow space, closing in on the main point of interest.

2. Try shifting your point of view so that the horizon is up high. Then try it down low before you decide which point of view best suits you. A high horizon line allows you ample ground space.

3. Let your eyes follow the lines and shapes that direct your attention to the focal point or points. They may be a road, fence posts, an alley, the side of a building, trees, the edge of a lake or river, and so on. Notice which shapes extend off the edges of the paper.

4. After you have chosen your scene, make quick thumbnail sketches to help you see how your composition looks on paper. Look for dark and light masses. Do any shapes in the foreground stand out against the sky? Will you use them to frame or be a focal point? Notice the direction from which the light is coming and the effect light has on the objects in your composition. Dappled light is different from harsh light. Light at different times of the day casts different lengths of shadows and can contribute to the mood of your artwork.

5. Instead of a viewfinder, use natural framing provided by a window, a hole in a fence, an arched door, a gate, an entry hall, and so on.

STRATEGIES FOR STIMULATING CHILDREN'S RESPONSES TO ARTWORKS

Children like to look at artworks and respond to them. When reproductions are placed before them, or when they visit a museum and see original artworks, or find sculpture and murals on corporate or public buildings in their own community, a guided dialogue can broaden their perceptions. When they describe, analyze, interpret, and make aesthetic decisions about an artwork, they learn a new visual/verbal vocabulary. Repeated encounters with a variety of artworks from global cultures as well as Western art will increase their response skills.

Large reproductions (often called *study prints* or *posters*), slides, overhead transparencies, books, and postcards of great artworks are available from distributors and museums and are relatively inexpensive. Calendars with large, first-rate reproductions of the works of well-known artists are readily available, and the Internet also is a resource for these works. This accessibility is an advancement from the past, when color reproductions were costly and limited in the number of selections available. Nothing can take the place of seeing original artworks; however, the difficulty of visiting distant and foreign museums is an obvious deterrent for many people.

With reproductions, students can compare three or four of one artist's artworks. Or the teacher can select three or four artworks by other artists that deal with the same theme. Student can then compare works that illustrate the four styles of art as described in Chapter 4 and discuss how each artist used the elements and principles of art to affect the composition, mood, and meaning of his or her artwork. Large reproductions have advantages over slides and overhead transparencies in the elementary classroom in that reproductions can be viewed in multiples in lighted rooms and left for extended periods of time for students to view. When large reproductions are used, children should be seated close to the work being described and analyzed. They need to know that the work is a reproduction, not the original.

The following dialogue suggests the sort of student remarks and teacher responses that could direct students' thinking to a greater understanding of the artwork *Sunday Afternoon on the Island of La Grande Jatte* by Georges Seurat (Colorplate 15).

A Model Dialogue between the Teacher and Students

T: Tell me what you see.

S: A lot of people.

T: Where are they?

S: On the grass. Maybe a park or something because I see some water, too. And I see a border, sort of like a frame painted all around the outside edge.

T: What are the people doing?

S: Just standing there or sitting. Oh, maybe walking. I see a lady with a little girl like she's walking toward me. They are really dressed up for a day in the park. They look like real people, but their clothes look like they're from an old-fashioned movie.

T: Yes, that's how people dressed at the time the artist Georges Seurat painted this artwork, more than 100 years ago. Which people are the closest to us?

S: That man and woman on the right.

T: You're right. The artist made them larger than any other figures and placed them lower on the canvas. That makes them seem closer to us. Which other figures seem close to us?

S: Those three on the left who are sitting on the grass. They are looking out toward the water. Maybe there is a sailboat race or something going on. Looks like the black dog is eating their lunch scraps.

T: Those figures are in the foreground, too. Can you see how the artist, Georges Seurat, has painted a shaded area here? What else do you see in the foreground?

S: Oh, I see a little monkey and a little dog running toward the black dog.

T: Let's take a little walk with your eyes back into the distance and find some more figures. How are they like the figures in the foreground?

S: Well, they are dressed like them. They're looking out at the water, most of them anyway, and I see some more parasols. Most of the people seem real quiet. I don't think it looks like a noisy place. I do see a man blowing a horn. Oh, I do see one little girl running.

T: Let's have several of you stand and sit in the same positions of the figures in the painting. Look carefully at the painting before you take a position. (Take timeout for this activity.)

T: Now let's look at the picture again and measure the figures you see in the middleground. (Hold a ruler or string upright to measure the heights of the couple on the right, then the central figure with the little girl, and then a figure in the background.) Seurat painted the figures that he wanted us to see as farthest away the smallest. When artists do this, we say they have used diminishing sizes to show deep space. He also placed them higher up from the bottom of the canvas. They are also lighter in color value. Can you see any other ways he made the figures seem farther away from us?

S: We can't see any stripes or ribbons or anything on their clothes.

T: Right, he made the details and textures less sharp and clear. Let's look and see how many places Seurat used curving lines and shapes. (Let a student use a pointer to do this.)

S: The skirts, the parasols, and hats, and even the tails on the animals. Oh, yes, the sailboat.

T: I'm glad you noticed that white, curving sail in the background. It is very much like part of the parasol. I think you may have noticed it because it was white, in contrast to the darker blue of the water. Can you find other places in the composition where the artist repeated white? This tends to add unity to the picture and lead our eyes around and throughout the complex organization. He has painted a shadow shape for almost each figure, and that adds unity, too. Describe the colors you see. Are they the same as you would see in nature?

S: Well, I see a lot of green, light green, a sort of a yellow-green, and some blue-greens. Quite a bit of blue, too. Then I see that reddish-orange color on the clothing and the parasol in the middle. They're probably the same colors the artist saw.

T: Good. Red and green are complementary colors on the color wheel. They are opposites and contrast strongly with each other. Let's talk about the surface quality of the painting. Do you see it as being smooth or what?

S: It looks, well, kind of grainy when I think of the way most other paintings look, like the one by Gauguin we saw a few days ago.

T: Grainy is a good word because Seurat invented a new way to put the paint on his canvas; he called it **pointillism.** He applied the paint with many tiny dots, one color next to another color, so that when he was done and you, the viewer, stepped away from the artwork, your eyes would mix the colors together. If a lot of white dots are applied with only a few blue dots, your eyes see a light blue.

S: That must have taken him a long time. How large is that painting in the original?

T: It is about 8 by 10 feet in size!

S: Wow! Did he make very many paintings during his life?

T: Only about 60 because he died in 1891, when he was only 31, of a throat infection. He was working with another artist named Signac, who carried on the experiments with pointillism. Look at the way Seurat arranged the people and trees. It all seems very casual and lifelike, yet he was very careful to create a feel of visual balance. We call the kind of symmetry he used informal. One side is not exactly like the other side. The two large figures in rather dark clothing on the right tend to balance the three seated figures and the dog on the left. Can you find other things that balance each other?

S: (Student uses pointer.)

T: What do you see as the focal point in this painting? What leads your eye to it?

S: I see the lady in the center, the one with the little girl in the white dress. I think it's because she is in the center and is the only one facing us. Then, too, her red

parasol contrasts with the green foliage of the trees above her.

S: I don't agree. My attention goes to the couple on the right. They're the largest figures. Their clothing is dark, and the line of the parasol and cane kind of point to them.

T: Do you like looking at this painting?

S: Yes. There are so many things to see. My eyes keep moving back and forth, imagining what the people were saying. It looks like a warm day. It is almost like a photo, but then again, the people all look like they aren't moving—like they're posing and still as statues. Most of the shapes and lines are vertical, the tree trunks and the people. Maybe that's why it looks quiet and peaceful.

S: And I like the new way Seurat painted, that pointillism. It's neat. Could we try making a picture like that . . . only not 8 by 10 feet!

Activities for Stimulating Children's Responses to Artworks

1. Tap very young children on their shoulder with a "magic paintbrush" to enable them to have "magic eyes" that see things in a picture. (To make a "magic paintbrush," cover the handle of a paintbrush with white glue and glitter dust. Also use the brush as a pointer to direct students' attention to a diagonal line, a geometric shape, converging lines of perspective, and so on. Use the brush to demonstrate how artists create brush strokes. Try other pointers, such as long feathers when discussing birds, glitter wands when discussing kings and queens, a twig for discussing trees, and so on.

2. A pair of artist eyeglasses (empty decorated frames) may give very young or somewhat shy children the confidence to describe the special colors, shapes, or subject matter they see. Children take turns wearing the glasses while they make comments.

3. Use a hand puppet to initiate a conversation with very young students about a painting.

4. Have children respond to questions by taking turns talking into a pretend microphone.

5. Show students a real object (a mango, beads, feather) that is in one of the paintings on display. Have scraps of textured materials (satin, lace, burlap, wood, etc.) to use in discussing the simulated textures in artworks. Tell the children to watch for the textures or for one of the objects.

6. You may want to dress in special clothing and use props that are appropriate to the artworks being discussed— for instance, a clown's costume for a circus painting by

Seurat, or a cowboy hat for a Remington or Russell painting.

7. Use plastic clips to attach a piece of clear vinyl to the reproduction to protect it from any accidental marks made with a water-based Vis-a-Vis marking pen. Cut out one or more openings in a piece of white butcher paper. Then cover a reproduction with the paper so that small details can be seen through the openings. Let students guess what the rest of the picture might be. Have students try completing the picture on the butcher paper.

8. Use a clear piece of vinyl the same size as a reproduction. Then use a Vis-a-Vis pen to convey certain concepts. For example, draw around all the round shapes, the contour lines, the perspective lines, all the places where the artist used red, the distorted shapes, and so on. Wipe the vinyl clean with a damp paper towel, and use again.

9. Have students look quietly at a picture for a minute or so, and then ask them to make up a good title for it. This calls for description and interpretation. Or tell the children the name of the picture, and then have them explain why they think the artist gave it that title. If you are showing several artworks, write the names of all the pictures on the board. Let students guess which title goes with which reproduction.

10. Ask children to imitate a pose, movement, or facial expression that they see in one of the pictures. Have several students imitate a group position. Have other students guess which picture each pose is imitating.

11. Ask students to enter a painting and take a walk with their eyes, telling what path their eyes follow and what lines, shapes, and colors direct them. This analysis helps children find a focal point and understand how the artist organized the composition.

12. Have students write or discuss what they think a person in a figure painting would write in his or her journal or diary that night. Or let one student interview a person in a picture, and have another student stand behind the reproduction and answer questions.

13. Ask individual students to pretend to be the artist. You might bring along a small artist smock, hat, and palette for role-playing. Ask the students to imagine preparing to paint the picture. Ask them what they, as the artist, probably did first when they made the picture. Where did they go to paint the picture? Who posed for the picture? What meaning or message was intended? What did they want to succeed in doing? What would they change, add, or "erase," or would they leave the picture just as it is? This activity involves reconstructing skills and helps students to think like an artist.

14. Have students imagine that the artist is alive today. Discuss where they would take the artist and what conversations they would have over the course of one day. What questions would they ask? What would they like to show the artist in today's America? How do they think the artist would react? What in today's world would the artist find especially interesting as subject matter for his or her work? What would they most like to tell or ask the artist?

15. Have two students imagine a conversation that might occur if two artists could meet and talk to each other today. Would the artists argue? On what would they agree? Would they be surprised at anything? What themes might they paint in today's world?

16. Play tic-tac-toe on the chalkboard. Divide the class into two teams. Ask questions at the end of a presentation about a painting. Let teams take turns answering, placing an X or O for each correct response.

17. Use a set of "art cards" (short descriptive phrases related to the elements and principles of art, technical qualities, emotional interpretation, and styles of art). Select appropriate art cards that could be applied in describing or interpreting the art reproductions at which the class is looking. Distribute one or two to each student at the end of a discussion about the reproductions and have them choose which pictures best typify the descriptive terms on their cards.

18. Have students write short Japanese poems—*cinquains* (sin canes), *haiku* (hi koo), and *tankas* (tangh kahs)—about artworks they have discussed. Model this activity first by writing a poem on the board as students suggest lines. Groups of students can work together to write a poem, with each group choosing a different painting. The lines should express their responses to what they see, feel, and know about the selected painting.

Cinquains: These poems have the following format:

Line 1   (two syllables): State the subject with one word (usually a noun).
Line 2   (four syllables): Describe the subject with two to four words (often nouns and adjectives, or all adjectives).
Line 3   (six syllables): Describe the subject's action with three or four words (often verbs).
Line 4   (eight syllables): Express an emotion about the subject with four to eight words.
Line 5   (two syllables): Restate the subject with another single word, reflecting what you have already said (usually a noun).

An example of a cinquain:

Green Violinist, Marc Chagall (Colorplate 37)
Fiddler

Bright coat, green face

Sitting, singing, playing

Happy tunes for the earth and sky

Russian

Haiku: These poems use only three lines to create a word picture and mood. Students should use the following format to express their responses to what they see, feel, and know about a painting:

Line 1:   Five syllables
Line 2:   Seven syllables
Line 3:   Five syllables

An example of a haiku:

Cow's Skull, by Georgia O'Keeffe (Colorplate 34)

Red stripes on the sides

Blue blazing in the background

The cow's skull shouts white.

Tanka: These short poems are made up of five lines in the following format:

Line 1:   Five syllables
Line 2:   Seven syllables
Line 3:   Five syllables
Line 4:   Seven syllables
Line 5:   Seven syllables

An example of a tanka:

The Bath, Mary Cassatt (Colorplate 36)

She wears a striped robe

As she holds the little girl

A pitcher nearby

Holds water to wash the feet

Of the child who played in sand.

19. A *preposition poem* may be developed as a group activity or as an individual project. Students choose a reproduction and write one-line phrases, each beginning with a different preposition (in, to, on, of, over, with, for, beside, under, above, below, behind, etc.). After four or five lines, they may close the poem with a final line that doesn't begin with a preposition but that completes the thoughts in the poem.

An example of a preposition poem:

American Gothic, Grant Wood (Colorplate 21)

With pitchfork in hand

Beside a woman

With a cameo on her dress

In front of a Victorian house

Beneath a pale blue sky

Stands a farmer in overalls.

BOOKS: VERSATILE PARTNERS WITH ART

1. Books may be used for taking a closer look at how the artist used one or more of the elements and principles of art as well as for their illustrative content, learning to describe and analyze the illustrations from several viewpoints. For instance, *Baby Rattlesnake*, told by Te Ata, a Native American, adapted by Lynn Moroney and illustrated by Mira Reisberg, tells of a little rattlesnake who cried because he didn't have a rattle. The repetition of shapes, colors, and lines throughout the book makes for a rich source of seeing a great variety of colorful patterns. *Who's in Rabbit's House* by Verna Aardema, with pictures by Leo and Diane Dillon, winners of the Caldecott Medal, tells a Masai tale. The many masked figures, shown in action-filled repetition, provide a great variety of poses. Seeing how a book illustrator shows motion can help students in their own artwork, such as the use of slanted, repeated, action lines; distorted bodies; and bent arms and legs. The wonderfully drawn lines in books illustrated by Peter Parnall—such as *The Great Fish* and *Annie and the Old One*—can help students see possibilities for improving the line quality in their own work.

2. An abundance of books on art and artists relate art to other areas of the curriculum. A science unit on birds would hardly be complete without books such as *First Impressions: John James Audubon* by Joseph Kastner and *John James Audubon: Wildlife Artist* by Peter Anderson. During a study of flowers and plants, *A Jungle Expedition* by Susanne Pfleger would awaken students to the imaginative plant forms created by Henri Rousseau after his many visits to the botanical gardens in Paris. In *Looking at Paintings: Flowers* by Peggy Roalf students will see works by Manet, van Gogh, Monet, Klee, O'Keeffe, Rivera, and others. An art book related to social studies is *Jacob Lawrence: American Scenes, American Struggles* by Nancy Shroyer Howard, which shows and tells of this African-American artist's determination to depict slavery in the South, the migration north, and life in Harlem in the 1920s. Lawrence also painted heroic people who fought for freeing the slaves, such individuals as Harriet Tubman, John Brown, Frederick Douglass, and Toussaint L'Ouverture. In a study of American history, *Buffalo Hunt* by Russell Freedman would be useful. It contains works by such artists as Albert Bierstadt, Charles Russell, Karl Bodmer, and George Catlin and tells the story of the demise of this beast by the white man and how Indians had depended on the buffalo for nearly everything they needed to stay alive.

3. Books are especially recommended for children when they are becoming acquainted with art from diverse

cultures. *Honoring Our Ancestors*, with its autobiographical stories and pictures by 14 artists, helps children learn how these artists honor the ancestors who touched their lives. *In Search of the Spirit of the Living National Treasures of Japan* by Sheila Hamanaka and Ayano Ihmi introduces students to the great variety of artworks in today's Japan.

4. If students are involved with painting, they could analyze and enjoy books that were illustrated with paint, thereby perceiving the medium and technique and not just the image as illustrative. When students are involved in cut-paper activities, they could benefit from and enjoy books that were illustrated with cut paper that has been textured and patterned, such as *The Dust under Mrs. Merriweather's Bed* by Susan Grohmann, which is entirely illustrated with rich cut-paper pictures. Books by Eric Carle have abundant illustrations cut from paper that the artist has painted and textured in a variety of ways.

5. When children are engaged in drawing, painting, or making prints or cut-paper artworks dealing with specific subject matter as horses, dogs, cats, dancers, the sea, portraits of each other, or self-portraits, the teacher may show the class one of the many books that deal with single subjects, such as the *Looking at Paintings* series by Peggy Roalf. For instance, *Self-Portraits* by Roalf features 19 paintings by well-known artists along with a page write-up of each. Such books show children that artists for many years have engaged in this activity, and some of these pictures will help them know what people looked like long ago. They will also gain the concept that portraits may be made with paint, crayon, cut paper, or even clay. They will see that some portraits are very realistic, while others are more abstract or expressive. *Mona Lisa: The Secret of the Smile* by Letizia Galli tells the story behind the world's most famous portrait. Another such series is *The World of Art through the Eyes of Artists* by Wendy and Jack Richardson.

6. A number of books for young readers include those dedicated to the life and work of one artist or perhaps a period of time or school of art. *A Boy Named Giotto* by Paolo Guarnieri, with its lovely illustrations, tells of the artist who is credited with giving impetus to the early days of the Italian Renaissance. Young readers learn how Giotto herded his father's sheep and was discovered when he was 8 years old by a leading artist, Cimabue, and became his apprentice. Children like to hear about the childhoods of famous artists: *Pablo Picasso* by Ibi Lepscky and *Leonardo da Vinci* by the same author are intriguing for the very young child as are books in the *Famous Children* series by Tony Hart, featuring Picasso, Lautrec, and others. Mike Venezia's series, *Getting to Know the World's Greatest Artists*, includes numerous books on different artists and all are richly illustrated and easy to read. In *Portraits of Women Artists for Children: Georgia O'Keeffe*, Robyn Montana Turner celebrates in pictures and words the amazing life of this American artist. For the older student, the *Eyewitness Art* series has an intense in-depth look at a particularly powerful movement in the history of art: *Impressionism* by Jude Welton, in association with the Art Institute of Chicago. Numerous color illustrations and text guide the older student in learning about these artists and the influences that shaped their work.

7. A number of fine books have been published that prepare children for a museum visit. *Squeaking of Art: The Mice Go to the Museum* by Monica Wellington contains much helpful and delightful content in relation to engaging the child in looking for specific items in the illustrations. Other such books include *Visiting the Art Museum* by Laurene Krasny Brown and Marc Brown, *Katie's Picture Show* by James Mayhew, and *Smudge* by Mike Dickinson. Through books of this sort, children will learn what they can expect to see and that museums are marvelous places where important and sometimes very old objects are kept, objects that often help us know about the past and understand the present.

8. Museum-related books are also available in which art production activities for students are paired with famous works of art. The National Gallery of Art in Washington, DC, publishes *Move Over, Picasso! A Young Painter's Primer* by Ruth Aukerman and *My Journey through Art: Create Your Own Masterpieces* by Kathryn Cave. *All My Own Work: Adventures in Art* by Carole Armstrong and Anthea Peppin is published by the National Gallery in London. The Brooklyn Museum has published an especially valuable art and activities book called *The Native American Book*.

9. Books may be selected for their rich verbal and visual imagery—stories or poems—for children to use as springboards for drawing and painting. After listening to a story or poem they may choose which part they would like to draw or paint.

10. Simple bookbinding techniques may be utilized by children when they write and illustrate their own stories in their choice of media: cut paper, paint, crayons, and markers.

INTERACTIVE EXTENSIONS

1. Use the Lesson Plan Format on page 112, and write two integrated strategies as described and modeled on pages 113–119. Focus one of the lessons on lower grades and one on upper grades.

2. Select one of these books, and report on its chapter on children's artistic growth to your class.

   Chapman, Laura H., *Approaches to Art in Education* (New York: Harcourt Brace Jovanovich, 1978).

   Day, Michael, and Al Hurwitz, *Children and Their Art*, 6th ed. (New York: Harcourt Brace Jovanovich, 1995).

   Eisner, Elliot W., *Educating Artistic Vision* (NAEA reprint, 1997, Archival series).

   Gardner, Howard, *Artful Scribbles: The Significance of Children's Drawings* (New York: Basic Books, 1980).

   Herberholz, Barbara, and Lee Hanson, *Early Childhood Art*, 5th ed. (New York: McGraw-Hill, 1995).

   Lowenfeld, Viktor, and W. Lambert Brittian, *Creative and Mental Growth*, 8th ed. (New York: Macmillan, 1987).

3. Observe two- to four-year-old children as they make marks. Then collect three or four of their artworks. Talk with the children about their drawings after they have finished. How does this information add to your understanding of how children of this age are developing in their artistic expression?

4. Collect drawings by children in the symbol stage, and look for differences and similarities in how they use color, shapes, figures, and space.

5. Collect three or four artworks by children, ages nine to twelve, and compare their use of color, line, and shape.

6. Collect three children's artworks from each of the three stages of artistic growth, and compare how the children have shown emotional expressions and what meanings the child was developing.

7. Do some research on safety in relation to the use of art materials. For example, review the health hazards in such books as *Safety in the Art Room* by Charles A. Qualley (Worcester, MA: Davis Publications) or check state requirements regarding health standards in relation to art materials.

8. Write two lesson plans, one for the lower grades and one for the upper grades, after reviewing the overall concepts exemplified in the six lesson plans in this chapter. Use the Lesson Plan Format on page 112.

9. Cooperate with an elementary teacher in presenting one of the strategies described in this chapter. Then guide the students in assessing their work according to the guidelines also found in this chapter.

10. Volunteer in an elementary school to assist several teachers in arranging a display of children's artwork. Consider how the works should be matted or mounted, what labels and brief explanations should appear to explain the goals of the various lessons, and what learning was achieved.

11. Read and report to your class on three children's books that exemplify three different ways the books could be used in your elementary classroom as described on pages 127–28.

A Lesson Plan Format

Students' Guided Tour for: Lower Grades   Upper Grades (circle one)

Focus: Mapping the Directions

Curriculum Integration

The Journey

Side Trips

Destination: Personal

Assessment.

1.

2.

3.

4.

6
CHAPTER

New Directions for the Twenty-First Century
Technology and Curriculum Design

Chapter Outline

TECHNOLOGY AND CURRICULUM DESIGN

The first part of this chapter contains a view of new technology and the role it plays in changing the manner in which art can be taught in the twenty-first century. Explanations are given as to how these new approaches enrich existing art programs already in place and develop higher-level art experiences and expectations.

The second part of this chapter explains how the National Standards for the Visual Arts have become the outcome of the educational reform effort generated in the 1980s and fueled by the publication of *A Nation at Risk*. With these Standards in mind, major publishers have produced visual art curriculum materials for elementary classrooms—packaged programs as well as children's textbooks along with teacher editions and supplementary materials. New directions that are within the scope of the Standards as well as how these materials can be developed and incorporated in elementary art classes are covered in this section. Future classroom teachers will be introduced to ways of developing their own comprehensive and integrated art lessons.

NEW TECHNOLOGY IN ELEMENTARY ART CLASSES

New technologies—computers, digital cameras, scanners, hypermedia, multimedia, laserdiscs, CD-ROMs, telecommunications, and computer networks—have become an important part of today's busy culture and workplace. In response to the growing presence of these technologies in our daily lives, our educational system has made technology integration a priority in efforts to revitalize teaching and learning in our nation's schools.

As computers and other emerging technologies find their way into elementary schools, it becomes the responsibility of classroom teachers to find effective ways of incorporating these new tools into existing curricular programs. While it is common practice among elementary teachers to use computers to advance instructional goals in such areas as reading and math, there are also exciting possibilities offered by new technologies in the area of art education.

The purpose of this section is to demonstrate ways elementary teachers can introduce new technology into their art lessons. This emphasis is not intended to imply, however, that new technologies should replace older tools and materials currently used in many art classes. For example, the use of computer graphics software may provide students with new image-making possibilities; but they should still learn how to use a pencil, a brush, scissors, and paper for personal creative expression. Elementary teachers can best serve their students by promoting the use of a wide range of tools,

materials, and processes to further the goals of art education in their classrooms.

Broadly speaking, technology serves two functions in art classes: (1) as media for creative expression and visual communication; and (2) as sources of art information and understanding. Applications of technology in each of these areas may vary according to the particular curricular goals and school context in which art instruction and learning take place. Some of the potential uses of newer technologies in art are presented below.

TECHNOLOGY AS EXPRESSIVE ART MEDIA

Among the tools and materials more commonly used as expressive art media in elementary classrooms today are brushes, chalk, clay, construction paper, crayons, markers, pastels, pencils, scissors, and water-based paints. The popularity of these media reflects, for the most part, certain economical and practical issues as well as the preferences of elementary teachers who hold traditional art practices in high esteem. Unfortunately, some young students eventually become turned off to art-making by their perceived lack of success with traditional art media. They often get discouraged when their initial attempts at representational drawing seem to be visually unrewarding. For elementary teachers who are sensitive to this problem, the computer offers a possible solution. By using computers and other new technologies to expand the range of possibilities for creative expression in the classroom, each student has a better chance of finding a medium that works well for him or her. This is already happening in many elementary schools today.

To date, the most frequent practice of using computers in elementary art classes has been to have students work with digital paint software that enables them to emulate traditional drawing and painting techniques on the computer screen. This approach is sometimes augmented with the use of a digital camera or scanner to capture photographic images that students then enhance or manipulate with the digital paint software and sometimes with conventional art media. Two of the more popular digital paint software programs used in elementary classrooms today are *Kid Pix* for younger students (grades K–3) and *Art Dabbler* for older students (grades 3–5). Each of these programs offers a range of art tools and techniques for image-making purposes.

Making pictures on computers with digital paint software has certain advantages over traditional art media. It appears to spark student interest and excitement; also, the novelty and ease of the digital-imaging process releases inhibitions. Students afraid of drawing with a pencil are often quick to try their hand at drawing with a computer. Students can quickly create images that are stored in the

Lyndsey and her sister Hailey work on the computer to create a personal Mother's Day card. The sisters scanned images, manipulated them on the screen, and presented the card to a happy mom.

computer's memory or on disk. They can then try out different ideas and easily "undo" them if they aren't pleased by the result. This feature is thought to make the computer more conducive to experimentation and risk-taking than traditional art media.

Advances in hardware and software capabilities over the past two decades have greatly expanded the possibilities of using computers for creative expression and visual communication. Where personal computers were once limited to displaying text and simple graphics, they are now able to easily deal with video, animation, sound, and high-quality photographic images. The multimedia capabilities of newer computers have added another creative dimension to elementary art classes today.

For example, in many elementary art classes, computers are being used by students to create real-time animation and motion graphics with sound accompaniments. By interfacing the computer with a video camera and VCR, students are able to combine computer animation with live-action imagery and transfer their creative productions onto video cassettes. Two popular multimedia programs used in elementary schools today are *Kid Pix Studio Deluxe* (which includes the digital paint program previously described) and *HyperStudio*. Both software programs can be successfully used in all elementary grades.

The use of computers as an expressive art medium can also be highly beneficial in inclusive classrooms by providing teachers with new possibilities in addressing the needs of exceptional students. A number of technologies are now available that enable children with severe disabilities to engage in the creative art process.[1] Likewise, children who are deemed gifted or talented in art may find working with digital paint software and multimedia programs challenging and personally rewarding.

In the end, whatever technologies are brought to bear on the creative art process, students must learn to use the tools and materials they have available to think, to imagine, to create, to play with ideas, to explore, and to feel what it means to be human. As teachers, seeing to it that this kind of authentic learning takes place in our classrooms may be the greatest investment we can make in our children's future.

TECHNOLOGY AS SOURCES OF ART INFORMATION

In addition to incorporating computers into elementary art classes as a new medium for creative expression, new technologies offer intriguing opportunities for assisting in the instruction and study of historical art content. In many elementary art classes today, students are able to view and discuss slides and reproductions of works of art; watch videotaped programs on artists, art techniques, and historical art periods; and read about artists and the history of art in books, magazines, and other printed materials. In this sense, newer technologies in the form of CD-ROMs and the World Wide Web offer an enormous wealth of digital resources designed to support art instruction and learning in the classroom or home.

There are a number of art-related CD-ROMs available today that can serve as a starting point for an art lesson, as a supplement to an art lesson, or as stand-alone resource used by students for individual research and study. CD-ROMs are able to store large databases of high-quality photographic reproductions, archival film footage, video segments plus accompanying text, sound, and voice clips. In addition to the multisensory nature of CD-ROMs, their most useful feature is that they are interactive, thereby allowing students to take control over the presentation of material and to access the stored information in a number of ways.

One of the most popular art-related CD-ROMs used in elementary classrooms today is *With Open Eyes: Images from the Art Institute of Chicago*, which contains high-quality full-screen graphics of over 200 works of art from the world-class collection of Chicago's Art Institute along with accompanying sounds, music, and spoken explanations. The selection of works consists of a variety of images from Egyptian mummy cases to Picasso portraits and is searchable by geography or time period. Other features include an automated slide show option, a zoom-in tool for examining small details in works, a scrapbook that can store selected works for later viewing, and a number of interactive games that reinforce learning in fun and ingenious ways.

CD-ROMs like *With Open Eyes* can be valuable classroom resources for promoting critical analysis of works of art and understanding the historical and cultural context in which a work of art is made. Whether used by individual students or in small groups, it is up to the teacher to determine how to best apply the new advantages for art learning that such interactive multimedia can provide.

The most effective approach involves arranging authentic classroom projects in which students use technology to think and work like adult professionals do in the world of art. For example, students in an elementary art class could be asked to assume the role of a museum curator and design an electronic art exhibition around a chosen theme by reviewing, selecting, and organizing works of art from a CD-ROM. Offering students opportunities to explore interesting and challenging projects like this is the key to promoting successful learning experiences in art involving new technology.

With an Internet-connected computer in the classroom, the availability of art resources for purposes of instruction and learning greatly expands. The arrival of the World Wide Web in the classroom brings immediate access to a multitude of people, places, things, and ideas that can inform and inspire both teachers and students alike. Given the significance and numerous possibilities this new technology offers for art education in elementary classrooms, a more in-depth look at the Internet and the World Wide Web follows.

TEN WAYS TO USE THE INTERNET IN ELEMENTARY ART CLASSES

The decade of the 1990s saw an expanding presence of the Internet in our nation's schools. According to the U.S. Department of Education, Internet access grew from 35 percent in 1994 to 95 percent of America's public schools being online in 1999 (National Center for Education Statistics, February 15, 2000). The surge in school Internet use is largely due to the growth and popularity of the World Wide Web.

The invention of the World Wide Web (WWW or the Web) in 1990 gave the Internet a user-friendly interface that offers point-and-click access to text, graphics, sound, and video files stored on host computers around the world. Web documents or files can be stored on one computer or on several computers in different locations that are interconnected through *hyperlinks*. By clicking on a link, or "hot spot," on a Web page, one can easily jump to other computers around the world.

The Internet with its vast collection of Web-based materials and new telecommunication tools has become a significant educational resource in all areas of the school curriculum. In art education, the Internet can enhance many traditional classroom practices as well as open up new avenues for teaching, learning, and alternative curricular arrangements. By becoming familiar with a few online tools and resources, elementary teachers will be in a better position to decide how to restructure existing classroom practices in order to take full advantage of what the Internet has to offer.

This section describes 10 ways to use Internet tools and resources in elementary art classes. The uses presented range from those that augment and support traditional models of art education to those that may significantly change how teachers teach and students learn in the classroom.

1: Communicate with Other Educators around the World

The Internet can be used by elementary teachers for a number of professional development activities, ranging from communicating with colleagues and experts to participating in online courses and workshops for graduate credit. Through private electronic mail correspondence (e-mail) and online discussion groups, teachers share curriculum ideas, lesson plans, and instructional strategies; receive early notification of national developments in education and pending governmental legislation; get assistance with emerging technologies, including new art-making tools and techniques; participate in online courses that advance their knowledge and skills; and obtain current information on educational research, grants, and other support services.

There are numerous *listservs* devoted to art education where teachers can ask questions and share ideas with colleagues and art education professionals. Since 1995, for example, the Getty Education Institute for the Arts has sponsored *ArtsEdNet Talk* (www.artsednet.getty.edu/ArtsEd Net/Connection), an electronic discussion group for those interested in discipline-based arts education. This popular online forum has close to 1,000 participants from around the globe who regularly exchange ideas and information concerning a wide range of topics and issues of mutual interest.

2: Collaborate with Other Teachers on Student Art Exchanges and Joint Classroom Projects

One of the easiest ways for elementary teachers to make immediate use of the Internet involves arranging exchanges of student artwork with other schools around the globe. Work completed with traditional art materials may be sent via postal mail or scanned and transmitted electronically over the Internet. Work done with the aid of a computer may also be sent over the Internet. Such exchanges typically involve students in each location creatively responding to a common theme and then sharing the resulting work. The following examples illustrate this form of low-impact use of the Internet in art classes:

- Elementary students from Florida and Iceland participated in a "mail art" project that was facilitated through e-mail exchanges between the two schools. Each student created an art postcard based on the common theme of the "ocean," which was then sent separately to a student at the other school through the postal service. In addition to the postcard exchange, each group generated a list of questions they had about children's lives in the other country. These questions were exchanged and then answered via e-mail.[2]

- Second-grade students in Fort Worth, Texas, and in Los Angeles, California, studied a David Bates painting titled *Grassy Lake* and then used the software program *Kid Pix* to create electronic postcards with images and text about the place where they lived. The postcards were then exchanged between the two schools over the Internet.[3]

- In a more ambitious project, a Wisconsin teacher arranged a national exhibition of student artwork at her middle school in conjunction with "Youth Art Month" by initially posting requests for submissions on the Internet. This exhibition, entitled "Art across America," included 70 pieces from 35 schools in 30 states. A traveling version of "Art across America" is currently visiting all participating schools.[4]

3: Promote Your Art Program on a Global Scale

With the arrival of the Web, elementary teachers now have the opportunity to promote their classroom activities on a global scale by placing curriculum materials and student artwork online. Such advocacy can not only lead to worldwide recognition of a school's art program but can also foster student learning, motivation, and pride by making their work available for viewing by a worldwide audience.

Elementary teachers looking for guidance in this area should visit websites developed by other teachers for possible ideas. For example, the site for Hoffer Elementary School in Riverside, California (cmp1.ucr.edu/exhibitions/hoffer/hoffer.homepage.html) includes several online exhibitions of student artwork made with traditional materials and new technologies. Also, Urbana Middle School's art department in Urbana, Illinois, maintains an excellent online student art gallery (www.cmi.k12.il.us/Urbana/projects/UMSart/gallery/gallery.html) featuring claymation *quicktime* movies, scanned 3-D artwork, and computer-generated mask images.

4: Use Online Resources to Support Art Instruction

The Web offers a wealth of historical and contemporary art images, video and audio files, lesson ideas, critical art essays, and other textual information that can support art instructional activities. Of special interest is the growing number of art museums worldwide that have established an Internet presence in the form of image databases that provide online access to selected works in their collections. For example, the Smithsonian American Art Museum (AmericanArt.si.edu) allows visitors to browse through its online collection of over 3,000 digitized works that can be searched by subject or by artist. Online versions of a number of past and present museum exhibitions are also available on the site.

With such immediate access to the world's art treasures, teachers have a seemingly unlimited collection of digitized images at their disposal. However, it is important to abide by copyright restrictions placed on the use of these images. Museums generally provide "conditions of use" statements that indicate that all the images and text stored on their websites are for personal, educational, noncommercial use only. Since many school districts also have policies regarding use of online resources, teachers should consult with their administration or computer support staff before incorporating digitized images harvested from the Web into their classroom presentations.

In addition to museum websites, there are a variety of art curriculum resources available online that contain lesson plans and related images. Elementary teachers searching online for art lesson ideas may find the following sites of interest:

- *ArtsEdNet* (www.artsednet.getty.edu)
- *NGA Teacher Exchange* (www.nga.gov/education/teachexc.htm)
- *North Texas Institute for Educators on the Visual Arts* (www.art.unt.edu/ntieva)

5: Take a Virtual Field Trip to an Art Museum or a Public Art Site

Perhaps the greatest benefit of having access to the Internet in schools is that it enables students to learn about things that cannot be directly experienced in the classroom or home. In art classes, students can tour current and past exhibitions at art museums around the world and visit public art sites in different cities and countries. In addition to providing images of artwork, many of these websites offer textual information that place the artwork on view in a historical or aesthetic context. Where such information is not available, the teacher may need to provide it or encourage students to do further research in order to promote such contextual understanding. Some of the many world-class museums and other websites that present art to the public online include:

- The *Chauvet-Pont-d'Arc Cave* (mistral.culture.fr/culture/arcnat/chauvet/en/gvpda-d.htm) is a recently discovered decorated cave in France that includes over 400 paintings and engravings dating to the Paleolithic era (between 32,000 and 30,000 years ago).

- The *National Gallery of Australia* (www.nga.gov.au) features a searchable database of the museum's collections along with several special online exhibitions for children.

- The *Kyoto National Museum of Japan* (www.kyohaku. go.jp) includes one of the most comprehensive collections of East Asian art on the Internet. Visitors can search through a database containing over 10,000 images of over 3,200 objects.
- The *Montreal Museum of Fine Arts* (www.mmfa.qc. ca/lundi/a-cyber-lundi.html) allows visitors to explore the museum's collections online according to themes such as family portraits, summer landscapes, fruits and flowers, and more.
- The *National Gallery of Art* in Washington, DC (www.nga.gov) offers a large searchable database of works from the museum's collections on its website along with several special online exhibitions and tutorials featuring selected works.
- *Torn Notebook* by Claes Oldenberg and Coosje van Bruggen (www.pbs.org/net/tornnotebook) is an unusual public sculpture in Lincoln, Nebraska, that was inspired by Oldenberg's lifelong process of developing his ideas in small notebooks that he carries with him everywhere.

6: Promote Student Dialogue with Their Peers at Other Schools

Through e-mail correspondence, elementary students can exchange views and information with their peers around the globe. This is a simple classroom activity, but one that can reap valuable educational benefits. It involves electronically linking individual students or groups of students of similar age across geographic boundaries for the purpose of collaborative learning. For example, the Smithsonian American Art Museum arranged an Internet-based project involving students in Maryland, Kansas, and Colorado using e-mail to discuss selected landscape paintings and photographs and to compare the landscapes of their different geographical regions. Among the more significant outcomes of this project were that students began to look at the land around them and became genuinely interested in learning about the places where other students lived. Their discussions crossed subject boundaries in the curriculum.[5]

7: Allow Students to Learn Online from Art Experts

Internet access in the classroom, electronic mail, and videoconferencing are powerful classroom tools for accessing art experts from around the world to motivate and teach students. Formal and informal online exchanges between students and working professionals serve to meld the classroom with the "real world" and are excellent ways to

supplement the art curriculum with current information. The following examples illustrate the potential of this type of online learning in art classes:

- *Ask Joan of Art* (www.nmaa.si.edu/referencedesk)—Art information specialists at the Smithsonian American Art Museum will answer questions about American art.
- *Interview with Jim McNeill, Tessellation Artist* (www.art.unt.edu/ntieva/news/vol_9/issue3/inter.htm) —Fifth-grade students in Forth Worth, Texas, studied the tessellation work of New Jersey artist Jim McNeill and formulated a series of questions that were sent to him and subsequently answered through e-mail. The students then used McNeill's answers to write a collaborative article that was published online and in the January 2000 issue of *School Arts* magazine.[6]

8: Promote Student Research and Active Learning in Art

The use of the Internet as a tool for conducting remote research opens new avenues for enhancing student learning in the areas of art criticism and art history. It offers instant access to catalogs and archives of many of the world's major libraries, electronic galleries of professional and student art work, the collections of world-class art museums, arts organizations, arts professionals, online art journals and newspapers, image archives, and much more. With access to a Web-connected computer, students can tap into these global resources that complement traditional local research tools like the school library.

In order to use the Internet successfully for a class research project, students need to learn how to search online for specific information or images. Sorting through the incredible array of online art resources for a relevant article or specific image can be a daunting challenge for even the most experienced Internet user. While just "surfing the Web" can itself lead to interesting self-discoveries, such wandering through cyberspace consumes valuable classroom time and raises the possibility that students will access offensive or inappropriate material along the way. There are several ways that teachers can ensure that students' classroom time on the Web is well spent in meaningful and focused activity:

Bookmarks and Curriculum Resource Pages.
Elementary teachers who make online resources accessible to students should first locate and evaluate relevant websites themselves. Once identified as useful resources, these sites are "bookmarked" or linked to a Curriculum Resources page and made available to students. For example, the Omaha Public Schools Art Web site has a links page (www.ops. org/art/links) that lists images and museum collections that support the district's art curriculum goals as well as teacher and student research.

Search Engines and Web Directories. There are a number of online search tools available to assist teachers and students in locating items of interest on the Internet. Search engines and Web directories allow users to browse through Web pages identified by topical selection or by free keyword search. Teaching students how to work with these search tools can help build their confidence in using the Internet to find the information they need for a school project or for personal research.

Search engines use *robots* or *spiders* to scour the Web on a regular basis for words, rather than subjects, on specific Web pages and then update their databases automatically. As a result, using a search engine like *AltaVista* (www.altavista.com) or *HotBot* (www.hotbot.com) can produce a seemingly endless list of Web pages—many are of questionable value and some are possibly offensive. Learning how to narrow a keyword search can produce more limited and useful results.

Web directories have databases of Web pages grouped according to broad topic categories and specific subcategories. Web directories vary in the focus and the scope of their listings. They are managed by human workers and may not include recent websites or pages in an area. The most popular directory on the Web is *Yahoo!* (www.yahoo.com). There is also *Yahooligans* (www.yahooligans.com), which is designed for use by elementary and middle school students.

Online References. In addition to online search tools, there are a growing number of Web resources that students can use to find information on various topics. These resources usually take the form of an online encyclopedia, database, tutorial, or links page. The following websites illustrate some study resources available to students in art:

- *Compton's Encyclopedia Online* (www.comptons.com/encyclopedia/)
- *Museum Suite* (www.museum.suite.dk)
- *Study Art Page* (www.sanford-artedventures.com/study/study.html)
- *The Vincent van Gogh Information Gallery* (www.vangoghgallery.com)
- *Watson and the Shark* (www.ngs.gov/feature/watson/watsonhome.html)
- *WebMuseum–Artist Index* (metalab.unc.edu/wm/paint/auth)

Virtual Treasure Hunts and WebQuests. Teaching students how to search for information on the Internet can be presented as a learning game or challenge, making the online experience both fun and educational. Such activities typically take on one of two structures, each of which is intended to familiarize students with the kinds of information available while helping them to develop their Internet search skills.

Virtual treasure hunts are like scavenger hunts, only they require students to access preselected websites for pieces of information that provide answers to certain questions. The complexity of the search and questions posed should take into account the developmental level of the students and their previous online experience. A virtual treasure hunt designed for students in art can be found at www.arts.ufl.edu/art/rt_room/treasure_hunt.html.

WebQuests are designed as inquiry-oriented activities "in which some or all of the information that learners interact with comes from resources on the Internet" (Dodge, 1996, edweb.sdsu.edu/courses/EDTEC596/About_WebQuests.html). WebQuests maximize students' time on the Internet and engage them in activities requiring higher-order thinking skills. They typically revolve around six attributes, including (1) an introduction; (2) a task that is doable and interesting; (3) a set of information resources needed to complete the task; (4) a description of the process students should go through to accomplish the task; (5) helpful pointers or guidance in organizing the information acquired; and (6) a closure activity in which students review what they have.

Due to their structure and focus, WebQuests have become one of the more popular online educational activities in classrooms today. There are literally hundreds of WebQuests available covering most subject areas in the school curriculum. The following WebQuests demonstrate how this structure can be used to promote student learning in art:

- *African Art WebQuest* (www.aquiline.com/realms/africa.html)
- *Colonial American Art* (ttt.teachtheteachers.org/~JSmall/amerart/index.htm)
- *Getting to Know Pablo Picasso* (www.hazelwood.k12.mo.us/~cdavis01/ webquests/mcw)

While having access to the Internet in the classroom opens up exciting avenues to promoting student research in art, it also offers students a growing number of online resources that can foster art appreciation, critical analysis, and historical understanding of works of art. The best of these resources take advantage of the interactive and multimedia capabilities of the Web and present content in an engaging, game-like or inquiry-based format. Here is a sampling of online interactive art education resources:

- *A Pintura: Art Detective* (www.eduweb.com/pintura)
- *Art Safari* (artsafari.moma.org)
- *NGAkids* (www.nga.gov/kids/kids.htm)

9: Publish Student Research and Class Projects on the Web

In addition to accessing existing Internet resources, elementary students can become "content providers" themselves by creating online art resources for others to use. One of the Web's most potent applications for classroom learning is as an electronic publishing tool. Given the potential of a world-wide audience, students are often eager to do their best in gathering, organizing, and presenting information in a useful and visually appealing online resource that will be shared with other teachers and students around the globe.

In designing and publishing their own Web resources, students can work individually or collaboratively with their classmates. Whether creating their Web pages directly in HTML format or by using a Web-authoring program (like *Claris Homepage*, *SiteCentral*, or *Web Workshop*), students need to learn the basics of constructing a well-designed website. In order to communicate effectively on the Internet, students must also learn how to manipulate the language of this new technology. This language—images, sound, movement, drama, and text—is also the language of the arts. Elementary teachers can build on this connection by incorporating Web-publishing activities in their curricula. The following exemplary sites demonstrate the kinds of online art resources that students are publishing:

- *Art Rights and Wrongs* (library.thinkquest.org/J001570)
- *African-American History through the Arts* (cghs.dade. k12.fl.us/africanamerican/index.htm)
- *Chinese Calligraphy: Language as Art* (tqjunior. advanced.org/3614)
- *Virtual Ancient Civilizations* (www.cmi.k12.il.us/ Urbana/projects/AncientCiv)

10: Allow Students to Use the Web as a Creative Expressive Medium for Their Ideas

While the Internet can be used to showcase student artwork done with traditional art media, it has greatly expanded the potential of using computers for creative expression and visual communication. The virtual space of the Internet offers unparalleled multimedia possibilities for merging animations, graphics, photographic images, video, music, voices, and textual content along with the capability of engaging viewers through interactive arrangements. Most students are quite adept in working with digital tools and often find the labor required to bring their creative endeavors online intrinsically rewarding. Teachers need to take advantage of these built-in motivations by arranging Web-based classroom projects that will enable students to discover the artistic possibilities offered by this new medium.

An excellent place to view examples of student-produced digital art, interactive multimedia, and Web pages is at the *Telecommunity* website (www.telecommunity.org). The *Telecommunity Project* has organized and participated in several youth cultural exchanges at Pittsburgh-area institutions and schools as well as at other locations around the world. Through this innovative project, young people explore local and planetary concerns, seek imaginative solutions, experience cultural differences, and form global friendships by participating in collaborative art activities involving networked painting, 3-D design, computer/fax art exchanges, computer/video conferencing, screen-sharing, and a host of other creative online activities. In sum, the young people involved in this project are pioneers who are exploring the edges of the Internet as the first artistic medium of the twenty-first century.

TECHNOLOGY GLOSSARY

This glossary provides brief definitions and explanations for some of the technical terms and special words that teachers will encounter when working with computer technologies.

application software A program written to create or manipulate data for a specific purpose (such as word processing or page layout).

baud rate The transmission rate or speed at which information is sent or received by a modem.

bit The smallest possible unit of digital information that a computer processes (either 1 or 0). Eight bits equal one byte.

browser A software program that allows users to retrieve and interpret hypertext documents on the World Wide Web. Netscape and Internet Explorer are the most common browsers used.

byte A unit of information in a computer system that is composed of adjacent bits—usually eight. Some newer computer systems can read 16 or 32 bytes at one time, which enable them to access more memory faster.

CD-ROM Refers to "compact disk/read-only memory"; a small, nonerasable optical disk that is capable of storing and playing back large amounts of digital information (e.g., text, graphics, and sounds).

CPU The "central processing unit" or microprocessor that controls the main activity of a computer.

cyberspace A term coined by William Gibson in his novel *Neuromancer* to represent a universe of interlinked computers; often used today to refer to the Internet.

default settings The automatic settings in a software program. They are the choices typically used such as standard margins and tabs in a word-processing program. They can be changed by the computer user.

digital Information stored as binary data (1s and 0s) so that it can be accessed and manipulated with a computer.

digitize Converting analog or real-world information into digital form.

download The transferring of data from a remote system to a user's local computer.

DPI Dots per inch (e.g., 72 dpi).

electronic mail A method of sending and receiving messages via computers over a network.

ethernet A standard for local area network hardware that offers fast data transfer.

file compression A way of saving files in order to economize on disk space or on transmission time of data.

file format The way in which a particular computer or application program saves data.

file server A computer on a network with special software that enables network users to access applications and documents stored on it.

file transfer protocol (FTP) An Internet-based program used to download files (such as free software, electronic publications, maps, software documentation, sound files, and images) from a distant computer to your own computer.

frequently asked questions (FAQs) A file maintained by most discussion groups on the Internet of commonly asked questions on a given subject. New members of the group should consult this file to avoid posting repetitive questions.

freeware A generic term used to describe software in the public domain that is free of copyright restrictions.

hard drive A magnetic high-volume storage medium that is fitted internally in a computer or connected to the computer as an external device.

hardware A generic term for the physical equipment of a computer environment (e.g., the keyboard, CPU, printer, and monitor).

home page The document that is first displayed when you open a Web browser (like Netscape) or the first document you come to in a collection of documents on a website.

HTML (hypertext markup language) The programming language used to create World Wide Web documents.

hypertext A programming concept that links multiple forms of data in both linear and nonlinear ways.

image-processing A generic term associated with programs that allow the user to enhance, edit, and manipulate the elements of a photographic image that has been scanned into a computer.

import To place data created with one software program into another software program so that it can be used.

initialize The process of formatting or preparing a blank disk (or hard drive) so that it can store information files.

inkjet printer A printer that uses a high-speed stream of electrically charged ink droplets deflected by a magnetic field to output a computer-generated document onto paper.

input To enter images, text, sounds, or code into a computer by whatever means.

interface cable The connecting cable that allows a computer and a peripheral such as a printer, videodisc player, or CD-ROM drive to communicate with one another.

Internet A vast electronic system that links thousands of different computer networks throughout the world together.

I/O Input/output.

kilobyte (K) Approximately 1,000 bits of storage capacity on a floppy disk or computer (e.g., 64K of RAM means roughly 64,000 bits of random-access memory). One kilobyte is equivalent to about 170 words.

LAN A local area computer network.

laser printer A printer that uses a laser beam and toner to output a computer-generated document onto paper.

listserv Short for list server. An automated mail service running on a BITNET computer that handles all the list administrative functions such as subscribing and unsubscribing people to and from a discussion group.

MB Short for "megabyte." Approximately 1,000 kilobytes of storage capacity on a disk or computer. One megabyte is equivalent to about 175,000 words.

modem Short for modulator/demodulator. A device that enables a computer to send and receive information over standard telephone lines.

multimedia The activity of combining or linking different forms of communication such as text, motion video, still images, graphics, and sound in one informational source, and the applications that allow a computer user to do this.

peripheral A generic term that refers to a hardware device such as a modem, printer, synthesizer, or mouse that is connected to a computer.

pixel Refers to "picture element." The higher the resolution of a computer image, the smaller the size of the pixels.

PostScript A "page description language" used by a laser printer to interpret the digital code comprising a computer-generated image or text file which it then re-creates on paper.

public domain A generic term used to describe any item of "intellectual property" (including software programs) that is free of all copyright restrictions.

Quicktime A file extension from Apple Computer that is installed in the system folder on a Macintosh computer. It allows users to take a cut-and-paste approach to integrating video, sound, and animations in their presentations.

RAM Short for "random access memory." The area in a computer where the application program currently in use and the document being produced are stored. RAM is automatically erased when the computer is switched off.

real time An event occurring on a computer in actual clock time, with little or no noticeable lag (e.g., a text character appearing on screen the moment its corresponding key is pressed).

resolution Refers to the crispness of the image on the computer screen. The more pixels there are per inch (dpi) on the screen, the smaller they are and the better the resolution.

ROM Short for "read-only memory." Data stored in ROM can only be read from and not written to.

scanner A device that optically converts flat art into a digital representation so that it can be manipulated or used within a computer.

shareware A generic term used to describe software that is obtained from a secondary source (such as a colleague, friend, or user group) and paid for (by mailing a check to the author) only if the program is found to be beneficial.

site license A special purchase agreement with a software company that allows a consumer to make multiple copies of a software program for use at a particular location (such as a school computer lab).

telecommunications The use of telephone lines and satellites to exchange information between people via computers.

universal resource locator (URL) An address of a document on the World Wide Web.

virtual reality (VR) A term associated with computer programs that allow users to simulate entry—through bodily peripherals such as data gloves and head-mounted graphic displays—into a 3D multisensory environment that includes sound effects, dynamic graphics, and sometimes tactile simulations of a real-life environment.

virus A mischievously written program that copies itself from computer to computer (i.e., via floppy disks or over networks) where it can cause problems such as repeated system crashes, files to disappear, or other similar malfunctions.

World Wide Web (WWW) An information presentation system written in hypertext that allows users to easily access different resources and information on the Internet (e.g., text, pictures, sound, music, and video documents).

COMPUTER SOFTWARE PROGRAMS

The following software programs are recommended for use in elementary classes. All programs listed are available for both PC and Macintosh computers, unless otherwise indicated.

Digital Painting Software

Art Dabbler (grades 3–up)—Corel

Kid Pix (grades K–3)—Broderbund

Multimedia Software

HyperStudio (grades K–up)—Knowledge Adventure

Kid Pix Studio Deluxe (grades K–3)—Broderbund

Website Development Software

Home Page (grades 3–up), for Macintosh only—FileMaker, Inc.

Microsoft FrontPage (grades 3–up), for PC only—Microsoft

SiteCentral (grades 2–up)—Knowledge Adventure

Web Workshop (grades 2–up)—Sunburst Communications

Photo-Imaging Software

Adobe Photoshop (grades 4–up)—Adobe

Microsoft Graphics Studio—Picture It! (grades 3–up), for PC only—Microsoft

Art CD-ROMs

A Passion for Art (grades 3–5)—Corbis Publishing

A Is for Art, C Is for Cezanne (grades K–3)—The Philadelphia Museum of Art

Look What I See! (grades K–3)—The Metropolitan Museum of Art

The Louvre: Museums of the World for Kids (grades 3–5)—The Voyager Company

Van Gogh: The Starry Night (grades 4–up)—The Voyager Company

With Open Eyes: Images from the Art Institute of Chicago (grades K–5)—The Voyager Company

NATIONAL STANDARDS FOR ARTS EDUCATION

The *National Standards for Arts Education* are the outcome of the educational reform effort generated in the 1980s and fueled by the 1983 publication of *A Nation at Risk*. In 1990, national education goals were announced, and these were in turn written into law with the passage of the *Goals 2000: Educate America Act*. In this document the arts are named as a core academic subject, as important to children's education as English, mathematics, social studies, science, and foreign language. In 1994, the voluntary National Standards for Arts Education were published, covering the four arts disciplines of dance, music, theater, and visual arts. These articulate what every young American should know and be able to do in the arts.

The National Standards are founded on the value and importance of the arts for the well-being of students and society as a whole. An education in the arts benefits students

> because it cultivates the whole child, gradually building many kinds of literacy while developing intuition, reasoning, imagination, and dexterity into unique forms of expression and communication. This process requires not merely an active mind but a trained one.[7]

An education in the arts benefits society because students who are educated in the arts, as stated in the National Standards, gain tools for:

- Understanding human experiences, both past and present.

- Learning to adapt to and respect others' (often very different) ways of thinking, working, and expressing themselves.

- Learning artistic modes of problem solving, which bring an array of expressive, analytical, and developmental tools to every situation.

- Understanding the influences of the arts, for example, in their power to create and reflect cultures, in the impact of design on virtually all we use in daily life, and in the interdependence of work in the arts with the broader worlds of ideas and action.

- Making decisions in situations where there are no standard answers.

- Analyzing nonverbal communication and making informed judgments about cultural products and issues.

- Communicating their thoughts and feelings in a variety of modes, giving them a vastly more powerful repertoire of self-expression.[8]

The National Standards, furthermore, address the needs of all students, as in an increasingly technological environment overloaded with sensory data, the ability to perceive, interpret, understand, and evaluate such stimuli is critical. The arts help all students to develop multiple capabilities for understanding and deciphering an image- and symbol-laden world.[9]

National Visual Arts Standards

Within the National Standards for Arts Education, each arts discipline is treated with its own content standards: Dance has seven content standards; music, nine; theater eight; and visual arts, six. The six visual arts content standards are

1. Understanding and applying media, techniques, and processes.

2. Using knowledge of structures and functions.

3. Choosing and evaluating a range of subject matter, symbols, and ideas.

4. Understanding the visual arts in relation to history and cultures.

5. Reflecting on and assessing the characteristics and merits of their work and the work of others.

6. Making connections between visual arts and other disciplines.

The national visual arts standards are articulated according to three grade-level groups: kindergarten–grade 4, grades 5–8, and grades 9–12. In the kindergarten–grade 4 standards, the achievement standards are formulated with reference to the developmental levels of these students:

In kindergarten–grade 4, young children experiment enthusiastically with art materials and investigate the ideas presented to them through visual arts instruction. . . . Creation is at the heart of this instruction. Students learn to work with various tools, processes, and media. . . . They learn to make choices that enhance communication of their ideas. . . . As they move from kindergarten through the early grades, students develop skills of observation, and they learn to examine the objects and events of their lives. At the same time, they grow in their ability to describe, interpret, evaluate, and respond to work in the visual arts. . . . Through these efforts, students begin to understand the meaning and impact of the visual world in which they live.[10]

As students move beyond the primary grades, their abilities increase, and these advanced abilities are reflected in the achievement standards for grades 5–8:

In grades 5–8, students' visual expressions become more individualistic and imaginative. The problem-solving activities inherent in art-making help them

develop cognitive, affective, and psychomotor skills. They select and transform ideas, discriminate, synthesize, and appraise, and they apply these skills to their expanding knowledge of the visual arts and to their own creative work. Students understand that making and responding to works of visual art are inextricably interwoven and that perception, analysis, and critical judgment are inherent to both.[11]

In the current standards-driven educational environment, states are looking to the National Visual Arts Standards for guidance and are formulating or revising already established standards. Each state is aware of the National Standards but must also consider the work, created locally before the advent of the National Standards. Thus, state standards correlate with the National Standards but, in some cases, are organized differently.

DEVELOPING VISUAL ARTS CURRICULUM

In preservice education, future teachers routinely learn how to develop and write general and subject-specific lesson plans. When engaging in the process of writing visual arts lessons or units, elementary teachers should consult the National Visual Arts Standards as well as consider the possibilities for integrating art with other subject areas.

Integration

Why should teachers consider **integration**, when the arts are important in their own right? After all, the Goals 2000 name the arts as a core, academic subject. The first and most compelling reason for integrating visual arts with other subject areas resides in the fact that there is simply too much content in the school curriculum and not enough time to teach it.

By identifying the mutual interests of subject areas and exploring such curricular devices as thematic units, educators have amplified their opportunities for cooperation, collaboration, and consolidation. Such changes may even have enabled some teachers to end up with additional time for their subject areas within the context of integrated or interdisciplinary study.[12]

A second persuasive argument for integrating the arts is the emphasis in the current educational climate on reading and writing and on standardized testing. In fact, the performance of teachers, in some districts, is measured by the scores that their students receive on these tests. Under these circumstances, teachers are simply not willing to include subjects that will not help them prepare students for these tests.

VISUAL ARTS LESSON DESIGN

Outline for Individual Lesson Plan

The components of a visual arts lesson plan are listed in Table 6.1, Outline for Individual Lesson Plan. In the *Overview of Lesson*, the teacher notes the artwork(s) that will be used during the lesson and the discipline(s) that will focus the lesson, whether art criticism, art history, art production, aesthetics, or a combination of them. The teacher indicates the subject area that will be integrated and also records the general direction of the lesson in the overview.

Lesson Objectives are a statement of what the teacher wants students to understand, learn, or be able to do as a result of the lesson.

Materials and Resources refer to the materials that will be needed by students to participate in the lesson and to the resources that the teacher will use to both prepare for and teach the lesson. All of the above components, *Overview of Lesson*, *Lesson Objectives*, and *Materials and Resources*, correlate with the components *Focus: Mapping the Directions* and *Curriculum Integration* that were used in the model strategies presented in Chapter 5 of this text.

In *Procedures*, the teacher documents the planning for the lesson, how the lesson will proceed (body of lesson), and how the lesson will be brought to closure. *Vocabulary* lists the new words used within the lesson that students need to learn. Procedures and Vocabulary as components correlate with *The Journey* of the Chapter 5 model strategies. *Formative Assessment* is an informal judgment of whether or not students did indeed understand, learn, or were able to do what was stated in the objectives of the lesson. Formative assessment[13] can be as simple as asking students to respond on an index card to the following prompt: What are the three most important ideas you gained from today's lesson? The component *Destination* of the Chapter 5 model strategies corresponds to *Formative Assessment* in the Outline for Individual Lesson Plan.

In writing lesson plans, teachers need to refer to the National Visual Arts Standards and record what specific standards were utilized in the lesson. This practice is a worthwhile endeavor for teachers so that they know they are addressing the national standards. It is also valuable information for parents and the community to know. In the current standards-driven environment, when parents know that their students are learning a defined body of knowledge that is specified in the form of standards, they begin to understand the importance of the arts. The final component *Interdisciplinary Extensions* presents an opportunity for teachers to consider other activities, involving other subject areas, which would enrich or extend the lesson as presented. *Interdisciplinary Extensions* correlate with *Side Trips* of the Chapter 5 model strategies.

Table 6.1
Outline for Individual Lesson Plan

Overview of Lesson
- Focus artwork/s
- Focus discipline/s (art criticism, art history, art production, aesthetics)
- Curriculum integration

Lesson Objectives

Materials and Resources

Procedures
- Planning
- Body of lesson
- Summary/closure

Vocabulary

Formative Assessment

National Visual Arts Standards

Interdisciplinary Extensions

Lesson Plan Outline Correlated with Chapter 5 Model Strategies

Outline for Individual Lesson Plan	Chapter 5 Model Strategies
Overview of Lesson	Focus: Mapping the Direction
Lesson Objectives	Curriculum Integration
Materials and Resources	
Procedures	The Journey
Vocabulary	
Formative Assessment	Destination
National Visual Arts Standards	
Interdisciplinary Extensions	Side Trips

Concept to Classroom: An Integrated Lesson Plan, Visual Arts and Language Arts

Overview of Lesson: In a fourth-grade lesson based on Harry Fonseca's *The Creation* (Colorplate 29), the teacher utilized the disciplines of art criticism and art history to integrate visual arts and language arts. This lesson provided an opportunity to address the description and persuasive writing genres, included in language arts standards.

Objective: Students will understand the meaning of the artwork.

Procedures: To begin the lesson, the class was divided into collaborative learning groups of five students each. The teacher distributed reproductions of Fonseca's *The Creation* to each group, and the group worked together to identify symbols and their meaning. Each group reported back, while the teacher charted the responses.

It quickly became clear that certain symbols, such as the stick figures, were identified and interpreted by all students in the same way, whereas other symbols, such as the wavy lines and the arched forms, were interpreted differently by the groups. Some saw the wavy lines as snakes, others as water. To some groups the arched forms appeared as rainbows; to others, as caves.

After this initial viewing of *The Creation*, the teacher presented contextual information about the artist and this particular work. She related that while the artist Harry Fonseca was enrolled in a Native American art course, he interviewed his uncle Henry Azbill and learned about the Maidu creation story. As a culmination of the course, Fonseca submitted a painting about this creation story. This one assignment resulted in a body of work dedicated to the Maidu creation story, and this work, investigated by the fourth-grade students, was part of this creation story series. From the interview documented by the artist, the teacher rewrote the narrative into grade-level appropriate language and divided the proper names into hyphenated names for ease of pronunciation. The class read together and discussed this narrative to ensure that everyone understood the story:

Maidu Creation Story

The most important figure is Helin-maideh. Helin-maideh created water, misty air, animals, and plants. In the beginning, Helin-maideh has only one friend, Turtle. They float along on a raft. Since they are only two, they become lonely. Because they are lonely, Kodo-yam-peh is created. Helin-maideh tells Kodo-yam-peh that his job is to create earth and people. Turtle dives into the water and brings up dirt under his nails. From this dirt Kodo-yam-peh makes the earth. Now he needs to make people.

Helin-maideh tells Kodo-yam-peh to sleep with two straight willow branches under each arm. In the morning Kodo-yam-peh finds a man and a woman in place of the willows. Kodo-yam-peh continues and creates the seasons, assembly halls, and songs but no dances. The dances come later. At first only the spirits dance.

In another part of the Maidu creation story, the short story of two young boys is told. At the time of this short story, everyone is forbidden to watch the spirits dance. Two young boys see two spirits dancing:

one spirit was covered with meat and the other spirit was covered with vegetables. Because the two young boys saw the two spirits dancing, they died. The story continues with other short stories.[14]

Once the students understood the written text, they returned to their small group work with the reproduction. This time their assignment was to return to the reproduction with the story in mind and decide which parts of the Maidu creation story had actually been represented by the artist in the painting. They were also directed to determine how the story was told in the painting: Was there an order to the story as depicted in the painting? If yes, what was that order? After working in collaborative groups, the teacher asked selected groups to report their findings and other groups to report new and different ideas to the ones already recorded. At the end of the discussion, the teacher asked students the following question: What would you like to ask the artist if he visited the class?

Formative Assessment: After summarizing the conclusions reached by the class, the teacher gave the following writing assignment:

Write a newspaper review on the newly acquired painting, *The Creation*. There will be no room for a picture of the artwork, so you will need to describe the work. Help readers understand what this work means. Convince them to visit the museum to see this new work of art.

After completion of writing, students shared their work in small groups. The teacher also read at a later time individual student writing to make certain that students had understood the meaning of the artwork.

National Visual Arts Standards: 2, 3, 4, 5, and 6.

In the above lesson plan, all of the components of a visual arts lesson plan were addressed, with the exception of the *Materials/Resources*, *Vocabulary*, and *Interdisciplinary Extensions*. The reader can infer these from the procedures as described. The lesson is primarily a visual arts lesson but has been integrated with the language arts curriculum. Almost any multilayered narrative work of art, like Fonseca's *The Creation*, can provide an opportunity for the classroom teacher to address the grade-level language arts curriculum. Allowing students a first encounter with a work of art elicits first impressions, many of which are informed by what students actually know about artworks and by what connections students discover between the work of art and their own life.

Before students encounter the artwork a second time, the teacher can either introduce some contextual information for younger students or the teacher can assign older students reading materials or topics for research in the library or on the Internet. The informed second look will then deepen the students' understanding and lead to richer and expanded student writing. The teacher can then take this first draft writing and work with students to refine and complete the writing in a language arts lesson. Such an integrated lesson is planned from the beginning with the standards for each subject area in mind, that of visual arts and that of language arts, and thereby the integrity of each subject is respected.

VISUAL ARTS UNIT DESIGN

Backward Design

Curriculum writers from all subject areas are currently exploring the ideas of Grant Wiggins and Jay McTighe whose *Understanding by Design*[15] has been published by the Association for Supervision and Curriculum Development. Wiggins and McTighe advocate a "backward design" process for creating curriculum that includes three stages:

1. Identify desired results.

2. Determine acceptable evidence.

3. Plan learning experiences and instruction.

In the first stage, the teacher needs to ask the following questions: What should students know, understand, and be able to do? What is worthy of understanding? What enduring understandings are desired? In the second stage teachers determine what kind of evidence will demonstrate student understanding and proficiency. In other words, teachers develop an assessment plan during this second stage, instead of designing lessons and activities next. With the results (i.e., assessment) clearly in mind, then the teacher can plan the learning experiences and instruction during the third and final stage. At this time, the teacher considers the knowledge and skills that will be needed by students to achieve the desired results, the activities that will teach these required knowledge and skills, and the materials and resources that will be needed.

Outline for Visual Arts Unit Development

Working with this backward design process, administrators and mentors of the Transforming Education through the Arts Challenge (TETAC), an arts education initiative funded in part by the J. Paul Getty Trust and the Annenberg Foundation, explored a curriculum design process for visual arts units of study under the guidance of curriculum consultant Dr. Marilyn Stewart. Several conceptual designs were formulated by collaborative groups, composed of administrators and mentors from the six organizations[16] involved in the initiative, and from these, the California Consortium for Arts

Table 6.2
Outline for Visual Arts Unit Development—Correlated with the Three Stages of Curriculum Design from Wiggins and McTighe

Outline for Unit Development	Wiggins and McTighe
Generate and brainstorm ideas	
Develop an enduring/big idea	
Formulate key concepts or essential questions	Stage 1
Define key art ideas for selected artworks	
Develop unit goals	
Formulate a summative assessment plan	Stage 2
Develop an instructional plan	Stage 3

Education developed the Outline for Visual Arts Unit Development, Table 6.2.

The first five steps from the Outline for Visual Arts Unit Development constitute the first stage of backward design, identifying the desired results. In the beginning, the teacher considers curricular topics, state proficiencies, themes, national visual arts standards, and possible cross-curricular connections along with related works of art to begin the process of deciding what enduring understandings will be the focus of the unit. The **enduring/big idea** of the visual arts unit will be the primary focus of the unit, the idea that is threaded through all of the lessons. This enduring idea will be an idea or theme that has lasting value beyond the classroom.

In order to clarify the enduring idea for students, teachers can break down the overarching, enduring idea into smaller areas of investigation. **Key concepts** are the ideas that are implicit in the enduring idea. For example, an elementary unit, developed by a second-grade team at Grand View Elementary School in the Manhattan Beach Unified School District, focused on the enduring idea of "all life works interdependently in a community." Key concepts for their enduring idea included

1. A community is dependent on the relationships and responsibilities of its members.

2. Every community has a system.

3. Tradition and culture provide structure for a community.

Table 6.3

Joseph Fitzpatrick Was Our Teacher: **Summative Assessment Rubric for Unit Goals 1 and 2**

Criteria	1	2	3	4
Autobiographical: Homage to high school art teacher; Andy Warhol, also student **Multicultural theme:** Bob Marley, Chinese calligraphy, Japanese cereal packaging **Gulf War:** 1992, Pax (peace), bring the troops home **Tiananmen Square:** Civil rights **Heroes:** Charlie Parker, Martin Luther King, Jr., Malcom X, Marie (mother) **Symbols:** Hearts, crosses, number 8, colors red and black	Incomplete, incorrect information; may describe a few art elements, but events, symbols, and experiences that influence Raymond Saunders and give meaning to this work are not noted	One or two events, symbols, or experiences that have influenced Saunders are noted, but information is lacking; focus is mostly on the art elements and design properties that comprise the work	Able to clearly write about three or four events, symbols, and experiences that have influenced Saunders; gives adequate information about the art elements and formal design properties of the work	Shows excellent understanding of the work and artist; gives detailed information about many events, symbols, and experiences of Saunders and relates them back to the work; clearly describes the art elements and formal design properties and ties them to the meaning of the work

Heidi Hayes Jacobs prefers to use **essential questions** to communicate the ideas implicit in the overarching, enduring idea. She feels that a question engages the learner more than a statement.[17] A question invites investigation and inquiry. Whether a teacher uses key concepts or essential questions is not important—what is important is that both strategies provide paths toward understanding the overarching, enduring idea that is the focus of the unit of study.

Inherent within the artworks selected for the unit will be **key art ideas** that form the foundation of the arts. For example, key art ideas include the following: artists can and often intentionally push artistic boundaries with form, media, techniques, and subject matter; art making is about making artistic choices for expressive purposes; artists often use symbols to express their experiences. Key art ideas permeate the arts and are repeated throughout different curriculum units.

All of the above (enduring ideas, key concepts/essential questions, key art ideas) comprise the conceptual foundations for the visual arts unit, thereby providing a rationale for the unit and answering the question: Why is this curriculum unit important for students to study? Meaningful reasons for the study of a visual arts curriculum unit include the following: the unit will result in learning that has lasting value beyond the classroom; the unit will address national and state visual art standards and contain key art ideas; the unit, if integrated, makes cross-curricular connections so that students learn in a more holistic manner. The unit goals of the visual arts unit that are formulated at this point represent the answer to the question posed by Wiggins and McTighe: What do we want students to know? Once these unit goals have been formulated, Wiggins and McTighe's first stage of backward design is completed.

The next step is summative assessment planning. This planning represents the second stage of backward design: determine acceptable evidence. The teacher decides exactly what evidence will demonstrate the understanding of the enduring idea. **Summative or formal assessment**[18] occurs at the end of the unit and can best be accomplished by creating a rubric for this specific purpose.

Only after the summative assessment has been formulated is the teacher ready for the final stage in backward design: plan the learning experiences and instruction. At this point the teacher considers the knowledge and skills that will be needed by students, the activities that will teach these, and the materials and resources for teaching. Each lesson in the visual arts unit will require a separate lesson plan, as shown in Table 6.1, Outline for Individual Lesson Plan.

Concept to Classroom: A Visual Arts Unit

What does a visual arts unit look like, if a teacher follows the Outline for Visual Arts Unit Development? Linda Faircloth is a sixth-grade teacher in the San Juan Unified School District in California. She developed a unit of study with the following enduring idea: our experiences make us who we are. The primary artwork at the center of her unit is Raymond Saunders's *Joseph Fitzpatrick Was Our Teacher* from 1991 (Colorplate 38). The essential questions that developed the enduring idea were the following: What types of experiences make us who we are? What events or experiences have influenced Raymond Saunders? How have your experiences influenced or changed your life? She addressed the following key art ideas: personal experiences can be expressed through art, and symbols are often used to represent and reflect an artist's experiences.

Following Table 6.2, Outline for Visual Arts Unit Development, the teacher now developed three unit goals:

1. Students will understand that artists are influenced by events and experiences.

2. Students will learn that artists often use symbols to express their experiences.

3. Students will become aware that they are influenced by their experiences and can express them in their artwork.

Designing summative assessment for unit goals 1 and 2, the teacher decided that after several criticism explorations students would write about Raymond Saunders's *Joseph Fitzpatrick Was Our Teacher*, using the following prompts: What events and experiences influenced Raymond Saunders to create *Joseph Fitzpatrick Was Our Teacher*? How do you know? What did you see in the painting that made that clear? What symbols did Raymond Saunders use?

For summative assessment of the third unit goal, students would be asked to create a collage using symbols that reflect the experiences and feelings of their sixth-grade year. At the conclusion of the collage, students would write a reflective piece about the symbols they created to represent their feelings and experiences. They would be asked to express why and how they selected the symbols, to what degree the work expressed the experiences and feelings of sixth grade, and if and how they might change the work to better express themselves. A rubric, developed by the teacher, would assist the students in self-evaluation (see Table 6.4).

After the teacher had formulated her summative assessment, she began to develop an instructional plan. Following Table 6.1, Outline for Individual Lesson Plan, she composed six lessons, all of which are referenced to the National Visual Arts Standards.

Lesson 1

Introduction of Raymond Saunders's *Joseph Fitzpatrick Was Our Teacher*

Objectives:

• Students will understand that Raymond Saunders used meaningful symbols and that events and experiences influenced the work.

• Students will understand the meaning of the artwork.

Procedures: This art criticism lesson was designed to take place over several days and was divided into three distinct teaching segments. In the first segment, students were divided into collaborative learning groups of five or six for careful observation and discussion of the artwork. After small group dialogue, a whole class discussion ensued along with the charting of a master list of possible symbols by the teacher.

In the second segment, the teacher began to ask the questions, What does it mean? and How do you know? All student responses were directed back to the painting and substantiated by the work. The teacher shared some information about the people and events represented in the work:

Andy Warhol, Ziggy Marley, Marilyn Monroe, Malcolm X, Gulf War, Tiananmen, Harlem Renaissance, etc. As these people and events were explored, the teacher was generating a list of topics that were assigned to individual students for further research in the library, at home and on the Internet. Individual topics were assigned to more than one student.

The third segment of this lesson involved the students' reporting back on the research topic to small groups. The teacher closed this final segment by facilitating a discussion about the meaning of the artwork after small group discussion.

Summative Assessment for Unit Goals 1 and 2: Students were asked to write about: what events and experiences influenced Raymond Saunders to create this artwork? How do you know? What did you see in the painting that made that clear? Table 6.3 shows the rubric, developed specifically for this summative assessment activity.

National Visual Arts Standards: 2, 3, and 5.

Lesson 2
Introduction of Additional Artworks, Using Symbols

Objectives: Students will learn that artists often use symbols to express their experiences.

Procedures: Before this art criticism and art history lesson, the teacher studied background information about each of the artworks. The teacher then led a discussion about two additional artworks that used symbols: Henri Matisse's *Beasts of the Sea* and Gericault's *The Raft of the Medusa*. During the discussion students explored first one work and then the other, looking for symbols and trying to interpret them. Using the background information, the teacher kept the students focused on the search for symbols.

Formative Assessment: Students chose one of the comparison works to write about in their journal, listing the symbols and writing about the events and experiences that influenced the artist.

National Visual Arts Standards: 2, 3, 4, and 5.

Lesson 3
Aesthetic Discussion

Objective: Students will engage in higher-order thinking, choosing an opinion and supporting their opinion with reasoning.

Procedures: The teacher reviewed the three works presented in the last lesson and posed to the class a series of aesthetics questions. Students were to discuss the questions, state an opinion, and defend it:

- How do we know what the symbols were meant to represent?
- Are symbols always easy to interpret?
- Do we need to have background information to decipher symbols?

- Is it important to know what a symbol represents?
- Can we understand a work without knowing the meaning?

After the large group discussion, the last question was discussed further in small groups.

Formative Assessment: Students wrote about their opinion about the last question and supported their opinion with reasoning.

National Visual Arts Standards: 2, 3, and 5.

Lesson 4
Creating a Collage

Objective: Students will create a personal visual diary, using symbols that represent the experiences and events of their sixth-grade year.

Procedures: The entire art production lesson took place over a series of days to allow time for students to reflect and revise. Students began by making a list of the events and experiences that meant the most to them during the school year. They were to create symbols for each of the experiences next. The teacher presented a lesson in design techniques and in collage to prepare students for the making of their own collage. Several periods of time were given to develop and reflect on the process of creating the work.

Formative Assessment: Students kept a process journal as they selected events, designed symbols, and created their work of art. Students wrote for about five minutes at the conclusion of each session to the following prompts:

- What is the task?
- What are your ideas?
- What problems have you encountered?
- What is your solution?

National Visual Arts Standards: 1, 2, 3, and 5.

Lesson 5
Presentation of the Student Collages

Objective: Students will recognize how they have been influenced by the events and experiences of sixth grade and will present their visual diary to others.

Procedures: In this art criticism activity, students presented their artwork in small groups of five to six students. They related the events/experiences of sixth grade that influenced them, symbols they created, and the ongoing process of creating.

Summative Assessment for Unit Goal 3: Students wrote a reflective piece about their work of art and how well their visual diary reflected the experiences/events that had meaning for them. They self-evaluated their collage with the teacher developed rubic. Table 6.4 shows this rubric, developed especially for this summative assessment task.

National Visual Arts Standards: 2, 3, and 5.

Lesson 6
Aesthetics Discussion

Objective: Students will be able to discuss their opinion pertaining to a personal aesthetics question and then use the experience to support their opinion on an aesthetics problem.

Procedures: Teacher posed the following question: How would you feel if someone's interpretation of your work was totally different from what you intended? Would it matter to you if your symbols and meaning were misinterpreted? The teacher modeled an example of a misinterpretation, using a student work. Students discussed the questions in small groups.

Formative Assessment: Students wrote in their journals, using reasoning to support their opinions, to the following prompts:

- Can we understand a work of art without knowing the meaning of the symbols and the background of the artist?
- Can we enjoy a work of art without knowing the same information?
- Are understanding and enjoying (the work of art) the same thing?

National Visual Arts Standards: 2, 3, and 5.

Table 6.4
Joseph Fitzpatrick Was Our Teacher, Lesson 5:
Summative Assessment Rubric for Unit Goal 3

Criteria	1	2	3	4
Symbols are simple and easily understood	No symbols evident	Some symbols evident, unclear what they represent	Symbols are used and they are easily understood	Unique, creative symbols are used; easily understood
Design uses variance of size, repetition, overlapping, running object off the edge, and color theme	None or only one of the design principles is evident	Some, but not all, of the criteria have been met	All criteria are met, but in a flat, uncreative manner	Unique design is created that utilizes all criteria
Technical craftsmanship is neat, shows knowledge of media; work is complete	Work is incomplete, messy; media not used correctly	Work is complete, but media has an unfinished quality	All criteria are met	Work shows creative, inspired use of media; all criteria are met

The teacher provided many instances for students to work in small groups and to construct their own knowledge. This "teaching through inquiry" or collaborative group learning strategy is grounded on the concept of the teacher as facilitator and not as presenter, the more traditional role for a teacher. If used in the lower elementary grades for short periods of time and with increasing frequency, students will be well prepared to construct knowledge on a meaningful level by the upper elementary grades. The construction of knowledge is one of the basic skills of lifelong learning, a primary goal of general education.

This teacher's unit of study demonstrates quite clearly that a visual arts unit includes ample opportunity for both reading and writing exercises. Expanding one of the writing assignments from the first draft stage to a completed piece integrates language arts into this primarily arts unit. Whenever classroom teachers decide to make connections between the arts and other subject areas, they must take care that the connections are meaningful and not superficial.

Concept to Classroom: An Integrated Curriculum Unit, Visual Art and Social Studies

A second-grade visual arts unit entitled "Working Together," mentioned above and developed by a team of second-grade teachers, was written to enrich the Manhattan Beach Unified School District social studies curriculum of "Depending on Others." In their rationale, these teachers state quite clearly why this unit was important for students to study:

If the world today is a global village, it is important that students begin early to understand our enduring idea: All life works interdependently in a community. During this unit, we want to increase our children's awareness of their roles and responsibilities in relation to themselves, their families, their community, and the world around them. They will also recognize that the actions of each member of a community will have an impact on the community as a whole. Our interdependence is most noticeable in our cultural celebrations, since celebrations are a vital part of every culture. Through studying the artworks *Village Feast* by Miguel Vivancos, and *The Sunflowers Quilting Bee at Arles* by Faith Ringgold, children will learn that celebrations reflect a community's cultural traditions.[19]

How did this team of teachers link the works of art to the social studies curriculum? Miguel Vivancos's *Village Feast* is a colorful painting that shows members of a community interacting in various activities in the setting of a town square or plaza: two musicians play on a platform; children ride on a merry-go-round while an organ grinder plays music; a woman sells oranges; several groups of men and women appear to be dancing; the plaza is decorated with bright, colorful paper lanterns and flags strung above the square; and so on. The two unit goals for "Working Together" were

- Students will understand that cooperative efforts are necessary to build communities.
- Students will understand that celebrations reflect a community's cultural traditions.

In the introductory art criticism lesson, teachers introduced the painting to the students who looked at the work, analyzed its characteristics, and explored the concept of a community and how that community celebrated its traditions.

The formative assessment for this lesson was based on the following prompt: We need to imagine that a student was absent from school today and he or she did not get to learn about *Village Feast*. What would we need to share with them about the painting? Students were to write down three things that they remembered from the discussion about the painting that would help the classmate to learn about it. They were directed to include as many details as they could remember about the painting.

The second lesson began the connection with the district second-grade social studies curriculum "Depending on Others."

Objective: Students will begin to explore the concept of interdependence by writing about an individual's role in the celebration depicted in the artwork.

Procedures: The teacher began by reviewing what had been explored in the previous lesson. Then the students were directed to imagine that they could step into the shoes of any person in the painting. Which person would they choose to be? What are they doing? Teachers added the idea that in preparing for community celebrations, everyone has a role or responsibility to make the celebration happen. Students were then asked: What is your responsibility or role in preparing for the village feast?

Students then described in writing who they were and where they were in the painting; what did they see, hear, smell, taste, and feel; what was their responsibility or role in preparing for the village feast? And lastly students were reminded that the village could not have had the feast without their help and participation. Students wrote from the point of view of the person they had chosen, using the word "I" in their writing. After the writing was completed, each student's photo was scanned into a computer and superimposed onto a figure in the painting, which had previously been scanned as well. The writing was then displayed next to a superimposed picture of each student as they appeared in the painting.

Formative Assessment: Selected students read their written work. After each student had finished reading, the class was asked to identify the person in the artwork that was described.

National Visual Arts Standards: 2, 3, 5, and 6.

The social studies connection was continued in the homework assignment, given at the conclusion of lesson 2: Students were to bring to class the following day a family photo of a celebration and answer the following four questions: What is the celebration or event called? When is it cel-ebrated, or when did you attend this event? Why do you celebrate it, or why do you attend this event? How did you, your family members, or your friends help create or plan for this celebration or event? In lesson 3 students shared and discussed their family photos and discussed how families celebrate traditions. They also created a collage that depicted the celebration, after teachers demonstrated the collage process. As a formative assessment for this lesson, students worked in pairs and exchanged their completed collages, using a checklist for the collage criteria and the following prompt: What do you remember about your partner's collage? Write two things that you remember and explain them. Students were also asked to respond to their own artwork with the following prompts: Which celebration/holiday did you include in your collage? What do these celebrations show us about our/your culture and its tradition?

In subsequent lessons teachers introduced the second artwork of the unit, Faith Ringgold's *The Sunflowers Quilting Bee at Arles*. This work of art expanded students' concept of community to include a group of people with like-minded ideas and goals. As a culmination to their unit, students were directed to synthesize the relationship between a community and its traditions by creating a holiday/celebration for their community, writing about the roles needed in their holiday celebration, and designing a poster to advertise their imaginary holiday. Throughout this unit, the district second-grade social studies curriculum "Depending on Others" guided the planning of the unit as much as national content standards for the visual arts. Both the visual art and the social studies curriculum were addressed in meaningful ways. Students learned about multilayered works of art, created their own works, and investigated their roles and responsibilities to themselves, their families, their community, and the world around them.

Both teacher-developed visual arts units, described above, illustrate clearly the process of curriculum design that results in deep and important understandings for students. A visual arts unit of study not only involves an in-depth look at multilayered works of art but also is centered on an enduring idea that has value beyond the classroom. The unit is, furthermore, integrated with other areas of the classroom curriculum, thus enabling students to learn more holistically. Following the step-by-step process of the Outline for Visual Arts Unit Development, Table 6.2, ensures a solid conceptual foundation for the unit and a well-conceived plan for assessment before individual lessons are designed. The Outline for Individual Lesson Plan, Table 6.1, takes the process the next step by making clear what needs to be addressed in individual lessons. Each lesson plan concludes with a reference to the National Visual Arts Standards, thus ensuring that each lesson meets the National Standards for Arts Education.

INTERACTIVE EXTENSIONS

1. Select and implement one of the 10 ways to use the Internet in the elementary art classes and report to your class on what you found to be useful.

2. Select one of the paint software programs, Kid Pix, Art Dabbler, or a similar program, use it to make an art product, and bring your art product to class for discussion.

3. Review one of the Art CD-ROMs, on page 140, discuss it with your class, and relate how you would use it in your future classroom.

4. Consult the National Visual Arts Standards and find the visual arts content standards for grades K–4. List the achievement standards for each of the six visual arts content standards.

5. Consult the National Visual Arts Standards and find the visual arts content standards for grades 5–8. List the achievement standards for each of the six visual arts content standards.

6. Look back in the chapter and locate the fourth-grade visual arts and language arts lesson that focused on Harry Fonseca's *The Creation*. Work through the lesson as presented, and write a newspaper review as suggested.

7. In a small group, select another subject area. Propose an integrated visual arts lesson that integrates with this second subject area. Select works of art for your visual arts lesson. Be sure to consider the content standards for both visual arts and the other selected subject area.

8. Write a lesson plan for the integrated visual arts lesson you proposed in the previous question. Use the Outline for Individual Lesson Plan, Table 6.1. Don't forget to include the National Visual Arts Standards.

9. Look back in the chapter and find the sixth-grade visual arts unit, which focused on the artwork *Joseph Fitzpatrick Was Our Teacher* by Raymond Saunders. In a small group of three to five students, complete the first lesson of this unit and the summative assessment for unit goals 1 and 2. Evaluate your performance with the rubric, Table 6.3.

10. In a collaborative group of five students, develop the conceptual foundations for a visual arts unit of study. Consult the Outline for Visual Arts Unit Development, Table 6.2, and determine the following:

    • An enduring idea and associated works of art to be studied.
    • Key concepts or essential questions.
    • Key art ideas.
    • Unit objectives.
    • Summative assessment for the unit objectives.

    Complete the assignment by writing a rationale for the proposed unit that explains why this unit is important for students to study.

11. Continue work on the visual arts unit you proposed in the previous question. Develop an instructional plan of four to six lessons. The lessons you develop should be comprehensive and address art criticism with an emphasis on finding meaning, art history, aesthetics, and art production.

CHAPTER

A Narrative Time Line of World Art:
Looking at Western and Non-Western Artworks

Chapter Outline

Art history attempts to classify developments in art by time period and style. This primarily linear approach identifies clusters of ideas and stylistic conventions as keys to recognizing the visual language of one period and culture as distinctive from another. Just as words and visual symbols carry specific meaning, depending on the time and place in which they are used, the art style has to be decoded in its historical context. The ideal proportions of the human figure in classical Greek art differ from the ideal nude portrayed by a Flemish artist of the **baroque** period. A belching smokestack in a nineteenth-century urban view celebrates the progress of the Industrial Revolution; in the twentieth century the same image portrays an ecological system in peril or the vices of corporate greed. Values, as conveyed through artistic conventions, are influenced by geography, politics, economics, religion, and so on.

An art historical survey presents guideposts to reading the values and conventions of the culture in which the work was produced. But this progressive view of presenting art—one style succeeding another—can also be limiting or misleading. The latter is particularly true when comparing Western and non-Western art and in viewing art produced since the second half of the twentieth century. However, viewing art of other times and other cultures within its context is an excellent way to engage students of all ages in a sensory-rich, interactive exploration of the values and ideas of past, present, and future generations.

Some key differences between Western and non-Western art:

Western Art

>   Rooted in ancient Greece and Rome.
>   Presented as an expression of ideas, emotions, experimentation, and invention.
>   Based on perceptual illusion of the three-dimensional real world from the Renaissance until the late nineteenth century.
>   Distinguishes fine art from functional arts.
>   Considers the importance of the artist as an individual from Renaissance forward.

Non-Western Art

>   Rooted in Asia, sub-Saharan Africa, indigenous art of the Americas, and Oceania.
>   Links spiritual and secular daily life.
>   Values continuity and tradition over invention.
>   Not based on conventions or realistic illusions of three-dimensional world (laws of perspective).
>   Historically blurs distinction between fine and functional arts.
>   Not based on artist as celebrity or importance of the individual.

This brief chronological guide noting the major periods and styles of art and important artists begins with the earliest achievements of humankind and moves through the cen-

Figure 7.1 **Bull, detail of ceiling painting, ca. 12,000 B.C. From the Caves of Lascaux near Montignac, France, 18 ft. long.**
Courtesy of French Government Tourist Office.

turies to artworks created in modern times. This chapter is a reference only, a point of departure for locating more in-depth information in both visual and written materials. Numerous books, videos, the Internet, and other resources go beyond the scope possible within this book.

Though artistic achievements of the Western world—that is, Europe and the United States—receive much attention, students should also be aware of the non-Western world's rich history of remarkable artistic accomplishments. Today's culturally diverse population needs to be acquainted with popular art forms as well as with those of folk artists around the world. The importance of the traditional arts of Mexico, Japan, China, India, Islam, Africa, Australia, Latin America, and other regions must not be overlooked. A study of ethnic art forms from around the world can help us gain insights into our own backgrounds as well as the heritage of other cultural groups. In addition, students need to develop a sensitivity to the art forms that surround us and enhance the quality of our lives—shopping center and mall designs; highway, park, and home landscaping; container, utensil, and packaging designs; jewelry; furniture; clothing; cars; magazines; photographs; advertisements; and films and video.

WHEN ART BEGAN

Discoveries in fairly recent years, the first being in 1875, have revealed humans' earliest attempts in prehistoric times to visually represent their ideas and feelings. Cave paintings in France and Spain, as well as in North America, show the human form represented as a stick figure, although careful attention is given to the details of the animals shown. The first paintings from these hunting economies were done about 30,000 years ago in the Old Stone Age. They are found on the roof of the Altimira cave in Spain. Other caves in Spain, as well as some in France, have revealed marvelously painted animals.

Figure 7.2 **Cheops pyramid and sphinx. Giza, Egypt.**
Historical Pictures Collection/Stock Montage, Inc.

The people who made these wondrous depictions of bison, deer, boars, and elephants, as well as symbolic figures of themselves engaged in the hunt, probably did not call their works "art." These early artworks were likely efforts to control the enormous, fierce creatures upon which these people depended for meat and furs. These Stone Age hunters had only the crudest weapons. How such lifelike images, many depicting animals in motion, could have been created in the dark underground caves is difficult to understand. Perhaps the artists were initially inspired to make these images when they observed the bulging contours of the stone interiors of their caves; when they traced a few lines of the creatures, they may have imagined they saw a more tangible form. These early paintings often show arrows and spears pointing at the animals. Early artists used natural colors—pigments they found in different earths, charcoal, and such—and mixed them with fat, blood, egg, or plant juice. They made brushes of animal fur, feathers, moss, and leaves.

Prehistoric humans also fashioned simple stone and bone tools for utilitarian purposes. Even in these earliest implements, we recognize humans' special need to embellish and make beautiful practical objects. During these pre-historic times, both human and animal figures were carved from horns, stones, and other materials. The famous *Venus of Willendorf*, with her broad hips and breasts, represented fertility and was probably called upon to ensure the survival of the tribe.

ARTWORKS IN ANCIENT TIMES

Art of the earliest times—the ancient world—gives us some idea about how people lived and what they valued and believed. We know from artworks that from about 30,000 to 2500 B.C., people lived in groups, had a language, made and wore clothing, lived in dwellings, and had distinguishing ways of decorating their containers, utensils, and homes. When people learned to use such metals as bronze and copper, about 3000 or 4000 B.C., civilization as we know it began. People abandoned caves and built shelters. They grew food and raised domestic animals. They invented reading and writing for keeping records and for exchanging information over distances. People lived in larger communi-

Figure 7.3 **Portrait head of Queen Nefertiti, ca. 1370 B.C., New Kingdom, eighteenth dynasty. Painted limestone, ht. 20 in.**
State Museums of West Berlin.

ties, even cities. Ancient art reached through several cultures, some contemporary with each other. Many of these ancient peoples lived near the Mediterranean Sea and Middle East Asia, extending as far as China and Japan. They all left magnificent artistic achievements.

By about 3000 B.C., the four major civilizations had developed in Egypt, China, India, and Mesopotamia. One of the best known of these early civilizations appeared about 3500 B.C. in Egypt. The Nile River made the Egyptians prosperous, and the surrounding deserts and the Mediterranean protected the inhabitants. Egyptian civilization, with its art and architecture suggesting stability and permanence, changed little for more than 3,000 years, making it not only one of the earliest but the most long-lived civilization in history. Most of what we know of ancient Egypt comes from the tombs of royal families. The Egyptians believed that life on earth, at least for the nobility, continued after death. Thus, the bodies of the nobility were preserved as mummies and the tombs painted with scenes of the pleasures of daily life. The size and exactness of the pyramids are amazing. One pyramid is made up of more than two million blocks of stone, each stone weighing more than 2½ tons. The modern

world was fascinated when the untouched tomb of Tutankhamen, brimming with remarkably rich artworks, was discovered in 1922.

Egyptian art is divided into three major kingdoms: the Old Kingdom, the Middle Kingdom, and the Empire. The pyramids of Giza are examples of the powerful architectural accomplishments of the first period. The pharaohs represented deity figures on earth, and the tombs they built contained stone sculptures, pottery, jewelry, and useful objects they would need in the afterlife. The Egyptians believed that spirits of their gods dwelt in certain animals and birds, such as the cat and the hawk, and they worshiped these images. An Egyptian pharaoh is often shown in the form of an animal, or at least with some features of an animal. For example, the sphinx has a human head and the body of a lion. The Egyptians often depicted a beetle or scarab pushing the sun across the sky in the manner of a dung beetle pushing its egg in front of it. The magical powers of the scarab in a piece of jewelry placed in Tutankhamen's tomb was thought to protect the dead pharaoh.

Elaborate temples built in honor of the ruling emperors characterized the art of the Middle Kingdom and the Empire. The artist, architect, and builders worked together in constructing these edifices, making decorative colonnades, walled surfaces, furniture, and implements. The Egyptians began using the post-and-lintel system in constructing their temples. Sculptural forms were often part of a building's structural support. Also attributed to this splendid age are magnificent examples of metalwork, furniture, pottery, and glassware. The most famous of these temples were uncovered at Luxor and Karnak. Some of the memorable artworks from Egypt include a bejeweled sculpture portrait of Queen Nefertiti wearing an ornate headdress and the coffin cover for King Tutankhamen, dating to 1340 B.C. and made of gold and semiprecious stones. Hieroglyphs (picture writing) on the walls of tombs and on scrolls contain figures and objects that represent words or sounds. Architecture and sculpture were the major art forms, with some paintings surviving today on tomb walls. The typical Egyptian stance for figures shows a profile view of the head, arms, and legs, and frontal views of the body and eyes. Important people were painted larger than slaves and servants.

During this time, Mesopotamia (the land between the Tigris and Euphrates Rivers; now called Iraq) was occupied by the Sumerians, the Babylonians, the Assyrians, and the Persians. Mesopotamia was a melting pot of different cultures, each passing on its religious beliefs, customs, knowledge, and skills. The land was flat, and the people built shrines on top of manufactured mountains, where they placed offerings to the gods whose forces they believed controlled the universe. They also placed images of the rulers and priests who they believed could ask the gods for mercy and favors.

Here, the Sumerians recorded accounts of how they believed their world began, stories with which ancient Hebrew writers were almost surely familiar when they wrote parts of the Old Testament. The Sumerians developed a cuneiform system of writing and also developed the world's first legal codes. Mesopotamia lacked wood and stone in any quantity; thus, the Sumerians used mostly sun-dried clay bricks to build temples and palaces replete with relief sculpture, metalwork, and frescoed murals. They seemed to be more concerned with the here and now than with an afterlife. These accomplished builders explored the possibilities of the archway in their architectural constructions. They made glazed tiles for wall decorations. Their most notable achievement in palace construction was a colorful tower called a *ziggurat*. For the most part, Sumerian art tells us about a vigorous artistic society.

The main accomplishments of Assyrian art date from 1000 to 600 B.C. and are seen in the architecturally magnificent palaces that house many fine sculptures and wall paintings. The Assyrians carved gods and animals on walls to protect the king. Statues were worshiped as gods throughout the ancient world. The militant, warlike nature of the people was reflected in their art, with scenes of battles, wounded animals, and monsters found in both sculpture and wall paintings. Assyrian art shows traces of Sumerian art but on a much grander scale. Unlike the stiff, stylized approach seen in the art of the Egyptians, the Assyrians expressed life with vigor and brusqueness. The Assyrians destroyed and rebuilt Babylon; its luxury under King Nebuchadnezzar was legendary, and the Hanging Gardens became one of the Seven Wonders of the World. The walls of the city boasted glazed bricks depicting huge reliefs of fierce lions.

The Minoans on the island of Crete and the Mycenaeans, who lived on the nearby Greek mainland, developed civilizations between 2000 and 3000 B.C. that were quite different from those of Egypt and Mesopotamia. These two groups were fishermen, seafarers, traders, and pirates. The ruling classes lived in fine palaces and villas complete with bathrooms and walls covered with bright paintings. Though they built no temples, the Minoans and Mycenaeans worshiped a mother goddess and sacrificed bulls to her. A double axe and the horns of a bull are symbols that often marked their shrines. Bull leaping was a popular sport that both young men and women practiced. A famous wall painting from Crete, dated 1500 B.C., shows an acrobat grasping the bull's horns while another athlete somersaults over the bull's back. Women played an important part in Minoan religious ceremonies. A well-known terra-cotta figure shows an elaborately dressed, bare-breasted woman holding a snake in each of her upraised hands. The Mycenaeans built massive stone walls to protect their cities and in time conquered the Minoans and absorbed a good deal of their culture. Disaster came about 1100 B.C. in the form of earthquakes, fires, and invading by armies from the north. The glories of these

Figure 7.4 Exekias, *Achilles Slays the Amazon Penthesileia*, ca. 540 B.C. Black-figured neck amphora, ht. 16⅓ in. *Reproduced by courtesy of the Trustees of the British Museum.*

lands are remembered in Homer's epic poems.

Another ancient civilization was that of Persia, with its exciting examples of woven and ceramic ware that can be traced as far back as 5000 B.C. Another culture, some 1,500 years before Columbus sailed to the New World—the Maya—flourished in Central America. The Maya developed a writing system and a refined and notable architecture; they also made spectacular achievements in the world of mathematics and astronomy. Though they lacked metal, wheels, or beasts of burden, they built towering temples and developed agriculture. Most Mayan art is related to the gods they believed controlled the sun, rain, wind, water, and such. Corn was the basis of their life, and every stage of the crop's growth was marked with religious ceremonies. The corn god was the most revered of the deities, and many statues of him were placed in tombs and temples. When the Mayan civilization declined, the Aztecs of Mexico and the Incas of Peru came into dominance, the latter being in control until Spanish conquerors brought horses and cannons and took over Incan lands in the sixteenth century.

Figure 7.5 **Parthenon, ca. 447–32 B.C. Acropolis, Athens.**
Photo by Barbara Herberholz.

CLASSICAL ARTWORKS

The Greeks

Western civilization and arts begin in ancient Greece. The arts and sciences together defined the laws of balance, harmony, and perfection. The earliest Greek vase design consisted of geometric patterns (tenth century B.C.), while later works (eighth century B.C.) incorporated stylized human and animal forms, painted in bands or friezes around the object. Later, vase paintings and murals involved figures in narrative form, stories of gods and mythic heroes, and contemporary scenes of warfare and entertainment. Furthermore, the elegant vase forms of the Greeks each conveyed the specific function for that vessel. An amphora, with its two handles and large neck, was the vessel type used for storing wine, honey, corn, and such.

By 600 B.C., the Greeks no longer worshiped animal gods but fashioned gods in their own image who had the traits of humans, both bad and good, and could be understood in human terms. A marble statue (originally painted with bright colors) of a youth, Kouros, was made early in the development of Greek sculpture, 525 B.C., before anatomy was clearly understood. In time, artists developed an understanding of anatomy and learned how muscles and bones control the body positions. This lifelike art in classical Greece was accompanied by the belief that spirits could inhabit images. Classical sculptors were not interested in expressing emotions in the faces of their figures because they believed that idealized mortals were almost divine and did not indulge in ordinary passions. Two of the most famous sculptures are *Winged Victory* (the goddess Aphrodite) and the *Venus de Milo*, both made late in the classical period and showing lifelike figures of perfect beauty. Some of the names of Greek sculptors are known to us, the most influential being Phidias, Myron, Praxiteles, Polyclitus, and Lysippus.

Architecture, too, conveyed ideals of perfection and grandeur. The Parthenon, built from 448 to 432 B.C., exemplifies these stylistic and mathematical inventions. Columns were bent and curved slightly but convey the illusion of straight lines. Built under the leadership of the statesman

Figure 7.6 *Procession*, **detail of *Ara Pacis*, ca. 10 B.C. Frieze, 63 in. wide.**
© Alinari/Art Resource, New York.

Figure 7.7 *Lady Antonia*, **36 B.C. Marble, ht. 27 in.**
Reproduced by courtesy of the Trustees of the British Museum.

Pericles, this structure was sacred to Athena and stands on the Acropolis, a hill overlooking Athens.

At about the time Greece was reaching its most glorious period, the Etruscans, with their fierce warriors and skilled metalworkers, came into power in Italy, north of the Greek colonies. They worshiped a number of different gods and placed in tombs everything they deemed necessary in the afterlife. We know that music and dance were important to these peoples from the paintings on tomb walls. The rulers wore purple robes as symbols of office and laid out their cities on a gridiron plan, as did the Romans who followed them.

The Romans

The Etruscan city-state of Rome was organized in 753 B.C. Etruscan rulers were overthrown about 400 B.C., and the Roman Republic was established. According to legend, the abandoned twins Romulus and Remus were suckled by a she-wolf; when they were grown, they founded the city of Rome at the place where a shepherd had found them. A famous bronze sculpture commemorates this legend. Within a few centuries, the Romans, with their talent for government and their desire to conquer, expanded into the largest empire ever known in the world. Initially, they borrowed ideas from all the peoples they conquered. In time, though, Romans developed more realistic, literal interpretations of the human figure. They replaced the ideal image that Greek sculptors used with a realism that showed every sagging muscle and wrinkle. Idealized features were reserved for

portrait busts of emperors and politicians. In addition to statues and busts, Roman sculpture also took the form of narrative reliefs or friezes. In this sculptural format, the carved figure emerges from, and remains clearly attached to, a background. Details of features, and the folds of garments, create crisp linear patterns across the surface. This linear frieze format lent itself well to visually unfolding heroic events along columns and building facades.

They were great engineers, constructing roads, waterways, and public baths. Their engineers were the first to use the arch and concrete in constructions. The Roman Colosseum, built from A.D. 70 to 82, remains one of the largest structures ever built. Despite its massive size, the Romans created balance by harmonizing rows of vertical columns—a different design for each story—and with horizontal bands of arches, creating both a visual rhythm and humanizing scale to the building. Designed to seat more than 50,000 spectators, the Colosseum form is the basis for the present-day stadium structure.

On the interior walls of villas and houses of the aristocracy were paintings of landscapes, still lifes, animals, and religious and historical subjects. The best known of these survive in the cities of Herculaneum and Pompeii because volcanic ashes covered these towns in A.D. 79, thereby preserving them for centuries.

Cultures in the East and West were unaware of each other's existence until the middle of the first century B.C. At this time, Roman armies, in pursuit of a Parthian army, suffered a major defeat. Their introduction to the Far East came in the form of the silk flags and banners of their opponents. From this contact, a silk trade developed, finding a ready market in Rome.

The power of Rome, once the largest and wealthiest empire on earth, gradually diminished after several hundred years of peace, and by the fifth century, the medieval period, or Middle Ages, began. The fall of Rome in the fifth century was the end of an era, but not the end of classical influences.

Figure 7.8 **Colosseum, Rome (aerial view).**
Photo © Robert C. Lamm.

WESTERN ART

Medieval Art

This 1,000-year period, from approximately A.D. 400 to 1400, and its remarkable artistic expressions can be summarized by the shift in values from the pleasures of earthly pursuits to the concern with spiritual salvation. Realistic interpretation in painting and sculpture was no longer the guiding principle in medieval art. Stylized forms and symbols laden with meaningful content were directed to a largely illiterate population. Christianity, after centuries of persecution, was now the dominant religion in Europe, and theologians were the source of power and influence. Therefore, the design of architecture, sculpture, manuscript illumination, and other art forms was intended to conform to religious conventions and to inspire religious devotion.

Art of the period is usually divided into at least three styles: Byzantine, Romanesque, and Gothic. The earliest form, Byzantine, takes its name from the eastern Mediterranean city of Byzantium, which became the center of Christianity and art in the fourth century. In A.D. 313, when the emperor Constantine converted, Christianity became the official religion of the Roman Empire. Constantine moved his court from Rome to the town of Byzantium, which he renamed Constantinople. Here, the distinctive Byzantine style of art developed. Mosaics rich with decorative patterns showed figures with long faces and unusual gestures. Paintings were flat and decorative, with figures representing saints and holy people, as well as the emperor and empress, depicted in frozen, rigid positions. These images were called *icons*, and in the eighth century, people called *iconoclasts* (image breakers) disapproved of them and destroyed all they could find. Such artists as Cimabue and Duccio worked with the stiff, formal patterns and flat backgrounds typical of the Byzantines. The flat handling of paint and the decorative style may have been influenced in part by a desire to discard the paganistic influences of Greece and Rome, where realism and humans had been considered of utmost importance.

In the fifth century A.D., barbarians overran the Roman Empire in the West, and for a while learning continued only in the monasteries. Because the printing press had not yet been invented and most people were illiterate, the church used art to instruct and inspire the people. Monks kept the glow of culture alive with their illuminated manuscripts of sacred and scholarly texts. They worked in rooms called *scriptoriums*, copying the Bible in Latin by hand on fine parchment called *vellum* (animal skin). Decorations and pictures appearing in the margins and used for initial letters were called *illuminations*. Gold leaf beaten so thin that you could see through it, and sometimes impressed with a pattern, was attached to these paintings and illuminated manuscripts. The Book of Kells, made in Ireland about A.D. 800, is a beautiful example of this art form.

Economic and social conditions were such during the Middle Ages that people had to devote full time to survival. The church was the binding source of artistic inspiration and achievement. Its power was felt in law, science, economics, literature, and the Crusades (military expeditions that sought to reclaim the Holy Land from the Muslims).

In the sixth century, Pope Gregory declared that paintings were useful for teaching people about the Bible. Altar pictures painted on three panels were called *triptychs*. Brightly painted sculptures and colorful stained-glass windows also were used to inform and inspire people. Giotto's innovative painting techniques, on both altar pieces and frescoes on church walls, foreshadowed the coming Renaissance. In A.D. 800, the pope crowned the French king Charlemagne as the first Holy Roman Emperor. Charlemagne hoped to restore his Christian homeland to the glory and grandeur of the past, so he imported scholars and artists. To guide them in their work, he brought in manuscripts and

Figure 7.9 **Cathedral at Amiens, ca. 1225.**
© *Scala/Art Resource, New York.*

works of art from the ancient world. In the latter part of the medieval years, skilled metalworkers made suits of armor for knights to wear in combat or in tournaments; other craftspersons wove tapestries filled with symbols and stories to hang on the cold stone walls of castles and churches.

Another notable artwork from this period is the *Bayeux Tapestry*, an embroidered pictorial account of the Norman conquest of England in A.D. 1066. Many women stitched the hundreds of figures on the 230-foot-long fabric background of this tapestry.

The **Romanesque** style is associated with the great wave of church construction that began about A.D. 1050. Borrowing from Roman precedents, builders and designers of this period added stone vaulting and constructed spaces to accommodate throngs of pilgrims who traveled between these sacred spots.

Toward the end of the Middle Ages, especially in the twelfth century, the old feudal systems began to deteriorate, and towns began to grow and become centers of learning, with the church providing strong leadership. The **Gothic**

style, introduced about A.D. 1200, led to some of the most innovative and daring building designs ever seen. Buildings such as the Cathedral at Amiens incorporated soaring interior spaces, intricately ornamented exteriors, pointed arches, exterior flying buttresses, richly decorated sculpture, and stained glass windows designed to emit an unearthly, graceful light. Builders, sculptors, and painters were skilled craftsmen who worked in guilds. Such a system did not recognize the artist as an individual. No artist's name is found on the carved stones, painted frescoes, illuminated parchment, stained and leaded glass, and such.

As the Middle Ages neared its end, the lords who constantly engaged in war between the city-states were intent on ensuring that future generations would remember their glorious battles. **Paolo Uccello** (1397–1475) was the master of these military paintings. He painted an enormous work recalling a Florentine victory in 1456 for Cosimo de'Medici.

Renaissance

Literally meaning a "rebirth," the Renaissance (approximately 1400–1500) appeared first in southern Europe. It signaled a revival of interest in classical art and thought as well as renewed interest in humanism. The classical formulae developed in earlier Greek and Roman architecture were reintroduced in Renaissance structures. Subject matter in painting opened beyond the figure to show the world, the beginning of interest in landscape painting. Artists of Northern Europe, such as Albrecht Dürer, retained some of the conventions of the Gothic style such as an emphasis on linear qualities, distorted perspective, and minute detail. Portraits were often painted in profile, like the heads portrayed on Greek and Roman coins. Printmaking, a new medium, developed in Northern Europe during this time. The oldest technique, woodcuts, emerged in 1400 and engraving followed in about 1430. Dürer elevated the art of engraving to its most sophisticated possibilities, creating light and spatial illusions unequaled by his generation.

Artists who worked in Florence—where the Renaissance began—introduced warmer, more human emotions in their interpretation of sacred subject matter. In time, they revealed the personality of their subjects. Even though they continued to paint religious subjects, they emphasized the lives of human beings and their accomplishments on earth. They studied anatomy to learn how the body works so that their artworks would be more lifelike and realistic.

It was also during this period that artists demonstrated a new-found concern for accurately portraying the three-dimensional world on a two-dimensional surface through the laws of perspective. Three other significant milestones of this period include the development of the oil paint medium, the use of light and shadow to convey the illusion of modeling (called *chiaroscuro*), and the triangular or pyramid arrangement of figures or objects in a composition to create symmetrical balance.

Figure 7.10 Giotto, *Lamentation*, 1305–6. Fresco, 7 ft. 7 in. × 7 ft. 9 in. Arena Chapel, Padua, Italy.
© *Alinari/Art Resource, New York.*

The Florentine painter **Cimabue** (ca. 1240–1302) represents a transition from the medieval to Renaissance style. He began changing some of the old Byzantine methods by incorporating a feeling of movement in their gestures and faces and by adding a sense of three-dimensionality to his artworks. He retained the gold background and patternlike arrangements of figures and objects. It remained for the great artist and architect **Giotto** (ca. 1266–1337) to break away from the Byzantine tradition and lay the foundation for the Renaissance. In his scenes of the lives of Christ and Mary, he showed real emotions, naturalism, and human warmth. He shaded the figures and put deep shadows in their clothing. He painted with egg tempera, a medium that uses an egg as the binding agent for powdered pigment and that was perfected by the fourteenth-century Florentines. Egg tempera was the dominant medium for painting until oil paints almost completely replaced it in the sixteenth century. People had been accustomed to dark colors in the Byzantine panels, and the clearness and brightness of Giotto's works gave the impression of soft daylight on a scene and paved the way for later artists.

Active commerce gave Italy money to sponsor art on a magnificent scale. Both painters and sculptors created lifelike portraits of recognizable individuals. No longer were artists considered little more than capable workers, as they were during the Middle Ages. Master artists, who belonged to guilds, took on youths as apprentices in their workshops. Church officials, the nobility and ruling classes, and wealthy merchants commissioned most artworks. The most important patrons of the arts were the Medici family of Florence.

Noted artists of the Italian Renaissance included the sculptor **Donatello** (ca. 1386–1466). His *David* was the first life-size, bronze, freestanding nude since ancient days. It combined classicism with realism. **Masaccio** (1401–1428) revolutionized painting in his short lifetime. In *The Tribute Money*, a famous fresco, he placed solid, modeled figures in a landscape that had great depth. Fresco, in which pigment is applied to wet plaster, was a popular medium during the Renaissance. Large murals painted in this manner could be viewed from any angle without glare. They also were washable. Assistants helped the artist, since the work was done in sections and had to be completed while the plas-

Figure 7.11 **Leonardo da Vinci, *The Last Supper*, ca. 1495–98. Mural, oil, and tempera on plaster, 14 ft. 5 in. × 28 ft.** *Refectory of Sta. Maria della Grazie, Milan. © Alinari/Art Resource, New York.*

ter was still wet. Masaccio is believed to have learned perspective from **Filippo Brunelleschi** (ca. 1377–1446), a great Florentine sculptor and architect. **Lorenzo Ghiberti's** (1378–1455) bronze designs for the massive doors of the Baptistery in Florence won a landmark competition and assured him a place in history.

Sassetta's (ca. 1392–1450) delightful paintings are small, narrative, and reminiscent of medieval book illustrations. The paintings of **Fra Angelico** (ca. 1387–1455), a priest, were made in the traditional manner of the early Renaissance, with decorative patterns and lesser concern for perspective. By the mid-fifteenth century, **Andrea del Verrocchio** (1435–1488) was producing innovative and important sculptures, paintings, and metalworks in his studio and attracting many young artists, among them Leonardo da Vinci. **Andrea Mantegna** (1431–1506) used perspective and foreshortening in a daring and startling manner. *Primavera* and the famous *Birth of Venus*, with their flowing, rhythmic lines, are examples of **Sandro Botticelli's** (ca. 1444–1510) masterpieces.

With the Italian High Renaissance came such artists as **Leonardo da Vinci** (1452–1519), whose genius embraced the arts and sciences and who worked in a variety of media (Colorplate 31). His fresco *The Last Supper*, painted in 1495–1498, demonstrates a new-found concern for accurately portraying the three-dimensional world on a two-dimensional surface using the laws of perspective.

Another important development near the end of the Renaissance was the expansion of patronage from the religious to the secular world. Up to this period, the Catholic Church supported the arts and therefore dictated the subject matter and themes.

The influence of the Italian Renaissance spread throughout Europe, with artists from northern Europe coming to Italy to learn and then returning to their homelands. The center of art and culture moved from Florence to Rome during the sixteenth century. The popes saw to it that artists worked to glorify the city with their paintings and sculpture. **Michelangelo** (1475–1564) took four years to paint 342 figures from the Bible on the ceiling of the Sistine Chapel. Regarding himself primarily as a sculptor, he at first refused to accept the pope's assignment. He developed a monumental style of painting solid, three-dimensional figures.

Another artist of great importance was **Raphael** (1483–1520). A popular young painter who died at age 37 from overwork, Raphael was known as the painter of "sweet Madonnas." He also painted murals in the Vatican. **Bellini** (ca. 1430–1516) was one of the first Italian painters to use oil on canvas. Artists from Flanders had visited Bellini's city, and from them he learned of Flemish experiments with oil paint and with painting on canvas rather than wood panels. **Giorgione** (ca. 1478–1510) and **Titian** (ca. 1488–1576), the most famous of all Venetian painters, were students in Bellini's workshop. Mastering the oil-on-canvas technique, Titian painted with warm, rich colors, sacrificing details for the sweeping effect of the entire painting. His rich

Figure 7.12 Michelangelo, *Pietà*, 1498–1500. Marble, 68½ in. *St. Peter's, Rome. © Alinari/Art Resource, New York.*

colors were built up with layers of contrasting glazes. He enjoyed the esteem of popes and princes and helped make full-length portraits fashionable. Giorgione, one of the first artists to paint small pictures for private collectors, integrated figures and landscapes to create moods filled with a poetic reverie. He greatly influenced Venetian painting, especially that of young Titian.

For sixteenth-century women to have careers in art or otherwise was unusual, but **Sofonisba Anguissola** (ca. 1532–1625) became the first well-known woman artist. She and her five sisters came from a wealthy Italian family and were well educated. Anguissola not only painted self-portraits but also created a new kind of picture that showed people in scenes of everyday life. She was invited to paint for King Philip in Spain. Two other women who achieved success as artists during this time were **Lavina Fontana** (1552–1614) and **Artemisia Gentileschi** (1593–1652). Fontana's father taught her to paint, and she became the first woman to make paintings for large public places. The pope invited her to Rome to paint religious works. Many fashionable people had her paint their portraits because she was so skilled in showing their fine clothing and jewelry. Many believe that Gentileschi was the greatest Italian female artist. She often depicted powerful and courageous women from ancient myths, the Bible, or history. Some of her artworks were more than 6 feet high.

Veronese (1528–1588) made paintings that used cool, clear colors and showed many figures, richly dressed in silk, velvet, lace, and jewels. He arranged the figures in large compositions with elegant backgrounds of classical antiquity, nature, or Venetian interiors. His sumptuous style set the standards for eighteenth-century Venetian decoration.

Jean Fouquet (ca. 1420–1477) was a French court painter. His portraits were monumental in construction, full and rounded in contour, and well composed, ranking him among the first Renaissance painters north of the Alps and making him the founder of a French tradition that was to be developed in the sixteenth century. The last great sixteenth-century Venetian artist was **Tintoretto** (1518–1594). His works anticipated the coming baroque style. He worked directly on his canvases without making sketches or underpaintings first. He even distorted and exaggerated shapes for the sake of the composition and the drama of the scene.

Much of what we know about these Renaissance artists comes from the writings of **Vasari** (1511–1574), an artist himself who gathered his information by traveling all over Italy. His first work was published in 1550, and an enlarged edition followed in 1568.

The Late Renaissance dates from about A.D. 1530 to 1600. The art of the High Renaissance was thought to be so perfect that young artists found it difficult to improve on the past. So some of them broke Renaissance rules and distorted the figures and spaces in their compositions; the results were dramatic, and the style was called **mannerism**. **Parmigianino** (1503–1540) achieved this effect in his *Madonna of the Long Neck*. Other mannerists attracted attention by exaggerating the proportions of the human figure and showing their subjects in unusual postures. **El Greco** ("the Greek" (1541–1614) came to Venice from Crete to study art. He later moved to Spain, where the Byzantine art he had seen in Crete and the masterpieces of the Italian Renaissance blended with the grimness of Spanish art to influence his work. He made many realistic yet mystical religious works, as well as portraits of the aristocracy. His elongated figures became easily recognizable as the work of El Greco. Typical of these is *The Burial of the Count Orgaz*. His dramatic *View of Toledo* shows a moody storm raging over the city.

The Renaissance also took place in northern Europe—in Flanders (now part of northern France and Belgium) and in Germany in the fifteenth and sixteenth centuries. It was a period of intellectual ferment stirred up by challenges to the Catholic faith. There, Martin Luther ignited the Protestant revolt. In breaking with the dogma and iconography of Catholicism, many of the emerging reformers banned religious images from their homes and churches. So without the patronage of the church, artists in northern Europe turned to nonreligious subjects, such as landscapes, still lifes, portraits for wealthy merchants, and scenes of everyday life.

Here, artists made paintings filled with details and jewel-like colors. Italian ideas spread there later. Ghent and Bruges were centers for the wool and weaving trades, and

Figure 7.13 **Pieter Brueghel, the Elder, *The Wedding Dance*, ca. 1566. Oil on panel, 47 × 62 in.**
The Detroit Institute of Arts, City of Detroit Purchase. Photograph © 1984 The Detroit Institute of Arts.

many people—merchants and aristocrats—had money to spend on paintings. Flemish artist **Jan van Eyck**, who died in 1441, is generally credited with developing a new oil-painting technique. He started a trend in realism that depicted details with a minute precision that was to be typical of Flemish painters for many years. This came about because oil paints, a mixture of dry pigments, oil, and sometimes varnish, lengthened the drying time and let artists work at a more leisurely pace. Van Eyck produced an enormous altarpiece for the cathedral in Ghent, Belgium. Many Flemish artists used the techniques of Renaissance Italian painters; others continued with the Flemish tradition of **genre** scenes from everyday life. **Hieronymus Bosch** (ca. 1450–1516) had a vivid imagination and invented weird, grotesque creatures in his works reflecting the broader interests of a new market.

Pieter Brueghel the Elder (ca. 1530–1569) worked in the Flemish manner but used perspective and other Renaissance techniques in his depictions of stout, rustic peasants at work or enjoying life. These depictions of ordinary folk engaged in everyday activities are called *genre paintings.* His two sons—**Jan Brueghel** (1568–1625) and **Pieter Brueghel the Younger** (ca. 1564–1638)—also became artists. It was not the Elder who taught them art, but their grandmother, a skilled watercolorist in her own right. **Rogier Van der Weyden** (ca. 1399–1464), an influential early Flemish painter, worked in an extremely natural manner,

using warm colors and subtle tonalities in emotional presentations of religious scenes. **Lucas Cranach** (1472–1553) is remembered for his late Gothic mythological scenes and landscapes with figures, the latter showing precise technique and details of German clothing and landscapes. His paintings are quite small, decorative, and jewel-like.

Important German painters of the sixteenth century were **Albrecht Dürer** (ca. 1471–1528) and **Hans Holbein the Younger** (ca. 1497–1543), whose father was also an artist. Dürer has been called the northern Leonardo because he was a learned man in many fields and had traveled to Italy. He is said to have been vain and handsome, and he painted many self-portraits. He was one of the first great engravers. Holbein, well known internationally, made many portraits, especially in England, where he painted members of the royal household of King Henry VIII as well as designed jewelry, hall decorations, and costumes for pageants.

Baroque Art

The baroque style, which took many forms in Europe, began in Rome, and dates from about 1550 to 1700. Leaders of the Catholic Church commissioned churches, sculptures, and paintings to portray a passionate, highly emotional form of religious art to counteract the forces of Protestantism. This movement was called the *counter-Reformation*. While the

Figure 7.14 **Hans Holbein the Younger,** *Edward VI as a Child*, **probably 1538. Oil on panel, 22⅜ × 17⅜ in.**
National Gallery of Art, Washington, Andrew W. Mellon Collection, Photograph © 2002 Board of Trustees, National Gallery of Art, Washington.

Figure 7.15 **Facade of the Cathedral de Compostela in Galicia, Spain, 1667–1750.**
Photo courtesy of the National Tourist Office of Spain.

Renaissance was equated with classical and the rational, the baroque style was rooted in fervor and ecstasy. It is characterized by dynamic, often violent movement, flamboyant emotion, unusual curving compositions, swirling figures, dramatic lighting, and exaggerated gestures.

In Holland, a predominantly Protestant country, the subjects of still life, portraiture, and landscapes prevailed. Interest in everyday life gave rise to genre subjects. The increasingly wealthy and worldly middle class demanded a wider range of subject matter without the overbearing moral tone of religious art. However, still-life painting embodied hidden symbolism. Flourishing blooms next to wilting petals carried the message of the fleetingness of life, or the "vanitas" theme. Technical abilities to render flowers and other objects with nearly flawless precision were the highest virtues of a still-life painter. **Caravaggio** (1573–1619) used strong contrasts of light and dark to make exciting portrayals of people. The classical landscapes of French artist **Claude Lorrain** (1600–1685) show hills, plains, and the ruins of Rome with tiny figures of people. The greatest of baroque painters was **Peter Paul Rubens** (1577–1649). Rubens was also an international diplomat with boundless

energy. His works were in such demand that he developed a "factory" of helpers. **Anthony van Dyck** (1599–1641) ranks as one of the greatest of all portrait painters.

Another well-known artist of the seventeenth century was **Diego Velázquez** (1599–1660). Court painter to King Philip IV of Spain, he used rich, harmonious colors. His remarkable brushwork created illusions of rich fabrics and flesh. Later, French impressionists admired the manner in which Velázquez made small, roughly textured brush strokes that showed the play of light on a surface.

Baroque painting took another turn in Holland. Since Holland was a farming country, domestic animals and landscapes were popular subjects for painters, as were genre paintings that showed the interiors of tidy, comfortable Dutch homes. Some artists specialized in still lifes showing fresh flowers, food, and dishes. A great deal of Holland's wealth came from sea trade, so pictures of ships and the sea were also popular. **Frans Hals** (ca. 1580–1666) has been called the first great painter of the seventeenth-century Dutch school. His portraits, with their quick, flashing brush stokes, almost seem to be spontaneous snapshots showing exuberant people with dancing eyes, happy laughter, and joyful gestures. Although fewer than 40 of **Jan Vermeer's** (1632–1675) artworks remain, his remarkable handling of

Figure 7.16 **Sir Peter Paul Rubens,** *The Assumption of the Virgin,* **ca. 1626. Oil on panel, 49⅜ × 37⅛ in.**
National Gallery of Art, Washington, Samuel H. Kress Collection, Photograph © 2002 Board of Trustees, National Gallery of Art, Washington.

Figure 7.17 **Diego Velázquez,** *Maids of Honor (Las Meninas),* **1656. Oil on canvas, 10 ft. 5 in. × 9 ft.**
Prado Museum, Madrid. © Alinari/Art Resource, New York.

light influenced artists for several generations. He painted humble scenes of daily life, often embedded with symbolism and mostly showing one or more people in cheerful, sunlit rooms filled with household objects. **Pieter de Hooch** (1629–1688) was an important genre painter who usually depicted interiors of Dutch homes that showed rooms and receding rooms with a precise perspective. His colors were softly warm and the scenes quiet in atmosphere.

Several women achieved measurable success at this time in northern Europe, the most famous probably being **Judith Leyster** (1609–1660). While in her 20s she became the only female member of the Harlem painters' guild and achieved renown for expertly painted still lifes, genre scenes, and portraits in her native Holland (Figure 3.8). She married an artist but kept her maiden name, signing her works with her initials J. L. and a star that stood for her last name "Lodestar." For many years, some of her works were believed to have been created by artist Frans Hals.

One of the most remarkable artists of all time was the Dutch painter **Rembrandt van Rijn** (1606–1669), whose amazing talents captured human emotions in ways never seen before. His many self-portraits chronicle the happy and sad times of his long life. He built up his paintings with many layers of color and dramatically lit important areas. One of his first important commissions was a group portrait called *The Anatomy Lesson of Dr. Tulp.* His best-known work is another enormous multifigured portrait called *The Night Watch.* He also painted Bible stories and scenes from ancient history, and he achieved great success as a printmaker.

In Germany, **Maria Sibylla Merian** (1647–1717) combined art and science by creating paintings and writing books about insects and plant life. She even traveled to South America with one of her daughters and lived in a jungle so she could paint flowers, birds, and insects. **Rachel Ruysch** (1664–1750) became interested in flowers and insects after watching her father, who was an anatomy and botany professor. She and her husband were invited to be court painters for a German ruler. She made many beautiful paintings of fruit and flowers.

French artist **George de la Tour** (1593–1652) is noted for his night scenes that are dramatically lit by candles and torches. The scenes show primarily religious subjects, seen in quiet moods. The opulence of the era is seen in architecture and the lifestyle associated with Versailles.

Figure 7.18 **Jean-Honoré Fragonard, *The Bathers*, ca. 1772–75. Oil on canvas, 25¼ × 31½ in.** *Louvre. Réunion des Musées Nationaux, Paris.*

The Eighteenth Century

With the beginning of the eighteenth century, leadership in art shifted from Italy to France. Societies were formed to sponsor painting exhibits, some sites later becoming public galleries. Rich connoisseurs built private collections. Academies established in European capitals taught students how to paint according to strict rules. The first artist to explore the special uses of chalk to make pastel portraits popular was **Rosalba Carriera** (1675–1757). When a French art collector invited her to leave Venice and come to Paris, Carriera introduced pastel portraits to France and was invited to become a member of the French Royal Academy of Painting. Carriera was also a member of the academy in Rome.

This period witnessed several art movements and philosophies within a relatively short historical period. In France, the ostentatious pomp of the baroque style, associated with Louis XIV and Versailles, evolved into the lighter, more frivolous style of the **rococo**. Flemish-born **Antoine Watteau** (1684–1721), a court painter to King Louis XV, was one of the first to break away from the grandeur of baroque, but his career was cut short when he died of tuberculosis at age 37. Painters such as **Jean-Honore Fragonard** (1732–1806) showed the aristocracy at play in bucolic settings or garden parties. Often these compositions incorporated figures from Greek and Roman mythology to underscore the lack of engagement with the real world and lack of serious content in the art. **Francois Boucher** (1703–1770) moved almost exclusively in the world of the French court. He decorated royal architecture and became the most popular painter of his day, with his influence extending not only to painting but also to interior decoration, tapestries, and porcelain. Boucher painted historical and mythological works, portraits, and pastoral scenes, for which he is most famous.

The smaller rooms or salons of aristocratic patrons needed smaller paintings. Smaller scale decorative arts—furniture, clothing, ceramics, metalwork, and even carriages—rose to higher prominence. The characteristics of this style include the sinuous "s-curve" and "c-curve," shell motifs, ribbon-like scrolls, and lighter silvery and pastel colors. Later in the century, the style spread to northern and central Europe.

The rococo spirit was challenged during the Age of Enlightenment, or the Age of Reason. Authority was fearlessly questioned, and long-held conventions that had governed lives were discarded. Political and social revolutions took place. The American Revolution of 1776 was followed by the French Revolution of 1789. Napoleon's victories and defeats brought about world-shaking developments. People in Mexico and other Latin American countries were also striving for greater freedom. The Industrial Revolution was changing lives.

Jean-Baptiste-Siméon Chardin (1699–1779) painted still lifes and pictures of ordinary people doing their domestic routines or enjoying simple pleasures. His goal was to show goodness and truth in everyday life. **Elisabeth Vigée-Lebrun** (1755–1842) made portraits of most of Europe's royalty, including Marie Antoinette, the queen of France. She painted more than 900 portraits during her long life and is remembered as one of the best portrait painters of the late eighteenth and early nineteenth centuries. Her fame allowed her to be one of the only three women invited into the French Royal Academy of Painting.

Another famous female artist during this time was **Angelica Kauffman** (1741–1807). Though born in Switzerland, Kauffman traveled as a young girl to Austria and Italy with her artist father. Later, she created many historical scenes and helped introduce **neoclassicism**. At this time, it was thought that only men could paint historical artworks, but Kauffman refused to accept this idea. She also painted many portraits of royalty, became wealthy, and was one of the founders of the British Royal Academy of Painting.

Popular Venetian artist **Canaletto** (1697–1768) was the leading view-painter of the eighteenth century. He was a prolific painter, and his panoramic views of cities, canals, churches, bridges, and palaces included much photographic detail.

Francisco Goya (1746–1828) was the official court painter of the king of Spain. He continued to paint even after he lost his hearing in midlife. Napoleon's invasion, with its mercilessly cruel killings, dramatically influenced Goya's artworks. From that point on, his work reflected profound disillusionment with human beings.

William Hogarth (1697–1764), one of the most original and influential of British artists, was the son of a schoolmaster who, during the boy's youth, was imprisoned for debt, an experience that marked Hogarth's later art production. He is best remembered for making a series of storytelling pictures and a series of engravings in which he

Figure 7.19 **Francisco de Goya, *Y No Hay Remedio (And There Is No Remedy)*, from *Los Desastres de la Guerra*, 1814. Etching.**
The Metropolitan Museum of Art, New York. Purchase. Rogers Fund and Jacob H. Schiff Bequest, 1922 [22.60.25(15)].

ridiculed the outlandish behavior of Britain's upper classes. He was perhaps the first artist to use his art for social criticism and to direct his work to a large, unsophisticated public. He was also an excellent portrait painter.

Another English artist, **Thomas Gainsborough** (1727–1788), was both a landscapist and portraitist, often placing his figures in light, feathery landscapes. In *Blue Boy* he showed his profound appreciation and understanding of Flemish portrait painter, **Anthony van Dyck** (1599–1641). Gainsborough's closet competitor was **Sir Joshua Reynolds** (1723–1792). His paintings are composed harmoniously and are completely unified, never being merely pretty or sentimental. Reynolds sought to raise the standing of art and artists.

The Nineteenth Century

In Europe The discovery of the classical ruins of Pompeii and Herculaneum and Napoleon's fascination with ancient Egypt gave rise to one of three major art movements of the first half of the nineteenth century: neoclassicism. Once again the arts turned to the rational symmetrical elegance of the ancient world for inspiration. Line took dominance over color; order took dominance over emotion.

The most important of all neoclassical artists was **Jacques-Louis David** (1748–1825). His work incorporated not only the stylistic features of classicism but its philosophical tenets as well, such as heroism and self-sacrifice. Classicism permeated architecture, interiors, decorative arts, and painting. In such an order, history and classical mythology dominated all other subject matter.

However, the volatility of politics, economics, and society of this era was mirrored in competing movements in the arts. In France, artists rebelled against the Academy. This rejection of old hierarchies and stylized classicism gave rise to the romantic movement. Imaginations fueled by new freedoms, improved travel, and access to exotic cultures expressed themselves in passionate coloration, dramatic compositions, and panoramic landscapes imbued with wonder and awe. Literary references, contemporary heroic events, and one's spiritual relation to nature provided sources for artistic interpretations.

Théodore Géricault (1791–1824) is generally credited with creating the **romantic** style. He emulated the exuberant works of Rubens and showed much spontaneity in his drawing and painting. His *Raft of the Medusa*, which tells of a frigate that sank in 1818, killing many people, was painted when he was 27 and made him famous. Géricault influenced **Eugène Delacroix** (1798–1863), whose numerous artworks showing horses testify to his ability to portray dynamic action. A favorite theme of the romantic painters was showing the power and grandeur of nature—lofty mountains, strong storms, and rough seas, with human beings pictured as small and defenseless. English painter **Joseph M.W. Turner** (1775–1851), who worked in oils and watercolors, tried to give the viewer a feeling of being present at a scene rather than showing how it actually looked.

The third movement to shape the nineteenth century reacted against the grandeur and passions of the romantic movement: realism. In **realism**, artists sought a more truthful interpretation of the world around them, whether in rural or urban settings.

English landscapist **John Constable** (1776–1837) painted directly from nature to produce realistic views of the countryside. His works influenced the Barbizon school of landscapists, a group of French artists who were a part of the romantic movement that lasted from about 1820 to 1850. Working near the village of Barbizon, they sketched out-of-doors and completed their artworks in their studios. Often this interest in realism extended to portraying people at work, thereby elevating the mundane or ignored to prominence. **Jean-François Millet** (1814–1875) created an iconic figure for the movement in his painting *The Sower*. Such feeling for their subjects, though, also tapped into the romantic sensibilities of the realist artists.

Eugene Boudin's (1824–1898) paintings are light and tender in quality, fresh in color and in the portrayal of light and reflections on people and landscapes. He painted luminous skies and gave peaceful impressions of a pleasant landscape. Such artists as Corot, Courbet, Sisley, Manet, and Monet admired Boudin's work. **Honoré Daumier** (1808–1879) was widely known for his political cartoons and today is considered one of the foremost French painters of his century. He was a confirmed realist, but to stress the true character of his subjects, he resorted to distortion. **Gustave Courbet** (1819–1877) was the foremost proponent of

Figure 7.20 **Jean-Francois Millet, *The Sower*, 1814–75. Oil on canvas, 40 × 32½ in.**
Gift of Quincy Adams Shaw through Quincy A. Shaw Jr. and Mrs. Marian Shaw Haughton. Courtesy Museum of Fine Arts, Boston.

Figure 7.21 **George Caleb Bingham, *Fur Traders Descending the Missouri*, 1845. Oil on canvas, 29 × 36½ in.**
The Metropolitan Museum of Art, New York, Morris K. Jesup Fund, 1933 (33.61).

realism. He emphatically rejected idealization in favor of painting the world as he saw it, even its unpleasant and harsh sides. He sometimes applied his paints with a palette knife and worked with only a few somber colors. The landscapes of **Jean-Baptiste Camille Corot** (1796–1875) reflect his love of nature. His early luminous paintings from nature greatly influenced figure landscapists and placed him among the more original artists of the nineteenth century.

French artist **Rosa Bonheur** (1822–1899) was one of the most popular artists of the nineteenth century. A doll in her likeness was even created for little girls. She loved painting animals and did it so well that royalty all over Europe gave her medals for her work.

In America Art served a variety of purposes in fast-growing America from the eighteenth into the nineteenth centuries. Sir Joshua Reynolds's teaching of the importance of historical painting greatly influenced American artist **Benjamin West** (1738–1820). West, one of the early neoclassicists, trained briefly in Philadelphia and then left in 1760 to study in Rome. Three years later, he settled in London, where his studio soon became a gathering place for American students abroad. His painting of *Penn's Treaty with the Indians* shows figures dressed in the clothing of their day rather than in the Roman togas fashionable with the neoclassicists.

John Singleton Copley (1738–1815) was one of the greatest eighteenth-century American artists. He was largely self-taught and made excellent likenesses of his countrymen, including a portrait of Paul Revere in his work clothes and holding a silver teapot he was making. **Gilbert Stuart** (1755–1828) is famous for his portraits of George Washington, one of which appears on the one-dollar bill. **Charles Willson Peale** (1741–1827) was one of several family members, both male and female, who were artists. His niece, **Sarah Miriam Peale** (1800–1885) was the first American woman to support herself with the money she earned painting. The most extraordinary American painter of this period was a Pennsylvania Quaker named **Edward Hicks** (1780–1849). Trained as a coach-and-sign painter, Hicks is most famous for his religious works, especially the approximately 70 variations on the theme of a kingdom in which animals and people live peaceably together.

American artists **William Michael Harnett** (1848–1892) and **John Frederick Peto** (1854–1907) carried realism to the point that the objects they painted seemed like real objects rather than painted images. This kind of art is called *trompe l'oeil*, meaning "to trick the eye."

In America, another group of artists sought inspiration from the unique natural wonders of the "new world" and consciously turned their backs on the influences of Europe. Linked to this thinking, Jacksonian democracy created a new pride in the American wilderness. **John James Audubon** (1784–1851) pictured the birds of America in their natural habitats in a highly realistic and beautiful way. At nearly the same time, **George Catlin** (1796–1872) left his law practice to devote his life to the portrayal of Native Americans. **George Caleb Bingham** (1811–1879) painted genre scenes of the Missouri River, showing male figures as

Figure 7.22 **Cast sculpture showing the western theme typical of Charles Russell's work.**
Collection of the authors.

Figure 7.23 **James McNeill Whistler,** *Arrangement in Gray and Black, No. 1*, **ca. 1877. Oil on canvas, 57 × 64½.**
The Louvre, Paris. Réunion des Musées Nationaux, Paris.

they talked, relaxed, danced, made music, fished, or played cards. The unique contribution of American artists was the focus on landscape, a subject that did not have as high stature among European artists.

The **Hudson River School**—a term that defines a style rather than a school—is associated with sweeping panoramic scenes of the wilderness, sometimes with diminutive figures of humans or animals to emphasize nature's dominance over them and acknowledgment of a supernatural force as creator. Often, these scenes incorporated symbolic religious references. The acknowledged leader of the Hudson River School, **Asher Brown Durand** (1796–1886), depicted landscapes with an engraver's close attention to detail and remarkable poetic sensitivity to the scene. **Thomas Cole** (1801–1848), who first traveled long the Hudson River in 1825 to sketch the Catskills, later walked through the Adirondacks, the White Mountains, and the old Northwest Territory to find his subject matter. His view of the countryside was highly emotional and patriotic. Artists such as **Albert Bierstadt** (1830–1902) (Colorplate 25) painted majestic scenes of the west—the Rocky Mountains, Yosemite, and such. **Frederic Church** (1826–1900), the only student of Thomas Cole, sought more exotic subject matter such as tropical scenes of Central and South America.

Although not associated with the Hudson River School, **Albert Ryder's** (1847–1917) almost mystical scenes of the ocean, with their strange, often yellowish, lighting, were painted in a manner that paralleled the romantic style. Like several artists who painted later in the nineteenth century, **George Inness's** (1825–1894) early work was influenced by the Hudson River School, but later, after contact with the

Barbizon School, he abandoned precise detail for broader style, using glowing light and indistinctly massed forms that gave a mystical view of nature.

Like their European counterparts, a number of artists moved beyond romanticism into realism. **Winslow Homer** (1836–1910) became best known for his paintings of the sea. Many works featured the rugged Maine coast, but he is equally well known for compelling views of rural and urban life. **Thomas Eakins** (1844–1916) paid unblinking attention to facts when he painted, recording honestly and precisely the reality he saw and remarking at the beauty of the wrinkles in an old woman's skin. His interest in anatomy is reflected in his celebrated work *The Gross Clinic*. Philadelphia-born impressionist artist **Cecilia Beaux** (1863–1942) had a vibrant, fluent style, using whites, yellows, and lavenders against a strong black. She married Eakins in 1884.

In the latter part of the nineteenth century, **Nathaniel Currier** (1813–1888) and **James Ives** (1824–1895) formed a partnership to produce inexpensive lithographs that recorded nineteenth-century life in America. More than 4,000 Currier and Ives prints by various artists were issued, and they depicted steamboats, trains, landscapes, newsworthy events, and life on the frontier. In this way, scenes of rural and urban America spread throughout the country and extended patronage to an affordable level.

Other American artists focused their efforts on other aspects of the American frontier. **Frederic Remington** (1861–1909), foreseeing an end to the Wild West, painted cowboys and Native Americans amid scenic grandeur. Likewise, **Charles Russell** (1865–1926) spent years as a trapper and cowboy, drawing and painting the frontier life he saw around him for amusement in idle moments. He was surprised when his works began to sell, and when he married, his insightful wife persuaded him to settle down to art.

Some of the best-known American artists of the late nineteenth century worked abroad, such as **James A. M. Whistler** (1834–1903). He was a socialite, a celebrated wit, and the first American artist to belittle the importance of subject matter, claiming art was for art's sake. He stressed formal, decorative patterns, called the famous painting of this mother *Arrangement in Gray and Black*. His younger American contemporary **John Singer Sargent** (1856–1925) also spent much of his life abroad, painting portraits of fashionable people. When he painted for his own pleasure, he created dazzling watercolors.

In recent years, the contributions of African-American artists have gained appropriate respect and attention. Among the earliest to gain professional stature was **Joshua Johnson** (1765–1830), who painted family portraits on commission, which have a charming modern appeal. Working in the Hudson River School style, **Robert S. Duncanson** (1817–1872) was recognized in his own time as an outstanding landscape painter. **Edward Mitchell Bannister** (1828–1901) became known in artistic circles in both Boston, Massachusetts, and Providence, Rhode Island. He felt compelled to be an artist after reading in a newspaper that while "the Negro may harbor an appreciation of art, he is unable to produce it." Only a handful of his paintings depicted blacks, with most of his works being landscapes in the Hudson River School tradition. Bannister won a gold medal at the Philadelphia Centennial Exposition. Also winning an award at the Philadelphia Exposition was **Edmonia Lewis** (1843–1909), whose marble sculptures in the neoclassical style reflected her feelings against racial prejudice and slavery. Her father was an African American, and her mother was a Chippewa Indian. She was the first African American to become known throughout the world as a sculptor. **Henry O. Tanner** (1859–1937) was a student of Thomas Eakins and was the first African-American artist to achieve an international reputation when he was elected to the French Royal Academy of Painting.

Impressionism

Each of these movements—neoclassicism, romanticism, and realism, and the forms they took in Europe and America—struck a resonant chord with the public and the larger art world and set the tone for the emergence of numerous approaches to modernism by the second half of the century. What began among a small group of French painters as a search for a more accurate understanding of visual perception grew into one of the most revolutionary art movements in history. Many of them insisted on painting outdoors and were called **plein air** painters. These artists also shared the common struggle for a number of years of trying to win critical and public acceptance. When **Claude Monet**

Figure 7.24 **Joshua Johnson, *The Westwood Children*, ca. 1807. Canvas, 41⅛ × 46 in.**
National Gallery of Art, Washington, Gift of Edgar William and Bernice Chrysler Garbisch. Photograph © 2002 Board of Trustees, National Gallery of Art, Washington.

(1840–1926) exhibited a seascape named *Impression: Sunrise*, an art critic derisively called the group of artists *impressionists*, and the artists adopted the name for themselves. When these artists were rejected from showing their works in the prestigious salons (the official exhibitions of the French Royal Academy of Painting), they joined together and sponsored eight of their own shows.

Many adapted their ideas of perspective—elevated point of view, diagonal arrangements, cropped scenery—from Japanese prints that were circulating through the marketplace at the time. Up to that point, Western art built itself upon only Western sources and European conventions. Through impressionism, Western art was thereafter open to a multitude of new influences and experimentations. Although the influences and stylistic features of impressionism's broken light and dabbed brush strokes continued well into the twentieth century, as a formal movement it lasted for fewer than 20 years. Some artists continued as impressionists even though they broke with some of the earlier features of the style.

Early on, **Edouard Manet** (1832–1883) shocked people with his colorful contrasts and unusual techniques. When one of Manet's paintings was first exhibited, a man tried to slash it with his cane. He inspired younger artists who worked in the impressionist style. **Claude Monet** (1840–1926) painted about 40 pictures of the facade of the Rouen Cathedral under many different lighting conditions. He worked rapidly, seizing a particular moment by not mixing different colors on his palette before applying them to his canvas. His strokes of pure colors allowed the eye to blend them. Monet also painted the water lilies and the gardens in his home in Giverny many times. **Camille Pissarro** (1830–1903) studied with Corot before meeting Monet in 1859. Pissarro was a kindly father figure who helped younger artists and introduced them to his friends.

Edgar Degas (1834–1917), who was fascinated with motion, specialized in painting ballet dancers and horses. He preferred to paint indoor scenes and even had a wooden horse in his studio to serve as a model. He was interested in a new invention, the portable camera. With this device, he could capture unposed action, take pictures from unusual angles, and show cropped edges. He worked closely with **Mary Cassatt** (1845–1926), an American artist born into a wealthy Pittsburgh family. Cassatt lived and worked in Paris and is especially known for her portraits of women and children (Colorplate 36). She helped the impressionists gain acceptance in America by urging her well-to-do friends to purchase their works.

Pierre-Auguste Renoir (1841–1919) worked in his youth at a porcelain factory. He is well known for his shimmering effects with light and for his pictures of young women and little girls (Colorplate 32). **Alfred Sisley** (1839–1899) spent most of his life in France, painting landscapes with a delicate sensitivity and careful composition. He remained faithful to impressionism throughout his life, but in addition to recording atmospheric changes in light, he captured the movement of foliage, the shimmer of water, and the textures of cloudy skies. **Berthe Morisot** (1841–1895) was the first woman to join the impressionists, and she persuaded her brother-in-law, Edouard Manet, to take up plein air painting (painting outdoors). She shared the impressionists' love of iridescent light but did not use their short, broken brush strokes. Instead, she developed a fragile, feathery technique.

Postimpressionism

After initial experiments with the perceptual qualities of impressionism, some artists felt that they had exhausted its potential. Others felt, specifically, that impressionism had sacrificed form for color to its detriment. One of the primary forces in this **postimpressionist** movement was **Paul Cézanne** (1839–1906) (Colorplate 16). To Cézanne, all in nature could be reduced to a cone, a cylinder, or a cube. In other words, form mattered. However, Cézanne and others retained the impressionists' interest in light and color. (Pablo Picasso and Georges Braque later pursued Cézanne's method of building up simple geometric forms in a style known as *cubism*.) Cézanne liked to paint still lifes because he could concentrate on the basic forms. He also made many paintings of a favorite landmark, Mont Sainte-Victoire.

Vincent van Gogh (1853–1890), though awakened to the brighter colors that impressionists used when he first came to Paris from Holland, soon reacted against the realism of the impressionists. For him, color, form, and movement

Figure 7.25 **Claude Monet, *On the Seine at Bennecourt (Au bord de l'eau, Bennecourt)*, 1868. Oil on canvas, 31⅞ × 39½ in.** *Mr. and Mrs. Potter Palmer Collection #1927.427. Photograph © 2002 The Art Institute of Chicago. All rights reserved.*

Figure 7.26 **Camille Pissarro, *Boulevard des Italiens, Morning Sunlight*, 1897. Oil on canvas, 28⅞ × 36¼ in.** *National Gallery of Art, Washington, Chester Dale Collection, Photograph © 2002 Board of Trustees, National Gallery of Art, Washington.*

were vehicles for vivid emotional and artistic expression. He put strongly contrasting colors such as blue and yellow next to each other to express his intense feelings more vividly. He loaded his brush and tools with paint and applied the pigment in swirling ridges to create a dynamic tension across the surface of his canvas (Colorplate 14). Van Gogh spent time in the south of France, producing landscapes, flowers, and portraits. His swirling brush strokes easily identify his works. His short, 10-year career as an artist ended at age 37.

Paul Gauguin (1848–1903) was a close friend of van Gogh. Gauguin gave up his family and a successful career as a stockbroker in Paris to become a full-time painter. Most of his time as an artist was spent in the South Seas, where he applied brilliant, arbitrary colors to large, flat areas separated by dark lines. He liked to paint exotic subjects, such as native women set in tropical surroundings ("drawing from nature by dreaming in her presence").

Georges Seurat (1859–1891) was a superb draftsman who invented a new method of painting called **pointillism**. Seurat pushed the analytical approach to color even further than the impressionists. Taking a precisionist's approach, he laboriously applied small dots of pure color over the canvas, juxtaposing complementary colors to stimulate an effect of coloring mixing in the eye of the viewer. His best-known work, *Sunday Afternoon on the Island of La Grande Jatte* (Colorplate 15) took at least two years to produce and was one of only seven works completed in his lifetime. **Paul Signac** (1863–1935) also worked in this manner.

Henri de Toulouse-Lautrec (1864–1901) observed and drew the life in music halls, theaters, circuses, and cabarets of Paris. Born into a wealthy, noble family, he had a normal torso but stunted legs due to childhood accidents. He excelled not only in painting and drawing but also in **lithography**, making posters that advertised music hall performances.

Until he retired in 1885, **Henri Rousseau** (1844–1910) worked as an official in a Parisian tollhouse and hence is often known as "Le Douanier" (customs official). He is usually categorized as primitive or naive, since he never had any formal art training. He never wavered in his belief in the grandeur of the contribution he would make to French art. Ridiculed by the public and critics, Rousseau was acclaimed by a number of his peers, and his work continues to receive delighted responses from surrealists, pop artists, and the public today. His exotic jungle fantasies were based on sketches he made in the botanical gardens and zoo of Paris. He had a superb intuitive sense of design and detailed pattern.

Edvard Munch (1863–1944) went even further than van Gogh in infusing color and form with powerful, expressive quality. His work, such as the well-known image *The Scream*, produced near the end of the century, exemplifies a style known as *expressionism*, which inspired several successive movements well into the twentieth century.

Another shattering influence on traditional approaches to art during the nineteenth century came from the invention of photography in 1839. The discoveries of **Louis-J. M. Daguerre** (1787–1851) in France and **William Henry Fox Talbot** (1800–1877) in England presented artists with extraordinary ways to capture images from the world around them and new ways to speak to their audiences. French artist **Paul Delaroche** (1797–1856) declared, "From this day, painting is dead!" In fact as history has proven, the pictorial arts did not capitulate to this new technology, but instead, photography pushed painting, drawing, and printmaking into new realms of interpretation and picture making.

The Twentieth Century

The post–Industrial Revolution age is characterized by rapid change, particularly in technology, and by profound effects on society and the arts. Artistic developments and styles of the twentieth century are more difficult to define and evaluate, in part, because as an audience we do not have the same analytical distance that we have for previous periods. Classifying artists into "ism" compartments can be confusing also because artists do not always fit neatly into a style, and if they do, they did not necessarily continue in that mode for their entire career. It is clear though that art of the twentieth century represents the most significant break from its precedents and broader cultural interaction than ever before. Developments in the emerging field of psychology had as profound effect on the arts as any other scientific advance. Exploring the landscape of the interior held more potential for artistic invention than relying only on the landscape of the exterior.

Fauvism The first avant-garde movement of the twentieth century to gain international attention occurred in 1905 in Paris with the introduction of fauvism (wild beasts). Inspired by retrospective exhibitions devoted to Cézanne, van Gogh, and Gauguin, a small group of artists charged forward with the idea that color did not have to imitate nature, but that it could express powerful emotions. In addition, artists such as **Henri Matisse** (1869–1954) and **Andre Derain** (1880–1954) were collecting African masks at this time. Exposure to these non-Western influences and to the terrain already explored by the impressionists, postimpressionists, and expressionists encouraged many artists to seek new inspiration for their own work. The general public, as well as the critics, were outraged by this form of visual defiance. Collectively, their work featured bright, discordant colors, distorted form and space, flattened planes, and aggressive brush strokes, which is how they earned the label, "wild beasts."

Later, Matisse's work evolved from this style to rich, decorative patterns suggesting the Persian carpets that influenced him. He is also famous for his cut-paper collages. Others associated with the fauves include **Georges Rouault** (1871–1958), who later turned from bright to more somber colors. His apprenticeship in a stained-glass shop in his youth may have inspired his use of dark outlines to separate areas of color.

German Expressionism At virtually the same time in 1905, a small group of German artists also felt the zeal of redefining art. Calling themselves *Die Brücke* (The Bridge to the Future), their work exploited distortions of color,

Figure 7.27 **Pablo Picasso, *Guernica*, 1937. Oil on canvas, 25 ft. 5¾ in. × 11 ft. 5½ in.**
Alinari/Art Resource, New York. © 2002 Estate of Pablo Picasso/Artists Rights Society (ARS), New York.

form, and space as well, but their purpose was more point-ed. They wanted to expose the psychological tensions and social ills that they associated with the old order. In addition to vividly charged, colorful canvases, they inspired renewed interest in printmaking, specifically the wood-cut medium. Artists associated with this movement include **Ernst Lud-wig Kirchner** (1880–1938), **Karl Schmidt-Rottluff** (1884–1976), **Max Pechstein** (1881–1955), and **Emil Nolde** (1867–1956). Nolde's friend **Käthe Kollwitz** (1867–1945) was sympathetic to the poor and oppressed in her lithographs and sculpture, often showing sad and suffer-ing women (her only son was killed in World War I and her grandson in World War II). The independent spirit of Ger-man artist **Max Beckmann** (1884–1950) is manifested in the stark, heavily outlined, massive figures of his paintings and in his numerous self-portraits. Their work became the cornerstone of German expressionism.

Following soon afterward, another group of forward-thinking artists formed *Der Blaue Reiter* (The Blue Riders) and exhibited together. Led by **Wassily Kandinsky** (1866–1944), they felt that the visual arts should be as abstract as music. Another member of the group, **Franz Marc** (1880–1916), used pure line and color as well as flat-tened planes to portray simplified animal forms, his linger-ing reference to nature (Colorplate 24). **August Macke** (1887–1914) was also a founder of the group but died in World War I. **Alexei von Jawlensky** (1864–1941), although never formally a member, was close to the aims of Der Blaue Reiter. The movement's most significant contribution

to modernism was Kandinsky's abandonment of all refer-ence to figure or nature and his breakthrough to pure **nonob-jective** art (Colorplate 30).

Futurism Futurism was an Italian art movement that began in 1909. One of its key artists was **Umberto Boccioni** (1882–1916). The futurists wanted to incorporate the dynamism of speed, motion, and modern technology into art. **Giacomo Balla** (1871–1958) captured the comic move-ments of a little dog on a leash in a manner that reminds us of stop-frame photography.

Cubism Another breakthrough of the early twentieth cen-tury is seen in a style termed *cubism*. In its purest form, cubism lasted only from 1908 to 1914. The style took two forms: analytical cubism and synthetic cubism. In analytical cubism, the artist usually worked in a muted palette and shattered form into fragments across the picture. This approach suggested the ability to see three-dimensional form in one plane, or all parts at once. In synthetic cubism, artists reassembled objects into their essential structures. Artists **Pablo Picasso** (1881–1973), **Georges Braque** (1882–1963), **Juan Gris** (1887–1927), and **Fernand Léger** (1881–1955) each contributed in unique ways to these inno-vations. Picasso, Braque, and Gris also introduced collage— glued and layered scraps of paper, cardboard, stencil letters, and such—as a medium for cubist expression.

Although most often associated with his experiments with cubism, Picasso's range exceeded any one style. Con-sidered one of the most inventive and influential artists of all time, he expressed himself in several media. Works such as *Girl before a Mirror* (Colorplate 33) demonstrate his continuing evolution beyond cubism into new realms of abstraction. Picasso also pushed beyond "art for art's sake." He understood the power of art to bring attention to political and social conditions. His most powerful work, *Guernica*, brought attention to the atrocities of the Spanish Civil War, which up to that time were unknown or ignored by the rest of the world.

Modernism in the United States Although most of the influential breakthroughs in the twentieth century are defined through French and German art movements, artists in America also pushed the boundaries of style and content. One of the more uniquely American movements in the early part of the century was known by the number of artists involved, *The Eight*. Led by **John Sloan** (1871–1952) and **Robert Henri** (1865–1929), The Eight also included **Maurice Prendergast** (1859–1924), **Arthur Davies** (1862–1928), **George Luks** (1867–1933), **William Glackens** (1870–1938), **Ernest Lawson** (1873–1939), and **George Bellows** (1882–1925). They were also known as the **Ashcan School** because they portrayed the more raw and gritty side of urban life. A critic once labeled Prendergast's work as "spotty canvases" and "artistic tommyrot." With his later success, Prendergast felt vindicated, remarking that he was "glad they've found out I'm not crazy." All but Davies sought to interpret city life and human conditions in American cities. Many of the artists came from a journalism background and imbued their work with an authentic urgency typical of big city newspaper reporting. Based in New York, they worked together from 1908 to 1913.

The independent spirit of The Eight spread after 1908 and culminated in the opening of the **Armory Show** in New York in 1913. Maurice Prendergast, one of The Eight, helped organize the exhibit. The Armory Show, viewed by about 30,000 people, has been called the starting point of modern American art. Approximately a third of the works shown were foreign; they were included to point out the evolution of modern art. This section included works by Delacroix, Corot, Courbet, Goya, Ingres, and a number of the impressionists and postimpressionists. Some of the works shocked the public. For instance, **Marcel Duchamp's** (1887–1968) *Nude Descending a Staircase* created such a furor that a frenzied mob threatened to destroy it. In this artwork, Duchamp depicted a female form in a manner that suggested rapid motion, as seen in multiple-exposure photography. One critic likened it to an explosion in a shingle factory. The press endorsed the public's hostile attitude toward the exhibit; nevertheless, the exhibit was a huge success, stirring up curiosity as it traveled to the Chicago Art Institute and Boston. The exhibit managed to find a few supporters and became the subject of somewhat penitent comments from its critics after it closed. From this time on, modern art found a larger audience in the United States.

Figure 7.28 **John Sloan, *The City from Greenwich Village*, 1922. Oil on canvas, 26 × 33¾ in.**
National Gallery of Art, Washington, Gift of Helen Farr Sloan. Photograph © 2002 Board of Trustees, National Gallery of Art, Washington.

Alfred Stieglitz (1864–1946) was one of the most influential leaders of modernism in the United States. He produced extraordinary photographs of New York's urban life and he operated galleries in New York that advanced American and European work beginning in 1905. He arranged the first exhibitions of Matisse (1908) and Picasso (1911) in his Gallery 291 and encouraged many emerging American painters (such as his future wife, Georgia O'Keeffe) and photographers in their path toward modernism.

New York also launched a later movement from the end of World War I through the 1920s, whose influences lingered throughout the century: the **Harlem Renaissance**. A movement made up of African-American writers, poets, musicians, and artists, it also revealed that American artists were well aware of the European movements. However, the figures and scenes were unique, mining the depths of the African-American experience through epic murals, biblical scenes, narrative series, and contemporary urban and rural experiences. Painters **Aaron Douglas** (1899–1979), **Palmer Hayden** (1893–1973), and **William H. Johnson** (1901–1970), sculptor **Sargent Johnson** (1887–1967), and photographer **James Van DerZee** (1886–1983) were some of the key figures of this vibrant movement. Palmer Hayden was the first recipient of the Harmon Foundation's Gold Medal for distinguished achievements by an African American in the fine-arts field. **Charles Alston** (1907–1977) headed up the influential Harlem Art Workshop in the mid-1920s, which launched the careers of a number of young African-American artists. One of the youngest artists associated with this movement and to come from the workshop was **Jacob Lawrence** (1917–2000), who continued to create strong and vibrant work through the twentieth century (Colorplate 35).

Following shortly afterward was a group of exceptionally independent artists. **Arthur Dove** (1880–1946) combined an advanced degree of abstraction with mystical images of natural forms. **John Marin** 1870–1953) often represented the rugged coast of Maine and the towers of Manhattan in his spontaneous watercolors marked with slashing brush strokes. **Edward Hopper** (1882–1967) showed the lonely desolation of empty streets and isolated people and of lighthouses and seacoasts in his starkly realistic scenes, in which light provided a dramatic element.

Precisionists These American artists worked together in the 1920s, moving beyond a search for contemporary content to further concerns with form. Although they never abandoned reference to the figure, they were known for reducing form to its most essential geometric elements. Italian-born American painter **Joseph Stella** (1877–1946) painted a dynamic series of kaleidoscopic views of the Brooklyn Bridge. **Lyonel Feininger** (1871–1956) painted in a distinctly personal style that is both cubist and architectural in derivation. His buildings, cityscapes, and seascapes are constructed of translucent, overlapping, geometrical planes. Along with artists such as **Charles Sheeler** (1883–1965), **Charles Demuth** (1883–1935), and **Georgia O'Keeffe** (1887–1986), they synthesized the tenets of abstraction and produced a machine age aesthetic. O'Keeffe was outspoken in wanting to push beyond what had been done before. She continued to produce original work throughout her life, from interpretations of city life in the 1920s, to magnified floral and skeletal shapes, to the landscapes of her beloved New Mexico (Colorplate 34).

European Modernism Several European artists were influenced early on by the experiments of fauvism, expressionism, and cubism and then developed their own unique contributions to modernism.

In 1919, German architect **Walter Gropius** founded the **Bauhaus**, a school of architecture, design, and craftsmanship. Its goal was to reunite all forms of artistic efforts—sculpture, painting, and the applied and decorative arts—and to reintegrate them into architecture. It introduced a new concept of art inspired by the memory of the old craftsmen's guilds. Before the Nazis closed the Bauhaus in 1933, it had exerted an enormous and lasting influence. Its teachers included Kandinsky, Klee, Feininger, Moholy-Nagy, Albers, and others.

Other artists working in Europe at this time included **Suzanne Valadon** (1865–1938), who became a painter after an accident while working as a circus acrobat. She used strong lines and bright, contrasting colors in her paintings of landscapes and still lifes. **Maurice Utrillo** (1883–1955) was Valadon's son. She brought him painting materials and postcards of city scenes while he was being treated for alcoholism at age 18, so he took up painting. He is known for his street scenes, many of which show thick brush strokes and white tones.

Maurice de Vlaminck (1876–1958) was an energetic giant of a man whose early works were painted in brilliant orange, red, and blue. He experimented with cubism and showed a preference for pure whites and deep blues. After 1915, he began painting strong, stormy landscapes, overcast skies, and lonely villages in a turbulent style. **Amedeo Modigliani** (1884–1920) was born in Italy but spent most of his short life in Paris. African sculpture, as well as the works of Cézanne and Picasso, inspired the distorted and elongated forms in Modigliani's painting and sculpture. Dutch artist **Piet Mondrian** (1872–1944) carried the idea of using geometric shapes to the extreme of using only straight lines and the three primary colors. The paintings of **Paul Klee** (1879–1940) are filled with signs and symbols that give flight to the imagination. Klee endeavored to capture the spontaneous gaiety of children's art.

Surrealism Although founded in Europe following World War I, surrealism spread throughout Europe and America during the 1920s and 1930s. Introduced by the poet Andre Breton, the term suggests going "beyond realism," which in intellectual terms meant exploring dreams and the unconscious. Like many other movements it grew from earlier experiences (**dadaism**) and eventually took different forms throughout different artists.

Odilon Redon (1840–1916) was a precursor of surrealism in painting and in the exploration of the symbols of the subconscious. Spanish painter **Joan Miró** (1893–1983), classified as a surrealist, practiced a form of visual improvisation to release all conscious control of form or content. Other European artists such as **Salvador Dali** (1904–1989) and **René Magritte** (1898–1967) used a meticulously realistic approach to present the absurd. Dali distorted the familiar, such as limp clock faces draped across unrelated objects in an eerie landscape, to achieve surreal, dreamlike-nightmarish scenes (Colorplate 19). **Giorgio de Chirico** (1888–1978) painted solitary figures, often in incongruous arrangements with a train, tower, or lighthouse, in empty Italian cityscapes. The works of Dutch artist **Maurits C. Escher** (1898–1972) often abound in bizarre metamorphoses and optical illusions that blend elements of surrealism with mathematics.

Although he did not consider himself a surrealist, the work of **Marc Chagall** (1887–1985) also explored the realm of dreams and memories. Rather than tapping into the darker areas of the unconscious, Chagall drew upon his Jewish heritage, the Bible, and his devotion to the folk tales of his Russian childhood. Throughout his career, he fused these potent sources into works composed of recognizable abstract elements (Colorplate 37).

American Scene/Regionalism During the 1930s, with America in the throes of the Great Depression, **regionalist** artists **Thomas Hart Benton** (1889–1975), **John Steuart Curry** (1897–1946), and **Grant Wood** (1892–1942) turned their attention to the American farmer and factory worker. By celebrating the virtues of hard work and its rewards, these artists sought to inspire native pride and confidence at a time of great desperation. In paintings, murals, and photography, the worker was portrayed as hero. No other image speaks more strongly and directly to these virtues than Grant Wood's *American Gothic* (Colorplate 21). **Charles Burchfield** (1893–1967), also a painter of midwestern landscapes, based his early, rather mystical works on childhood emotions and memories of the world of nature. After 1943, Burchfield's works showed a Nordic mysticism in jagged shapes that created a menacing element.

Social Realism Working during this same period, other artists and photographers selected the same subject matter— celebrating the working classes—but with the purpose of showcasing injustices to inspire reform. Also rooted in realism, these artists—such as **Ben Shahn** (1898–1969) and **Reginald Marsh** (1898–1954)—used exaggerated scale and color to convey emotion. The paintings of **Philip Evergood** (1901–1973) depicted the hunger, social discrimination, unemployment, and political oppression of the Great Depression, placing Evergood in the ranks of the social realists. He was one of the hundreds of artists employed by the Federal Public Works Project.

One of the most prominent artists of this movement and this period was a Mexican artist, **Diego Rivera** (1886–1957). Rivera, who studied art in Europe, abandoned modernist content and instead embraced and celebrated the indigenous art of his native country. Starting in 1921, a period of artistic renaissance in Mexico, Rivera and fellow artists **Jose Orozco** (1883–1949), who created savage caricatures dealing with the Mexican Revolution, and **David Siqueiros** (1896–1974), who was the most politically active Mexican artist, gave visual expression to popular political viewpoints of the working classes through murals and graphic arts. Rivera's extensive skills as a muralist brought him international notice and numerous commissions in the United States. His mural series for the Detroit Institute of Arts (Colorplate 26) is considered one of his masterpieces.

Two other Mexican artists made significant contributions to twentieth century art from this period forward. **Rufino Tamayo's** (1899–1991) best works are his easel paintings in which he blended European styles with Mexican folklore. **Frida Kahlo** (1910–1954) (Colorplate 39) was born in Mexico; her father was an immigrant German Jew and her mother a native of Mexico. She nearly died at age 15 in a streetcar accident and spent her life in constant pain. Best known among her works are expressive and soul-searching self-portraits. She was married to Diego Rivera.

Photography, Mid-Century Photography, a medium that never lost power since its introduction 100 years earlier, became a vehicle for social empowerment. In the 1930s, the federal government hired Roy Strkyker, who in turn enlisted a group of photographers to work with him, to pro-

Figure 7.29 **Dorothea Lange,** *Migrant Mother***, 1936. Gelatin-silver print, Nipomo, Calif., 12½ × 9⅞ in.**
The Museum of Modern Art, New York. Purchase. Copy Print © 2001 The Museum of Modern Art, New York.

vide eloquent visual evidence of the plight of the rural laborer. One of that group, **Dorothea Lange** (1895–1965), produced a moving body of work focusing on California migrant workers. One of the images from that series, *Migrant Mother*, became the iconic figure for the impact of the Depression on American families.

In addition to the work of the WPA (Works Progress Administration) photographers, there were many others whose brilliant work defined new directions for this medium. Early on, **Edward Weston** (1886–1958) gained recognition from his romantic, soft-focus pictures. He is remembered, though, for his "straight photography," dramatic straight-forward close-up images of peppers, roots, shells, and other objects. **Ansel Adams's** (1902–1984) landscapes of western America show fine details, a full range of tonal values, and great depth of field. **Berenice Abbott** (1898–1991) is best known for her photographs of New York's architecture, transportation, and people. **Margaret Bourke-White** (1904–1971) photographed industry and cities, as well as natural disasters and World War II. Other notable photographers of this era were **Imogene**

Figure 7.30 **Horace Pippin,** *Victorian Interior,* **1945. Oil on canvas, 30 × 24¼ in.**
The Metropolitan Museum of Art, New York. Arthur H. Hearn Fund, 1958 (58.26).

Cunningham (1883–1976), **Man Ray** (1890–1976), **Paul Strand** (1890–1976), and **Gordon Parks** (1912–).

African American Artists after the Harlem Renaissance

The Harlem Renaissance—which influenced all of the arts, with the help of publishing efforts and dedicated patrons—energized African-American artists working in other areas of the country and in succeeding generations. **Horace Pippin** (1888–1946) taught himself to paint but, unlike his French counterpart Henri Rousseau, was acclaimed in his own lifetime. **Hale Woodruff's** (1900–1980) most famous work is a three-panel series showing a slave revolt on a Spanish ship in 1839, with the slaves being returned to their homeland by John Quincy Adams and other abolitionists. **Richmond Barthe** (1901–1989) was a prolific sculptor who made portraits of famous actors and racial allegories. **Lois Maillol Jones** (1905–) painted cityscapes in the spirit of Cézanne and designed textiles.

Archibald Motley, Jr. (1891–1980) was primarily a genre painter of modern black life and was one of the first African Americans to have a one-man exhibit in the United States. His paintings were often derived from African-American culture and had intensely colored surfaces and images culled from urban sources. **Alma Thomas** (1891–1978) became a full-fledged artist after teaching in the public schools in Washington, DC. **Allan Crite** (1910–) has been called an "artist reporter" for re-creating small but important details of life in the predominantly African-American Roxbury neighborhood in Boston. **Romare Bearden** (1914–1988), whose family home became the social center for key figures of the Harlem Renaissance, used painting and collage techniques to express themes related to African-American life in the rural South and the urban North. He incorporated cubist principles and showed the influence of African sculpture. **Hughie Lee-Smith** (1915–) had parents who encouraged his artistic production. His paintings of aging neighborhoods where old buildings stand isolated and empty often convey a sense of desolation and alienation.

Like Hale Woodruff and Jacob Lawrence, **Charles White** (1918–1979) worked during the Great Depression for the WPA Art Project. He was a strong social critic, working in the style of Mexican muralists Rivera and Siqueiros. **Elizabeth Catlett** (1919–) was active in the civil rights movement and has produced work concerned with social needs. Los Angeles–born **Betye Saar** (1929–), influenced by African-American folk culture and myths, uses many found and earth-oriented materials, such as leather, wood, straw, and cloth, for her assemblage constructions and imaginative tableaux. **Faith Ringgold** (1930–) (Colorplate 17) was born in Harlem. Her story-quilts reflect her childhood experiences and African-American heritage by combining needlepoint, braided ribbon, beads, and painting. A leading member of a movement called *blackstream*, **Benny Andrews** (1930–) makes powerful works that attack American junk culture and show that African-American artists are creating art as unique as American jazz.

Sculpture The twentieth century has also seen important and significant developments in sculpture by artists whose work transcends many of the styles and isms more easily applied to painters. The nineteenth-century sculptor **August Rodin** (1840–1917) is called the "father of modern sculpture" because he constantly experimented with new techniques and ideas. He imbued expression and astonishing realism into full-size figures as well as "fragments." Sometimes, he carved part of a body from a stone and left much of the block uncut and unpolished. Rodin's work served as inspiration for several artists whose work bears little resemblance to his.

Constantin Brancusi (1876–1957), born in Romania, explored an ovoid theme throughout his life, abstracting into stone or metal the essence of physical life forms. American sculptor **Alexander Calder** (1898–1976), with his engineering background, created incredible animated toys before he became widely known for his freestanding metal stabiles and his mobiles with moving elements.

English sculptor **Henry Moore** (1898–1986) carved and cast enormous reclining and seated figures, often using the theme of mother and child. Such natural forms as driftwood, polished stones, and shells, as well as archaic Mexican sculpture, influenced Moore. In 1929, he began piercing holes through solid masses in his works to create negative spaces. He liked his works to be displayed outdoors. Also from England, **Barbara Hepworth** (1903–1975) moved from biomorphic to geometric forms, exploring the interplay of voids and solid masses and reducing her forms to simple shapes with subtle finishes.

David Smith (1906–1965) is known for his cubiform elements of stainless steel—polished, abraded, and arranged at odd angles—that command extraordinary authority. **Alberto Giacometti** (1901–1966), a Swiss sculptor, cast sticklike figures of varying scale, often placing them in dramatic groups. **Louise Nevelson** (1899–1988), an American of Russian Jewish origin, made sculptures composed of found objects, usually wood, arranged in boxes or shelves and occupying a wall taller than the spectator. The assembled sculpture was often sprayed in a solid color, such as black. As a child, **Marisol** (1930–) often traveled to Venezuela and New York with her wealthy French parents. Her brightly painted sculptures of boxy figures are made of wood plaster and found objects, and they satirize contemporary customs and manners (Colorplate 20). **Judy Chicago** (1939–), though trained as a painter, gained enormous recognition with her large, collaborative projects that show feminist content. *The Dinner Party* tells women's history through 39 place settings arranged on a triangular table, each dedicated to a great woman in the past.

Abstract Expressionism European artists, forced to leave their native countries during the 1930s, encouraged interest in **abstract expressionism** in the United States. German-born **Hans Hoffman** (1880–1966) pioneered in the method of freely poured pigment and the theories behind the dynamic "push-pull" impulses of contrasting colors in an abstract composition. Armenian-born **Arshile Gorky** (1905–1948) created fluid forms that coagulated and merged to show a personal surrealism verging on abstract expressionism. By 1942, Gorky's free **calligraphic** brushwork often had no figurative reference.

It was American artist **Jackson Pollock** (1912–1956) who truly liberated the painting surface and dismissed the need for recognizable imagery. With the introduction of Pollock's abstract expressionist style in the late 1940s, New York decisively wrenched the center of art from Europe to the United States. Working with commercial paints, Pollock often poured pigment directly onto his canvas that he placed on the floor. This improvisational approach, also called ***action painting***, earned Pollock the nickname of "Jack the Dripper."

From this point, abstract expressionism developed further through artists **Franz Kline** (1910–1962), **Robert Motherwell** (1915–1991), **Mark Tobey** (1890–1978), **Clyfford Still** (1904–1980), and **Joan Mitchell** (1926–). Tobey's work paralleled the abstract expressionist movement, but he was highly influenced by Japanese Zen philosophy and painting. His works show a kind of calligraphic, spontaneous brushwork called *white writing*. Other developments from the abstract expressionistic base came in the form of *color field* painting. Artists such as **Mark Rothko** (1903–1970), **Barnett Newman** (1905–1970), **Helen Frankenthaler** (1928–), and **Morris Louis** (1912–1962) made color the focus of their work, whether freely formed or more geometrically constructed. Frankenthaler, who stud-

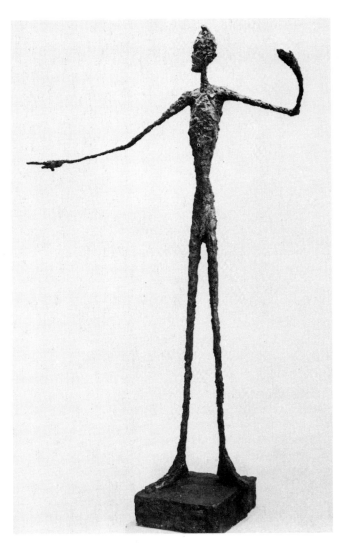

Figure 7.31 Alberto Giacometti, *Man Pointing*, **1947. Bronze, 70½ in. × 40¾ × 16⅜ in.**
The Museum of Modern Art, New York. Gift of Mrs. John D. Rockefeller 3rd. Photograph © 2001 The Museum of Modern Art, New York. © 2002 Artists Rights Society (ARS), New York/ADAGP, Paris.

ied with Hoffman, often uses washes of color, pouring the thinned paint directly onto unprimed canvases. Her abstract artworks contain no recognizable objects; instead, they glow with color and movement. Frankenthaler married and later divorced Robert Motherwell. **Willem de Kooning** (1904–1997) used the expressionistic approach of the others but retained his reference to the figure.

The most significant reaction to abstract expressionism came in California where a group of artists led by **David Park** (1911–1960), **Richard Diebenkorn** (1922–1993), and **Elmer Bischoff** (1916–1991) developed the Bay Area Figurative School.

Pop Art Inevitably for some artists, abstract expressionism ran its course within a decade. From the reactionary

Figure 7.32 **Judy Chicago, *The Dinner Party—Judy Chicago*, 1979. Mixed, 47 ft. per side.**
© Judy Chicago, 1979. Photo by Donald Woodman.

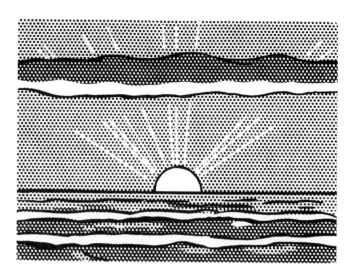

Figure 7.33 **Roy Lichtenstein, *Landscape*, 1964. Pencil and touche on paper, 16⅞ × 21¼ in.**
San Francisco Museum of Modern Art. Gift of John Berggruen. © Estate of Roy Lichtenstein.

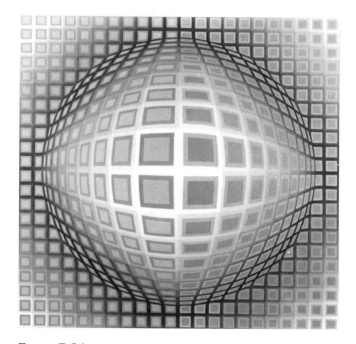

Figure 7.34 **Victor Vasarely, *Vega-Nor*, 1955. Oil on canvas, 78¾ × 78¾ in.**
Albright-Knox Art Gallery, Buffalo, New York. Gift of Seymour H. Knox, 1955. © 2002 Artists Rights Society (ARS), New York/ADAGP, Paris.

movements emerged such artists as **Jasper Johns** (1930–). In one of his best-known works, *Three Flags*, he called attention to an American icon and questioned its meaning, and further, he questioned the meaning of art. This intellectual, seemingly detached approach set the groundwork for pop art. Borrowing directly from popular culture and the iconography of the consumer culture, this next group of artists presented fresh, clean, hard-edged, color-charged mechanical imagery to the public. **Roy Lichtenstein** (1923–1997) adapted his art directly from the pages of battle and romance themes in comic books. To heighten the irony, he used pure, primary colors in a comic strip format and re-created benday dots as his background.

Andy Warhol (1930–1987) utilized everyday consumer products such as soup cans, Coke bottles, and celebrities as his subjects. By eliminating all sense of the artist's involvement in image making—often repeating an image to the point of visual saturation—Warhol called attention even more directly to the public's fascination with consumer culture and the individual's loss of identity within this culture.

Also in the mid-1960s, **op art** emerged. This type of abstract art exploits the optical effects of pattern. Hard-edged, black-and-white, or colored compositions seem to vibrate and change shape as we look at them. **Victor Vasarely** (1908–1997), born in Hungary, is known as the "father of op art." British artist **Bridget Riley's** (1931–) closely packed, curving parallel lines create a strong impact on our eyes.

Minimalism The work of artists such as **Donald Judd** (1928–), **Carl Andre** (1935–), **Sol Lewitt** (1928–), and **Richard Serra** (1939–) rely on clean, bare, machine-made materials to convey what they consider is essential to art. Although the ideas resonate with pop art and apply to the work of several painters, minimalism is linked to hard-edged sculpture. Such work is devoid of expression and image.

This movement was another reaction to the perceived expressive excesses of abstract expressionism.

Realism and Photo-Realism Despite the fascination with abstraction and the various reactionary styles, several artists continued to devote themselves to realism, seeking new challenges within that approach. **Wayne Thiebaud** (1920–), whose sumptuously painted vignettes of food and other everyday objects initially linked him to pop art, is actually a throwback to realists such as Chardin, Hopper, and Eakins. His chief concern is not to portray the inner qualities of his subjects, be they food or figures. His primary interest is in manipulating the formal elements, sometimes returning to the same work and same subject over the course of several years. Recently his subject matter has expanded to dynamic interpretations of San Francisco street scenes and color-charged, elevated views of the rural landscapes of northern California (Colorplate 27).

Richard Estes (1936–) was the first of several artists to use the projected photographic image as the source for his work. Rendering hyperrealistic views of everyday objects and highly reflective surfaces of windows, this approach often echoed advertising art.

Like the work of minimalists, the primary intent of photo-realist artists was to establish an objectively revealed view of the object, not to engage the viewer in specific meaning or reaction. Artists such as **Maria Winkler** (1946–) (Colorplate 40) achieve the sumptuous realism of Estes and others, yet because she selects subject matter with special meaning, a subjective interest enters her work. **Chuck Close's** (1940–) monumental-scale close-ups of faces create the illusion of photo-realism when viewed at a distance, and up close, they dissolve into complicated abstracted patterns of color dots or fingerprints. Such obsession with pattern and the effect of visual perception remind one of Seurat's pointillist technique.

Some realists work in three dimensions, such as **Duane Hanson** (1925–1996), who created his photo-realist sculptures from plaster casts of actual people. His ability to tap into the look and stance of people who are usually taken for granted—guards, tourists, bus riders, and such—creates astonishing reactions in viewers.

Conceptual Art For the past four decades, a number of artists have contended that the idea, or concept, is more important than the object. In this case, media is incidental and at times ephemeral. This category can encompass other categories such as process art (the act of doing is more important than the end product), installation art (objects assembled and intended to collectively convey a statement may be temporary), performance art (staged event with the artist as performer), and environment art (out-of-doors, site-specific, usually to disappear/return to original materials).

Robert Smithson (1938–1973), known for using land as a work of art, was part of a movement termed *earthworks*. This movement rejected commercialism and embraced ecology. In works such as *Spiral Jetty*, massive amounts of rocks and earth were moved to create sculpture-like mounds. **Bruce Nauman** (1941–) has been involved in several forms of conceptual art such as performance art (the artist's body is the medium) and art video neon. The artwork, which may often be ephemeral, is documented in photography or video. **Jenny Holzer** (1950–) uses printed messages to communicate her art, such as billboards, stickers, or electronic panels/signs. Her short, often pithy messages, are ambiguous or clever plays on words. Perhaps the best-known conceptual artist is **Christo** (1935–), whose *Running Fence* and *Umbrellas* projects call attention to the process of arranging the works as much as to the visual impact created.

Postmodernism It will probably take a full generation to reflect upon and sort out the many artistic ideas that currently fit under a term that gained momentum in the late 1980s: **postmodernism**. Most people in the art world define this term as referring to art of the past (before modernism) to create a new statement (after modernism). Eclecticism, appropriation of imagery from previously existing sources, and socially engaged content are just some of the characteristics of this movement. Traditional art subjects such as landscape and portraiture find a place along with computer-generated imagery and video art. Distinctions between genres are blurred or ignored. Appropriation of imagery calls into question the importance of "originality."

Artist **Cindy Sherman** (1954–) appropriates some of the masterpieces of past artists by re-creating the composition and then photographing herself, in costume, as the central figure in this setting. Often, Sherman manages to imbue her re-created images with a provocative message. She calls her work "pictures of emotions personified." **Barbara Kruger** (1945–) combines text and graphic images in a convincing mock-advertising style, taking her viewers off guard to deliver strong, politically charged messages. Further blurring the distinction between high art and low art, **Keith Haring** (1958–1990) used graffiti imagery on subways, billboards, and canvases.

Although his work does not fit into this category of high/low art, **Raymond Saunders** (1934–) has created a rich and eloquent body of work that blends tradition and improvisation, appropriation and invention. In one of his finest works, *Joseph Fitzpatrick Was Our Teacher* (Colorplate 38), Saunders layered elegant chalk-like drawings, heavy slashes of paint, and collaged drawings and posters onto a black background, calling to mind the surface of a blackboard or urban wall. The work carries several recurring symbolic references to his childhood, his heroes, and his mother. The work embraces several global messages as well, including references to the Persian Gulf War and Japanese advertising. At a deeper level, referred to in the title, the work pays homage to an art teacher, Joseph Fitzpatrick.

Figure 7.35 **Frank O. Gehry, *Solomon R. Guggenheim Museum Bilbao*, Bilbao, Spain, 1993–1997.**
The museum is 257,000 square feet with 112,000 square feet of gallery space; it stands on the site of an old factory and parking lot. Its postmodern construction was part of an urban renewal project for Bilbao and cost $100 million.

Andy Warhol also attended classes taught by Fitzpatrick, and Saunders makes reference to Warhol as well with his images of Marilyn Monroe, Elvis Presley, and Coca-Cola bottles.

Architecture Through the medium of architecture, some of the most creative and inventive thinking of this century can be appreciated. The invention of the elevator and the development of steel for structural skeletons were major breakthroughs in architecture. **Louis Sullivan** (1856–1924) was a turn-of-the-century American pioneer whose work led to the evolution of the skyscraper. Sullivan observed that "form follows function" and led architects in rethinking their designs from the inside out. **Le Corbusier** (1887–1965) solved urban design problems with steel columns and reinforced slab constructions. In Europe, a new international architecture that rejected decorative ornamentation and traditional materials evolved between 1910 and 1930. **Walter Gropius** (1883–1969) used these principles in designing the Bauhaus in Germany, a building that shows the interior and exterior simultaneously in opaque and **transparent** overlapping planes. Between 1956 and 1958, **Mies van der Rohe** (1886–1969) and **Philip Johnson** (1906–) designed and built the elegant, austere Seagram Building in New York, with vertical lines emphasizing the feeling of height and providing a strong pattern.

    Frank Lloyd Wright (1869–1959), one of the most influential American architects, designed bold and elegant homes and public buildings, often harmonizing his meticulous attention to design detail with nature and the surrounding site. **Buckminster Fuller** (1895–1983) was a forward-thinking inventor, architect, and structural engineer. Polyhedrons found in nature inspired Fuller's development

of the geodesic dome. The fantastic and striking buildings by **Frank Gehry** (1929–) have become a part of the postmodern scene, his design for the new Guggenheim Museum in Bilbao, Spain, being a fine example. The design is complex with an unusual variety of shapes. Its curvilinear roof forms have been called a "metallic flower."

Artists and the Public

The rapidity with which ideas evolve results in a single artist working through several styles and several levels of discovery within his or her life span. Artists today have become increasingly less dependent on wealthy, influential patrons, which can allow even greater freedom of ideas and expression. However, the question of public support for the arts in the late twentieth and early twenty-first centuries, whether at the local or federal level, has injected an unprecedented level of interest on the part of the general public to define "art."

NON-WESTERN ART

African Art

The art of Africa usually refers to that produced in sub-Saharan Africa, where the influences, materials, and spiritual context are distinct from that of the areas bordering the Mediterranean Sea. The geography, climate, racial groups, religions, and languages of this vast continent are just a few indicators of the diversity of the people and their art. Environments range from grasslands to rain forests, from high mountains to flat, dry plains. There are more than 50 countries that make up the African continent today. Most scholars speak in terms of West, South, or Central Africa. The art of West and Central Africa differs from that of the other regions. The people of East Africa are traditionally nonsedentary, and because of this lifestyle, they are not known for producing sculptures or masks. On the other hand, most of the forests are located in West and Central Africa, providing an abundant supply of wood for sculpture, masks, and such. Most of the art known to Western audiences, and collected by museums, comes from these areas. Each of the many African tribes and kingdoms has its own customs, religion, and language, and each has its own special art. African art varies from realistic to abstract, depending on its function, the particular tribal culture, and the individual artist. Africa's largest art-producing tribe in terms of both quantity and forms is the Yoruba.

    Art, rather than being a separate entity in Africa, is an integral part of the harmonious blend of the tribe's spiritual and social life. Much African art has been made for social and religious ceremonies—ceremonies to ensure good harvests, to protect the tribe, to honor ancestors, to ensure fertility, to cope with natural forces, and to instruct and

Figure 7.36 **Yoruba headdress, nineteenth to twentieth century, Nigeria. Wood, paint, nails; ht. 15¹⁵⁄₁₆ in.**
The Metropolitan Museum of Art, New York. The Michael C. Rockefeller Memorial Collection. Bequest of Nelson A. Rockefeller, 1979 (1979.206.192).

Figure 7.37 **Nimba mask, Baga tribe of Guinea. Wood, ht. 46½ in.**
The Metropolitan Museum of Art, New York. The Michael C. Rockefeller Memorial Collection. Bequest of Nelson A. Rockefeller, 1979 (1979.206.17).

motivate daily life. Art objects relate to the spiritual realm; transmit the laws, moral codes, and history of each tribe to its young; and facilitate communication between the people and the world of the supernatural. They also indicate their owners' wealth and status. The objects made serve a vital purpose while also beautifying the environment. Some of the art objects are not made to be permanent but are used for an occasion and then discarded.

Tribes are modeled on an enlarged family, with the family being the basic unit. The leader or chief represents authority and embodies the tribe's power and wealth. The chiefs and councils of elders and subchiefs try to preserve tribal customs, with many rituals to promote fertility and to appease the unknown that might bring death, disease, and disaster. Ritual acts of purity are intended to cleanse an individual of evil forces, strengthen the life force, and restore order after disruption. A priest or medicine man usually supervises rituals. Many ceremonies are directed toward ancestors, who are part of the tribe's power and who may

mediate between the natural world and the supernatural. A type of ritual sculpture common to most African groups is a fetish. Fetishes are endowed with special powers for particular purposes, perhaps to ward off evil spirits or to attract good ones.

The wearing of masks and headdresses during ceremonies is believed to ensure that the dancer will be possessed by the spirit or force being portrayed. Tribes place great importance on the ability of these masks to influence the spirit world. Three types of masks are (1) the face mask, worn to hide the identity of the person wearing it; (2) the helmet, or shoulder mask—a large, carved mask that rests on the wearer's shoulders and sometimes weighs 75 pounds and makes the wearer appear 8 feet tall; and (3) the head-

Figure 7.39 *Stool with Caryatid*, **nineteenth century, Luba tribe, Zaire. Wood, glass beads; ht. 23¼ in.**
Boltin Picture Library.

Figure 7.38 **Antelope headpiece, nineteenth to twentieth century, Bamana tribe, Mali. Wood, ht. 35⅔ in.**
The Metropolitan Museum of Art, New York. The Michael C. Rockefeller Memorial Collection. Gift of Nelson A. Rockefeller, 1964 (1978.412.435).

piece or headdress, worn like a cap. Mask wearers are entirely costumed while performing with dance and music. Masks are used for major community life events and the life cycle of birth, puberty, marriage, and death. Decorated instruments—drums, harps, ladles, and staffs—are also used in rituals. Deities called *orishas*, along with myths, societies, and cults, require a great variety of masks. Masks can also be a mark of authority, with an actual officer or magistrate wearing a police officer's or a judge's mask. Masks have been carved for special functions, rituals, initiation ceremonies, funerals, and agricultural rites. They are designed to give the wearer courage, to frighten the enemy, and to fight evil forces. Some masks are worn for entertainment.

In addition to masks, sculptures of the human figure are dominant African art forms, although animals may lend features and characteristics of special powers. Sculpted figures are usually tranquil, static, and frontal. Monumental in form, if not in size, they are usually made of a single piece of wood with planes that emphasize contrasting shadows. Figures may be divided into abstract pole types (Sudanese) and naturalistic rounded types (Guinea Coast and Congo). Some sculptures honor past tribal members and the dead. These works are quite abstract, showing amazing creativity and imagination. The sculptures are believed to hold the spirits and energies of the people they honor, since the sculptures do not show how people actually looked. Ancestor figures are not themselves worshiped; rather, they are intermediaries, and many ceremonies are directed toward ancestors. Reliquaries, or grave figures, are sculptural forms placed above containers holding the bones of ancestors.

Much of African sculpture is made of wood, often a single log, with a natural oil finish that not only brings out the beauty of the grain but also is believed to enrich the magical power of the carving. Finished carvings are often ornamented with paint, beads, seeds, and fibers. Many carvings were created in the nineteenth and twentieth centuries. Most of what we see today was created during the last hundred years since climatic conditions did not favor earlier preservation, but these works help us understand the art created by past generations.

Figure 7.40 *Areogun*, 1900–1910, African, Nigeria, Yoruba tribe, Village of Osi. **EPA Society mask, wood with polychrome painted decoration, ht. 49½ in.**
The Toledo Museum of Art. Purchased with funds from the Libbey Endowment. Gift of Edward Drummond Library.

In Mali, the village people of Dogon carve stools, jars, bowls, doors, and figures in both human and animal forms that blend geometric and organic shapes. The sculptural design of their houses and granaries, with their organic relationship to the natural contours of hillsides, inspired contemporary city planners.

The aristocratic Ife in Nigeria peaked between the

Figure 7.41 **Tiananmen Square, Beijing, China.**
Photo by Gene Sahs.

twelfth and fourteenth centuries. Here, bronze sculptures were made by the lost-wax method of casting, a skill probably learned in Egypt. To the south of Ife was the Benin kingdom, where outstanding cast bronze sculptures were created between the sixteenth and nineteenth centuries. The casting technique may have been learned from the Ife in southwestern Nigeria, which was the seat of the Yoruba kingdom from the eleventh until the seventeenth century. Both Benin and Ife sculptures may have roots in the Nok culture in present-day northern Nigeria, with pieces of Nok sculpture being dated between the fifth century B.C. and the second century A.D. Both Ife and Benin figure sculptures show much decorative repetition and are quite lifelike, although some are stylized and show distorted proportions.

Many African tribes carve ivory and make objects of clay. Goldsmithing occurs on the Guinea Coast. Weaving is done on simple horizontal or vertical looms, often in narrow bands. Figures may be woven in or stamped on later.

Unlike Western art, African art fulfills tribal needs, being used for specific purposes on special occasions. The non-Western perspective of African tribal art relies on formal, direct sculptural qualities, such as exaggerated proportions and emphasized heads, eyes, mouths, navels, and genitals, to express or embody its power. Mouths and curving horns of an animal may suggest food and survival as well as signify the animal's power. African art has had profound visual impact on a number of twentieth-century European artists. Picasso and Braque were inspired by these masks as they developed cubism, as was Modigliani when he painted and sculpted his elongated and distorted portraits.

African traditions began to change when trading, Christianity, and Western education were introduced. Cities began to grow, and modern technology created a separation between art and life. Since the beginning of the twentieth century, and the development of markets outside of Africa, a "tourist" aesthetic in many art forms has appeared, which incorporates and appropriates found objects from the industrial world. Contemporary art objects currently are being created more for their individual aesthetic appeal than for the traditional reasons of the past.

Chinese Art

With four times the population of the United States and a history that is 20 times longer, China has a cultural heritage as old as India's. Chinese art has influenced the art of Japan, Southeast Asia, Korea, and parts of Indonesia.

To understand and appreciate Chinese art—architecture, sculpture, painting, calligraphy, ceramics—it is important to understand the role of religion or belief systems throughout the country's history. Taoism, also referred to as "The Way," is the search for truth in the natural world and involves the elements of mysticism and nature worship. Confucianism, at times in conflict with Taoism, is concerned with how people should conduct their daily life, a code of ethics. In art, Confucian beliefs are revealed through order, symmetry, and formality. Buddhism arrived in China, from India, between the fourth and fifth centuries A.D. and reached its highest point during the seventh to tenth centuries. These belief systems fluctuated in importance over time and from region to region; but they influenced all of the arts. To understand these patterns, Chinese art is studied by dynasties, beginning with the Shang Dynasty in 1700 B.C.

In early China, the highest forms of expression were calligraphy, painting, and poetry. Students practiced calligraphy for years before becoming painters. By meditating and contemplating nature, the artist was able to translate natural forms with skillful strokes of the brush. These artists believed in Tao and sought to harmonize with nature. They used black ink on white paper or silk, which symbolized the Taoist idea of duality. Also guiding the artist in making landscape paintings were the cosmological principles of yin and yang, meaning the synthesis of two opposite forces.

Landscape paintings expressed many religious philosophies—the discipline and order of Confucius, the natural and romantic harmony of Tao, and the spiritual and metaphysical insights of Buddhism. The intense colors of Western artists were not available to early Chinese painters; instead, they used black and gray ink, earth colors, and mineral pigments. Of special concern to Chinese artists were trees and mountains, with artists endeavoring to capture their essence or nature. Predominantly horizontal and flat shapes were often stacked vertically to create a feeling of depth. Skilled use of the brush has long dominated Chinese painting.

Fifteen centuries ago, **Hsieh Ho** established a manifesto of six guiding principles that have unified Chinese artists' work ever since: (1) The work must be imbued with life and spirit; (2) the brush must be handled with vigor, giving inner strength to each line; (3) one must be truthful in depicting objects; (4) color should be as it appears in nature; (5) one must attend to harmony in composition and arrangement of

Figure 7.42 **Zhu Da, two sheets from an album of 10 paintings, Ch'ing dynasty, seventeenth century. Ink on paper, ht. 10¹⁄₁₆ in.**
Courtesy of Freer Gallery of Art, Smithsonian Institution, Washington, DC (55.21–B,H.).

the picture; and (6) one should endlessly copy and transcribe masters of the past. Chinese artists spent many years practicing quick, precise strokes, working to show the spirit and the form of the subject through simple, fluid lines that expressed movement, energy, and emotion. Artists were scholars and also used brushes to write.

Over the centuries, Chinese painting styles changed. The artists used three basic formats: (1) The album leaf was part of a sequential book that combined calligraphy, poetry, and painting; (2) the hanging scroll was vertical in format and stored in a roll (a scroll is a long roll of silk, parchment, or paper; the viewer starts at the bottom and moves the eyes upward); (3) the handscroll had a beginning, development, and an end and varied in length from 12 inches to 40 feet. Viewers of a handscroll meditated on each portion of the scene as it unrolled from right to left. Artist and owners added red seal stamps and sometimes wrote poetic thoughts in vertical rows of calligraphy.

After the eleventh century, an increased interest in landscape painting in which ink and watercolors were brushed on silk and paper showed that artists felt that strong colors did not reflect nature's colors and detracted from the brushwork. Line was all important, rather than the light and shadow of Western artists. Colors were softly blended, and if figures were present, they were infused in the surroundings. Buildings, boats, and people were tiny in comparison to the landscape. The Chinese saw the physical universe—earth and sky—as a unit; they believed that the earth was covered with heaven's canopy and that the stars controlled people's destiny.

The belief that people should live together peacefully and should respect their elders was reflected in the earliest Chinese paintings, which showed many images of people. After Buddhism came to China, however, Chinese art changed and instead emphasized Buddhist concepts of nature and meditation. Artists focused on a single idea or object so that they could realize the beauty of the idea or object while capturing its mood. The result was fewer people in paintings.

In their gardens, the Chinese used rocks and water as symbols and arranged trees and plant life symbolic of their beliefs concerning the body and the universe. Lords and kings could afford animals in their gardens to symbolize their wealth and power. By 300 B.C., however, gardens began to represent spiritual peace and served as places to worship in the Taoist and Buddhist traditions.

An outline of Chinese dynasties and the artworks representative of each follows. (A *dynasty* refers to a succession of rulers who were members of the same family.)

Prehistoric (ca. 5000–1700 B.C.) Tools and weapons made from stone and jade with polished and decorated surfaces are representative of the New Stone Age. Pottery was made to store grain, with painted pieces also being buried in tombs for use in the afterworld. The thin, fragile pots made later were used in rituals.

Shang Dynasty (1700–1111 B.C.) When they died, Shang rulers were provided with useful and ceremonial objects, as well as chariots, horses, servants, and family members. Bronze ritual vessels for wine or food were cast with inscriptions that told of the occasion of the vessel's creation. These objects were skillfully crafted and sometimes resembled suits of armor. During the Shang and Chou dynasties, many bronze tools, animal forms, vessels, and weapons were produced, all showing a variety of shapes and decoration.

Chou (1111–221 B.C.) In 1111 B.C., Chou people came from the west as conquerors, and images were substituted for live animals and people in the royal tombs. Objects made of jade were used in burials and were thought to be indestructible. Confucianism (ca. 550–478 B.C.) began. Confucius advocated respect for nature and also humility and patience. He advised that people not withdraw from society but take an active role in it. His thinking focused on human relations and the consequences of one's acts, emphasizing

Figure 7.43 **Attributed to Mu Qi, *Swallow and Lotus*, Chinese, Southern Sung dynasty, mid-thirteenth century. Hanging scroll, ink on silk, 91.8 × 47 cm.**
© *The Cleveland Museum of Art, 2002. Purchase from the J.H. Wade Fund, 1981.34.*

mutual responsibility as the basis of ethics and intellectual life. His Golden Rule predated that of Jesus by 500 years. Taoism (ca. 604 B.C.) emphasized the relationship of human beings to the universe and being in harmony with nature, a principle that is deeply planted in Chinese minds to this day.

Ch'In (221–207 B.C.) King Cheng, the first emperor of China, was a vicious tyrant who buried scholars alive and burned the classical texts. However, he united China, saving it from the internal conflicts of the Warring States (475–221

B.C.). He began the construction of the Great Wall as protection from invaders in the north. King Cheng's tomb, which was only recently discovered, was a huge complex of underground palaces and pavilions that contained 7,500 life-size soldiers and horses made of baked clay, using the slab and coil technique.

Modern Period: Han Dynasty (206 B.C.–A.D. 220) The modern period occurred at the same time as the Roman Empire. Buddhism was introduced from India, and the arts flourished under this new religious spirit. China's borders expanded north to Korea, south to Vietnam, and west to Afghanistan. Silk production increased tremendously, with trade routes reaching Rome and allowing contact with other cultures. Derived from observing the repetition of the seasons, the Chinese idea of duality—yin (darkness, dampness, softness, passiveness) and yang (brightness, dryness, hardness, action)—greatly influenced art.

The legends of Confucius and Taoism provided much of the material for the early art of the Han dynasty. The number of chambers in tombs increased, so that the tombs looked much like the Han houses of the living. Elaborate murals on the walls showed narrative storytelling scenes. Bronze mirrors with polished fronts and low-relief designs on the reverse sides were placed in tombs to bring the dead person into ultimate harmony. Technology improved, giving much vitality to art. Rubbings over carved reliefs became popular. Artisans carved elaborate designs in objects after hundreds of coats of lacquer had been applied. When the Han dynasty collapsed, China fell into chaos until the T'ang dynasty came to power about 400 years later.

Six Dynasties and Northern Wei (A.D. 221–618) For 300 years, China had many short-lived dynasties in the south. The Tartars (non-Chinese people) founded the Wei dynasty in the north. They adopted Chinese customs and Buddhism. Ninety percent of the people of northern China had adopted Buddhism by A.D. 400. Enormous Buddhas, relief carvings, and paintings represented a mix of Indian, central Asian, and Chinese cultures.

Monasteries and Buddhist temple complexes were established. Monks carved the famous Colossal Buddha into stone cliffs in the Gobi Desert, and other Buddhas were carved in caves and dwellings, the caves being used as way stations by travelers on the Silk Road. The temple complexes consisted of buildings arranged across a central axis within a walled compound. One of the buildings was a pagoda, a tower made up of several stories, which was the Chinese version of the Indian stupa. Another building housed the sculptures of the main deities. Small figures made of gilt bronze were objects of dedication and used in temples, shrines, and homes.

T'ang Dynasty (618–907) The T'ang dynasty became the largest and most powerful civilization in the world. Fine arts and decorative arts—goldware, textiles, and glass—

flourished. Thousands of household articles and human figures have been recovered from T'ang tombs. During this time, Chinese sculpture, expressing the new vigor of the Buddhist faith, flourished, although non-Buddhist art, with its lively ceramic horses and riders that represented the warriors who kept order at home and safeguarded the borders, perhaps tells more of T'ang's vigor. The horse has always been a popular image in Chinese art, and many stone carvings, clay modelings, and cast bronze horses were made at this time. A decorative style of landscape painting ("blue and green") and figure painting reached a high point. In the late T'ang period, poetic monochromatic landscapes painted in ink on silk appeared. Prints were carved from woodcut blocks and printed on large presses. Tea drinking became popular, necessitating the production of decorative ceramic ware. Porcelain, a hard, white, nonporous, translucent ceramic, was developed at this time, 800 years before it was produced in Europe.

Sung Dynasty (960–1127 [Northern]; 1128–1279 [Southern]) The powerful Sung dynasty is famous for its scrolls, which were often 50 feet long, and its classical examples of porcelain, each identified by the name of the village that produced it. Although landscapes were painted during the T'ang, the best examples were produced during the Sung dynasty. These works, with their deep, mystical space and airy landscapes, showed a reverence for nature combined with Confucian philosophy and the serenity of Buddha. Monumental landscape paintings, usually with a large mountain, were typical of northern Sung, while southern Sung paintings showed a sense of calm, peace, and humans' unity with nature. These scrolls were viewed in private, not displayed on museum walls as they are in the West. Also of high quality were the woven and embroidered silks and tapestries, along with lacquerware, carved jades, hardstones, and ivory carvings.

Yuan Dynasty (ca. 1280–1368) During the Yuan dynasty, cities grew, and silk and ceramic items were exported to other countries. The miserable situation of foreign domination brought a change of status for artists, and this period is one of individuality and inventiveness. Paintings were more assertive, with some artists discarding ink washes and substituting dry brush lines. Pottery became heavier, while the shapes became sturdier. Overglaze enamels and underglaze designs were introduced.

Ming Dynasty (1368–1644) Porcelain reached a high point during the Ming dynasty. Some painters produced in the conservative traditional manner, and others worked as individualistic scholar-gentlemen, basing their style on various sources. The Imperial Palace (Forbidden City) was established at this time.

Ch'ing Dynasty (1644–1911) The Ch'ing dynasty emphasized intricate patterns, bright colors, and technical perfection in ceramics. Thousands of workers produced

Figure 7.44 **Wu Zhen,** *Poetic Feeling in a Thatched Pavilion*, **Chinese, Yuan dynasty, 1280–1354. Hand scroll, ink on paper, 23.8 ×**
99.4 cm.
© *The Cleveland Museum of Art, 2002, Leonard C. Hanna Jr. Fund, 1963.259.*

ceramics for export to Europe. Courtyard gardens, through which people could walk in covered corridors while looking out lattice windows, became popular. Painting and calligraphy flourished.

The People's Republic of China (1949–Present)

China's art since 1949 has reflected the social and political life of the new government. Many posters have been produced, their themes related to political and popular heroes, defense, women-centered issues, minorities, and political propaganda. Images are representational, as there is no place for pure abstraction.

Japanese Art

Throughout history, Japanese artists have selectively assimilated external cultural influences, especially from China, and creatively absorbed and transformed these influences into unique Japanese art forms. The name Japan comes from Chinese characters that mean "Land of the Rising Sun." Japan has had many fiercely proud rulers who saw in art a means to political ends, as well as objects of beauty for beauty's sake.

Shintoism and Buddhism are Japan's two basic religions. Shintoism grew from a primitive form of ancestor worship and emphasizes reverence for family, race, and the rulers as the direct descendants of the gods. Buddhism was introduced in the sixth century from Korea.

The great theme of Japanese art has been the combination of human beings and nature and natural materials. Japan's wood buildings harmonize with natural settings. Both architecture and sculpture tend to be on an intimate human scale and show skilled craftsmanship. Inside the small Japanese houses of wood, paper, and fiber is often found a singular flower arrangement or a painting whose subjects reflect their love of nature. Early Japanese art served religious beliefs, but the art of the last 300 years increasingly shows the secular interests of many different classes of people.

Japanese art tends to be less formal and more expressive, concrete, particular, narrative, decorative, and public than Chinese art. In both countries, painting is closely related to writing, and calligraphy is considered a fine art. Chinese and Japanese paintings do not use Western ideas of perspective and shading, leaning toward linear rather than modeled form, using asymmetrical balance, and treating space as an active rather than a negative element. Japanese paintings often tell stories, and they tend to be more detailed and decorative than Chinese painting. Artists paint scrolls and screens with calligraphic brush strokes and use perspective to give the illusion of space. Japanese ceramics are well designed and skillfully crafted.

The vigorous and decorative Japanese landscape paintings strongly contrast with the subtle brush-and-ink landscapes of the Chinese. Japanese artists often applied colors in a flat manner in conjunction with a gold or silver background. The Japanese also were more interested than the Chinese in showing figures in storytelling situations. Although both countries made hanging scrolls, the Japanese hanging scrolls show more angular brushwork and a hard-edge technique. A tilted perspective in Japanese painting tends to give a bird's-eye view of buildings without roofs or walls. Around the eleventh century, screen paintings appeared and were used to brighten the interiors of homes and temples.

Zen, a religious sect focused on meditation, inspired the tea ceremony. Other notable Japanese art forms include flower arranging and garden design. Japanese dry gardens emphasize texture and pattern. Garden artists may use a large stone to symbolize an island and then rake sand in beautiful patterns to represent the waves of the sea. Bronze, wood, and dry lacquer show Buddhist influence. Some sculpture is decorated with inlaid stone, gilded, or painted. Dramas and dances call for the creation of unique masks. The architectural design of Japanese homes features modular walls and sliding screens. Huge castles, shrines, and palaces exemplify typical Japanese styles.

Figure 7.45 **Kung Hsien, two details of *Landscapes in the Manner of Tung Yuan*, Ch'ing dynasty, late seventeenth century. Handscroll, ink on paper, ht. 10½ in., full length 31 ft. 10 in. Top is Section 2; bottom is Section 6.**
The Nelson-Atkins Museum of Art, Kansas City, Missouri. (Purchase: Nelson Trust) 48-44.

Japanese woodblock prints (*ukiyo-e*, meaning pictures of the "floating world") captured scenes from everyday life. As early as the eighth century, these multiple prints were used to create inexpensive religious images and to illustrate books. During the Edo period (1615–1868), the Japanese made many of these affordable prints. A prosperous merchant class and changes in lifestyles produced the art of ukiyo-e. Games, theaters, festivals, love, fashion, music, dancing, and hairstyles were all subject matter for these artists. Though the school of ukiyo-e began with painting, thousands of these woodblock prints were produced for mass consumption and reflected rapid changes in tastes and styles. These popular pictures have been called "magnificent scraps of paper" and "poor man's art" because common folk could afford them. Japanese woodcut prints, especially those by Hiroshige, Hokusai, Harunobu, and Utamaro (1753–1805), are known worldwide. In the early days, professional wood carvers translated the artist's drawing. Hokusai was the only artist who could do his own carving. When trade with Europe opened in the nineteenth century, these artists learned of paintings that were done by single artists and began to make the entire print themselves. In turn, many Western artists—Cassatt, Gauguin, van Gogh, Matisse, and Monet, for instance—were intrigued and influ-

Figure 7.46 **Katsushika Hokusai, *Fuji in Clear Weather*, 1831–33. Japanese, Ukiyoye School, 1760–1849. Color woodblock print, 25.5 × 37.5 cm.**
© *The Cleveland Museum of Art, 2002, Bequest of Edward L. Whittemore, 1930.189.*

enced by Japanese woodblock prints, with their emphasis on linear elements, the flat use of color, the bird's-eye view, and space not used merely as background but as a part of the design.

Utamaro (1753–1806) created a standard of sensuality and worldliness in his female subjects, using expressive lines and a plain background. **Hokusai** (1760–1849), born in Edo, the capital of Japan, was adopted by an important artisan family because he was a younger son. As an apprentice to a mirror maker, he learned engraving and later applied his skills to cutting woodblocks. He tried his hand at a number of occupations and had more than 50 different names during his life. He became Hokusai when he was 46. Most of the work for which he is famous was done after he was 70 years old. Hokusai experimented with Western motifs and techniques and led and created a renewal of interest in the Japanese landscape. In later years, he signed his works "Old Man Mad about Drawing." He died at age 89. **Hiroshige's** (1797–1858) landscapes were more realistic than Hokusai's, and he often depicted seasons and changes in weather.

Important periods in the history of Japanese art follow.

Archaic Period (Pre-Buddha) Jomon Culture (5000–200 B.C. [in the South]) Clay pottery with incised or cord-impressed designs (4000–250 B.C.) are the earliest art objects from Japan. These were found at pit dwellings of the Neolithic hunter-gatherers called Jomon. Also found were small clay or stone figures, decorated bracelets, earrings, and blades of bone, ivory, and horn. Pottery figures with animal and human features guarded grave sites.

(Pre-Buddha) Yayoi Culture (200 B.C.–A.D. 300 [in the South]) Rice cultivation began, and wheel-thrown pots with smooth surfaces were made. The Yayoi culture is best known for its blades, mirrors, and swords and for its bronze ceremonial bells decorated with representations or abstractions of daily and ceremonial scenes. It also had pottery grave guardians (horses, warriors, and swords) that were more sophisticated than those of the Jomon culture.

(Pre-Buddha) Kofan (Old Mound) (A.D. 300–ca. 650) People of the Kofan culture built enormous, mounded tombs surrounded by moats for emperors and clan leaders. The tombs were elaborately equipped with fired clay miniatures of people, animals, and houses. Clay figures were placed around the mound as "guards." Jewels, iron weapons, and bronze mirrors were found in some tomb interiors. A new equestrian and military culture is seen in later artifacts. Asian cultural influences came to Japan.

Japanese reverence for nature is the basis of Shinto, the Way of the Gods. Shinto is the oldest practiced religion in Japan. Ancestors and Kami (gods in nature) are honored with prayers and gifts. Because Shintoists do not focus on an afterlife, ceremonies relate to such aspects of life as harvests, peace, and health. The wooden gate or entrance to Shinto shrines is made of two pillars holding an inverted arch, reminiscent of a pagoda roof. With the frame as a symbol for the sky, the structure's horizontal bar stands for the

Figure 7.47 *Guardian Figure*, **Kamakura period, 1183–1333, Japanese, Shiga Prefecture. Wood, ht. 168.5 cm.** *© The Cleveland Museum of Art, 2002, Leonard C. Hanna, Jr., Fund, 1972.159.*

earth. The Sun Goddess lives in a bronze mirror in the main buildings of the Great Shrine at Ise, the ancestral shrine of the imperial family and the most sacred Shinto shrine in Japan.

Asuke (555–710) The Japanese eagerly adopted Buddhism in 552 when a Korean king sent Buddhist scriptures, a bronze Buddha, and lavish gifts to the Japanese court. Buddhists believe that humans are at one with nature. Buddhism brought to Japan a sophisticated and complex religious doctrine, complete with cultural traditions and developed art forms. Prince Shotoku (592–622) was instrumental in the spread of Buddhism, importing Chinese artistic, literary, philosophical, and political forms. Large temple complexes built for ceremonies incorporated pagodas (towers several stories high, with roofs curving upward at the corners, that contained relics of Buddha). Mainly built of wood with tile roofs, these temples were different in design from their counterpart, the Indian stupa. Painted or gold-leafed wood was the favored sculptural material. Since Buddhism originated in India, many of the images show Hindu influences. Early sculptures were modeled of clay, and some were carved in wood and cast in bronze. When new emperors came into power, they would have a new Buddha cast, each ruler trying to have his Buddha made larger than any before to demonstrate the emperor's important position.

Nara (710–794) The capital was moved to Heian in 784, and a golden age began, with Japan adopting much of Chinese culture at this time. The dominant clan, the Fujiwaras, surrounded the court with artists who created lacquered wooden carvings and high-quality painted scrolls. Painting and sculpture adapted Chinese Buddhist themes. The T'ang style predominated in Buddhist architecture, painting, and sculpture. Large, lifelike sculptures were produced in dry lacquer and bronze, along with unfired clay sculptures, which originated in India. Most buildings were made of wood, which fire, weather, and wars easily destroyed. Buildings were often rebuilt and changed, the architecture never being completely static. Roofs were massive, elaborate, and supported by huge pillars. Most walls, interior and exterior, were moving panels that could be rearranged. Gardens contained many views, landscapes, and visual surprises, and provided artistic and spiritual balance, expressing themes based on philosophies of beauty or the meaning of life. Gardens had several elements: rocks, which represented islands, mountains, and so on; water, which stood for the continuity of life and the sea and also provided for the musical sound of waterfalls; and shrubbery, which was shaped and trimmed as a piece of sculpture. Love of nature was seen indoors in the form of *bonsai* (dwarf trees) and *ike bano* (floral arrangements).

Heian (794–1185) When the Fujiwara clan gained control of the throne and moved the capital to the city of Heian, a native Japanese artistic style began to replace the heavily influenced Chinese technique. Early sculptures were carved from solid wood and left unpainted so as not to impair the wood's fragrance. The Japanese court ended diplomatic missions to China in 894, with the result that the Japanese began creating more of their own artworks—paintings of the numerous deities of new religious sects. The Pure Land sect favored light and graceful architecture to contain their seated Buddhas and his attendants. Temple complexes contained peaceful gardens, ponds, and large sculptures. Late Heian (Fujiwara, 897–1185) was marked by luxurious pomp and elegant court life. Illustrated novels on handscrolls had the text presented in calligraphy, which was considered as important an art form as the pictures. This style in Japanese art is thought of as the first pure example of Japanese art. Decorated screens for dividing rooms were another art form. In 1185, civil war ended what is called the golden age, ushering in political upheaval for 430 years.

Kamakura (1185–1333) Zen, a Buddhist sect introduced from China, spread during the Kamakura period. It was marked by strong self-discipline and meditation and was attuned to the active and violent samurai; the warrior class supported it. Zen advocated intuitive and emotional responses to life situations. It emphasized the Buddha-nature in humans and nature. Continuous warfare destroyed Buddhist temples, but a new military government later restored them. A new, vigorous, realistic style of art began, leading to portraits of warriors, priests, and common citizens. Sculptured temple guardians, lifelike in anatomy and color, and some possessing glass eyes, were vividly real to frighten evil spirits. The Guardian Figure, with its feeling of ferocity, energy, and movement, is typical of this period. Ukiyo-e, depicting scenes of Japanese life, was a new art style that emerged with the arrival of peace. Zen monks introduced new art forms, including scroll painting (*makimono*). These were elaborate depictions of warriors' exploits and daily lives, painted with bright colors and bold pattern. Art became more realistic, more colorful, and less religious. Sculpture, under Zen influence, declined. The harmony between works of human origin and natural objects influenced the design of homes, gardens, and temples.

Ashikaga (1336–1573) With a weak central government, the Ashikaga period (also known as the Muramachi period) was a time of violent social unrest and upheaval. Zen thinkers developed the starkly beautiful dry or rock gardens, using bright and dark rocks and carefully raked sand or pebbles to symbolize waves, the sea, ships, and islands. They carefully arranged elements in these remarkable artistic abstractions to create an illusion of movement. The first Europeans (Dutch and Portuguese) arrived and set up trading posts, and Christian missionaries began efforts to convert the people. The Japanese grew suspicious of these foreigners, thereby planting the seeds of Japan's fear of the outside world.

Momoyama (1573–1615) In 1573, the emperor expelled the military shogun and also destroyed monasteries and killed monks to break the political power of the Buddhists. Daimyo, the emperor's successor, brought together the great families, enabling Japan to have one rule after 250 years of disunity. Art was revitalized. Narrative and portrait painting flourished. The art of ink brush painting (*sumi*) was introduced, and puppet theater became popular. Daimyo built palace-fortresses, surrounded by moats and reflecting the grandeur and wealth of their masters, which soon became the new cultural centers. Official residences had brilliantly painted screens and sliding doors, while private homes had a subdued style with small teahouses. The tea ceremony, a graceful and beautiful ritual, reflected the subtle relationships of human beings to ritual and nature. The ceramics industry responded by creating many styles of pottery to meet the need, among them "Raku ware" and "Shino ware." In 1592, Korean potters introduced Chinese porcelain. The Japanese Kakiemon ware showed a greater freedom of design. The capital shifted to Edo, the future Tokyo,

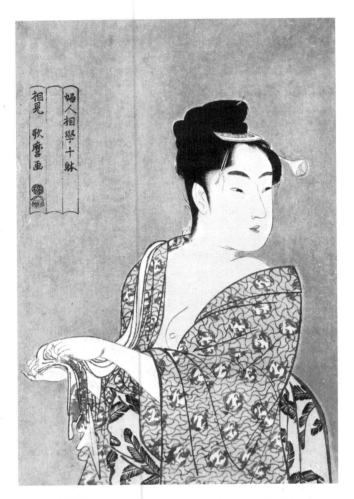

Figure 7.48 **Kitagawa Utamaro,** *Uwaki, Noso, Half-Length Portrait,* **Japanese, 1753–1806, Edo period. Color woodblock print, 36.2 × 25.4 cm.**
© *The Cleveland Museum of Art, 2002, Bequest of Edward L. Whittemore, 1930.218.*

after 1650. A prosperous society was united and strong. Traders were expelled, and Japanese Christians were strenuously persecuted, with thousands being killed. Foreign books and technical knowledge were outlawed. Japan was almost entirely cut off from the outside world.

Tokugawa (Edo) (1615–1868) The Tokugawa (Edo) period was named for a village that became Tokyo. At this time, Japan's isolation provided peaceful stability (Colorplate 22). Home design emphasized being surrounded by nature. Refined tea ceremonies provided time for contemplation and relaxation, with an emphasis on simplicity and humility. Japan's isolation radically changed in 1854, when Commodore Perry's war fleet appeared and forced the shogun to open Japanese ports to the West. A growing, wealthy middle class demanded artworks for their homes, and such masters as Hokusai, Hiroshige, Utamaro, and

Harunobu created inexpensive and easily reproduced woodblock prints. They originally portrayed actors and courtesans but soon began depicting all subjects. Utamaro introduced large head portraits of generalized beauties, focusing on the elements of shape and color. The energetic and imaginative Hokusai, with his 36 views of Mount Fuji, and the popular Hiroshige, with his poetic depictions of the country's weather and seasons, were two great landscape artists of the early nineteenth century. These late ukiyo-e prints of Japanese subjects show the influence of Western perspective and shading while symbolizing Japanese reverence for country and nature.

Meiji (1868–1912) The shogunate was discredited, and power was restored to the throne. This was the beginning of a period of rapid industrialization that quickly elevated Japan to a position of world power.

Taisho (1912–1926); Showa (1926–present) Contacts with the outside world during the late nineteenth century brought an increased interest in realistic art and the use of Western themes and techniques. Trade with Europe created a demand for woodblock prints, textiles, metalwork, painted fans, screens, inlaid lacquer, and metalwork. Ideas from Europe and America replaced the isolationist policies of the Tokugawa military overlordship. The Nihonga style developed as a synthesis of East and West, old and new. Japan's contemporary art forms show this harmonious relationship in a reverence for nature and beauty. During this time, the appeal of ukiyo-e (or "floating world" paintings), a popular art form since the early 1500s, increased in the form of woodblock prints, many showing Kabuki actors, courtesans, and such.

Korean Art

Although Korean art is not explored in depth in this survey, its place in Far Eastern Asian Art should be noted. Korea shares its northern border with China, and over the centuries, its art and philosophies have been shaped by Confucianism, Taoism, and Buddhism (introduced from China in the fourth century A.D.). Korea has also embraced Shamanism, a form of nature worship native to that country. In this belief system, spirits lived in mountains and rocks, which explains the importance of this imagery in Korean art. Its parallel folk art is distinctive.

Korea's achievements in ceramics were extraordinary. Works produced during the Unified Silla Dynasty (A.D. 668 to 935) were primarily produced for tombs or temples. Examples from this period reveal the unique Korean aesthetic which, unlike its neighbor China, did not value symmetry or perfection. Ceramics of the Koryo Period (935 to 1392), known for their subtle celadon glazes—which originated in Korea before spreading elsewhere—and elegant incised designs, were the finest of any period.

Islamic Art

About A.D. 600, a new religion that was to become one of the world's largest took shape about 2,000 miles east of India in the city of Mecca. Followers of Islam are called Muslims. Within 100 years, the Islamic religion spread westward from Arabia (now Iran) to Spain and east to India. The Arabian prophet Muhammed, a merchant who, in A.D. 613, started preaching a faith that centered on one god called Allah, founded the Islamic religion. Muhammed incorporated his beliefs in the Koran. The calligraphy (beautiful writing) in this book is alive with flowing letters, circular gold decorations, and arabesques. Arabesques are decorative, flat, abstract designs of plant life done in swirling geometric patterns. Muhammed eliminated slavery, gambling, and wine, and he taught that people were accountable for their deeds, reaping punishment in the afterlife. The five Pillars of Islam are faith, prayer, alms-giving, fasting, and a once-in-a-lifetime pilgrimage to Mecca.

Mosques are Muslim houses of worship and they must be oriented toward Mecca. Each mosque has a wall with niches called *mihrabs*, a staired pulpit, and at least one tower, called a *minaret*, from which the faithful are called to prayer five times a day. Islamic architectural works have achieved a high degree of beauty. Mosques are covered with mosaics and filigree in geometric designs on the carved walls and on stained-glass windows. Designs for these geometric patterns are called *tessellations*, meaning that the repeated shapes fit together perfectly.

Early Muslim teachings did not allow depictions of animals or humans, and these images are only seen in art about everyday life or about the court. Thus, arabesques and other geometric designs are used to decorate tiles, rugs, miniature paintings, and many craft objects. Rich calligraphy, Persian rugs, elaborate compositions, and highly decorative and stylized landscapes are typical of Islamic art. Islamic artists strongly desired to fill all spaces with patterned motifs. Since the representation of nature and even the human form is forbidden, Islamic art is rich in abstract symbolism. Persian carpets serve as prayer rugs, floor coverings, blankets, cushions, and saddle bags. They are often designed in a medallion pattern of rich colors, incorporating abstract flowers and animals.

The first Moors landed in Spain in A.D. 771, and the last left in 1492. In 1248, when they controlled much of Spain, they built a famous palace, worship place, and citadel—the Alhambra—using the characteristic filigree and tile on the many walls, ceilings, and arches. During the 800s, Spain had some 300 Muslim mosques. The architecture is slightly ethereal, with sequences of arches, spindly columns, and pierced stone screens.

During the fifteenth to the seventeenth centuries, Persian miniatures were at their height. Due to the restriction on depicting the human figure, these miniatures were highly

Figure 7.49 Soga Shokahu, *Orchid Pavilion Gathering*, **Edo period, 1730–81, Japanese. Hanging scroll, ink on silk, 122.5 × 55.5 cm.**
© *The Cleveland Museum of Art, 2002, Purchase from the J. H. Wade Fund, 1979.53.*

decorative and were hidden in books. Rules, mostly from China, required that artists use no shading and no perspective, with the views being from slightly above and with the horizon at the top and all the figures the same size. Different scenes are sometimes within one composition. Landscapes and architecture may be seen in the backgrounds. Colors are decorative rather than realistic, and variations in proportion often show a servant smaller than his master. Because of rules established by Islamic laws, faces show no emotion, even though a scene might be romantic or violent, because this might disturb the desired peaceful effect. The unifying use of tiny patterns to fill in the background tends to create a lack of deep space. For the paints, finely ground minerals were sifted through silk before being mixed with a binder. Silk and linen paper was polished with a crystal egg or mother-of-pearl.

Indian Art

Present-day India, only half the size of the United States, has a larger population than North and South America combined. As far back as 3000 B.C., a Neolithic culture existed in the Indus Valley, in what is now Pakistan. It had large cities, paved streets, fortifications, and blocks of houses and public buildings. Excavations have located pottery, carved seals, and sculptures of small female figures, attesting to a mother-goddess cult. Small seals, used to sign legal documents and contracts, were carved in reverse and contain animal designs replete with anatomical detail; the human form is more abstract and simplified.

To understand the art of India, we need to understand something of this country's two leading religions—Hinduism and Buddhism—which have shaped India's art during the last 2,500 years. Hinduism incorporated earlier native beliefs and art traditions, with Hindu artists dealing with stories and legends about the major gods. Tribes from the north invaded India about 2000 B.C. and introduced the Vedas, hymns similar to the ancient Greek myths or the Old Testament poems. These became the Upanishads, marking the beginnings of Hinduism, the world's oldest religion. Much of Indian art is based on Hinduism, which began about 700 B.C. It has many gods and is rich in images. Not having a single leader, Hinduism is a collection of the beliefs and ideas of many peoples and various cultures. Reincarnation (rebirth in another form) and karma (reward or punishment based on behavior in a previous life) are two strong Hindu beliefs. Hinduism is based on an identity of humans with nature. Hindus believe that people can learn about the universe through worship. The goal is to find the true nature of the self in light of the only real Existence, or Brahma, with all people on a cycle of reincarnation until they finally become one with Brahma.

Cast metal Indian sculptures are filled with symbolic meaning, depicting Hindu gods and expressing the creative force of the universe. Indian art has many animal forms,

Figure 7.50 **Nataraja,** *Shiva as King of Dance*, **South India, Chola period. Bronze sculpture, eleventh century, ht. 111.5 cm.**
© *The Cleveland Museum of Art, 2002, Purchase from the J. H. Wade Fund, 1930.331.*

especially Ganesha, an elephant that symbolizes prosperity for his worshipers. Many early pieces of Indian art reflect the Hindu concept of reincarnation, as well as myths about Brahma, the creator; Vishnu, the preserver; and Shiva, the destroyer.

Many gods represent different aspects of nature. Especially important are Vishnu, the preserver of the world; Krisha, believed to be an incarnation of Vishnu; and Indra, a god of war with many arms that symbolize his inner energy. Shiva is a puzzling Hindu god and symbolizes creativity as well as the myth of death. The hand that points to the foot shows that the dance represents life; the fourth hand assures us that all is well and that death/life, or creativity and change, are part of our lives. Shiva is the god who destroys creation as old age destroys youth. Shiva is depicted as god of dance, god of bounty and of wrath, god of destruction and fertility. Many Shivas were made during the eleventh century.

Hindu gods have certain characteristics: Shiva has three eyes; Brahma has four faces; many gods have four arms. These attributes symbolize extraordinary knowledge and power.

Hindu architects cut great temples directly into solid "living" rock formations in the belief that rock was the matrix that contained the potential of all forms.

Figure 7.51 *Seated Buddha*, **India, Gandhara region, Kushar period. Gray schist sculpture, first half of third century** A.D. **100 × 29.5 cm.**
© *The Cleveland Museum of Art, 2002, Leonard C. Hanna, Jr., Fund, 1961.418.*

While Hinduism is rooted in prehistoric times, Buddhism emerged from it about 500 B.C. Siddhartha Gautama, the Enlightened One who established Buddhism, was born the son of a rich nobleman about 500 years before Christ. Until the gods arranged for him to see four signs depicting old age, illness, death, and hunger, he was kept from seeing any suffering. He preached a life of withdrawal from earthly individuality, one in which the goal was *nirvana*, the ultimate release from rebirth and entry into oneness with the universe. In early artworks, Buddha is represented symbolically, rather than as a human form, by the lotus, the wheel, the bodhi tree, the footprint, or the stupa. The first images of Buddha in human form appeared during the Kushan dynasty (ca. A.D. 50–320). Occupations by Alexander the Great's Greek legions had brought contact with Greek and Roman civilizations, and the style of the early sculptures of Buddha showed this influence. These early sculptures show Buddha

seated cross-legged (lotus position) and include a third eye on the forehead, long earlobes, and a hand motion. The third eye looks within. A bump on top of the head symbolizes enlightenment and wisdom. Long earlobes indicate the weight of heavy jewelry and tell that Buddha was once a prince. Sculptures of Buddha are still and static, focusing on peace, contemplation, and meditation.

Indian paintings are seen in temple murals, manuscript pages with miniature illustrations, and palm-leaf paintings. These paintings show a love of the ideal.

Buildings often are not painted in proportion to figures, since the events shown were considered more important. Perspective is often tilted, and shadows are lacking. Indian architects built *stupas*, beehive-shaped domed buildings that evolved from burial mounds, early on to honor Buddha and other important leaders. These burial mounds contain relics of Buddha's body and are pilgrimage sites for his followers. Stupas indicate Buddha's royalty and have four gates covered with relief sculpture (depicting Buddha's previous lives), through which believers enter and then walk around the dome while meditating and reading Buddhist teachings carved on the walls. The stupa, with its parts determined by rigid rules of magical proportions, is a cosmic symbol that is a small replica of the universe.

Buddhism and Hinduism have shared the same architectural styles. At Khajuraho, a number of sacred Hindu, Buddhist, and some Jainist (Jainist is a branch of Hinduism) temples were built around the eleventh century, yet all have similarities. With conical domes and elaborately carved surfaces, the impressive Hindu temple dedicated to Shiva as Mahadeva, Lord of Lords, reminds us of a group of beehives. Sanctuaries and halls are found within its walls. Most of the ancient temples employ post-and-lintel construction; that is, the walls, or columns or posts, support a heavy masonry ceiling.

The Gupta dynasty (A.D. 320–600) is called the golden age of Buddhist art. Artists began depicting Buddha with a bony protuberance on the top of his head, wheels on his palms and soles, webbed fingers, elongated ears, and a third eye. Wall paintings show detailed views of courtly elegance. Crowns, necklaces, bracelets, and patterned cloth show intricate designs and craftsmanship.

Hinduism revived in the latter part of the Gupta dynasty, and during the Pallava dynasty (500–750), sculptured temples with numerous deities were carved from rounded outcroppings of granite. High-relief sculptures show episodes in the lives of the more than 3,000 Hindu deities that represent symbols, aspects, or attributes. The greatest of all the rock temples was carved around 750 to 900 and is in western India at Ellura. It features a sanctuary, shrines, and enormous life-size elephants. During the Chola dynasty (ca. 907–1053), cast bronze sculptures achieved a high quality of excellence.

Muslims from Afghanistan arrived in northern India during the eighth century. Most of the area was united under

Figure 7.52 *Sita in the Garden of Lanka*, **from the** *Ramayana, Epic of Valmiki*, **ca. 1720, India, Pahari, Guler School. Gold and color painted on paper, 55.5 × 79 cm.**
© *The Cleveland Museum of Art, 2002, Gift of George P. Bickford, 1966.143.*

Mogul leaders by 1526. Muslims brought with them aspects of Persian culture that were changed somewhat by Indian concepts. Court painters copied European paintings and began using shading and showing depth. They depicted romances, epics, and historical events. In the Mogul's attempt to eliminate imagery, many Hindu and Buddhist temples were destroyed and replaced with palaces with formal gardens and mosques. These were made of marble and set with precious stones and mosaics. Painting studios were closed, and the weaving of gold cloth was banned during the declining years of the Mogul culture. The white marble Taj Mahal in India, built in 1632 in memory of a Muslim ruler's wife, is a well-known, elegant structure with its fine filigree, beautiful gardens, and reflecting pools.

Southern India escaped Mogul domination. During the Nayak dynasty (ca. 1550–1743), long, covered galleries were added to the existing temples. Enclosed by high stone walls and topped with towers, the temples featured many carved and painted Hindu dieties.

During the Rajput dynasty (1500–1800), a local literature developed that focused on love stories and heroes. Various illustration styles developed in different regions; some were quite colorful and highly patterned. Rajput paintings lacked perspective, illusions of depth, and shading.

Fabric arts are important in India and include the fine embroidery pieces, woven items, printed fabric, and fabric decorated by the batik process. Decorations are often intricate with overall patterns and borders. Batik, a wax-resist technique used for decorating fabrics, has reached a high degree of excellence in India. Designs are applied with melted wax, a dye is applied, and the wax is removed.

The British East Indian Company, and later the English Crown, developed trade during the nineteenth century. India became independent in 1947, with Pakistan being partitioned as a Muslim state. Many buildings in present-day India reflect British influence, but the art of India still depicts its religion principally in the traditional styles that are hundreds of years old.

ART OF THE AMERICAS

Mexican Art

Four cultural groups developed in ancient Mexico and Central America: the Olmec, West Mexican, Mayan, and Aztec. The Olmec culture, located in the swampy lowlands along the eastern coast, has been called the "mother culture" of Mexico because of its influence on all later civilizations. The Olmec lived about 3,000 years ago and are best remem-

Figure 7.53 Olmec head.
Museo de Antropolgia, Universidad Veracruzana, Jalapa Region, Vera Cruz, Mexico.

bered for their gigantic sculptured human heads that were used for religious ceremonies. Sculptures of Olmec gods had both animal and human elements—for instance, half-human, half-jaguar figures.

The next oldest culture was the West Mexican, centered in Colima. West Mexicans made small clay sculptures of dogs, called *effigies*, that were believed to have special powers in serving the dead.

Another group, the Maya, began to dominate the region called Teotihuacan in the central highlands north of today's Mexico City. They flourished from 300 B.C. to A.D. 800, which is approximately the same period as the Han and T'ang dynasties in China. Mayan nature worship centered around Tlaloc, god of rain, and Quetzalcoatl, a feathered serpent. The Maya built enormous, complex pyramids for their rituals. By A.D. 800, the great Mayan culture covered the Yucatan peninsula and areas in present-day Belize, Guatemala, and Honduras. The Maya built cities with huge temples and pyramids, some of them 175 feet high. They were advanced in both architecture and mathematics, having the most accurate calendar of any culture anywhere. Their shamans governed and also were mediums between the natural and spiritual worlds. The ancient Mayan city of Tikal, which occupied 50 square miles, was discovered in the late

nineteenth century. Archaeologists believe that about 55,000 people lived there. The relief carvings on monuments and buildings were complex and geometric, depicting human, animal, and plant forms.

The warlike and religious Aztec civilization represents the largest culture of ancient Mexico and Central America. Emerging between A.D. 1200 and 1325, the Aztec people followed the command of their god to leave their settled homes and begin anew wherever they saw an eagle perched on a cactus. And so they founded Tenochtitlan in 1325 on a swampy island that became the center of their great empire that spread over central and southern Mexico. This was the 25-square-mile city that Cortez and his Spanish soldiers conquered in 1519, what is today Mexico City. Enormous sculptures were carved for ceremonies for the 1,600 gods and goddesses in the Aztec religion. The Aztecs practiced human sacrifice because they believed that their sun god had died to create man and required repayment with human blood. Their intricately designed calendar stones, some 12 feet in diameter and weighing up to 24 tons, depicted signs for the 20 days of the Aztec months.

Mask-making is highly developed in Mexico because masks have been used in rituals and ceremonies to "transform" the wearer into a particular god and to give him or her the power of the animal or god that the mask symbolizes. In ancient Mexico, warriors wore masks depicting fierce jaguars and birds of prey to frighten their enemies. The earliest masks were made of clay, stone, and wood and decorated with gold, turquoise, jade, and other precious materials. The tradition of mask-making continues in Mexico today and shows a blending of Christian symbols with ancient ones. Often, mask-making skills are passed within families from one generation to the next. Masks combine creativity and imagination with traditional symbolism. Some masks combine two faces. Though wood is a popular mask-making material, many other materials are also used.

Following the Mexican Revolution of 1910, the Minister of Education implemented the idea of using murals as a way to teach the history of Mexico to large numbers of people who otherwise had little or no access to education. Mexico's famous muralists—**Diego Rivera** (1886–1957) (Colorplate 26), **José Clemente Orozco** (1883–1949), and **David Alfaro Siqueiros** (1896–1974)—were influenced by both pre-Columbian and colonial murals and by European muralists and fresco-painting techniques. They painted large artworks designed to tell the history and proud traditions of the native people and to arouse in them feelings of pride and desires for agrarian reform.

Throughout the centuries and up to the present day, traditional arts and crafts, usually referred to as *folk art*, have flourished in Mexico. Made for functional, social, personal, and religious purposes, the containers, masks, clothing, jewelry, and such have distinct and colorful character. Different regions tend to specialize in specific styles and media.

Figure 7.54 **Frog mask, Oaxaca, Mexico.**
Collection of the authors.

Paintings, prints, and posters from contemporary artists are rich in variety and form, and tell us much about the political and social lives, customs, religions, and values of Mexico's peoples.

Today, Chicano artists, especially in California and Chicago, continue the tradition of creating large, boldly expressive murals. (*Chicano* refers to first-generation persons born in the United States of Mexican heritage.) In the United States today, artists **Gilbert S. Lujan** (1940–) (nicknamed "Magu"), **Carmen Lomas Garza** (1948–), and many others are making cultural connections in their art production of traditional Mexican folk art—retablos, santos, carretas, diablito figures, and papel picado.

Posters were very important during the early consciousness-raising period of the Chicano art movement. Just as Chicano murals served to give pride to Chicano people, who previously had no idea of the indigenous civilization to which they were connected as offspring of Mexican parents, the Chicano posters announced rallies and meetings that dealt with Chicano issues and cultural events. Like the muralists, the poster artists had Mexican antecedents who had used inexpensive means to make multiple images available to large numbers of people. Chief among the Mexican graphic artists who influenced Chicano poster art was **José Guadelupe Posada** (1851–1913). Well-known contemporary poster artists working in the United States today are **Rupert Garcia** (1941–) and **Malaquias Montoya** (1938–).

Tribal Art of the United States and Canada

Tribal art of the United States and Canada includes the traditions, language, and art of hundreds of different groups spread out over the continental United States. Tradition is the manner in which a group of people views and uses its past, a past that has been passed on in oral accounts and visual images. Tradition, then, becomes those things that members of the culture both remember and emphasize. Some traditions may include elements of the past that are chosen to meet the needs of the present, needs such as identity, security, or well-being. This definition of tradition implies that change is an integral part of the cultural group and influences how the group adapts to its surroundings.

Before the arrival of European settlers, more than 300 tribes lived in what is now the United States and Canada, but they kept no written records. Diversity among the tribes was great, with many different languages being spoken. Although the cultures varied greatly from each other, they had many things in common. Two were a reverence for nature and the belief in many supernatural beings governing all aspects of life. Native Americans have always revered the forces of nature. They hunted, fished, gathered food, or farmed, so they needed the full cooperation of nature to survive. Rain and rich soil ensured good crops. Plenty of fish, deer, or buffalo provided sufficient food and skins for clothing and shelter. A drought or other natural disaster could mean starvation. Another commonality of Native Americans is that their art was and is practical as well as aesthetic. It includes everyday functional and utilitarian objects, as well as those created for religious or ceremonial purposes.

Native Americans have created many beautiful objects from local natural materials, such as wood, animal skins, bones, grasses, seashells, and clay. They decorate these objects with different designs and symbols that have special meaning for their particular tribes. The artworks of Native Americans provide visual information about tribal beliefs, customs, rituals, and way of life. The various art forms and craft objects that Native Americans make are as diverse as the tribes. Native American art is usually grouped in the following cultural/geographic categories: the Eastern Woodlands, the Southwest, the Eskimos, the Plains, the Pacific Northwest, and California.

Eastern Woodlands   The Eastern Woodlands comprises a large geographical region wherein dwelled hunters, fishermen, farmers, and fighters. Some tribes were nomadic. The Iroquois, in particular, were fascinating, being a confederated nation of six tribes that formed the largest cultural group of Native Americans. One of the interesting aspects of Iroquois religious practice was the False Face Society. Believing that spirits cause sickness, the Iroquois sought to overcome these evildoers through dance rituals involving various carved masks. The twisted and distorted features in these masks were meant to frighten away the evil spirits. In addition to these masks, which were carved directly from tree trunks, the Iroquois also braided masks from corn husks. Trees also gave the tribes shafts for spears and arrows, and bark for house walls, boxes, trays, canoes, cradle boards, snowshoes, and toboggans. Clothing of caribou, moose, and hare hides was decorated with moose-hair and porcupine-quill embroidery. Sometimes, the tribes also painted straight and curved lines on clothing. Other notable art objects from this region include the beadwork of the Huron and Ojibways and the quilled birchbark of the Micmac.

Southwest Twenty to thirty thousand years ago, early peoples are believed to have crossed the Bering Sea and settled in the Southwest. They learned to use the abundant clay to fashion beautiful coiled pots about A.D. 400 through trade with Mexico. They hunted and farmed and left rock paintings (pictographs) and carvings (petroglyphs) that they believed would help them capture an animal's spirit. In the Southwest, pueblos were functional and innovative and were the first apartment houses. They were several stories high and made of adobe bricks to help keep out the cold of winter and the heat of summer. The Pueblo people were peaceful farmers and fought only when the Apache and Navajo attacked.

The tribes in the Southwest used a variety of dance masks. The Hopi people made small, carved wooden figures called kachinas to represent hundreds of different kachina spirits—supernatural beings that oversee religious and social activities. The kachinas were used to teach the children about the different spirits. The Navajos developed sand paintings for religious ceremonies, and many of the designs were secret; only the artist and the medicine man were allowed to see them. Later on, after the Spaniards had introduced sheep, the Navajos borrowed weaving techniques from the Pueblos and began to create rugs, which were traded to white settlers and tourists. The Navajos are also well known for fashioning silver and turquoise jewelry, another skill learned from the early Spaniards.

Eskimos For thousands of years, the Eskimos of Canada and Alaska have survived their cruel environment. Recently, they have become especially well known for their prints and for their carvings from bone, ivory, and stone of the birds and animals native to the northlands. Before the Eskimos began to sell their products, their artwork was used mostly to decorate tools and other objects, such as harpoon heads, knives, needle cases, goggles, wooden bowls, and such. Wooden masks were made for religious ceremonies and represented spirits of both animals and people. In general,

Figure 7.55 **Ranchos de Taos Church, Taos, NM. Side view; adobe architecture.**
Photo by Severina Marsh.

Figure 7.56 **Hand-coiled Southwestern Pueblo terra-cotta pot shows bird and flower motif.**
Collection of the authors.

masks that realistically showed humans or animals were worn during secular dances, whereas the more abstract and stylized masks had religious significance. Masks were based on visions seen by shamans, but often they were fashioned by carvers working under the direction of the medicine man. Only the shaman who had seen the vision knew the mask's precise meaning, but others had a general idea of its significance, since each mask represented the spirit of the creature it depicted.

Lack of trees made it necessary for Eskimos to use driftwood or, more recently, lumber purchased at a trading post to build kayaks. A kayak may have no piece of wood more than one foot long in its framework. Animal bones were sometimes used in place of wood in the kayaks. The rest of the world has imitated the design of Eskimo kayaks. This has also been the case with Eskimo clothing, such as the fur parka, which is both functional and attractive.

Plains Indians The nomadic Plains Indians, made up of such tribes as the Arapaho, Cheyenne, Comanche, Crow, and Sioux, roamed from the Mississippi River to the Rocky Mountains. After obtaining horses and rifles from European explorers, they became excellent buffalo hunters. Today, many Americans live in a "throwaway" society in which many items go to waste, but the Plains people were more environmentally sound. The buffalo was used for food, shelter, moccasins, leggings, tepees, clothing, and shields. Designs painted on shields were believed to have magical powers and were the real means of protection. Buffalo hides were used as robes, which husbands and wives made together. The painting of these hides was a major development among Native Americans. The men painted the figures of warriors and horses, since only those who participated in these activities were allowed to paint representations of them. The women worked with nonrepresentational, geometric shapes. They also made items for personal adornment, such as head gear and necklaces, using feathers, hair, bones, horns, and claws. The Plains Indians are also known for their cradle boards, which they used to carry their young.

Another outstanding craft of the Plains Indians was quill embroidery, which is done nowhere else in the world. Porcupine quills take dyes well. They are softened with water and then flattened, and have a smooth, glossy surface somewhat like straw. Abstract and floral patterns prevail. Beadwork began on the Plains about 1800, but only after very small beads became available about 1850 did the craft progress rapidly. Pipes were carved from catlinite (named after American artist George Catlin, who sent samples east from Minnesota for testing) or pipestone and used for many purposes, some in ceremonies or private rites but many for pleasure alone.

Pacific Northwest Northwest Coast tribes, such as the Haida, Kwakitl, and Tlingit, lived along the Pacific coast from California to Alaska. Although they farmed, hunted, and gathered food, they mainly depended on ocean salmon for food. They used cedar planks to build gable-roofed houses. Wood was abundant and was used for canoes, which were needed for fishing and for travel. The clan's totems, or supernatural animal beings, were carved and often painted with stylized designs on tall totem poles that stood in front of homes as a sign of prestige. These totems were the center of the culture. People also entered houses through totem poles, especially on ceremonial occasions. A doorway for this purpose was carved in the base of the pole. These skilled carvers also decorated their canoes and made rattles, dishes,

Figure 7.57 **Eskimo Kuskokwim River mask, Alaska. Wood, ht. 36½ in. The mask represents Negakfok, the Cold Weather Spirit.**
Courtesy of The National Museum of the American Indian/Smithsonian Institution (#29613).

and masks, using stylized designs of figures and animals. Masks worn in the Northwest Coast tribes were believed to transform the wearer into chief of the undersea world. Religious rituals centered around the supernatural beings governing the sea and its inhabitants.

Handsome blankets were woven for the chiefs of a subtribe of Tlingit Indians called *Chilkats*. Male artists provided the designs, and the women did the actual weaving, using mountain goat wool and shredded cedar bark. Designs were based on family crests, inherited through the family clans.

California The California Indians produced some of the finest and most beautiful baskets in the world. They used

Figure 7.58 **Totem pole, Haida, British Columbia.**
Museum of Anthropology no. A50034, The University of British Columbia, Vancouver, Canada.

Figure 7.59 **Gina Gray, *Plains Warrior*, 1991, Pawhuska, Okla. 17 × 22 in.**
From the collection of the artist.

three basic methods: plaiting, twining, and coiling. Tribes in northern California used twining; these baskets were flexible and decorated with an overlay of fern stems and yellow bear grass. Central California tribes used both twining and coiling. Southern tribes used fine coiling with bundles of grass for fibers, lashed with rushes, grass, or wood splints. Indian women competed to see who could make the smallest basket; examples of these must be viewed with a magnifying glass! Chumash Indians of the Santa Barbara area produced sturdy canoes and created stone vessels, including large, thin-walled pots, and mortars with pestles and dippers. Their shell work included beads and pendants, often decorated with inlay, and finely carved bowls made from abalone.

In the 1880s, legislation known as the Indian Act was passed. It was based on the assumption that Native Americans were morally and culturally inferior to white people. Native Americans were required to register with government agencies, which then limited where Native Americans could live and work. Children were sent away to special schools, where they were forbidden to use their Native American language and customs. By the time they finished school, they found it difficult to fit into either Native American or white society. Certain Native American customs, such as the Northwest potlatch ceremonies, were outlawed. Some groups held them secretly but risked imprisonment if caught. By the time these laws were repealed in 1951,

Native American culture and identity had been seriously damaged.

Today, many Native American artists are working to keep their history and traditions alive. Traditional designs and motifs seen on Native American craft objects depict animals, figures, plants, and geometric shapes in a symbolic, stylized manner. Many Native Americans today, however, have chosen to take a new direction in their paintings and are using realistic styles in their portraits and landscapes, incorporating and infusing traditional symbols and themes for their rich cultural heritage.

Native Americans in the United States were introduced to poster and oil paints at the Indian Schools that the federal government established to train them to produce sellable art. As late as the 1970s, the Indian School in Santa Fe, New Mexico, stressed painting as an art form, in addition to pottery, sculpture, jewelry making, and weaving. One of the leading teachers there, **Fritz Scholder** (1937–), inspired many successful contemporary Native American painters.

INTERACTIVE EXTENSIONS—WESTERN ART

1. On a long piece of paper, make a chronological time line of important periods of Western art, leading artists/artworks, characteristics of the period/style, and concurrent events in science, math, music, drama, politics, and literature.

2. Study your art history time line from activity 1, and reflect on how art affected or was affected by the events of its time.

3. How did World War II affect art in the United States? Research and report on the major influences on art and the leading artists at this time.

4. From your time line in activity 1, select two periods and report on who supported the artists and how artworks reflect that sponsorship. Illustrate your report with slides or Xerox copies of artworks.

5. After researching the life and works of a particular artist, pretend to be that artist, and write a letter to a young relative, inviting her or him to spend a week with you. Tell your relative about the kind of artworks you do, how you do them, and why you think he or she would enjoy getting acquainted with you.

6. Because you are a famous artist, you are to be interviewed on the "Today" show, where you will discuss three or four of your artworks. Choose another student to serve as the interviewer, and supply this person with appropriate questions so that you can respond in a manner that will help the audience understand your work. In impersonating the artist, you can wear an appropriate costume and use props.

7. Find a quotation by an artist in a reference book. Use the quotation to make a small poster. Use calligraphy and illustrations in the manner of that artist. Design a border, and make an illuminated initial to begin the quotation.

8. Make a painting or drawing in the manner of one of the artists in the Color Gallery. However, choose subject matter that the artist never tried. For instance, paint a penguin in the manner of Picasso. Paint a butterfly the way Renoir might have painted it.

9. Make a crossword puzzle about one of the artists and his or her artwork in the Color Gallery.

10. Select an artwork with two or three large figures. Use the grid system to enlarge it on a large, heavy piece of foam board. Paint it with tempera. Then cut out the face areas, and let students peek through the openings to have their pictures taken.

11. Write a front page for a newspaper that might have appeared in the lifetime of an artist or of several artists who lived at the same period of time. Record news about the artists, as well as events that were happening at that time.

12. Make a book in which you write questions and answers about a particular artist, a poem you wrote about the artist, a short biography, and so on. Include postcard reproductions of the artist's works.

13. You and another student are artists visiting a Parisian cafe. Agree and disagree on your choices of subject matter and themes, your styles of art, your differences in techniques and paint application. Compare your working habits, childhood experiences, different personalities. Consider when and where you each lived and how this affected your work. Show three or four of your paintings that are typical of your oeuvre. Use them to tell what you were attempting to do and whether or not you feel you accomplished it. Why do you think you will be famous in 100 years?

INTERACTIVE EXTENSIONS—NON-WESTERN ART

1. Visit a natural history, anthropology, or art museum that has art objects from tribal and world cultures. Compare objects made from wood, clay, or fiber from two diverse groups. Or compare containers, clothing, body ornaments, masks, sculptures, paintings, and so on from two or more different groups. Think about why the objects were made, the construction techniques, the decorative effects, and the symbolism used.

2. In a museum or in library books, find two pieces of ceremonial art, and report on their cultural contexts. Tell about the values, ideas, expressive content, and symbolism that the objects transmit to the viewer. Find out when objects were made and if such objects are still being made and used by that cultural group.

3. In library books, find and make copies of four different objects from four different cultures that depict the human form (or animal forms), and compare differences and similarities, if any, from one culture to another. Is one more abstract? Does one show distortion, exaggeration of body parts or features? Does one show an extensive use of pattern and decorative elements? Do any show action? Which ones show a figure engaged in specific activities?

4. Attend a different culture's local festival or religious ceremony. Observe what art objects are important parts of the ritual. What symbolism is contained within the art objects? Are music and dance used, and if so, how are they integrated in the ceremony? How long has this particular festival or ceremony taken place? Has it been modified since it was brought to America from its original venue?

5. In library books, compare the shapes and forms used by African mask makers with the shapes and forms in temple carvings in India.

6. Find a picture of an art object from another culture, and tell why you think a museum should purchase it and make it available to future generations.

7. As early as A.D. 770, Japanese artists were making woodblock prints. Look in art books to find how other countries have used woodblock prints. Discover other ways of making prints in other cultures.

8. Find pictures of Greek temples and temples in Mexico or India. How are they different?

9. Find pictures of Spanish architecture, and note how it is indebted to Moorish art.

10. Find an example from the Book of Kells, and compare its calligraphy and illustrations with Islamic manuscripts.

11. Demonstrate an art form from another culture, and explain it in its appropriate context. For example, demonstrate how to make a Japanese dry garden, using a tray filled with fine sand, several small rocks, and a comb for raking patterns in the sand. Explain the cultural content and context of dry gardens.

12. Select a book that contains photographs of artworks from a culture with which you are unfamiliar. Choose one picture, and without reading any of the text, write a paragraph in which you endeavor to describe and interpret what you see. Then read to discover how and why the object was created, how it was used, and what symbolism is seen in it. Finally, write another paragraph about what you see and feel about the work.

13. Research and make a time line of the traditional arts of one of the following: China, Japan, India, Africa, or Native Americans.

14. Research and report on world cultures and how their religious beliefs influenced their visual images. How are some of the changes reflected in religious architecture? Explain.

15. Compare and contrast Mayan and Aztec pyramids, religions, calendars, and writing systems.

16. Compare and contrast Mexican, Chinese, and Japanese pottery, dolls, and costumes.

WWW INTERNET RESEARCH

The following is a selective list of some of the best museum websites for locating examples of artworks as indicated by collection areas. These museum websites provide images and contextual information on numerous works of art, based on the most recent available scholarship. Please note that these websites are frequently updated, and that addresses do change.

If you are looking for a specific museum address, you can access any museum by state at www.museumlink.com or through any reliable search engine.

Western Art

Art Institute of Chicago (www.artic.edu/aic/index.html)
  Greek/Roman; European art from medieval period through twentieth century; American art from the nineteenth century to present.

Brooklyn Museum of Art (www.brooklynart.org)
  Egyptian; Greek/Roman.

Detroit Institute of Art (www.dia.org)
  Greek/Roman, European art from Renaissance through twentieth century; twentieth century American art (including lesson plans for Diego Rivera mural).

Frick Museum (www.frick.org)
  European art from the sixteenth to nineteenth centuries.

Hermitage Museum (www.hermitage.ru)
  Egyptian, Greek/Roman, European art from medieval period.

Huntington (www.huntington.org)
  English and French art of the eighteenth and nineteenth centuries; American art from the eighteenth to mid-twentieth centuries.

Kemper Art Museum (www.kemperart.org)
  twentieth century American art.

Kimbell Art Museum (www.kimbellart.org)
  Egyptian; Greek/Roman; European art from the medieval period through nineteenth century.

Los Angeles County Museum of Art (www.lacma.org)
  Greek/Roman; European art from the seventeenth through nineteenth centuries; American art from the nineteenth century to the present (strong photography collection).

Louvre (www.louvre.fr)
  Egyptian; Greek/Roman; European art from medieval period through nineteenth century.

Metropolitan Museum of Art (www.metmuseum.org)
  Greek/Roman; European art from medieval period through nineteenth century.

National Gallery of Art (www.nga.gov)
  European art from medieval period through nineteenth century; American art from nineteenth and twentieth centuries.

Norton Simon Museum (www.nortonsimon.org)
  European art from medieval period through nineteenth century.

St. Louis Museum of Art (www.slam.org)
  European art from nineteenth and twentieth centuries (strong German expressionist collection); American art from nineteenth through twentieth centuries.

San Francisco Museum of Modern Art (www.sfmoma.org)
  European and American art from twentieth century to the present.

Sheldon Memorial Art Gallery (sheldon.unl.edu)
  American art from eighteenth through twentieth centuries.

Walters Art Gallery (www.thewalters.org)
  Greek/Roman; European art from medieval period through nineteenth century.

Non-Western Art

Art Institute of Chicago (www.artic.edu/aic/index.html)
  African art; Asian art; art of the Americas.

Asian Art Museum of San Francisco (www.asianart.org)
  Asian art.

Brooklyn Museum of Art (www.brooklynart.org)
  African art; Asian art; art of the Americas.

Buffalo Bill Historical Center (www.bbhc.org)
  art of the Americas (Plains).

Denver Museum of Natural History (www.dmnh.org)
  art of the Americas.

Detroit Institute of Art (www.dia.org)
  African art; Asian art; art of the Americas.

Freer Museum (www.si.edu/asia)
  Asian art.

Hermitage Museum (www.hermitage.ru)
  Islamic art; Asian art.

Indiana Museum of Art (www.ima-art.org)
  African art; Asian art.

Kimbell Art Museum (www.kimbellart.org)
  African art; Asian art; art of the Americas (pre-Columbian).

Los Angeles County Museum of Art (www.lacma.org)
  Asian art.

Metropolitan Museum of Art (www.metmuseum.org)
  African art; Islamic art; art of the Americas (pre-Columbian).

National Gallery of Canada (www.national.gallery.ca)
  art of the Americas (Inuit).

National Museum of the American Indian (www.si.edu/nmai/nav.htm)
  North American Indian art.

National Palace Museum, Taipei, Taiwan, Republic of China (www.npm.gov.tw)
  Asian art.

Nelson-Atkins Museum (www.nelson-atkins.org)
  African art; Asian art; art of the Americas.

Norton Simon Museum (www.nortonsimon.org)
  Asian art.

St. Louis Museum of Art (www.slam.org)
  African art; Asian art; art of the Americas (pre-Columbian and Southwest).

Walters Art Gallery (www.thewalters.org)
  Islamic art; Asian art.

Resources
Glossary

A

abstract Artworks that stress the arrangement of the elements and principles of art rather than subject matter.

abstract expressionism Twentieth-century style in which artists applied paint freely to show feelings and emotions. Strong dependence on accident and chance; no effort to represent subject matter.

additive process Building up a sculptural form with addition of clay or other material; opposite of subtractive sculpture such as wood carving.

aerial perspective Method of showing distance on flat surface, using lighter, duller tones.

aesthetics Branch of philosophy that has to do with the nature of art and beauty.

analogous colors Colors that are next to each other on the color wheel.

armature A framework serving as a support in making sculpture with clay.

Armory Show First large exhibit of modern art in America, New York City, 1913. Great impact.

Ashcan School Group of early twentieth-century Americans who painted city life, alleys, slums. Original name: The Eight.

asymmetrical balance Type of balance in which both sides are not the same but give viewer feeling of visual equality.

B

balance A harmonious arrangement of parts or elements in a design.

baroque Seventeenth century, between mannerism and rococo eras; characterized by dynamic movement, overt emotion; ornate, curving, and diagonal lines.

batik A process of applying melted wax to fabric or paper before a color dye is applied. The wax resists the dye, protecting the surface beneath. The wax is then removed to reveal the design.

Bauhaus Pronounced "bough house." German school of architecture, design, and craftsmanship, 1918. Great impact on modern concepts of design. Closed by Nazis in 1933.

Byzantine Art of eastern Roman Empire; paintings and mosaics showing rich use of color; figures seem flat and stiff; intended as religious lessons, presented clearly and simply.

C

calligraphic A kind of drawing made of flowing lines, curving shapes, like those used in calligraphy (beautiful writing).

chiaroscuro Italian term "bright-dark." A technique for modeling forms in a painting by shading with dark and light values. Leonardo and Rembrandt were leaders.

classical Originally, the art of ancient Greece. Later, works created from 600 B.C. till fall of Rome. Then used to describe artworks that were inspired by ancient Greek or Roman examples. Used today to describe perfection of form with emphasis on harmony and unity, restraint of emotion.

collage Artwork made by using variety of objects (paper, fabric), joined by adhering them to a flat surface.

color Element of art—hue; appearance of object that is created by the differing qualities of light it reflects.

complementary colors Colors that are opposite from one another on the color wheel and that contrast with each other.

contour line drawing Drawing showing outlines and edges of subject matter, both inside and outside.

cool colors Green, blue, violet, reminding us of cool places and feelings.

cubism Twentieth-century art movement developed by Picasso and Braque in which subject matter is broken up, analyzed, and reassembled in abstract form, often seen from several points of view.

D

dadaism French for "hobby horse," selected at random from dictionary; movement of revolt, 1915–23, aimed at destroying art as aesthetic cult and replacing it with shocking nonsense.

distort To change the way something looks to make it more interesting or meaningful, usually by twisting it out of its natural shape, or by exaggerating some of its features.

E

elements of art Basic ingredients in a work of art: line, color, shape/form, texture, space.

emotionalism See *expressionism.*

emphasis Viewer's attention is directed to focal point in an artwork.

encaustic Painting with pigments mixed with wax.

enduring/big idea An idea that has lasting value beyond the classroom. Enduring ideas provide the focus for visual arts units and are threaded through all the individual lessons of each unit.

essential questions Questions that are implicit in the overarching enduring idea of a visual arts unit and that help clarify the enduring idea for students.

expressionism Modern art movement in which artists communicated their strong emotional feelings. Flourished especially in Germany during late nineteenth and early twentieth centuries.

F

fantasy See *surrealism.*

fauves "Wild beasts," early twentieth-century style in France. Brilliant, unrealistic colors used in violent, uncontrolled way.

foreshortening Way of drawing an object or person so it seems to project directly toward viewer.

form Three-dimensional artwork such as sculpture, architecture, various crafts. Also shown by shading when drawing a 3-D form on a flat surface.

formal balance Symmetrical, same on both sides of artwork.

format Shape and size of artwork.

formative or informal assessments Refers to judgments made during a unit/course of study that enable the teacher to make mid-course changes before completion of the unit/course.

fresco Painting form, usually used for murals. Water-based paint is applied to wet plaster.

futurism Italian style of painting, early twentieth century; emphasizing machine-like quality of modern life.

G

genre Subjects and scenes from everyday life.

gesture lines Lines that capture movement, usually free-flowing and made with continuous hand movement.

Gothic Style of architecture, painting, and sculpture that developed in Western Europe, mainly France and England, in mid- and late twelfth century. Cathedrals had spires and pointed arches.

gradation Gradual step-by-step change, from dark to light, large to small.

H

Harlem Renaissance Explosion of African-American cultural achievement at its height in 1920s in Harlem, New York City.

Hudson River School Small group of American artists, 1825; created first truly American style of painting focusing on American landscapes.

I

impasto Thick, opaque paint applied with brush or knife, creating textural effect on surface of painting.

implied lines Lines you cannot see, but that direct eye.

impressionism A way of painting that started in France during 1860s. Artists painted candid glimpses of subjects emphasizing momentary effects of light on surfaces. Paint applied in dabs.

informal balance See *asymmetrical balance*.

integration The process of making meaningful connections between different subject areas of a school curriculum, so that the different subjects are taught in a more unified, holistic manner.

intensity Brightness or dullness of a color.

intermediate colors Colors created when a primary color is mixed with an adjacent secondary color on the color wheel.

K

key art ideas Ideas that form the foundation of and permeate the arts, such as artworks can have both personal and social value; artworks are objects for interpretation; art making is about expressing ideas; and so forth.

key concepts Statements that are implicit in the overarching enduring idea of a visual arts unit and that help clarify the enduring idea for students.

L

landscape Painting or drawing showing a scene from nature: mountains, trees, rivers, fields, outdoor scenery. Cityscapes show urban scenes; seascapes show the ocean.

line An element of art: mark on a surface created by a tool (pencil, pen, brush).

linear perspective When line is used to create illusion of depth on flat surface. If lines are extended, they meet at a point on the eye level line of the viewer called the *vanishing point*.

lithography Method of printing from prepared stone.

M

mannerism Period between High Renaissance and baroque. Heightened, often artificial style. Elongated or overly muscular figures, contorted poses, crowded composition, designed to create intense emotional response.

medieval From or of the Middle Ages in Europe, A.D. 500–1500.

medium Material used to create an artwork (oils, watercolor, clay, etc.). May also refer to various techniques such as collage, printmaking, or sculpture. Media is plural of medium.

mobile Sculptural art form invented by Alexander Calder in which shapes are suspended from supporting rods in a manner that turns slowly in the air.

monochromatic Using one color, including its tints and shades.

movement Motion; may be simulated or actual in an artwork.

mural Large artwork applied to wall or ceiling, usually done with fresco.

N

naive Painting in primitive untrained fashion; childlike, simplified style; literal depiction; much detail and decorative pattern; folk art.

negative space Empty space surrounding shapes or forms.

neoclassicism Nineteenth-century French art style that began as reaction to baroque. Sought to revive ideals of ancient Greece and Rome. Classical forms expressed ideas about courage, sacrifice, and so on.

neutral Term used for white, black, and gray and sometimes tans and browns.

nonobjective Without a recognizable object.

O

opaque Opposite of *transparent*. Tempera and oil pastels are opaque and may be used on colored background paper. (Water colors and crayons are usually applied to white paper in that they are transparent.)

op art Twentieth-century art style in which artists created an impression of movement on picture surface by means of optical illusion.

P

perspective Creating illusion of 3-D objects on 2-D surface.

plein air painting Painting outdoors in contrast to formal and controlled style of studio painting.

pointillism Nineteenth-century French paintings in which colors are systematically applied in small dots, producing vibrant surfaces.

pop art Art in which everyday, popular items are used as subject matter, such as comic strips, product packages, and so on.

positive shape Space that a form or shape occupies in an artwork.

postimpressionism French style of painting started in late nineteenth century, following impressionism. Stressed expressions of feelings and ideas.

postmodernism Style of art (ca. 1970–current) that borrows various compositional elements from works of art in the past and rearranges them in new combinations, often with a distinctive neoclassical flavor.

primary colors Red, yellow, blue. Secondary colors made by mixing two of them. Mixing primaries when using tempera are magenta, yellow, and turquoise.

primitive Early or undeveloped; also self-taught artist (see *naive*).

principles of art Ways in which artists compose elements of art: balance; emphasis; proportion; movement; rhythm, repetition and pattern; variety; and unity.

proportion Relationship of one part to another.

R

radial balance Design radiating outward from center of circle.

realism Representational art; mid-nineteenth-century style in which artists discarded formulas of neoclassicism and theatrical drama of romanticism to paint familiar scenes and events as they actually looked.

regionalism Style of art popular in the United States during 1930s; American scenes painted in a clear simple way.

relief Sculpture in which figures and objects protrude from a background slab.

relief print One of the four basic graphic arts, involving images printed from a raised, inked design cut into a block.

Renaissance Rebirth of art of classical Greece and Rome, emphasis on realism, cultural awareness, and learning; fourteenth and fifteenth centuries, particularly in Italy and northern Europe.

representational Realistic, as we see it in nature.

rhythm Sense of visual movement regular or harmonious pattern created by repetition of lines, shapes, or colors.

rococo Eighteenth-century style that emphasized carefree life of aristocracy, rather than heroes or pious martyrs. Love, romance, free graceful movement; playful use of line, delicate colors.

Romanesque architecture Architecture characterized by round arches; used by Egyptians and Etruscans and later the Romans. If rotated on its vertical axis, it forms a dome.

romanticism Art that flourished in early nineteenth century, emphasizing excitement, emotions, in a bold dramatic manner. Pictures filled with action, exotic settings.

rubric A formal plan for scoring a product or process.

S

sculpture Three-dimensional art form made by either additive techniques or subtractive techniques. May be a relief on a slab or freestanding.

secondary colors Colors made by mixing two primary colors: orange=red/yellow; violet=red/blue; green=yellow/blue.

shade Dark value of a color created by adding black to it.

shading Gradual change from light to dark to show three-dimensional forms on flat surface.

shape Element of art; two-dimensional area defined by line or color change.

space Element of art; usually related to showing foreground, middleground, and background on a flat surface.

still life Composition made up of objects that don't move; usually on table top.

subtractive process Sculpture in which parts are removed to create the form.

summative or formal assessment Refers to the evaluation of a completed unit of study, and answers the question of whether or not students gained the desired skills and understandings, as defined by the objectives of the unit.

superrealism Twentieth-century art in which emphasis is placed on photographic realism.

surrealism Twentieth-century art in which dreams and fantasy are subject matter. Often very realistic objects are seen in unusual or bizarre relationships.

symmetrical balance Seen when both sides of an artwork are identical.

T

tempera Thick, water-soluble opaque paint.

texture Element of art; actual texture is the way a surface feels; visual texture is the way it looks as if it would feel.

tint Light value of a color created by adding it to white paint.

tjanting A small funnel-shaped tool used in applying melted wax to fabric or paper when making batik.

transparent Opposite of opaque; able to see through it, such as watercolors and crayons that are used on white paper.

trompe l'oeil Pronounced "tromp loy." "Fool the eye" type of painting that is so realistic that viewer thinks objects are real.

U

unity Principle of art. Seen or felt when all parts of an artwork give viewer a sense of harmony and completion.

V

value Lightness or darkness of a color; color added to white to create tints; black added to a color to create shades.

vanishing point Point on eye-level line or horizon line where horizontal lines that are parallel to each other recede and meet.

variety Principle of art in which elements are different and combined in pleasing nonchaotic manner.

visual texture Texture in an artwork that imitates actual texture.

W

warm colors Red, orange, and yellow. Warm colors remind us of warm places and feelings.

wash Paint or ink thinned with water to be transparent.

Resources for Art Education

Student Textbooks for Elementary Classrooms

Barrett Kendall Publishing, Ltd., *Portfolios, A State of the Art Program*, K–8

Davis Publications, Inc., *Adventures in Art*, K–6

Davis Publications, Inc., *Connections in Art: The Interdisciplinary Curriculum*, 1–5

Harcourt Brace School Publishers, *Art Express*, K–5

SRA/McGraw-Hill, *SRA Art Connections*, K–5

Packaged Art Programs for Elementary Classrooms (videos, CD-ROMs)

Alarion Press, PO Box 1882, Boulder, CO 80306

Art Image Publications, PO Box 568, Champlain, NY 12919

Crizmac, PO Box 65928, Tucson, AZ 85728-5928

Crystal Productions, PO Box 2159, Glenview, IL 60025

Cuisenaire Dale Seymour Publications, PO Box 5026, White Plains, NY 10602-5026 (800-872-1100)

Davis Publications, Inc., 50 Portland St., Worcester, MA 01608 (800-533-2837)

Knowledge Unlimited, Inc., PO Box 52, Madison, WI 53701-0052

Wilton Programs, Reading and O'Reilly, PO Box 541, Wilton, CT 06897 (800-458-4274)

Reproductions of Artworks

Austin Reproductions, Inc., 815 Grundy Ave., Holbrook, NY 11741 (sculpture replicas)

Fine Art Distributors/Haystack Publishers, 80 Kettle Creek Rd., Weston, CT 06883

Knowledge Unlimited, Inc., PO Box 52, Madison, WI 53701-0052

New York Graphic Society, Ltd., PO Box 1469, Greenwich, CT 06482

Shorewood Reproductions, 27 Glen Rd., Sandy Hook, CT 06482

Starry Night Distributors, Inc., 15 Pin Oak Dr., Kinderhook, NY 12106

Universal Color Slide Co., 1221 Main St., Suite 203, Weymouth, MA 02190

University Prints, 21 East St., Winchester, MA 01890

Museum Catalogs (reproductions, art games, art-related items, etc.)

Metropolitan Museum of Art, Institutional Sales, Special Services Office, Middle Village, NY 11381-0001

Museum of Fine Arts, Boston, PO Box 244, Avon, MA 02322-0244

Museum of Modern Art, 11 West 53rd St., New York, NY 10019-5401

National Gallery of Art, Publications Service, 2000 B So. Club Drive, Landover, MD 20785

Magazines

Art Education, National Art Education Association, 1916 Association Dr., Reston, VA 22091

Arts and Activities, 591 Camino de la Reina, Suite 200, San Diego, CA 92108

Scholastic Art, Scholastic Inc., 902 Sylvan Ave., Box 2001, Englewood Cliffs, NJ 07632 (formerly *Art and Man*; for upper-grade students)

School Arts, 50 Portland St., Worcester, MA 01608

Crayola Kids (for upper grades), Meredith Corp., 1912 Grand Ave., Des Moines, IA 50309-3379

Muse, PO Box 7468, Red Oak, IA 5191-2468 (800-827-0227)

Art Supply Catalogs

Dick Blick, Dept. A., Box 1267, Galesburg, IL 61401

J. L. Hammett Co., Braintree, MA (800-333-4600)

Nasco, 901 Janesville Ave., Fort Atkinson, WI 53538; also 1524 Princeton Ave., Modesto, CA 95352 (800-558-9595)

Sax Arts and Crafts, PO Box 51710, New Berlin, WI 53151 (800-558-6696)

Triarco Arts and Crafts, 14650 28th Ave. North, Plymouth, MN 55447

United Art and Education Supply Co., Inc., Fort Wayne, IN (800-322-3247)

R. B. Walter, PO Box 920626, Norcross, GA 30092

Safety in Art

Babin, A., ed. *Art Hazards News* 17, no. 5 (1994)

Babin, A., P.A. Peltz and M. Rossol. *Children's Art Suppliers Can Be Toxic*. New York: Center for Safety in the Arts, 1992

Center for Safety in the Arts, 5 Beekman St., Suite 820, New York, NY 10038

Qualley, Charles A. *Safety in the Art Room*, Worcester, MA: Davis Publishing, Inc., 1986

Art Forms
Two– and Three–Dimensional

Artworks are either two-dimensional or three-dimensional. Two-dimensional objects have height and width. Three-dimensional objects have height, width, and depth.

TWO–DIMENSIONAL ARTWORKS

1. *Drawings* are made by moving an implement that leaves a mark across the flat surface of a material, usually paper. The following are some of the mainstream drawing media.
   a) Charcoal—available in vine, compressed, and pencil form.
   b) Colored chalk—for use on paper, not chalkboards.
   c) Conte crayons—available in black, brown, and sienna.
   d) Ink—used with pen or brush.
   e) Oil pastels—similar to crayons but softer, more opaque, and more intense in color; may be blended.
   f) Pastels—similar to chalk but finer and available in a wider range of colors.
   g) Pens of all sizes and colors.
   h) Pencils, black, from hard (H) to soft (B); colored.
   i) Wax crayons.

2. *Paintings* depend more on color than do drawings and usually are executed on paper or canvas. Pigment is a finely ground powder that is used to give color to paint. The binder is the liquid that holds the pigment together and causes it to stick to the painting surface. The solvent is the material used to thin or remove the paint. Paint media include
   a) Acrylics—quick-drying synthetic paint that was introduced during the 1950s; applied thinly or heavily in the manner of oil paint; solvent is water.
   b) Egg tempera—pigment is mixed with egg and water and applied to gessoed wood panels; applied in layers; very durable; in use before oil paints were invented.
   c) Encaustic—pigment is mixed with melted wax; ancient technique.
   d) Fresco—done with watercolors on moist plaster walls for murals.
   e) Gouache (pronounced "gwash")—opaque watercolor.
   f) Oil paint—pigment ground into linseed oil for the binder; turpentine is the solvent; colors may be blended on palette or directly on canvas; slow to dry. (The paint tube was invented in the nineteenth century, allowing artists to take their canvases outdoors and to paint directly from nature, rather than from memory and from sketches.)
   g) Tempera—used in schools; dries quickly; opaque; inexpensive and water soluble; generally used with stiff flat or round bristle brushes.
   h) Watercolor—transparent; used with soft brushes; available in trays or tubes; binder is gum arabic.

3. *Prints* are original artworks made in multiples. The Chinese developed printmaking 2,000 years ago. As early as A.D. 770, the Japanese were making woodblock prints. Prints are made on paper or fabric from the inked image of a prepared surface. An *artist's proof* is a trial print and is made first. Prints are signed at the bottom: on the right, the artist's name and date; on the left, the numerical order of each print, followed by the total number of prints made. Thus, the seventh print in an edition of 24 would be signed 7/24. Print techniques include
   a) Intaglio—image is scratched or etched into the surface, and ink is forced into the grooves; excess ink on the surface is wiped away and the image transferred by applying pressure so that ink appears on the paper; etching is an example of this process.
   b) Lithographs—image is applied with a greasy medium on a flat piece of limestone, aluminum, or zinc; when ink is applied, it sticks to the drawing and runs off the treated surface, enabling a print to be made of the image.
   c) Relief prints—image is raised from the background, and a special printing ink (oil or water-based) is applied to raised areas; linoleum, woodblock, potato, scratch-foam, card prints, eraser prints, and even fingerprints are examples of this popular printing activity.
   d) Serigraphs—silk is stretched on a frame; an image is transferred to the surface with the areas not to be printed blocked out so that the ink may be pressed through the silk onto the paper or fabric with a squeegee.

4. *Collages* are paper, fabric, photographs, string, and various found materials combined to adhere to a surface. Cubists, dadists, and a number of artists during the 1950s and 1960s were the first to make collages.

5. *Mosaics*—small pieces of glass, tile, stones, paper, and such, (called *tesserae*, meaning "tile") are adhered to background to create a unified pattern or image.

6. *Calligraphy* is "beautiful writing" that is usually accomplished with the skillful use of a chisel-tipped pen or a brush.

7. *Photography* (both black-and-white and color), computer art, films, and video are media that are the results of modern technology.

8. *Graphics* refers to designs that artists make for publication and other commercial uses, such as advertisements, logos, letterheads, brochures, wrapping paper, posters, greeting cards, and so on.

THREE–DIMENSIONAL ARTWORKS

1. *Sculpture* is freestanding and viewed from all sides. It may be additive (in which the artist adds parts as work progresses) or subtractive (in which the artist carves or takes parts away as work progresses). Bas-relief sculpture is usually mounted on a wall and is meant to be viewed from the front only. Artists work in clay, wood, stone, metal, plaster, wax, glass, plastics, and fibers. Sculpture media and processes include

a) Carving—stone or wood or other material are cut or chipped to create a solid form.

b) Modeling—clay is shaped into a form, usually over an armature.

c) Cast—a form is created; a mold made from the form is then filled with molten metal or other liquid, such as plaster or slip.

d) Assembled—different materials (wood, fabric, wire, cardboard, and so on) are collected and joined together to create a form.

2. *Crafts* are made by hand for a utilitarian function (to wear, to contain things, etc.) or objects made with traditional craft materials. They include

a) Ceramics—clay objects that are fired at a high temperature in a kiln; they may be glazed or left bisque; uses are containers, lamps, and so on.

b) Fibers—may be spun, dyed, woven, batiked, quilted, tie-dyed, printed, stitched; used for clothing, draperies, floor coverings, and so on.

c) Glass—blown by forcing air through a tube into globs of molten glass that are attached at the end of the tube; cut and formed, stained; used for containers, jewelry, lamps, windows; can also be cast.

d) Leather—dyed, imprinted, stitched, shaped; used for clothing, shoes, belts, purses.

e) Metal—pounded, welded, soldered, cast, enameled; used to form bowls and plates and flatware, belt buckles, containers, jewelry.

f) Plastic—cast, cut, adhered; used for containers, furniture, architecture.

g) Wood—carved, painted, glued, pegged; used for furniture, containers, jewelry.

3. *Product design* concerns furniture, appliances, housewares, tools, dishes, clothing, automobiles, and such that are made commercially and mass produced after a product designer working with engineers plans them.

4. *Architecture* concerns spaces where we dwell, worship or meditate, meet, learn, work, and play. Materials, site, climate, intended use, budget, and sometimes cultural tradition determine actual form. Interiors are designed to enhance space. Landscape design is an important factor. City planning is vital to the design and future growth of urban and suburban areas.

5. *Theater design* includes stage design, costuming, and lighting.

Pronunciation Guide

A

Angelico, Fra (An JAY lee koh, Frah)
Anguissola, Sofanisba (Ahn GWEES so la, So fah NISS bah)

B

Balla, Giacomo (BAHL la, JAH koh moh)
Barlch, Ernst (BAHR lahk, Airnst)
Bellini, Giovanni (Bel LEE nee, Joh VAH nee)
Bierstadt, Albert (BEER tstaht, AL bert)
Boccioni, Umberto (Boh CHO nee, Oom BER toh)
Bonheur, Rosa (Bahn uhr, ROS ah)
Bonnard, Pierre (Bo NAHR, Pee EHR)
Bosch, Hieronymus (BOSH, Heer AHN ni mus)
Botticelli, Sandro (Bot ti CHEL lee, SAN droh)
Boucher, François (Boo SHAY, Fran SWAH)
Boudin, Eugene (Boo DINH, Uh ZHEN)
Brancusi, Constantin (BRAHN koo see, KAHN stuhn teen)
Braque, Georges (BRAHK, Zhorzh)
Brueghel, Pieter (BROY gel, Peter)
Brunelleschi, Filippo (Brew nell LESS kay, Fee LIP po)

C

Canaletto (Kah nah LET toh)
Caravaggio, Michelangelo (Kah rah VA joh, Mee kel AHN jay lo)
Carriera, Rosalba (Car ree AYE rah, Rose AHL bah)
Cassatt, Mary (Cah SAT)
Cézanne, Paul (Say ZAHN)
Chagall, Marc (Shah GAHL)
Chardin, Jean-Baptiste (Shar DAN, Zhahn Bap TEEST)
Cimabue (Tshee ma BOO aye)
Copley, John Singleton (COP lee)
Corot, Jean (Caw ROH, Zhahn)
Courbet, Gustave (Koor BAY, Goos TAHV)
Cranach, Lucas (KRAN uck)

D

Dali, Salvador (DAH lee, SAHL van dore)
Daumier, Honoré (Dohm YAY, Oh noh RAY)
David, Jacques-Louis (Dah VEED, Zhahk Loo EE)
de Chirico, Giorgio (de KEY ree co, JOHR jyo)
Degas, Edgar (Duh GAH, ed GAHR)
de Hooch, Pieter (dee HOKE, Peter)
de Kooning, Willem (duh KOE ning, VILL em)
Delacroix, Eugène (Duh lah KWAH, Uh ZHEN)
De La Tour, Georges (Duh lah TOOR, Zhorzh)
Demuth, Charles (Duh MOOTH)
Derain, André (Duh RAN, ON dray)
Diebenkorn, Richard (DEE ben korn)
Donatello (Dah na TELL lo)
Duccio (Do tshee yo)
Duchamp, Marcel (Doo SHAHM, Mahr SELL)
Dufy, Raoul (DEW FEE, Rah OOL)
Dürer, Albrecht (DUHR er, AL brekt)

E

Eakins, Thomas (A kinz)
El Greco (El GREH coh)
Escher, M. C. (ESH uhr)

F

Feininger, Lyonel (FINE in gurr)
Fouquet, Jean (Foo KAY, Zhahn)
Fragonard, Jean-Honoré (Frah goh NAHR, Zhahn Oh noh RAY)
Frankenthaler, Helen (Frank en TALL er)

G

Gauguin, Paul (Goh GINH)
Gentileschi, Artemisia (Djen tee LESS kay, Ar tay ME zee a)
Géricault, Théodore (ZHAY re koh, TAY oh dor)
Ghiberti, Lorenzo (Ghee BAIR tee, low RENT soh)
Ghirlandaio, Domenico (Geer lahn DAH yoh, Doh MAY nee koh)
Giacometti, Alberto (Jah ko MET tee, Ahl BAIR toh)
Giorgione, Giorgio (John JOY nay, Johr joh)
Giotto di Bondone (JOHT toh, dee Bohn DOH nay)
Gorky, Arshile (GOR kee, ARSH shul)
Goya, Francisco (GAW Yuh, Fran SIS coe)
Gris, Juan (GREES, Wahn)
Gropius, Walter (GRO pih us, Wall tur)
Grunëwald, Mathis (GREWN vahlt, MAH tis)

H

Hals, Frans (HALLS, Frahnss)
Hofmann, Hans (HOHF mahn, Hans)
Hogarth, William (HOE garth)
Hokusai (Hohk SY)
Holbein, Hans (HOHL bine, Hahns)

I

Ingres, Jean (INH gr, Zhahn)
Inness, George (IN us)

J

Jawlensky, Alexei von (Yah VLENS key, Ah LEX)

K

Kandinsky, Wassily (Kan DIN skee, VAH see l'yee)
Kirchner, Ernst Ludwig (KEERKH ner, Airnst LOOT vik)
Klee, Paul (Clay)
Kokoschka, Oskar (Koh KOSH kah)
Kollwitz, Käthe (KAHL wits, Kate uh)

L

Laurencin, Marie (Loh rahn sinh)
Le Corbusier (Luh Core boo zee ay)
Léger, Fernand (Lay ZHAY, Fair NON)
Le Nain, Antoine and Louis (Luh NINH, Ahn TWAHN, Loo EE)

Leonardo da Vinci (Lay oh NAR doh da VIN chee)
Leyster, Judith (LIE ster)
Lichtenstein, Roy (LICK ten steen)
Lipchitz, Jacques (LIP sheets, Zhahk)
Lippi, Fra Filippo (LEEP pee, Frah Fill LEEP poh)
Lorrain, Claude (Luh RAN Klohd)

M

Macke, August (MACK uh)
Maes, Nicolaes (MASS, NIK o lay)
Magritte, René (Muh Greet Ruh NAE)
Maillol, Aristide (MY yoh, AH ris teed)
Manet, Edouard (Man AY, Eh doo arh)
Mantegna, Andrea (Man tay nya, Ahn DRAY ah)
Marin, John (MARE uhn)
Marini, Marino (Mah REE nee, Mah REE noh)
Marisol (Mah ree SOHL)
Masaccio (Mah SAH chyo)
Matisse, Henri (Mah TEES, On REE)
Medici (MED uh chee)
Merian, Maria Sibylla (MARE e uhn, MAH REE ah Suh BEE La)
Metsys, Quentin (MET sis, Kwen ten)
Michelangelo Buonarroti (My kel AHN jay loe, Bwoh nah ROE tee)
Mies van der Rohe, Ludwig (MEES vahn dair ROH-eh, Loot vik)
Millet, Jean-François (MEH yah, Zhahn Fran SWAH)
Miró, Joan (Mee ROH, Ho AHN)
Modigliani, Amedeo (Mo DEE lee ah nee, Ah meh DAY oh)
Mondrian, Piet (MOHN dree ahn, PEET)
Monet, Claude (Mo nay, Klohd)
Morisot, Berthe (Moh ree ZOH, Bairt)
Munch, Edvard (MOONK, ED var)
Muybridge, Eadweard (MY brij, ED wurd)

N

Nolde, Emil (NOHL duh, AY muhl)

O

Oldenburg, Claes (OLE den berk, Clays)
Orozco, José Clemente (Oh ROHS coe, Ho SAY Kleh MEN tay)

P

Parmigianino (Par me dji ah KNEE no)
Pechstein, Max (PEX stine)
Peto, John Frederick (PEE toh)
Picasso, Pablo (Pea CAH so, Pahb lo)
Pissarro, Camille (Pee SAH roh, Ka MEE)
Poussin, Nicolas (Poo SINH, NEE koh lahs)

R

Raphael (RAHF ay el)
Rauschenberg, Robert (ROW shen berg)

Redon, Odilon (Ruh DAWN, Oh dee YON)
Rembrandt van Rijn (REM brant van Ryne)
Renoir, Pierre-Auguste (Ren WAHR, Pee EHR oh GOOST)
Rivera, Diego (Ree VAY rah, Dee AY goh)
Rodin, François-Auguste (Roh DAN, Frahn swah oh GOOST)
Rouault, Georges (Roo Oh, Zhorzh)
Rousseau, Henri (Roo SO, On REE)
Rubens, Peter Paul (ROO benz)
Ruysch, Rachel (RO iss, RAH shell)

S

Saarinen, Eero (SAHR uh nen, EER oh)
Sassetta (SAHS SAY tah)
Schmidt-Rottluff, Karl (Shmeedt ROHT loof, Kahrl)
Scholder, Fritz (SHOWL duhr)
Seurat, Georges (Suh RAH, Zhorzh)
Shahn, Ben (Shawn)
Signac, Paul (SEEN yahk)
Siqueiros, David (See key AIR ohz)
Sisley, Alfred (SEES ley)
Stieglitz, Alfred (STEEG lits)

T

Tamayo, Rufino (Tah MAH yoh, Roo FEE noh)
Thiebaud, Wayne (Tee bo)
Tintoretto, Jacopo (Teen toh RET toh, Jah KOH poh)
Titian (TISH yan)
Toulouse-Lautrec, Henri de (Too LOOZ Lah TREK, On REE duh)

U

Uccello, Paolo (Oo TCHEHL loh, POH loh)
Utrillo, Maurice (Oo TREE oh)

V

van der Weyden, Rogier (van duh VIE den, ROW jay)
van Dyck (van DIKE)
van Eyck, Jan (van IKE, Yahn)
van Gogh, Vincent (van GO)
Vasari (Va SAHR ee)
Vaserely, Victor (Vah zuh RAY Lee)
Velázquez, Diego (Vay LAS kes, DEE AYE goh)
Vermeer, Jan (ver MAIR, Yahn)
Veronese, Paolo (Ver oh NEES, POH loh)
Verrocchio, Andrea del (Ver ROK kyoh, Ahn DRAY ah)
Vigée-Lebrun, Elisabeth (VEE zhaye lub run, Ale EE za bet)
Vlaminck, Maurice de (Vlah MANK)
Vuillard, Édouard (VWEE yahr, Ay Doo ARH)

W

Warhol, Andy (WOHR hohl)
Watteau, Antoine (Wah TOH, Ahn TWAN)

Children's Books on Art and Artists

Books in a Series

ABC Series, Florence C. Mayers: *Costumes and Textiles, Los Angeles County Museum; Egyptian Art from the Brooklyn Museum; Museum of Fine Arts Boston; Musical Instruments from the Metropolitan Museum of Art; the Museum of Modern Art* (New York: Abrams, 1991).

Adventures in Art (New York: Prestel, 1997–98).

Alphabet Animals, Charles Sullivan (New York: Rizzoli Publishing, 1991).

American Women of Achievement, various authors: *Louise Nevelson; Georgia O'Keeffe; Grandma Moses*; and *Mary Cassatt* (New York: Chelsea Publishers, 1989).

Art for Children, Ernst Raboff: *Marc Chagall; Leonardo da Vinci; Albrecht Dürer; Paul Gauguin; Paul Klee; Henri Matisse; Michelangelo; Pablo Picasso; Rembrandt van Rijn; Frederic Remington; Pierre-August Renoir; Henri Rousseau; Henri de Toulouse-Lautrec; Vincent van Gogh; Diego de Silva y Velazquez* (New York: J.B. Lippincott, 1969–95).

Art for Children, various authors: *Brueghel: The Story of a Clown and a Jug; Chagall: My Sad and Joyous Village; Da Vinci: The Painter Who Spoke with Birds; Degas: The Painted Gesture; Good Day, Mister Gauguin; The Impressionists; Matisse: The Essential Painter; Miro: Earth and Sky; Picasso: A Day in His Studio; The Renaissance; Rousseau: Still Voyages; van Gogh: The Touch of Yellow* (New York: Chelsea House, 1993–98).

Art for Young People Series, various authors: *Pablo Picasso*, Matthew Meadows; *Claude Monet*, Peter Morrison (New York: Sterling Publishers Co., 1996).

Art Revolutions, Linda Bolton: *Pop Art, Impressionism, Cubism, Surrealism* (New York: Peter Bedrick Books, 2000).

Artists, Susan and John Edeen; *Women Artists* by Susan and John Edeen and Kay Alexander (White Plains, NY: Cuisenaire Dale Seymour Publications, 1988, 1990).

Artists' Workshop, Penny King and Clare Roundhill: *Stories, Portraits, Animals, Landscapes* (New York: Crabtree Publishing Co., 1996).

Black Americans of Achievement, various authors: *Gordon Parks, Photographer; Romare Bearden, Artist* (New York: Chelsea House, 1995).

Come Look with Me, Glady S. Blizzard: *Enjoying Art with Children; Exloring Landscape Art with Children; Animals in Art; Exploring Native American Art with Children* (Charlottesville, VA: Thomasson-Grant, Inc., 1997).

Eyewitness Art, various authors: *Looking at Paintings; Color; Gauguin; Goya; Impressionists; Manet; Monet; Perspective; Post-Impressionist; Renaissance; van Gogh; Watercolor* (New York: Dorling Kindersley, 1992–94).

Famous Artists, Antony Mason: *Cezanne; Leonardo da Vinci; Matisse; Michelangelo; Miro; Monet; Picasso; van Gogh* (Hauppauge, NY: Barron's, 1992–94).

Famous Children, Ann Rachlin and Tony Hart: *Da Vinci; Picasso; Leonardo; Michelangelo; Lautrec* (New York: Barron's, 1994).

First Impressions: *Introduction to Art*, various authors: *John James Audubon; Mary Cassatt; Marc Chagall; Leonardo da Vinci; Francisco Goya; Michelangelo; Claude Monet; Pablo Picasso; Rembrandt; Andrew Wyeth* (New York: Abrams, 1990–92).

Getting to Know the World's Greatest Artists, by Mike Venezia: *Botticelli; Brueghel; Cassatt; Dali; Da Vinci; Gauguin; Goya; Klee; Michelangelo* (Chicago: Children's Press, 1988–94).

Great Artists, David Spence: *Renoir; van Gogh; Michelangelo; Rembrandt; Monet; Manet; Picasso; Degas; Gauguin; Cezanne* (New York: Barron's, 1997).

Hispanics of Achievement, various authors: *Diego Rivera; Salvador Dali; Frida Kahlo* (New York: Chelsea House, 1991–95).

How Artists See, Colleen Carroll: *Animals; People; Weather; Elements; Land; Buildings; Universe* (New York: Abbeville Kids, a Division of Abbeville Publishing Group, 1996).

Lerner Series, Sharon Lerner: *The Self-Portrait in Art; Kings and Queens in Art; The Warrior in Art; Farms/Farmers in Art; Portraits; Circus and Fairs* (Minneapolis: Lerner Publishing, 1965–83).

Looking at Paintings, Peggy Roalf: *Cats; Children; Circus; Dancers; Dogs; Families; Flowers; Horses; Landscapes; Musicians; Seascapes; Self-Portraits* (New York: Hyperion Books for Children, 1992–93).

Millbrook Arts Library, series Anthea Peppin: *Nature in Art, Places in Art, People in Art* (Brookfield, CT: Millbrook Press, 1992).

Museum Guides for Kids, Ruthie Knapp and Janice Lehmberg: *Impressionist Art; American Art* (Worcester, MA: Davis Publications, 1998).

Portraits of Women Artists for Children, Robyn Montana Turner: *Georgia O'Keeffe; Rosa Bonheur; Mary Cassatt; Frida Kahlo; Faith Ringgold; Dorothea Lange* (Boston: Little, Brown, 1991–94).

Series on Modern Art: *Colors*, P. Yenawine and Museum of Modern Art: *Lines; Shapes; Stories*. (New York: Delacorte Press, 1991).

Voyages of Discovery, various authors: *The History of Printmaking; Paint and Painting; What the Painter Sees; The Art of Sculpture* (New York: Scholastic Inc., 1994–96).

A Weekend with . . ., various authors: *Degas; Homer; Leonardo da Vinci; Matisse; Picasso; Rembrandt; Renoir; Rivera; Rousseau; van Gogh; Velazquez* (New York: Skira/Rizzoli, 1990–96).

What Makes a . . ., Richard Muhlberger: *Bruegel; Degas; Monet; Raphael; Rembrandt; van Gogh* (New York: Metropolitan Museum of Art, 1993).

The World of Art through the Eyes of Artists, Wendy and Jack Richardon: *Animals; Cities; Entertainers; Families; Natural World; Water* (Chicago: Children's Press, 1991).

Single Books on Art and Artists

Activities for Creating Pictures and Poetry, Janis Bunchman and Stephanie Bissell Briggs (Worcester, MA: Davis Publications, 1994).

Alphabet Animals, Charles Sullivan (New York: Rizzoli, 1991).

The American Eye: Eleven Artists of the Twentieth Century, Jan Greenberg and Sandra Jordan (New York: Delacorte Press, 1995).

Annie and the Old One, Miska Miles, ill. by Peter Parnall (Boston: Little, Brown, 1971).

Annotated Art: The World's Greatest Paintings Explored and Explained, Robert Cumming (New York: Kindersley, 1995).

Art Fraud Detective, Anna Nilsen (New York: Kingfisher, 2000).

Artistic Trickery: The Tradition of Trompe L'Oeil Art, Michael Capek (Minneapolis: Lerner Publishing, 1995).

Artist in Overalls: The Life of Grant Wood, John Duggleby (San Francisco: Chronicle Books, 1995).

Art of African Masks. Carol Finley (Minneapolis: Lerner Publishing, 1999).

The Block, Romare Bearden, poems by Langston Hughes (New York: Viking, Metropolitan Museum of Art, 1995).

The Blue Rider: The Yellow Cow Sees World in Blue, Doris Kutschbach (New York: Prestel, 1996).

A Boy Named Giotto, P. Guarnieri (New York: Farrar Straus Giroux, 1998).

Buffalo Hunt, Russell Freedman (New York: Holiday House, 1988).

C as in Cezanne, Marie Sellier (New York: Peter Bedrick Books, 1995).

Can You Spot the Leopard? African Masks, Christine Stelzig (New York: Prestel, 1997).

Celebrating America: A Collection of Poems and Images of the American Spirit, compiled by Laura Whipple, art provided by the Art Institute of Chicago (New York: Phiomel Books, 1994).

Chagall from A to Z, Marie Sellier (New York: Peter Bedrick Books, 1995).

A Child's Book of Art: Great Pictures, First Words, selected by Lucy Micklethwait (New York: Dorling Kindersley, 1993).

Color, Ruth Heller (New York: Putnam and Grosset, 1995).

The Color Box, ill. by Giles Laroche (Boston: Little, Brown, 1994).

Connections! Art: Discover the Connections through Questions and Answers, Andrea Finn and Julia Weiner (Chicago: World Book, Inc., 1996).

Degas and the Little Dancer, Laurence Anholt (New York: Barron's, 1996).

Diego, Jeanette Winter, text by Jonah Winter (New York: Alfred A. Knopf, 1991).

Dinner at Magritte's, Michael Garland (New York: Dutton Children's Books, 1995).

Dreaming Pictures: Paul Klee, Jurgen von Schemm (New York: Prestel, 1998).

Family Pictures, Cuadros de Familia, Carmen Lomas Garza (San Francisco: Children's Book Press, 1990).

A Fish That's a Box: Folk Art from the National Museum of American Art, M. M. Esterman (Arlington, VA: Great Ocean Publishers, 1990).

The Folk Art Counting Book, Abby Aldrich Rockefeller Folk Art Center (New York: Abrams, 1991).

Georgia O'Keeffe, Linda Lowery. (Minneapolis: Carolrhoda Books, Inc., 1996).

The Girl with a Watering Can, Ewa Zadrzynska (New York: Chameleon Books, 1990).

Go In and Out the Window: An Illustrated Songbook for Young People, Claude Marks, music edited by Dan Fox (New York: Henry Holt, in association with the Metropolitan Museum of Art, 1987).

Grandma Moses: Painter of Rural America, Zibby Oneal (New York: Puffin Book, 1971).

Great Painters, Piero Ventura (New York: G. P. Putnam's Sons, 1984).

Hailstones and Halibut Bones, Mary O'Neill (New York: Doubleday, 1989).

Harriet and the Promised Land, Jacob Lawrence (New York: Simon and Schuster, 1993).

Henri Rousseau: A Jungle Expedition, Susanne Pfleger (New York: Prestel, 1996).

History of Women Artists for Children, Vivian Epstein (Denver: VSE Publishers, 1978).

Honoring Our Ancestors: Autobiographies and Art by 14 Artists from Diverse Cultures, Harriet Rohmer, ed. (San Francisco: Children's Book Press, 1999).

How Artists See Animals, Colleen Carroll (New York: Abbeville Publishing Group, 1996).

How to Show Grown-ups the Museum, Philip Yenawine (New York: Museum of Modern Art, 1987).

I Live in Music, poem by Ntozake Shange, paintings by Romare Bearden (Welcome Book distributed by Stewart, Tabori and Chang, Inc., 1994).

I Spy—An Alphabet in Art, selected by Lucy Micklethwait (New York: Mulberry, 1992).

An Illustrated Treasury of Songs: Traditional American Songs, Ballads, Folk Songs, and Nursery Rhymes (New York: Rizzoli, in association with the National Gallery of Art, 1991).

Imaginary Gardens: American Poetry and Art for Young People, Charles Sullivan (New York: Henry N. Abrams, 1989).

Inspirations: Stories about Women Artists, Leslie Sills (Niles, IL: A. Whiteman & Co., 1989).

Jacob Lawrence, American Scenes, American Struggles, Nancy Shroyer Howard (Worcester, MA: Davis Publications, 1996).

John James Audubon: Wildlife Artist, Peter Anderson (New York: Franklin Watts, Dikvision of Groliefr Publishing, 1995).

The Journey of Diego Rivera, Ernest Goldstein (Minneapolis: Lerner Publishing, 1993).

Katie Meets the Impressionists, James Mayhew (New York: Orchard Books, 1999).

Katie's Picture Show, James Mayhew (New York: Bantam Books, 1997).

The Kids' Art Pack, Ron Van Der Meer and Frank Whitford (New York: Dorling Kindersly, Inc., 1995).

The Legend of the Indian Paintbrush, Tomie de Paola (New York: Putnam and Grosset, 1988).

Leonardo da Vinci, Ibi Lepscky (Woodbury, NY: Barron's, 1984).

Let's Go to the Art Museum, Virginia K. Levy (Pompano Beach, FL: Veejay Publications, 1983).

Lichtenstein: The Artist at Work, L. Walker and M. Abramson (New York: Dutton Lodestar, 1994).

Li'l Sis and Uncle Willie, Gwen Everett (New York: Rizzoli, 1991).

Linnea in Monet's Garden, Christian Bjork (New York: R&S Books, 1987).

Lives of the Artists: Masterpieces, Messes (and What the Neighbors Thought), Kathleen Krull (New York: Harcourt Brace, 1995).

Looking for Vincent, Thea Dubelaar and Ruud Bruijn (New York: Checkerboard Press, 1992).

Marc Chagall: Painter of Dreams, Natalie S. Bober (Philadelphia and New York: The Jewish Publication Society, 1994).

Matisse from A to Z, Marie Sellier (New York: Peter Bedrick Books, 1993).

Meet Edgar Degas, Anne Newlands (Toronto: Kids Can Press, 1988).

Meet Matisse, Nelly Munthe (Boston, MA: Little, Brown & Co, 1983).

Miro for Children, Helene Lamarche (Montreal, Canada: Montreal Museum of Fine Arts, 1986).

Miro (Great Painters for Children), Albert Delmar (New York: Trans-National Trade Development Corp., 1992).

Mona Lisa: The Secret of the Smile, Letizia Galli (New York: Doubleday, 1996).

Move Over, Picasso! A Young Painter's Primer, Ruth Aukerman. (New Windsor, MD: Pat Depke Books, in association with the National Gallery of Art, Washington, DC, 1994).

Museums, Muses and Me: A Sketchbook for Young Artists, Donna Vliet (Austin, TX: Archer M. Huntington Art Gallery, 1991).

My Journey through Art: Create Your Own Masterpieces, Kathryn Cave (Hauppauge, NY: Barron's, in association with the National Gallery of Art, Washington, DC, 1994).

My Name Is Georgia: A Portrait, Jeanette Winter (New York: Harcourt Brace, 1998).

Naming Colors, Ariane Dewey (New York: Harper Collins, 1995).

The Native American Look Book, Art and Activities, from the Brooklyn Museum, Missy Sullivan, Deborah Schwartz, Dawn Weiss, and Barbara Zaffran (New York: New Press, 1996).

Now You See It—Now You Don't: Rene Magritte, Angela Wenzel (New York: Prestel-Verlag, 1998).

Optical Illusions in Art, or Discover How Paintings Aren't Always What They Seem to Be, Alexander Sturgis (New York: Sterling Publishing, 1996).

Pablo Picasso, Ibi Lepscky (Woodbury, New York: Barron's, 1984).

The Painter's Eye: Learning to Look at Contemporary American Art, Jan Greenberg and Sandra Jordan (New York: Delacorte Press, 1991).

Painting: Great Lives, Shirley Glubok (New York: Chas. Scribner's, 1992).

Paintings, A First Discovery Art Book, Claude Delafosse and Gallimard Jeunesse (New York: Cartwheel Books, Scholastic Inc., 19XX).

The Patchwork Quilt, Valerie Flournoy (New York: Dial Books for Young Readers, 1985).

The Peaceable Kingdom, E. Zadrzynska (New York: M. M. Art Books, 1993).

Picasso and the Girl with a Ponytail, Laurence Anholt (New York: Barron's 1998).

Picture This: A First Introduction to Paintings, Felicity Woolf (New York: Bantam Doubleday Dell, 1992).

The Princess and the Painter, Jane Johnson (New York: Farrar, Strauss and Giroux, 1994).

Rembrandt's Beret, Johnny Alcorn (New York: Tambourine Books, 1991).

The Shapes Games, verse by Paul Rogers, pictures by Sian Tucker (New York: Henry Holt, 1989).

Smudge, Mike Dickinson (New York: Abbeville Press, 1987).

Squeaking of Art: The Mice Go to the Museum, Monica Wellington (New York: Dutton, 2000).

Starting Home: The Story of Horace Pippin, Painter, Mary E. Lyons (New York: Chas. Scribner's, 1993).

Story Painter: The Life of Jacob Lawrence, John Duggleby (San Francisco: Chronicle Books, 1998).

Take a Look: An Introduction to the Experience of Art, R. Davidson (New York: Penguin Books, 1993).

Talking to Faith Ringgold, Faith Ringgold, Linda Freeman, and Nancy Roucher (New York: Crown Publishers, 1996).

Tar Beach, Faith Ringgold (New York: Crown Publishers, 1991).

Understanding Modern Art: An Usborne Introduction, Monica Bohm-Duchen and Janet Cook (Tulsa, OK: EDC Publishing, 1992).

Usborne Story of Painting: Cave Painting to Modern Art, A. Peppin (Tulsa, OK: Hayes Books, 1980).

Vincent van Gogh, Sergio Bitossi, Eng. Adaption, Vincent Buranelli (New York: Silver Burdett, 1987).

A Visit to the Country, Herschel Johnson, paintings by Romare Bearden (New York: Harper and Row, 1989).

Visiting the Art Museum, Laurene K. Brown and Marc Brown (New York: E. P. Dutton, 1986).

The World of Art, Jacqueline Dineen & Nicola Barber (Parsippany, New York: Silver Burdett Press, 1997).

N. C. Wyeth's Pilgrims, Robert San Souci (San Francisco: Chronicle Books, 1996).

Recommended for Further Reading

Barrett, Terry. *Talking about Student Art*. Worcester, MA: Davis Publications, Inc., 1997.

Beattie, Donna Kay. *Assessment in Art Education*. Worcester, MA: Davis Publications, Inc., 1997.

Cornett, Claudia E. *The Arts as Meaning Makers: Integrating Literature and the Arts throughout the Curriculum*. Upper Saddle River, NJ: Merrill, an imprint of Prentice Hall, 1999.

Day, Michael, ed. *Preparing Teachers of Art*. Reston, VA: National Art Education Association, 1997.

Dobbs, Stephen Mark. *Learning in and through Art: A Guide to Discipline-Based Art Education*. Los Angeles: Getty Education Institute for the Arts, 1998.

Dorn, Charles M. *Thinking in Art: A Philosophical Approach to Art Education*. Reston, VA: National Art Education Association, 1994.

Edwards, Betty. *The New Drawing on the Right Side of the Brain*. New York: Jeremy P. Tarcher/Putnam, 1999.

Efland, Arthur; Kerry Freedman; and Patricia Stuhr. *Postmodern Art Education: An Approach to Curriculum*. Reston, VA: National Art Education Association, 1996.

Finn, David. *How to Visit a Museum*. New York: Harry N. Abrams, Inc., 1985.

Freeman, Julian. *Art: A Crash Course*. New York: Watson Guptill, 1998.

Gardner, Howard. *Art Education and Human Development*. Los Angeles: Getty Center for Education in the Arts, 1990.

Gilbert, Rita. *Living with Art*. 5th ed. New York: McGraw-Hill, 1998.

Greh, Deborah. *New Technologies in the Artroom: A Handbook for Teachers*. Worcester, MA: Davis Publications, Inc., 1999.

Herberholz, Barbara; and Lee Hanson. *Early Childhood Art*. New York: McGraw-Hill, 1995.

Horowitz, Frederick A. *More Than You See: A Guide to Art*. Orlando, FL: Harcourt Brace, 1997.

Hoving, Thomas. *Art for Dummies: A Reference for the Rest of Us*. New York: IDG Books Worldwide, Inc., 1999.

Hurwitz, Al; and Michael Day. *Children and Their Art: Methods for the Elementary School*. 6th ed. New York: Harcourt Brace College Publishers, 1995.

Hutchens, James; and Marianne Suggs, eds. *Art Education: Content and Practice in a Postmodern Era*. Reston, VA: National Art Education Association, 1997.

Jones, Arthur F. *Introduction to Art*. New York: Harper Perennial, 1992.

Kindler, Anna M., ed. *Child Development in Art*. Reston, VA: National Art Education Association, 1997.

McKim, Robert H. *Thinking Visually: A Strategy Manual for Problem Solving*. Belmont, CA: Lifetime Learning Publications, 1980.

Mittler, Gene A. *Art in Focus*, 2d ed. Mission Hills, CA: Glencoe Publishing Co., 1989.

Montanari, Sally. *Look Again! Clues to Modern Painting*. Washington, DC: Starrhill Press, 1997.

Moore, Ronald, ed. *Aesthetics for Young People*. Reston, VA: National Art Education Association, 1995.

Parks, Michael E. *The Art Teacher's Desktop Reference*. Englewood Cliffs, NJ: Prentice Hall, 1994.

Robinson, Waler. *Instant Art History from Cave Art to Pop Art*. New York: Fawcett Columbine, 1994.

Saunders, Robert J., ed. *Beyond the Traditional in Art: Facing a Pluralistic Society*. Reston, VA: National Art Education Association, 1998.

Sayre, Henry M. *A World of Art*, 2d ed. Upper Saddle River, NJ: Prentice Hall, 1997.

Simpson, Judith W.; Jean M. Delaney; Karen Lee Carroll; Cheryl M. Hamilton; Sandra I. Kay; Marianne S. Kerlavage; and Janet L. Olson. *Creating Meaning through Art: Teacher as Choice Maker*. Upper Saddle River, NJ: Prentice Hall, 1998.

Slatkin, Wendy. *Women Artists in History from Antiquity to the Twentieth Century*. 2d ed. Englewood Cliffs, NJ: Prentice Hall, 1990.

Smith, Nancy R.; with Carolee Fucigna; Margaret Kennedy; and Lois Lord. *Experience and Art: Teaching Children to Paint*. 2d ed. New York: Teachers College Press, 1993.

Smith, Ralph A., ed. *Readings in Discipline-Based Art Education: A Literature of Educational Reform*. Reston, VA: National Art Education Association, 2000.

Smolucha, Larry. *The Visual Arts Companion*. Englewood Cliffs, NJ: Prentice Hall, 1996.

Steves, R.; and G. Openshaw. *Europe 101: History and Art for the Traveler*. Santa Fe: John Muir Publishers, 1990).

Stewart, Marilyn G. *Thinking through Aesthetics*. Worcester, MA: Davis Publications, Inc., 1997.

Strickland, Carol. *The Annotated Mona Lisa: A Crash Course in Art History*. Kansas City, MO: Andrews and McMeel, 1992.

Thompson, Christine Marme. *The Visual Arts and Early Childhood Learning*. Reston, VA: The National Art Education Association, 1995.

Wachowiak, Frank; and Robt D. Clements. *Emphasis Art: A Qualitative Art Program for Elementary and Middle Schools*. 6th ed. New York: Longman, 1997.

Wigg, Philip R.; and Jean Hasselschwert. *A Handbook of Arts and Crafts*, 10th ed. New York: McGraw-Hill, 2001.

Wilson, Brent. *The Quiet Evolution: Changing the Face of Arts Education*. Los Angeles: Getty Education Institute for the Arts, 1997.

Zelanski, Paul; and Mary Pat Fisher. *The Art of Seeing*, 4th ed. Upper Saddle River, NJ: Prentice Hall, 1999.

National Visual Arts Standards

(GRADES K–4)

1. Content Standard: Understanding and applying media, techniques, and processes.

Achievement Standard

Students

a) Know the differences between materials, techniques, and processes.

b) Describe how different materials, techniques, and processes cause different responses.

c) Use different media, techniques, and processes to communicate ideas, experiences, and stories.

d) Use art materials and tools in a safe and responsible manner.

2. Content Standard: Using knowledge of structures and functions.

Achievement Standard

Students

a) Know the differences among visual characteristics and purposes of art in order to convey ideas.

b) Describe how different expressive features and organizational principles cause different responses.

c) Use visual structures and functions of art to communicate ideas.

3. Content Standard: Choosing and evaluating a range of subject matter, symbols, and ideas.

Achievement Standard

Students

a) Explore and understand prospective content for works of art.

b) Select and use subject matter, symbols, and ideas to communicate meaning.

4. Content Standard: Understanding the visual arts in relation to history and cultures.

Achievement Standard

Students

a) Know that the visual arts have both a history and specific relationships to various cultures.

b) Identify specific works of art as belonging to particular cultures, times, and places.

c) Demonstrate how history, culture, and the visual arts can influence each other in making and studying works of art.

5. Content Standard: Reflecting upon and assessing the characteristics and merits of their work and the work of others.

Achievement Standard

Students

a) Understand there are various purposes for creating works of visual art.

b) Describe how people's experiences influence the development of specific artworks.

c) Understand there are different responses to specific artworks.

6. Content Standard: Making connections between visual arts and other disciplines.

Achievement Standard

Students

a) Understand and use similarities and differences between characteristics of the visual arts and other arts disciplines.

b) Identify connections between the visual arts and other disciplines in the curriculum.

(GRADES 5–8)

1. **Content Standard:** Understanding and applying media, techniques, and processes.

Achievement Standard

Students

   a)   Select media, techniques, and processes; analyze what makes them effective or not effective in communicating ideas; and reflect upon the effectiveness of their choices.

   b)   Intentionally take advantage of the qualities and characteristics of art media, techniques, and processes to enhance communication of their experiences and ideas.

2. **Content Standard:** Using knowledge of structures and functions.

Achievement Standard

Students

   a)   Generalize about the effects of visual structures and functions and reflect upon these effects in their own work.

   b)   Employ organizational structures and analyze what makes them effective or not effective in the communication of ideas.

   c)   Select and use the qualities of structures and functions of art to improve communication of their ideas.

3. **Content Standard:** Choosing and evaluating a range of subject matter, symbols, and ideas.

Achievement Standard

Students

   a)   Integrate visual, spatial, and temporal concepts with content to communicate intended meaning in their artworks.

   b)   Use subjects, themes, and symbols that demonstrate knowledge of contexts, values, and aesthetics that communicate intended meaning in artworks.

4. **Content Standard:** Understanding the visual arts in relation to history and cultures.

Achievement Standard

Students

   a)   Know and compare the characteristics of artworks in various eras and cultures.

   b)   Describe and place a variety of art objects in historical and cultural contexts.

   c)   Analyze, describe, and demonstrate how factors of time and place (such as climate, resources, ideas, and technology) influence visual characteristics that give meaning and value to a work of art.

5. **Content Standard:** Reflecting upon and assessing the characteristics and merits of their work and the work of others.

Achievement Standard

Students

   a)   Compare multiple purposes for creating works of art.

   b)   Analyze contemporary and historic meanings in specific artworks through cultural and aesthetic inquiry.

   c)   Describe and compare a variety of individual responses to their own artworks and to artworks from various eras and cultures.

6. **Content Standard:** Making connections between visual arts and other disciplines.

Achievement Standard

Students

   a)   Compare the characteristics of works in two or more art forms that share similar subject matter, historical periods, or cultural context.

   b)   Describe ways in which the principles and subject matter of other disciplines taught in the school are interrelated with the visual arts.

Notes

Chapter 1

1. Eric David Tack, photography by Bruce Hucko, "Reweaving Tradition: New Trends in Contemporary Navajo Basketry," *Native Peoples, Arts and Lifeways*, September–October 2000, pp. 23–26.
2. Kurt Edward Fishback, *Art in Residence, West Coast Artists in Their Space* (Sacramento, CA: Solomon Dubnick Press, Blue Heron Publishing Co., 2000).
3. Gina Gray, letter to authors.
4. W. J. Strachan and Bernard Jacobson, *Henry Moore Animals* (New York: Aurum Press, 1983), p. 13.
5. Marie Mitchell, "Overlapping Traditions," *Crosswinds* (Native American Issue) 4, no. 8, p. 15.
6. Ibid.
7. Ibid.
8. Ellen H. Johnson, ed., *American Artists on Art from 1940 to 1980* (New York: Harper and Row, 1982), pp. 152–56.
9. Ellen Harkins Wheat, *Jacob Lawrence, American Painter* (Seattle: University of Washington Press, 1982), p. 41.
10. Cindy Nemser, *Art Talk* (New York: Charles Scribner's Sons, 1975), p. 179.
11. Diana MacKown, *Dawns and Dusks* (New York: Charles Scribner's Sons, 1976), p. 168.
12. Johnson, ed., *American Artists on Art*, p. 90.
13. Fishback, *Art in Residence*.
14. Dore Ashton and Jack Flam, *Robert Motherwell* (New York: Ashville Press, 1982), p. 12.
15. Irving Stone, ed. *Dear Theo, the Autobiography of Vincent van Gogh* (Garden City, NY: Doubleday, 1946).
16. Mitchell, "Overlapping Traditions," p. 15.
17. MacKown, *Dawns and Dusks*, p. 14.

Chapter 2

1. Betty Edwards, *The New Drawing on the Right Side of the Brain* (New York: Jeeremy P. Tarcher/Putnam Inc, 1999).
2. Ibid.
3. Ibid.

Chapter 4

1. E. B. Feldman, *Varieties of Visual Experience* (Englewood Cliffs, NJ: Prentice Hall, 1992).
2. Lynn M. Hart, "Aesthetic Pluralism and Multicultural Art Education," *Studies in Art Education* 32 (Spring 1991), p. 3.
3. Ellen Dissanayake, *What Is Art For?* (Seattle: University of Washington Press, 1990).
4. NAEA Advisory, "Censorship and the Arts," adopted by the National Art Education Association Board of Directors, Motion 17, September 1991.

Chapter 5

1. Gary L. Gerhart, "Motivational Techniques in the Elementary Art Class," *NAEA Advisory*, Fall 1987.

2. Tom Anderson, "Talking about Art with Children from Theory to Practice," *Art Education*, January 1986.
3. Howard Gardner, "Interview by Ron Brandt," *Educational Leadership*, December 1987/January 1988, pp. 30–34.
4. J. Piaget, *The Construction of Reality in the Child* (New York: Basic Books, 1954).
5. Viktor Lowenfeld and Lambert Brittain, *Creative and Mental Growth*, 8th ed. (New York: Macmillan, 1987).
6. Rob Barnes, *Teaching Art to Young Children, 4–9* (Boston: Allen and Unwin, 1987).

Note: The National Art Education Association provides art education books, standards, and flyers. Access to this comprehensive resource of usable information by writers and researchers may be found online at www.naeareston.org/publications.

Chapter 6

1. For more information on the use of assistive technology in art classes, see www.wati.org/assistiveart.html.
2. This project took place during the spring of 1999 between students at Williston Elementary School in Williston, Florida, and students at the Akureyri School of Visual Arts in Akureyri, Iceland.
3. "Electronic Postcards Link California and Texas Schools," in *ArtsEdnet OFFLINE Newsletter*, the Getty Education Institute for the Arts, no. 11 (Winter 1999), p. 10.
4. For more information on the "Art across America" exhibition contact Mary Bolyard via e-mail at gregjuli@execpc.com.
5. F. Powe, personal e-mail communication posted on *TEACHART*, Wednesday, July 12, 1995.
6. For a more detailed account of this online exchange, see "Connecting with an Artist" by Pam Geiger Stephens and Nancy Walkup in *School Arts* 99, no. 5 (January 2000), pp. 46–47.
7. *The National Visual Arts Standards*, National Art Education Association, 1994, p. 2.
8. Ibid., pp. 2–3.
9. Ibid., p. 3.
10. Ibid., p. 15.
11. Ibid., p. 18.
12. Stephen Mark Dobbs, *Learning in and through Art* (Los Angeles, CA: The J. Paul Getty Trust, 1998), p. 110.
13. For a comprehensive understanding of current ideas and practice in arts education assessment, please see Donna Kay Beattie, *Assessment in Art Education* (Worcester, MA Davis Publications, Inc., 1997).
14. The original commentary, from which this story was adapted, can be obtained from Jill Pease or K. D. Kurutz, directors of the California Consultancy for Arts Education, Sacramento, California.
15. Grant Wiggins and Jay McTighe, *Understanding by Design* (Alexandria, VA: Association for Supervision and Curriculum Development, 1998).

16. The six organizations, participating in the grant Transforming Education through the Arts Challenge initiative, are the California Consortium for Arts Education (now the California Consultancy for Arts Education), the Florida Institute for Art Education, Prairie Visions: The Nebraska Consortium for Arts Education, the Ohio Partnership for the Visual Arts, the Southeast Center for Education in the Arts, and the North Texas Institute for Educators on the Visual Arts.

17. Heidi Hayes Jacobs, *Mapping the Big Picture*: *Integrating Curriculum and Assessment K–12* (Alexandria, VA: Association for Supervision and Curriculum Development, 1997).

18. Donna Kay Beattie in her 1997 *Assessment in Art Education* discusses in-depth different forms of assessment, including formative, summative, performance, authentic, and so forth.

19. Second-grade teachers from Grand View Elementary School in Manhattan Beach, California, were Juliana Torchiana, Mischa Nall, Marilyn Berardo, and Kristina Carter. The mentor with whom they worked was Marilyn Wulliger.

Index